Harry R. G. Inglis

The 'Contour' Road Book of Scotland

Elevation Plans of the Roads, with Measurements and Descriptive Letterpress

Harry R. G. Inglis

The 'Contour' Road Book of Scotland
Elevation Plans of the Roads, with Measurements and Descriptive Letterpress

ISBN/EAN: 9783744729871

Printed in Europe, USA, Canada, Australia, Japan

Cover: Foto ©Andreas Hilbeck / pixelio.de

More available books at **www.hansebooks.com**

lecture — 1935

INDEX MAP
TO THE
ATLAS OF SCOTLAND.

The Numbers on the Maps refer to the Routes.

AYRSHIRE & GALLOWAY.

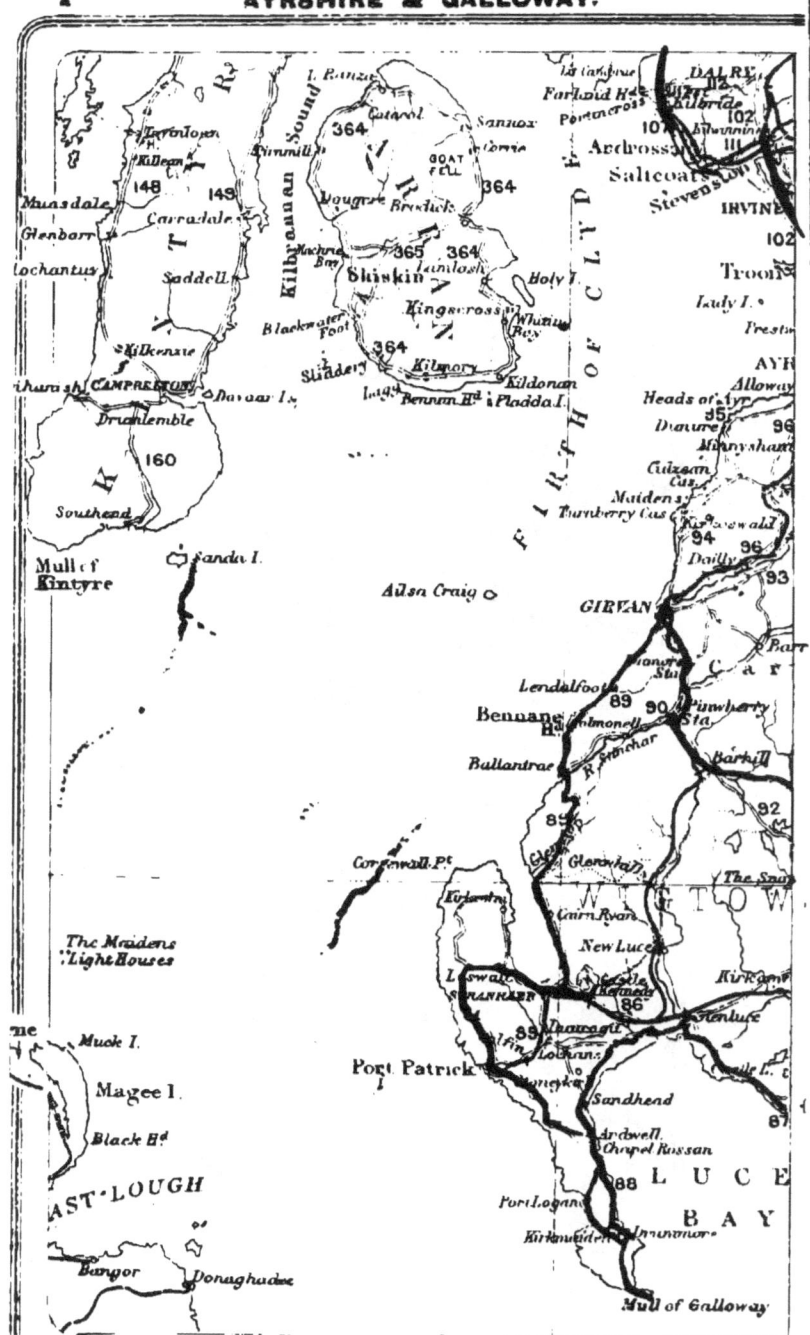

AYRSHIRE & GALLOWAY.

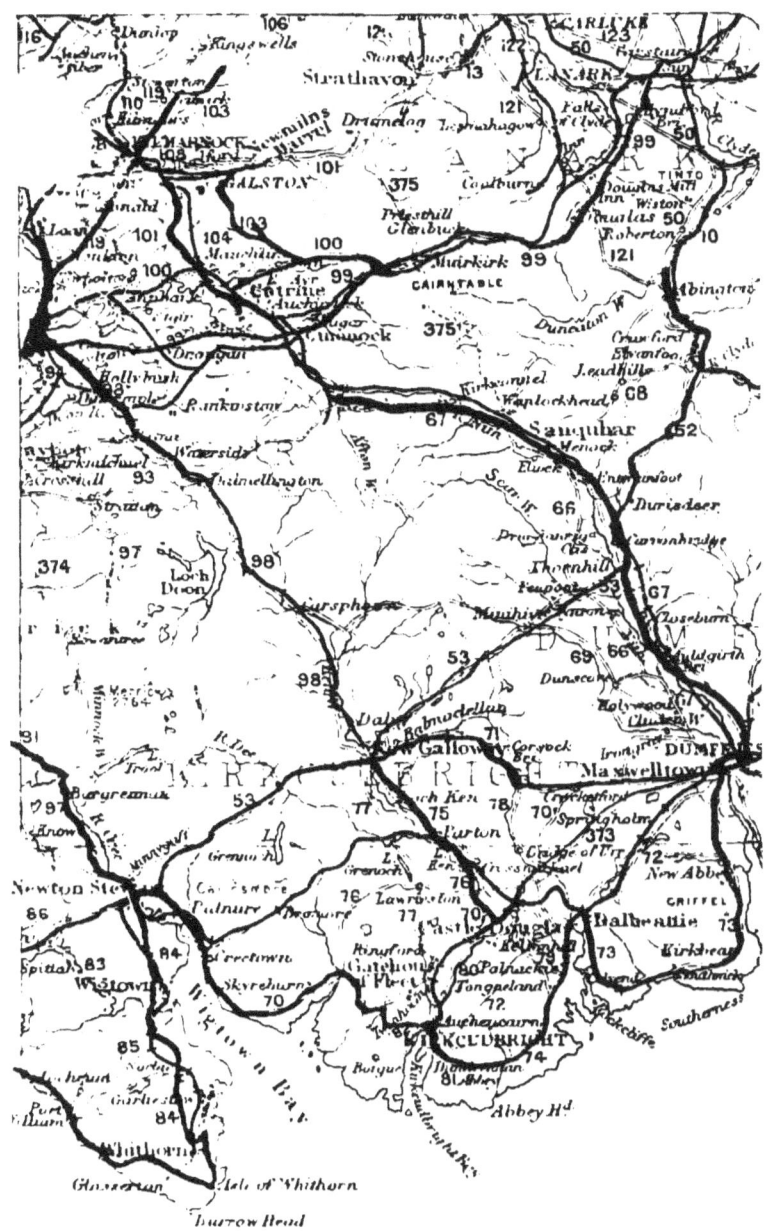

3 BORDER COUNTIES.

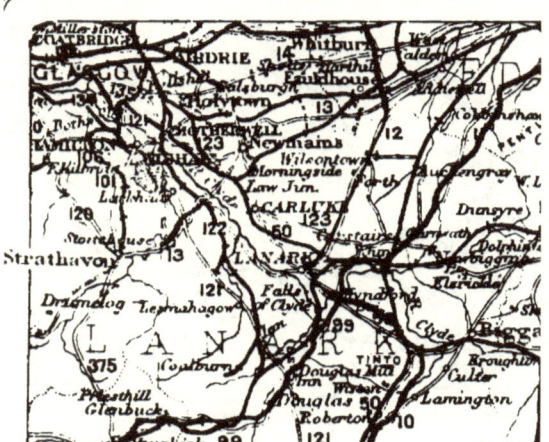

BORDER COUNTIES.

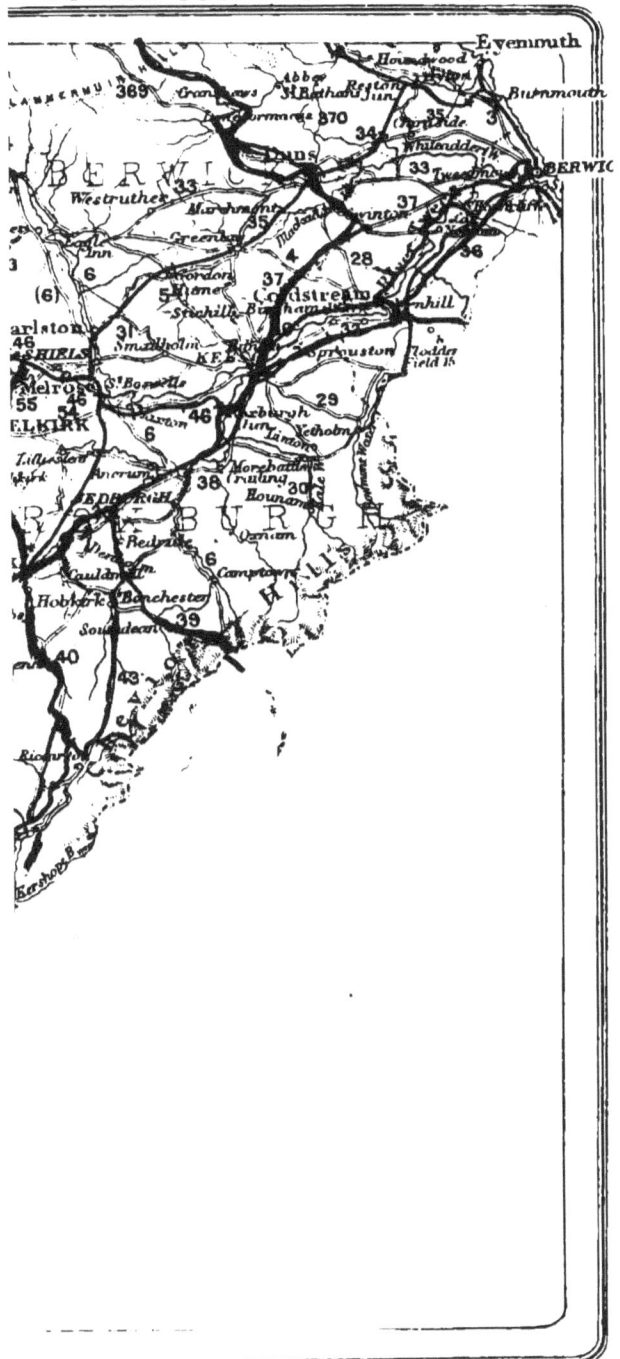

ARGYLESHIRE & GLASGOW.

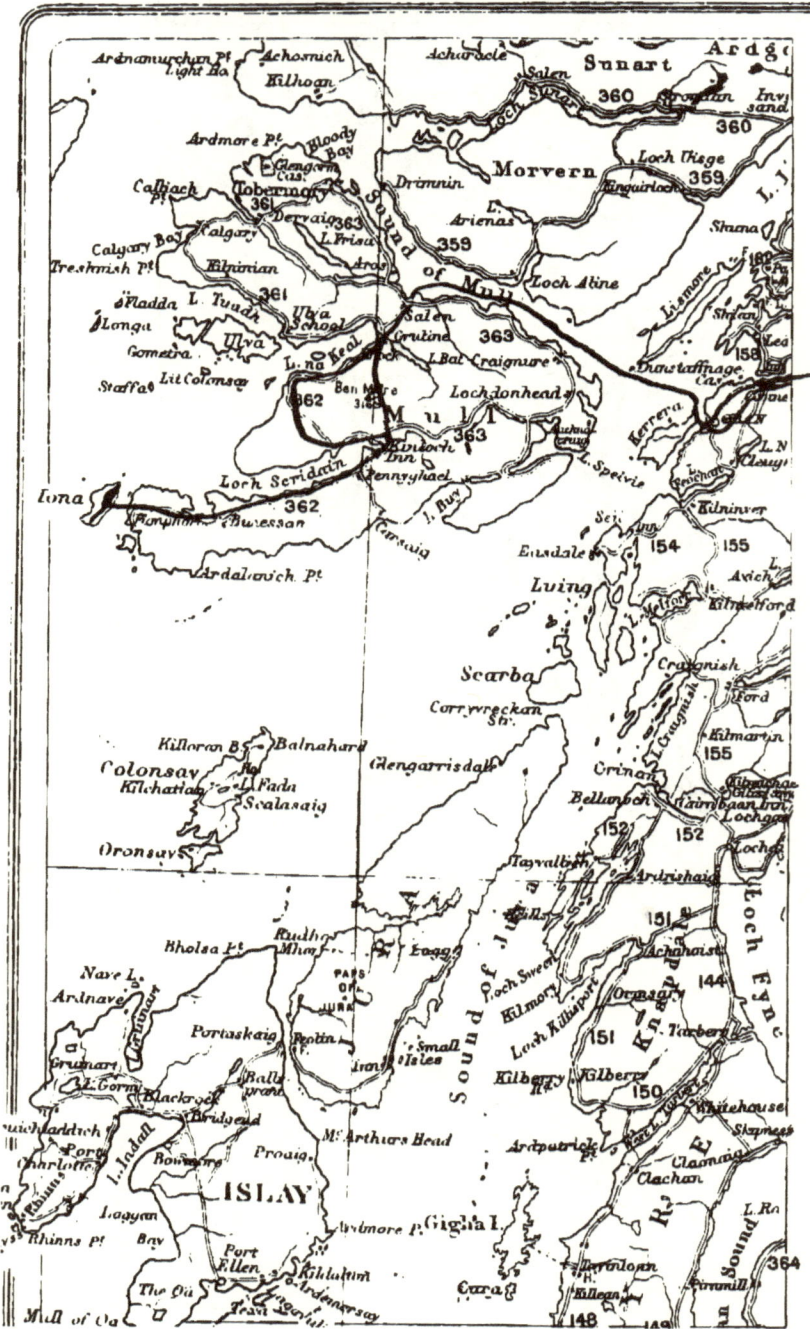

ARGYLESHIRE & GLASGOW.

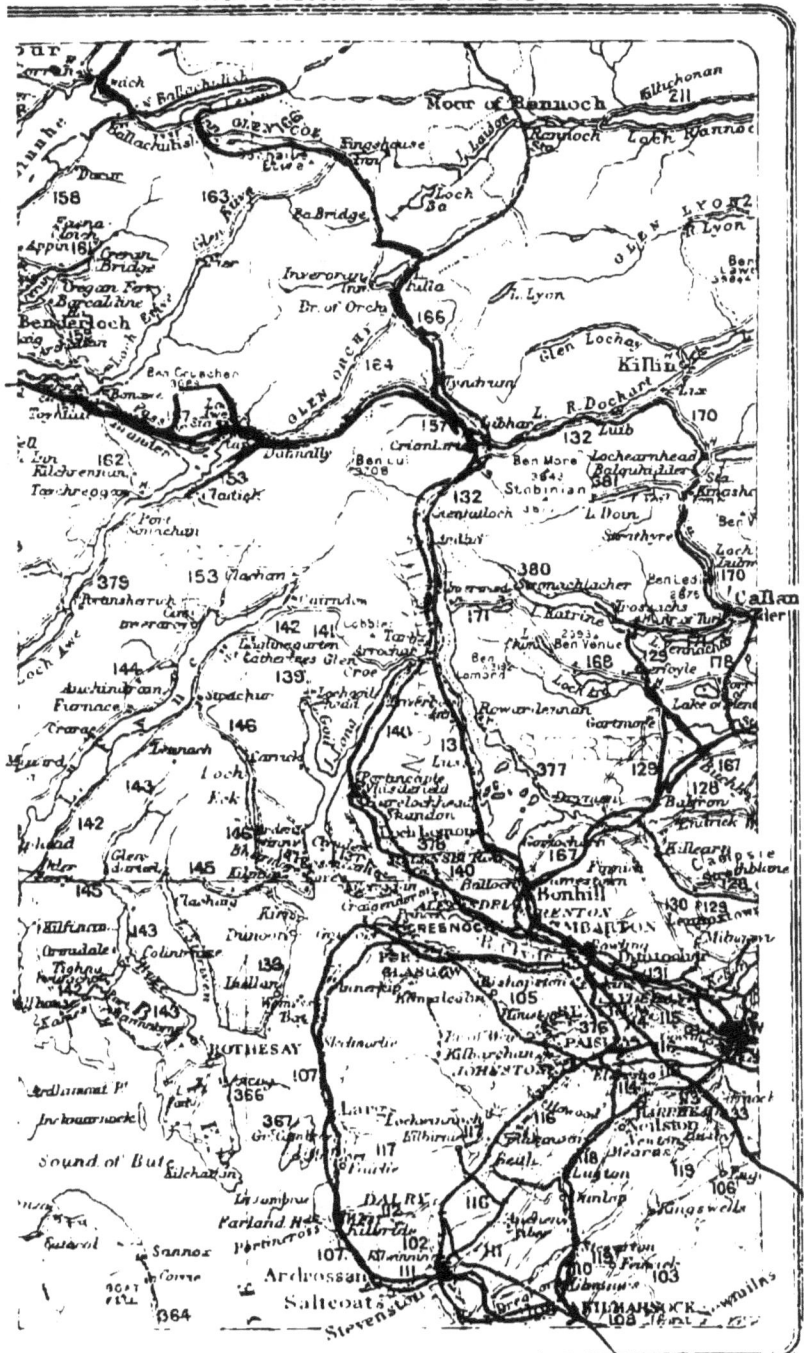

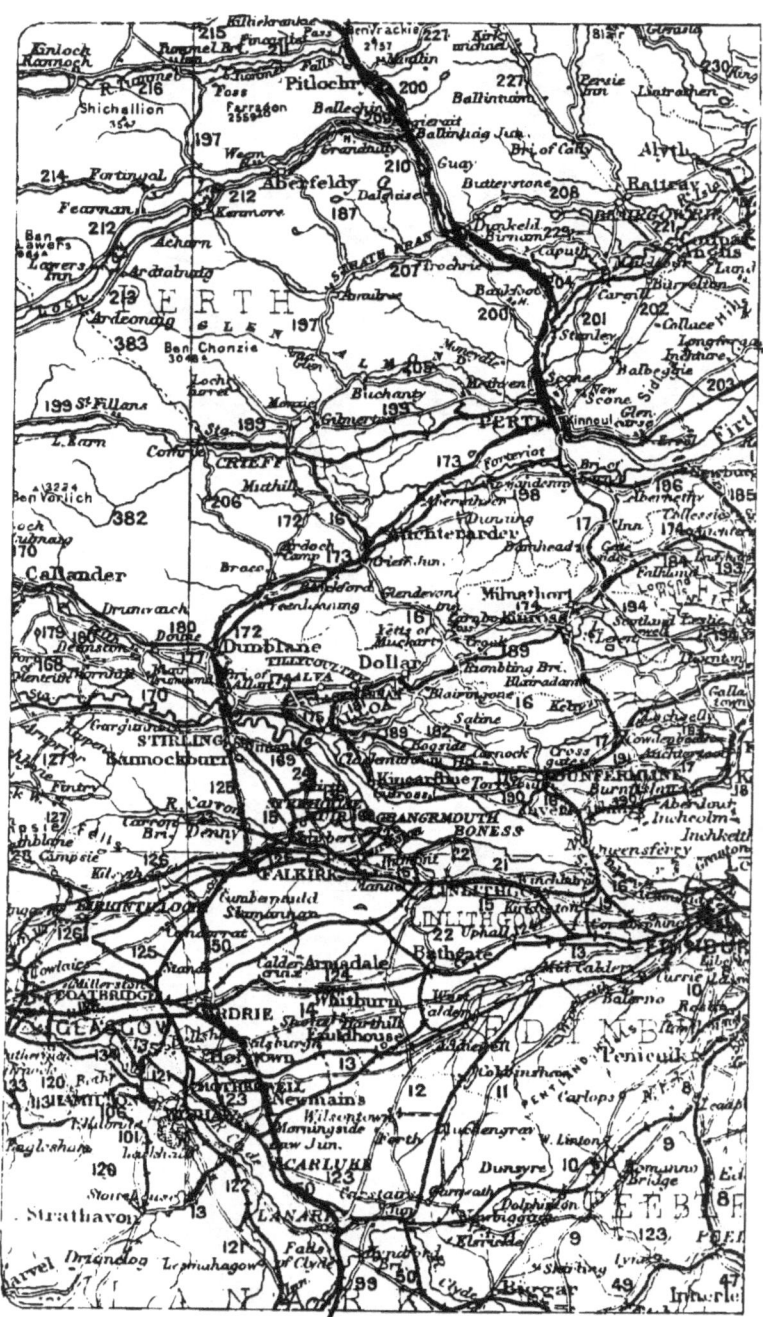

CENTRAL SCOTLAND.

8

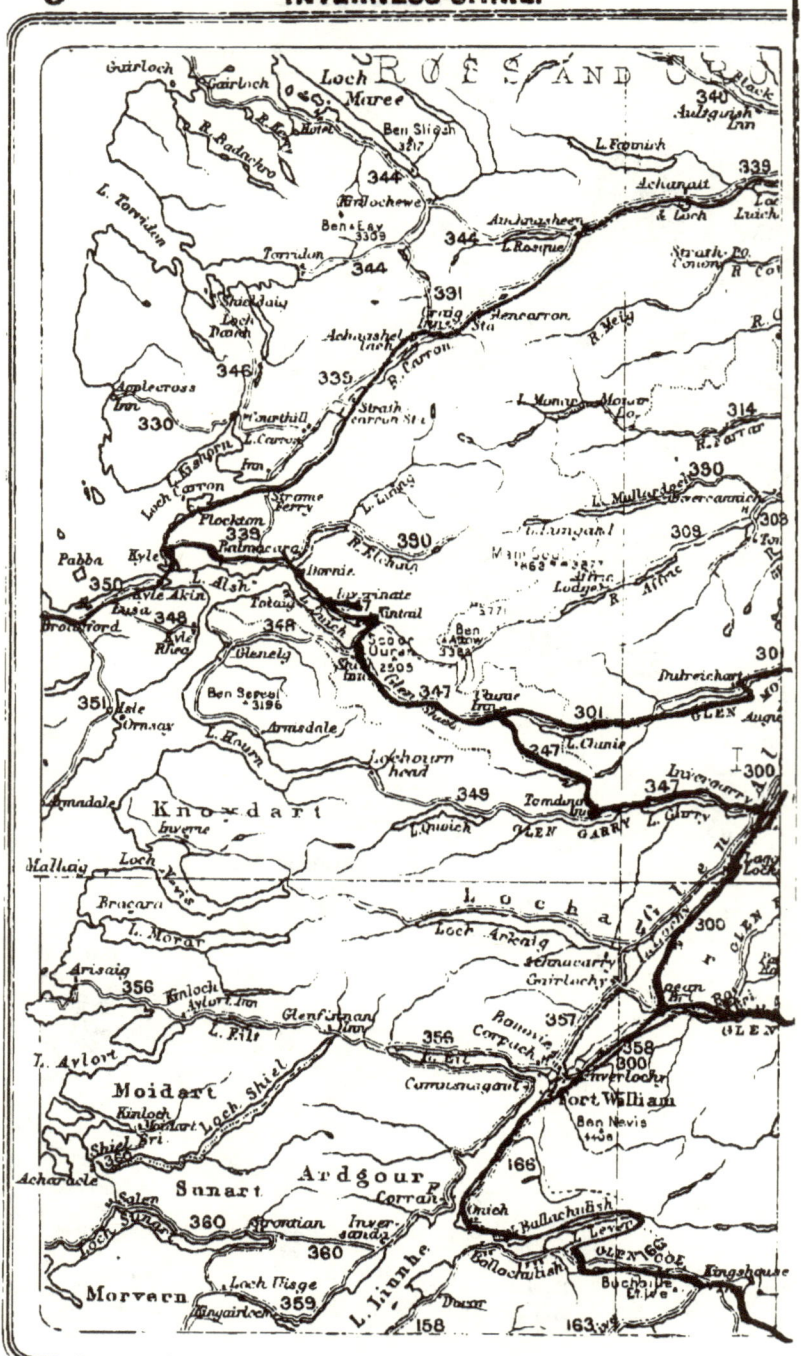

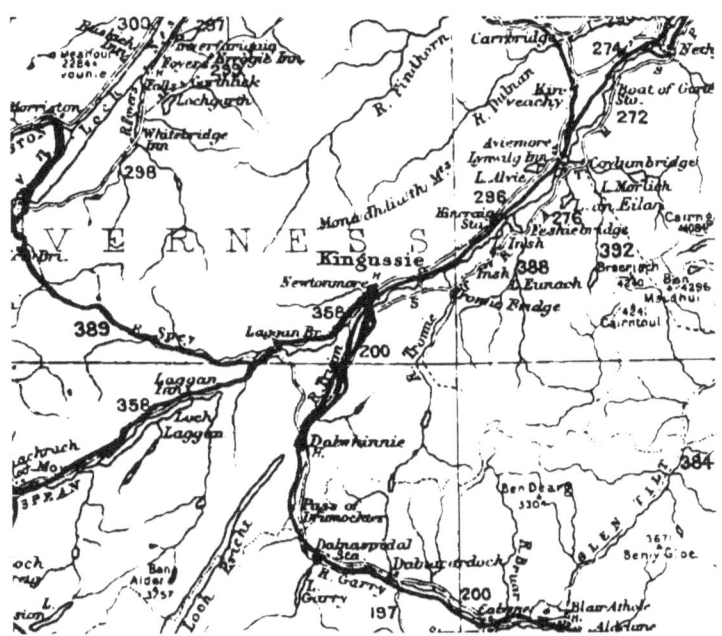

ABERDEEN, BANFF, AND ELGIN.

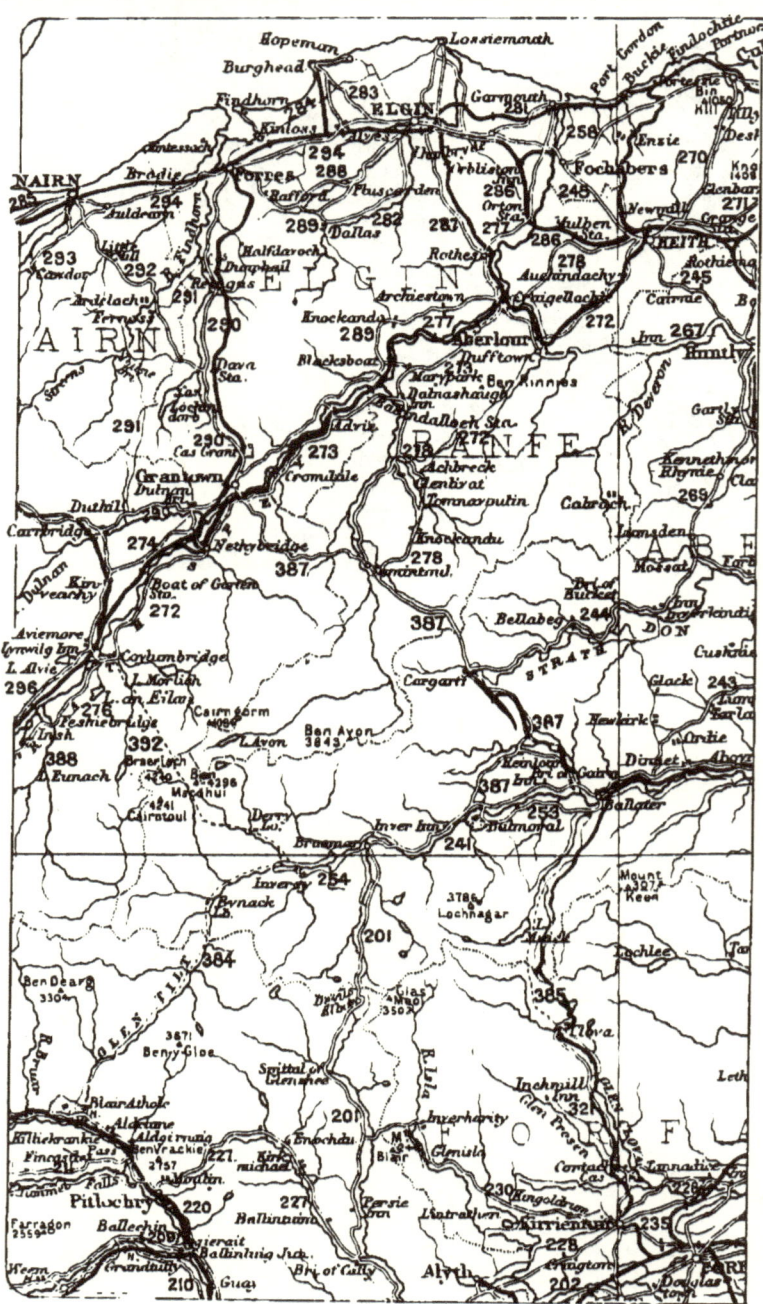

SUTHERLAND AND CAITHNESS.

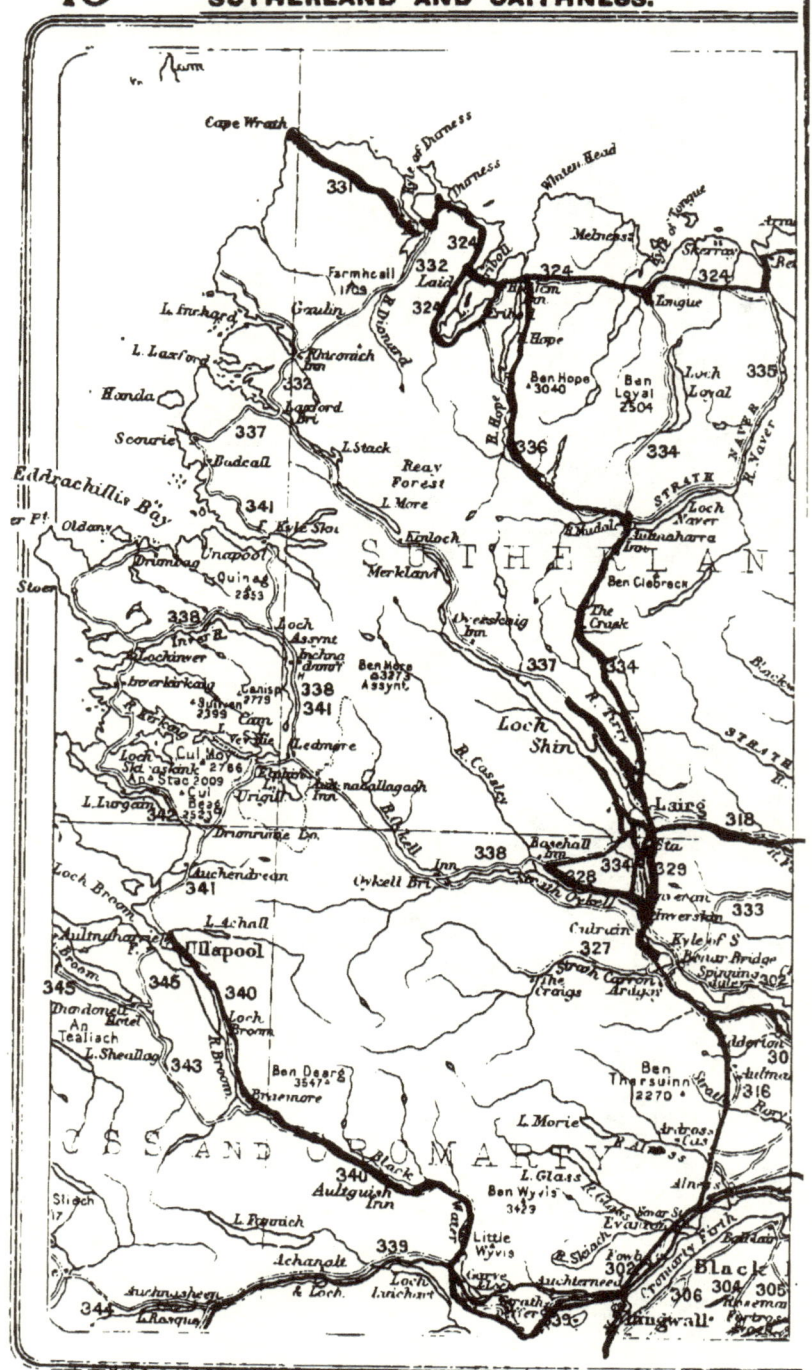

SUTHERLAND AND CAITHNESS.

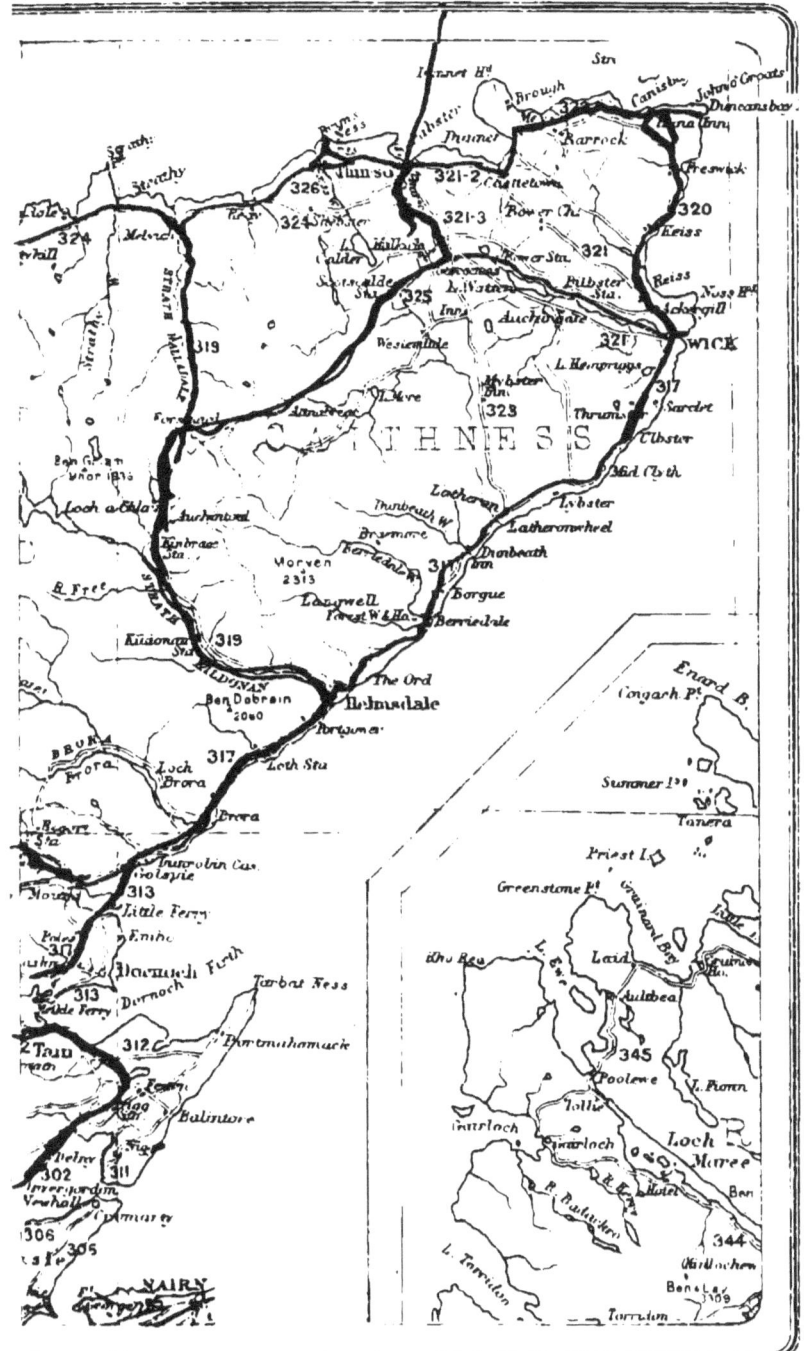

THE 'CONTOUR' ROAD BOOK

OF

SCOTLAND

A Series of Elevation Plans of the Roads, with Measurements and Descriptive Letterpress.

BY HARRY R. G. INGLIS.

With 500 Diagrams and Maps.

Edinburgh:
GALL AND INGLIS, 20 BERNARD TERRACE;
AND LONDON

1898
(Copyright.)

Uniform with this Volume.

The 'Contour' Road Book of England.

By HARRY R. G. INGLIS.

* * *

Northern Division.—Covering the Counties of Northumberland, Durham, Yorkshire, Cumberland, Westmorland, Lancashire and Cheshire.

South-East Division.—(London Section) Covering the Country East of Derby, Coventry, and Southampton, including the Counties of Derby, Nottingham, and Lincoln.

Western Division.—In preparation.

Preface.

The "Contour" Road Books—of which this is the first—form an entirely new departure in Mapping. There are numerous Road Maps in existence, but everyone has felt that even the best of these do not convey much more than a general idea of the course of a road, while the Road Books, however detailed they may be, can only give a very vague indication of the profile.

The Diagrams in this book were begun eight years ago, but the extensive and laborious work involved has prevented earlier publication. Neither time nor expense have been spared in the execution of details, and most of the Diagrams have been drawn out independently a second time, many three times, to minimise the chance of error.

The "Description" in this book has been drawn largely from personal observation, but we must express our indebtedness to a large circle of friends for assistance at various stages, to the Advocates' Library, Edinburgh, for permission to refer to numerous Maps and works of reference; and to many of the Road Surveyors.

Edinburgh,

The "Safety" Map of Scotland

Is a companion volume to this work, and by consulting it the Tourist can see at a glance the qualities of the Roads in any district. The Roads are indicated by distinctive colouring and marks, according to their quality.

Price 1/-; on Cloth 1/6.

CONTENTS.

The Routes are arranged Geographically from centres, so that the roads in each district are kept together.

As a general rule, the Route is from the larger place to the smaller.

Route. EDINBURGH, &c.
1. Edinburgh to N. Berwick.
2. ,, Drem.
3. ,, Berwick.
4. ,, Coldstream.
5. ,, Kelso.
6. ,, Jedburgh.
7. ,, Hawick.
20. ,, Lasswade.
8. ,, Peebles.
9. ,, Moffat.
10. ,, Abington.
11-12. ,, Lanark.
13. ,, Strathavon.
14. ,, Hamilton.
(24. ,, Glasgow.
15. ,, Stirling.
16 ,, Crieff.
17. ,, Perth.
18. ,, Dundee.
19. ,, St. Andrews.
21. Linlithgow to Queensferry.
22. Bo'ness to Bathgate.
26. Tranent to Gifford.
27. Aberlady to Gifford.

BORDER COUNTIES, &c.
28. Duns to Coldstream.
33. Berwick to Lauder, &c.
34. ,, Duns.
2. ,, Edinburgh.
35. Eyemouth to Greenlaw.
29. Kelso to Yetholm.
30. ,, Hounam.
46. ,, Galashiels.
31. ,, Earlston.
5. ,, Edinburgh.
32. ,, Cornhill.
36-37. ,, Berwick.
38. Hawick to Kelso.
39. ,, Carter.
40. ,, Newcastleton.
41. ,, Carlisle.
42. ,, St. Mary's Loch.
7. ,, Edinburgh.
43. Jedburgh to Annan.
6. ,, Edinburgh.
44. Selkirk to Ettrick.
45. ,, Moffat.
7. ,, Edinr. or Hawick.
54. ,, St. Boswells.
55. ,, Melrose.
56. ,, Walkerburn.

Route.
46. Galashiels to Kelso.
7. ,, Edinr. or Hawick.
47. Peebles to Galashiels.
48. ,, Tushielaw.
49. ,, Symington.
8. ,, Edinburgh.
123. ,, Glasgow.

DUMFRIESSHIRE.
50. Abington to Stirling.
51. ,, Carlisle.
52. ,, Thornhill.
68. ,, Sanquhar.
53. Thornhill to N'ton Stewart.
9. Moffat to Edinburgh.
45. ,, Selkirk.
60. Langholm to Eskdalemuir.
61. ,, Lockerbie.
41. ,, Hawick or Carl.
57. Annan to Lockerbie.
58. ,, Longtown.
64. ,, Moffat.
62. Dumfries to Carlisle.
63. ,, Annan.
59. ,, Lockerbie.
65. ,, Moffat.
66. ,, Penpont, &c.
67. ,, New Cumnock.
69. ,, Moniaive.

GALLOWAY.
70. ,, N'ton Stewart.
71. ,, New Galloway.
72. ,, Kirkcudbright.
73. ,, New Abbey, &c.
74. Dalbeattie to Kirkcudbright.
78. ,, Corsock.
75. Castle Douglas to Dalry.
76. ,, Lochenbreck.
79. ,, Auchencairn.
80. ,, Kirkcudbright.
77. Kirkcudb'ht to N. Galloway.
81. ,, Dundrennan.
82. ,, Gatehouse.
83. Wigtown to Kirkcowan.
71. N'wton Stewart to Dumfries.
84. ,, Whithorn.
85. ,, Port William.
86. ,, Stranraer.
91-92. ,, Girvan.
53. ,, Thornhill.
87. Isle of Whithorn to Glenluce.
88. Stranraer to Drummore.

v.

AYRSHIRE.

- 89. Girvan to Port Patrick.
- 90. ,, Ballantrae.
- 91-92. ,, Newton Stewart.
- 93. ,, Dalmellington.
- 94-5-6. Ayr to Girvan.
- 97. ,, Newton Stewart.
- 98. ,, New Galloway.
- 99. ,, Carstairs.
- 100. ,, Muirkirk.
- 101. ,, Hamilton.
- 119. ,, Glasgow.
- 102. ,, Dalry (Ayrshire).
- 103. Cumnock to Galston.
- 104. Kilmarnock to N. Cumnock.
- 109. ,, Troon.
- 110. ,, Lugton.
- 119. ,, Glasgow.
- 119. ,, Ayr.
- 108. Irvine to Galston.
- 111. Auchentiber to Ardrossan.
- 112. Dalry to West Kilbride.
- 113. Paisley to East Kilbride.
- 105. ,, Greenock.
- 106. Hamilton to Fenwick.
- 107. Greenock to Irvine.
- 114. Barrhead to Renfrew.

GLASGOW, &c.

- 115. Glasgow to Greenock.
- 116. ,, Dalry.
- 117. ,, Largs.
- 118. ,, Irvine.
- 119. ,, Ayr.
- 133. ,, Eaglesham.
- 120. ,, Strathavon.
- 134. ,, Hamilton.
- 121. ,, Abington.
- 122. ,, Lanark.
- 123. ,, Peebles.
- 135. ,, Holytown.
- 124. ,, Edinburgh.
- 125. ,, Stirling.
- 126. ,, Kilsyth.
- 127. ,, Kippen.
- 129. ,, Aberfoyle.
- 130. ,, Drymen.
- 131. ,, Arrochar.
- 128. Kilsyth to Buchlyvie.
- 136. Dennyloanh'd to Kincardine.
- 132. Tarbet to Killin.
- 140. Dumbarton to Arrochar.
- 131. ,, Tarbet.
- 167. ,, Stirling.
- 131. ,, Glasgow.
- 137. Garelochhead to Kilcreggan.

ARGYLESHIRE.

- 139. Inveraray to Lochgoilhead.
- 141. ,, Arrochar.
- 142. ,, Tighnabruaich.
- 143. ,, Rothesay.
- 144. Inveraray to Tarbert.
- 153. ,, Dalmally.
- 145. Dunoon to Otter.
- 146. ,, Inveraray.
- 147. ,, Ardentinny, &c.
- 138. ,, Toward.
- 148. Campbeltown to Tarbert.
- 149. ,, to ditto by E. Coast.
- 160. ,, Southend.
- 150. Tarbert to Kilberry.
- 151. Ardrishaig to Kilberry.
- 152. ,, Keills.
- 154. Oban to Easdale.
- 155. ,, Ardrishaig.
- 157. ,, Crianlarich.
- 158. ,, Ballachulish.
- 159. Round Benderloch.
- 161. Port Appin to Glen Creran.
- 162. Taynuilt to Cladich.
- 163. Lochetiveh'd to Kingshouse.
- 164. Dalmally to Bridge of Orchy.
- 166. Tyndrum to Fort William.
- 359. Corran to Morvern.
- 360. ,, Moidart.

STIRLING & FIFE.

- 15. Stirling to Edinburgh.
- 125. ,, Glasgow.
- 169. ,, Polmont.
- 50. ,, Abington.
- 167. ,, Dumbarton.
- 168. ,, Inversnaid.
- 170. ,, Killin.
- 177. ,, Doune.
- 172. ,, Crieff.
- 173. ,, Perth.
- 174. ,, St. Andrews.
- 175-6. ,, Dunfermline.
- 23. Falkirk to Bo'ness.
- 15. ,, Edinburgh.
- 126. ,, Kilsyth.
- 23. ,, Denny.
- 25. ,, Alloa.
- 181. Alloa to Dollar.
- 175-6. ,, Stirling.
- 175-6. ,, Dunfermline.
- 183. ,, Kinross.
- 182. Dunfermline to Dollar.
- 16. ,, Edinr. or Crieff.
- 175-6. ,, Stirling.
- 191. ,, Kirkcaldy.
- 190. Burntisland to Culross.
- 18. Kirkcaldy to Edin. or D'ndee
- 183. ,, Auchtertool.
- 191. ,, Dunfermline.
- 192. ,, St. Andrews.
- 19. ,, Crail.
- 184. ,, Bein Inn.
- 185. ,, Newburgh.
- 193. ,, Tayport.
- 194. Milnathort to Largo.
- 17. Kinross to Edinr. or Perth.

CONTENTS.

186. Cupar to Largo.
18. ,, Edinr. or Dundee.
174. ,, Stirling or St. Ands.
196. ,, Perth.
174. St. Andrews to Stirling.
19. ,, Crail or Tayport.
187. ,, Anstruther.
188. ,, Largo.
192. ,, Kirkcaldy.

PERTHSHIRE.
171. Callander to Inversnaid.
178. ,, Port Menteith.
179. ,, Kippen.
180. ,, Doune.
170. ,, Stirling or Killin.
170. Killin to Stirling.
132-157. ,, Tyndrum.
212-3. ,, Aberfeldy.
197. Crieff to Dalnacardoch.
199. ,, Perth or Comrie.
16. ,, Edinburgh.
172. ,, Stirling.
206. Comrie to Braco.
196. Perth to Cupar.
17. ,, Edinburgh.
198. ,, Dunning, &c.
173. ,, Stirling.
199. ,, Lochearnhead.
200. ,, Kingussie.
204. ,, Caputh.
201. ,, Braemar.
202. ,, Stonehaven.
203. ,, Dundee.
205. Methven to Buchanty.
210. Dunkeld to Aberfeldy.
207. ,, Amulree.
208. ,, Blairgowrie.
200. ,, Perth or Kingussie.
212-3. Aberfeldy to Killin.
214. ,, Glenlyon.
209. ,, Ballinluig.
227. Pitlochry to Blairgowrie.
211. ,, Rannoch.
200. ,, Perth or Kingussie.
215. Struan to Rannoch.
216. Rannoch to Aberfeldy.
227. Blairgowrie to Pitlochry.
228. ,, Kirriemuir.
208. ,, Dunkeld.
201. ,, Perth or Braemar.
221. ,, Dundee.
229. Coupar Angus to Dunkeld.

FORFAR & KINCARDINE.
18. Dundee to Edinburgh.
203. ,, Perth.
221. ,, Blairgowrie.
222. ,, Alyth.
223. ,, Kirriemuir.
224. ,, Forfar, &c.
225. ,, Aberdeen.
226. ,, Brechin.

230. Kirriemuir to Glenisla.
231. ,, Clova.
228. ,, Blairgowrie.
232. Forfar to Montrose.
233. ,, Carnoustie.
202. ,, Perth.
202-224. ,, Brechin.
234. Arbroath to Brechin.
235. ,, Kirriemuir.
225. ,, Aberdeen.
225. ,, Dundee.
236. Brechin to Lochlee.
202. ,, Stonehaven.
219. ,, Montrose.
202. ,, Perth.
217. Glamis to Newtyle.
218. Fettercairn to Drumlithie.
237. Edzell to Banchory.
219. Montrose to Brechin.
220. ,, Fettercairn.
238. ,, Fordoun.
225. ,, Aberdeen.
239. Stonehaven to Banchory.
252. ,, Mill Inn.
225. ,, Dundee.
202. ,, Perth.
225. ,, Aberdeen.

ABERDEENSHIRE.
225. Aberdeen to Dundee.
240. ,, Banchory.
241. ,, Braemar.
242. ,, Lumphanan.
243. ,, Tarland.
244. ,, Strathdon.
245. ,, Elgin.
246. ,, Banff.
247. ,, Methlick.
249. ,, Peterhead.
250. ,, Fraserburgh.
248. Newburgh to Culsalmond.
255. Inverurie to Tillyfourie.
251. ,, Forgue.
253. Ballater to Balmoral.
254. Braemar to Inverey.
256. Ellon to Methlick.
259. ,, Newbyth.
258. Peterhead to Elgin.
249. ,, Aberdeen.
249. ,, Fraserburgh.
260. Fraserburgh to Methlick.
261. ,, Turriff.
262. ,, Banff.
263. Turriff to Mintlaw.
257. ,, Bogniebrae.
264. ,, Keith.
265. Huntly to Banff.
266. ,, Portsoy.
267. ,, Craigellachie.
268. ,, Inverurie.
269. ,, Aboyne.
245. ,, Aberdeen or Elgin

CONTENTS

BANFF, ELGIN, & NAIRN.
262. Banff to Fraserburgh.
258. ,, Peterhead.
246. ,, Aberdeen.
265. ,, Huntly.
258. ,, Elgin.
270. Keith to Cullen.
271. ,, Banff.
272. ,, Glenlivat.
279. ,, Craigellachie.
277. Fochabers to Knockando.
278. Ballindalloch to Tomintoul.
281. Elgin to Garmouth.
258. ,, Peterhead.
245. ,, Aberdeen.
286. ,, Keith.
287. ,, Aberlour.
282. ,, Dallas.
288-294. ,, Forres.
283. ,, Burghhead.
284. Forres to Burghhead.
289. ,, Dalnashaugh.
290. ,, Grantown.
291. ,, Duthil.
273. Grantown to Aberlour.
274-5. ,, Aviemore.
280. ,, Carrbridge.
290. ,, Forres.
292. ,, Nairn.
292. Nairn to Dava.
293. ,, Daviot.
285. ,, Fortrose.
294. ,, Elgin or Inverness.
295. ,, Culloden.

INVERNESS.
276. Kingussie to Aviemore.
200. ,, Perth.
358. ,, Fort William.
296. ,, Inverness.
307. Inverness to Fort George.
294. ,, Elgin.
295. ,, Culloden, &c.
296. ,, Kingussie.
297. ,, Inverfarigaig.
298. ,, Fort Augustus.
299. ,, Whitebridge.
300. ,, Fort William.
301. ,, Clunie Inn.
302. ,, Dornoch.
303. ,, Invercannich.
304. ,, Invergordon.
305. ,, Cromarty.
308. Drumnadrochit to Invercan'ch
309. Invercannich to Affric.
314. Struy to Monar.
356. Fort-William to Arisaig.
357. ,, Loch Arkaig.
300. ,, Inverness.
358. ,, Kingussie.
166. ,, Tyndrum.

SUTHERL'D & CAITHN'S.
318. Dornoch to Lairg.
313. ,, Golspie.
302. ,, Bonar Bridge.
319. Helmsdale to Melvich.
320. Wick to John o' Groats.
321. ,, Thurso.
317. ,, Tain.
322. Thurso to John o' Groats.
323. ,, Latheron.
324. ,, Durness.
325. ,, Westerdale.
326. ,, Reay.
327. Bonar Bridge to Craigs.
328. ,, ,, Rosehall.
329. ,, ,, Lairg.
333. ,, ,, Mound.
334. ,, ,, Tongue.
302. ,, Dornoch or Inverness.
331. Durness to Cape Wrath.
332. ,, Laxford Bridge.
335. Aultnaharra to Bettyhill.
336. ,, Ereboll.
337. Lairg to Scourie.
338. ,, Lochinver.

ROSS-SHIRE.
310. Dingwall to Kessock.
339. ,, Kyle Akin.
302. ,, Inverness.
302. ,, Dornoch.
306. Conon to Cromarty.
315. Muir of Ord to Strathconon.
316. Alness to Bonar Bridge.
311. Tain to Cromarty.
312. ,, Tarbat Ness.
302 & 313. ,, Dornoch.
317. ,, Wick.
302. ,, Inverness.
340. Garve to Ullapool.
341. Ullapool to Scourie.
342. ,, Lochinver.
343. Braemore to Dundonnell.
344. Auchnasheen to Gairloch, &c.
345. Gairloch to Ullapool.
346. Strathcarron to Shieldag.
330. Tornapress to Applecross.
347. Invergarry to Balmacara.
348. Shiel Inn to Broadford.
349. Tomdoun to Kinlochhourn.

ISLANDS.
350. Portree to Kyle Akin.
353. ,, Dunvegan.
354. ,, the Quirang.
351. Broadford to Armadale.
352. Sligachan to Dunvegan.
355. Uig to Duntulm, &c.
361. Tobermory to Salen.
363. ,, Kinloch Inn.
362. Salen to Iona.
364 & 365. Arran.

General Notes.

The favourite districts of the Country for Tourists are:—Edinburgh, Stirling, Perthshire, The Clyde, Oban and Western Highlands, Inverness-shire, and Braemar. In some parts accommodation in the Season is difficult to obtain, and is apt to be at what are often considered pretty high rates. The South of Scotland, Skye, Ross-shire, and the districts adjoining those parts already named, also present considerable attractions to the Tourist.

In the Highlands, beyond the roads that are named in this book there are almost no others, and none should be reckoned on that are not marked on the "Safety" Map of Scotland.

It may be well to state here, that Glencoe is the Cyclist's "Bête Noir," the road generally being in a dreadful state, and that the Hotel-less 20 miles from Struan to Dalwhinnie, on the Perth and Inverness road, is best done by train.

In the Lowlands there are many other roads between the numerous towns and villages—they are mostly hilly, but very well kept. Travelling in the Coal and Iron District, of which Airdrie is the centre, is not very pleasant owing to the smoke-laden atmosphere.

A glance at the "Safety" Map will show the different qualities of the roads in the various parts of the country.

Ferries.—The length is given in Brackets after the name. For the shorter distances the fare is usually 3d. for one passenger—double fare if starting between 9 p.m. and 6 a.m., but Tarriff Boards are generally posted up, and should be consulted. The charge for a bicycle is usually 6d.

Railway Ferries ply between Granton and Burntisland, Hawes Inn and N. Queensferry, Tayport and Broughty Ferry, and there is also a steam ferry from Newport to Dundee.

On the Clyde, below the Broomielaw, there are large steam ferry boats crossing the river at various points, and there are large boats at Renfrew and Erskine Ferry. Further down, the Steamer Service is conducted with the frequency and regularity of trains from nearly every watering-place.

The rest of the ferries are relegated to small boats, and are conducted in a free and easy manner. Where the ferryhouse is on the other side, a smoke or the hoisting of a flag are the usual signals, and a long wait may be necessary.

On the following Fresh-water lochs, there are steamers, viz.:—Lochs Lomond, Katrine, Tay, Awe, Eck, Maree; also on the Caledonian and Crinan Canals.

Tourist Approaches from England.—Scotland is usually entered either from Berwick, Coldstream, or Carlisle, and from these towns there are excellent roads, that via Carter being very rough. Good steamers run to the principal ports from London, Hull, Newcastle, Liverpool, Bristol, &c.

Tourist Approaches from Ireland.—The ports of arrival of the Irish steamers are:—Stranraer, Ayr, Ardrossan, Gourock, Greenock, and Glasgow, but Tourists are advised that the journey from Greenock to Glasgow, up the River, is very tedious. From Stranraer a fine coast road leads to Glasgow, and a very fair one leads eastward to Dumfries. From Ayr there are fine roads, but those eastwards are hilly. From Ardrossan there is a favourite coast road to Greenock, where the Tourist should ferry across to Helensburgh, and so avoid the manufacturing part of the country. Tourists landing at Greenock should note this.

Explanation of Diagrams.

The line bordering the shaded portion of each diagram is a facsimile of the profile of the Route, and is divided by vertical lines into miles, and by horizontal lines into contours of 100 feet, so that distances and heights are ascertained quickly.

The blocks show the positions of the Villages and houses, while the signs (for explanation see page 3) are the road directions. The directions for the forward journey are above the road line, those of the reverse below, except in a few instances where lack of room has caused them all to be above the line.

The vertical scale has necessarily been enlarged out of strict proportion, as otherwise the ordinary Gradients would almost have been imperceptible.

Explanation of Letterpress.

The diagram should be consulted first, as the letterpress is appended to it. Places named in brackets are off the road.

The Description states the quality of the road, and it should be observed that the "Class" refers solely to the construction of the road, and not to its surface. Class I. is a superior, broad, and finely made road. Class II. is the ordinary main road. Class III. is of inferior construction, usually narrow, hilly, or rocky surface. Roads of this class are usually very old, or have been constructed in an inferior manner.

Gradients.—1 in 25; *i.e.*, 1 foot of rise in 25, is a fairly easy hill, 1 in 20 is stiff, 1 in 15 is steep. Cyclists usually walk up a hill of 1 in 17. A descent does not generally become dangerous till it is 1 in 15 and then only with a sharp turn, but with anything steeper the danger increases. A little experience of one or two hills will be a permanent guide. On nearly every hill the gradient varies every few yards. Those given here represent approximately the general slope, and in most cases the maximum is given.

Milestones.—As a general rule each county has its own set of milestones measured from its own centre; therefore in a route, when only one starting point is named, it may generally be concluded that the milestones are all measured from that point, but where there are two points, those near the county boundaries or in the centre are usually incorrect, the route having been measured from both ends.

Measurements.—The tabular form gives the distance from any one point to another, the number below the one name and opposite the other being the distance required. For clearness the furlongs have been put in the tables as ⅛ths. Places named in brackets, or in italics, are off the route.

Principal Objects of Interest.—These are only notes—details can be found in almost any guide book.

Hotels or Inns.—Those named in this heading are nearly all of a satisfactory kind, but it has been found difficult in many cases to decide whether certain small houses should be mentioned or not. The tourist, therefore, should not expect much of some of them, as they are the only accommodation available.

Historical Notes.

After long-continued wars with England, the crowns of the two countries were united in 1603, when James VI. of Scotland succeeded to the throne of England as James I. The parliaments of England and Scotland were united in 1707. Scotland sends seventy-two members to the House of Commons: and fifteen peers to the House of Lords, elected by their brother peers of Scotland.

Battlefields.

A.D.

1263.—**Largs,** Ayrshire: Alexander II. defeated Haco, king of Norway.
1296.—**Dunbar:** Edward 1. defeated John Baliol.
1297.—**Stirling Bridge:** Wallace defeated the English.
1298.—**Falkirk:** Edward I. defeated Wallace.
1314.—**Bannockburn,** near Stirling: Bruce defeated Edward II., and secured the independence of Scotland.
1383.—**Halidon Hill,** Berwickshire: Edward III. defeated the Scots.
1411.—**Harlaw,** near Invernry, Aberdeen: the Earl of Mar defeated Donald, Lord of the Isles.
1488.—**Sauchieburn,** near Bannockburn: James III. defeated by his nobles, and afterwards slain.
1547.—**Pinkie,** near Musselburgh: the English defeated the Scots.
1568.—**Langside,** south of Glasgow: the Regent Murray defeated Queen Mary.
1645.—**Philiphaugh,** near Selkirk: the Covenanters under General Leslie defeated the Marquis of Montrose.
1646.—**Kilsyth,** twelve miles west of Falkirk: Montrose defeated the Covenanters.
1650.—**Dunbar,** on the east coast of Haddington: Cromwell defeated the Covenanters under Leslie.
1679.—**Drumclog,** six miles south-west of Strathavon: the Covenanters defeated Viscount Dundee (Claverhouse).
1679.—**Bothwell Bridge,** nine miles south-east of Glasgow: the troops of Charles II. defeated the Covenanters.
1689.—**Killiecrankie Pass,** thirty miles north-west of Perth: Viscount Dundee defeated the troops of William III., but was himself slain.
1715.—**Sheriffmuir,** near Dunblane, Perthshire: Royalists under Argyle defeated the Jacobites under the Earl of Mar.
1745.—**Prestonpans,** eight miles east of Edinburgh: Prince Charles Edward defeated the Royalists under Sir John Cope.
1746.—**Falkirk:** Prince Charles Edward defeated the Royalists
1746.—**Culloden Moor,** six miles north-east of Inverness: the Duke of Cumberland finally defeated Prince Charles Edward.

Antiquities.

In various parts of Scotland many relics of ancient times are to be found. It is probable that they had their origin in different periods, and were the workmanship of different races; as, Picts, Scots, Scandinavians, &c. Such are—

The "**Standing Stones**" of Stennis, near Kirkwall, generally supposed to be the remains of a Celtic Druidical temple. The stones are of great size, and arranged in two circles. Similar remains are also found in the islands of Lewis and Arran, and elsewhere.

The "**Picts' Houses**" found in Orkney, Caithness, and Sutherland. These are curious circular buildings; some of them are underground, and are called Earth-houses. Cave-dwellings are found in Shetland and other parts.

The **Round Towers** of Brechin, Forfarshire, and of Abernethy, near Perth; these resemble the round towers of Ireland. Nothing is known with certainty of their origin. **Vitrified Forts** are found in most of the northern counties. They are supposed to have been used for defensive purposes. The stones of which they are composed are partially fused by the burning of wood-fires.

Many remains of **Circular Camps** are to be seen in various parts of the country; they are probably of native origin. Implements of flint, stone, and bronze have been found in great numbers in many places; also ornaments of bronze, gold, and silver.

Remains of the **Great Roman Wall of Antoninus** still exist near Falkirk and other places. It was constructed by the Romans between the Firths of Forth and Clyde, as a defence against the attacks of the Scots and Picts. The most perfect remains of a Roman Camp to be found in Great Britain are at Ardoch, near Dunblane, Perthshire. Other Roman Camps are found in Peeblesshire and Dumfriesshire; they were always built in the form of a square.

Ruins of Abbeys, Cathedrals, &c. The most ancient ecclesiastical ruins are in Iona, where Columba is said to have planted Christianity about 570 A.D. Elgin, Dunkeld, and St. Andrews have ruined Cathedrals; those of Glasgow; St. Giles, Edinburgh; Kirkwall, Brechin, Dunfermline, and Dunblane have been restored. There are beautiful ruined Abbeys at Jedburgh, Melrose, Dryburgh, Kelso, Coldingham, and Dundrennan.

Scotland abounds in ruined **Castles**, many of them exceedingly picturesque, but smaller than those of England. The most famous are—Dunnottar, near Stonehaven; Dunstaffnage, near Oban; Doune (which has been restored to its original appearance); Turnberry, near Maybole. The castles of Edinburgh, Stirling, and Dumbarton are in good preservation, and used as barracks for soldiers.

The royal palaces of Linlithgow; Scone, near Perth; and Falkland, in Fife, are ruined. Holyrood Palace, Edinburgh, is still maintained as a royal residence.

Heights of the Principal Mountains.

The heights of the more important hills will be found also on the small maps at the beginning of the volume.

The number before each name is the order of height, in this list.

Order.	Name.	Feet.	Order.	Name.	Feet.
13.	Ben Alder	3757	44.	Castel Abhail, Arran	2817
41.	„ Arthur	2891	52.	Cheviot	2676
22.	„ Attow	3383	41.	Cobbler	2891
8.	„ Avon	3843	73.	Criffel	1866
34.	„ Clibreck	(3154)	27.	Cuchullin Hills	3234
37.	„ Chonzie	3048	51.	Dollarlaw	2680
62.	„ Cleuch	2362	80.	Eildon Hills	1385
15.	„ Cruachan	3689	69.	Ettrick Pen	2269
18.	„ Douran	3523	55.	Farragon	2559
25.	„ Eay	3309	20.	Glasmeal	3502
39.	„ Hope	3040	43.	Goatfell	2866
24.	„ Ime	3318	53.	Hartfell	2651
57.	„ Loyal	2504	72.	King's Seat (Campsie	
6.	„ Lawers	3984		Fells)	1894
42.	„ Ledi	2875	79.	Knock	1409
31.	„ Lomond	3192	84.	Knockdolian	869
14.	„ Lui	3708	83.	Largo Law	965
9.	„ More (Perth)	3843	11.	Lochnagar	3786
32.	„ More (Mull)	3169	76.	Lomond Hills, Fife	1713
26.	„ More Assynt	3273	59.	Lowther	2403
2.	„ Macdhui	4296	75.	Lammermuirs	1733
1.	„ Nevis	4406	7.	Mam Soul	(3877)
46.	„ Resipol	2774	68.	Mealfourvonie	2284
49.	„ Rinnies	2755	47.	Merrick	2764
30.	„ Screel	3196	74.	Minchmoor	1856
29.	„ Slioch	3217	85.	Mormond	769
61.	„ Venue	2393	66.	Morven	2318
28.	„ Vorlich	3224	35.	Monadhliath M'ts.	3087
48.	„ Vrackie	2757	56.	Mount Battock	2555
21.	„ Wyvis	3429	58.	„ Blair	2441
16.	„ Y Gloe	3671	36.	„ Keen	3077
77.	Bennachie	1698	86.	North Berwick Law	612
12.	Bidean nam Bean	3766	54.	Paps of Jura	2569
81.	Birnam	1324	67.	Queensberry	2285
70.	Black Larg	2231	17.	Schichallion	3547
38.	Blaven	3042	40.	Scour Donald	2915
3.	Braeriach	4248	33.	„ na Gillean	3167
50.	Broadlaw	2723	19.	„ Ouran	3505
23.	Buchaile Etive	3345	82.	„ of Eigg	1289
5.	Cairngorm	4084	78.	Sidlaw Hills: Craig-	
65.	Cairnsmore	2331		owl	1493
71.	Cairntable	1912	10.	Stobinian	3827
4.	Cairntoul	4241	63.	Storr Rock	2360
72.	Campsie Fells	1894	60.	Suilven	2399
45.	Canisp	2779	64.	Tinto	2335

The Heights of the Road Passes.

MOSTLY ABOVE 1000 FEET.

Pass.	Height in Feet.	Position.
Southern Ranges—		
Carter	1371	Jedburgh to Newcastle.
Note o' the Gate	1250	,, Newcastleton.
Limekilnedge	1195	Hawick to Newcastleton.
Mosspaul	848	,, Langholm.
Foulbog	1096	Ettrick to Langholm.
Birkhill	1105	Selkirk to Moffat.
Tweedshaws	1348	Broughton to Moffat.
Beattock summit	1025	Glasgow to Carlisle.
Dalveen Pass	1140	Elvanfoot to Thornhill.
Wanlockhead summit	1531	Leadhills to Sanquhar.
Lochmuck	987	Ayr to New Galloway.
Shalloch	1421	,, Newton Stewart.
Nick o' the Balloch	1280	Maybole to Newton Stewart.
Mountbenger	1150	Peebles to Tushielaw.
Redstone summit	1416	Haddington to Duns.
Soutra	1192	Edinburgh to Lauder.
Tynehead	908	,, Galashiels.
Leadburn	931	Edinburgh to Peebles.
Linton summit	976	,, Abington.
Maidenwell	1080	,, Lanark.
Whitehouse	1024	,, ,,
Campsie Fells—		
Campsiemuir	1154	Glasgow to Kippen.
Grampians.—Main Range: Aberdeen to Inveraray.		
Cairn mon earn	757	Stonehaven to Banchory.
Cairn o' mount	1475	Fettercairn to Banchory.
Capel Mount (Path)	2275	Ballater to Clova.
Cairnwell	2199	Perth to Braemar.
Drumochter	1507	,, Kingussie.
Glen Tilt (Path)	1647	Blair Athole to Braemar.
Glencoe	1040	Tyndrum to Ballachulish.
Blackmount	1449	,, ,,
Tyndrum	895	,, Dalmally.
Southern Spurs—		
Whitebridge	1263	Aberfeldy to Dalnacardoch
Trinafour	1452	,, ,,
Lochnacraige	1339	Crieff to Aberfeldy.
Glenoglehead	948	Stirling to Killin.
Northern Spurs—		
Larig Pass (Path)	2771	Aviemore to Braemar.
— —	2091	Braemar to Tomintoul.
Monadhliath Mountains—		
Slochd Muicht	1333	Inverness to Kingussie.
Dava	978	Forres to Grantown.
Chlai	1257	,, Duthil.
Corrieyarrick (Path)	2543	Laggan Bridge to Fort Augustus.
— —	1275	Fort Augustus to Foyers.
Ross-shire, &c.—		
Fain	1101	Braemore to Dundonnell.
Mam Ratachan	1116	Shiel Inn to Glenelg.
— —	1424	Tomdoun to Clunie Inn.
Bealach	2053	Lochcarron to Applecross.

Lochs (Fresh Water).

These are very numerous: and being generally among the mountains, are remarkable for their grandeur and beauty. Most of the Highland lochs are long and narrow.

Heights of the principal Lochs, above sea-level.

Name.	Feet.	Name.	Feet.
Loch Achray	276	Loch Lomond	23
,, Ard	105	,, Loyal	369
,, Affrick	744	,, Lubnaig	395
,, Arkaig	140	,, Luichart	270
,, Assynt	215	,, Maree	32
,, Awe	118	,, Menteith	55
,, Ba (Mull)	41	,, Monar	663
,, Chon	291	,, Morar	31
,, Clunie	606	,, Muick	1310
,, Cobbinshaw	870	,, Mullardoch	704
,, Doon	660	,, Naver	247
,, Earn	305	,, Ness	50
,, Eck	67	,, Oich	105
,, Eilan	840	,, Ossian	1269
,, Ericht	1153	,, Quoich	555
,, Fannich	822	,, Rannoch	667
,, Frisa (Mull)	245	,, Shiel	16
,, Hope	12	,, Shin	270
,, Katrine	364	,, St. Mary's	803
,, Ken	145	,, Tay	350
,, Laggan	819	,, Treig	784
,, Laidon	924	,, Tummel	450
,, Lee	880	,, Vennachar	270
,, Leven	350	,, Voil	410
,, Lochy	93	,, Watten	58

Waterfalls.

The highest in Scotland are the Falls of Glomach, which descend some 300 feet in a very short distance. They are about a mile from 14¼m. in Route 390. The next are the famous Falls of Foyers, near Fort Augustus. Corra Linn—one of the Falls of Clyde—is about 90 ft. high, and, on account of the large volume of water and its situation, is worthy of the place of being the largest fall in Scotland. Other falls of great beauty are the Falls of Moness, and Acharn near Aberfeldy, Bruar and Tummel near Blair Athole, Falls of Turret near Crieff, Falls of Kilmorack near Beauly, Linn o' Quoich, Linn o' Dee, Linn of Corriemulzie near Braemar, Falls of Braan near Dunkeld, Falls of Rumbling Bridge near Dollar, Falls of Cruachan at Loch Awe, and the Grey Mare's Tail near Moffat; besides Stonebyres Falls, and Bonnington Linn on the Clyde.

Glossary.

The following Gaelic words will enable the Tourist to trace the meaning of many of the Gaelic names, both in the Highlands and Lowlands.

It will be observed that bh and mh are the same as v. Excepting in dhu (du) the letters dh are mute. Buidh is Bui.

Word.	Meaning.	Example.
Aber	River mouth (generally)	Aberdour.
Ach, or Auch	A field	Ach-na-cloich.
Aird, or Ard	A prominent height	Ardgour.
Alt, or Ault	A brook	Taynuilt.
An	Diminutive	Lochan.
An	Of the	Loch-an-Eilan.
Avon	A river	Avondhu.
Bal	A village or town	Balmacara.
Ban	White, fair	Banchory.
Barr	A projecting point	Dunbar.
Beath	A birch tree	Altbeath.
Bealach	A pass	Bealach-nam-bo.
Beag	Little	Glenbeg.
Ben, Bein or Ven	A rocky mountain	Benmore.
Blair	A plain	Blair-Athole.
Bo	Cattle	Bealach-nam-bo.
Breac	Spotted, brindled	Benvracky.
Buidh	Yellow	Loch Buie.
Cailleach	Old woman	Ben-na-cailleach
Cam, Cambus	Crooked, a creek	Cambusmore.
Carn	A heap of stones	Cairngorm.
Caol, or Col	A strait, or narrows	Colintraive.
Ceann, Can, or Kin	Head	Kintail.
Cro	A sheepfold	Glencroe.
Clach	A stone	Ach-na-cloich.
Clachan	Collection of houses	
Coire, or Corry	A hollow	Corrieyarrick.
Creag	A rock, a cliff	Craigard.
Cruach	A stack	Ben Cruachan.
Dal	A dale, a field	Dalwhinnie.
Dearg	Red	Bendearg.
Dhu, or Du	Black	Avondhu.
Dour	Water	Aberdour.
Drochaid	A bridge	Drumnadrochit.
Drum	A ridge	Drumnadrochit.
Dun	A fort	Dunbar.
Eas, or ess	A waterfall	Inver-ness.
Eilean	An island	Loch-an-Eilan.
Fearn	An alder	Fearn.
Fionn, or Fin	White, shining	Lochfyne.

Word.	Meaning.	Example.
Garve, or Garbh	Rough	Garvamore.
Gair	Short	Gairloch.
Glas	Grey	Glasven.
Glen	A narrow valley	Glenbeg.
Gorm	Dark blue	Cairngorm.
Inver	River mouth	Inverness.
Kin, or Ken	Same as Cean	
Kinloch	Head of the loch	Kinlochard.
Knock	A knoll	Knockandhu.
Kyle	See Caol	
Lon	A meadow	Tayinlone.
Leamhan, or Leven	An elm-tree	Lochleven.
Learg	The slope of a hill	Largs.
Mam / Meal	A rounded hill	Mam Soul.
Monadh	An upland moor	Moness.
Mor, Mhor, Vohr	Great	Morven.
Muck, or Muick	A sow	Glenmuic.
Na	Of the	Drumnadrochit.
Rath	A fort	Rathven.
Righ, ry or ree	A king	Dalry.
Ros	A projecting point	Ross of Mull.
Scuir, Scour	Precipitous hill	Scour Ouran.
Sron	A nose, a promontory	Stronachlacher.
Srath	A strath, broad valley	Strathmore.
Tigh	A house	Taynuilt.
Tilly	A knoll	Tillycoultry.
Tom	A mound	Tomintoul.
Uamh	A cave	Wemyss.
Uisge	Water	
Vohr, or Vor	Same as mhor	Uam Var.
Ven	Same as Ben	

Pronunciation of Names.

The general rule in pronouncing names of two syllables, is to place the emphasis on the first syllable of the word, as Ob-*an*, Al-*yth*, &c., but there are some exceptions to this notably *Ach*-arn, Dal-ry, Kin-ross, Kin-tail, Kil-lin, Port-ree, Dun-bar, and other names beginning with Dun.

We cannot attempt to give the Gaelic names and their pronunciation, as they are far too numerous to detail, but it will be found that as a general rule *dh* is almost mute (but sometimes has the value of *t*), while *bh* and *mh* both are pronounced *v*. In the glossary we have given a number of common Gaelic words which will show the English equivalents of many names.

Local and other Peculiarities of Pronunciation.

Aberchirder	is locally known as	Foggylone.
Avoch	,,	Auch.
Alyth	,,	Aylith.
Ballingry	,,	Balling-ary.
Balquhidder	,,	Balwhidder.
Cambuslang	,,	Camslang.
Cockburnspath	,,	Coburnspath.
Cuchullin Hills	,,	Coollin Hills.
Culross	,,	Cooross.
Durrisdeer	,,	Disdeer.
Edzell	,,	Edjell.
Fenwick	,,	Fenick.
Friockheim	,,	Freekem.
Glamis	,,	Glaams.
Grandtully	,,	Grantully.
Kilconquhar	,,	Kinneuchar.
Kilmalcolm	,,	Killmacomb.
Kingussie	,,	King-ussie.
Kirkcudbright	,,	Kirkoobri.
Meikleour	,,	Meeklour.
Milngavie	,,	Millguy.
Lochwinnoch	,,	Lochaneuch.
Moniaive	,,	Minny-ive.
Monzie	,,	Monee.
Muthill	,,	Muth-ill.
Montreathmont	,,	Monrummont
Row	,,	Roo.
Rutherglen	,,	Ruglen.
St. Ninians	,,	St. Ringans.
Salen	,,	Saalen.
Strachan	,,	Strawan.
Strathavon	,,	Stravon.
Sanquhar	,,	Sanchar.
Stincher	,,	Stinsher.
Tighnabrualch	,,	Tinnybruach.

The Contour Road Book of Scotland.

The Principal Objects of Interest in most of the following towns do not appear in the letterpress:—

Edinburgh.—Castle, Holyrood Palace, St. Giles' Cathedral, Parliament House, University, M'Ewan Hall, Scott Monument, Burns' Monument, Museums, National Portrait Gallery, Free Library.

Glasgow.—Cathedral, University, Municipal Buildings, George Square, Broomielaw. In vicinity: Langside.

Aberdeen.—Marischal College, King's College, Duthie Park, Brig o' Balgownie, Brig o' Dee.

Ayr.—*See Route 119.*

Dumfries.—Burns' Monument, Globe Inn, Bridge, Observatory, Mid-steeple, Lincluden Abbey.

Dundee.—Town Church, Albert Institute, Royal Arch, Dundee Law, Tay Bridge.

Hawick.—Mote Hill, Tower Hotel.

Inveraray.—Castle, Duniquoich Hill, Falls of Aray.

Inverness.—Castle, Islands, Tom-na-hurich.

Oban.—Dunollie Castle, Pulpit Hill, &c.

Perth.—*See Route 17.*

Selkirk.—Scott's Statue, Mungo Park's Statue, The Haining, Philiphaugh Battlefield, Ettrick, and Yarrow.

Stirling.—*See Route 15.*

LEITH.

Measurements.—From Leith Corn Exchange.
1¾m. Edinburgh, G.P.O.
6¼m. Cramond Bridge. 9½m. Queensferry, Hawes Inn.
1¼m. Newhaven Inn. 2½m. Granton Pier.
2¾m. Portobello, Town Hall.

1 EDINBURGH TO NORTH BERWICK, &c.

Description.—Class II. Between Edinburgh and Musselburgh only fair, on account of suburban traffic. The next three miles are very rough, but thereafter the road is very good and level. Good but hilly road to Dunbar. Class III.

Gradients.—At 20 m., 1 in 26; to N. Berwick 1 in 18; at 23m., 1 in 23; at 28¼m., 1 in 22; at 29½m., 1 in 20; at 29¾m., 1 in 14.

Milestones.—Measured from Old Post Office, Edinburgh. After N. Berwick the M.S. follow a very steep but more direct road to Whitekirk.

Measurements.

Edinburgh,* G.P.O.								
3¼	Portobello,* Town Hall.							
5⅝	2⅜	Musselburgh * Bridge.						
8¾	5½	3⅜	Prestonpans.*					
15¼	12	9⅝	6½	Aberlady.*				
20⅛	16⅞	14½	11⅜	4⅞	Dirleton Inn.			
22⅞	19⅝	17¼	14⅜	7⅝	2¾	N. Berwick,* Town Hall.		
28⅛	24⅞	22½	19⅜	12⅞	8	5¼	Whitekirk.	
35⅛	31⅞	29½	26⅜	19⅞	15	12¼	7	Dunbar,* High St.

Principal Objects of Interest. — MUSSELBURGH; Old Bridge; Pinkie House and Battlefield 1547. 8¾m., to S., Preston Tower; Battlefield, 1745. 14m., Gosford House. 20¼m., Dirleton Castle and Gardens. NORTH BERWICK; Priory. 25⅛m., Canty Bay, Bass Rock. 25⅜m., Tantallon Cas. 25¼m., Whitekirk Ch. 29⅜m., Tynninghame House.

Hotels or Inns at places marked * and at Levenhall, Cockenzie, and Gullane.

---

2 EDINBURGH TO DREM, &c.

Description.—Class II. To beyond Musselburgh, as above. Thence a fairly level road the whole way, but with medium surface.

Gradients.—At 7¼m. 1 in 24, thereafter nothing steep.

Milestones.—Measured from Old G.P.O. travel *via* Ravensheugh (Route 1), up a very steep hill, and join this Road at 8m.,—only tolerably correct.

Measurements.

Edinburgh,* G.P.O.					
5⅝	Musselburgh * Bridge.				
9	3⅜	Preston.			
12¾	7⅛	3¾	Longniddry P.O.		
17⅝	12	8⅝	4⅝	Drem P.O.	
20⅝	15	11⅝	7⅞	3	Dirleton Inn.

Principal Objects of Interest.—To 6m. as above. 9m. Preston Tower. 9¾m., Battlefield, 1745.

Hotels or Inns at places marked * and at Portobello and Levenhall.

Route 1. Edinburgh to North Berwick, &c.

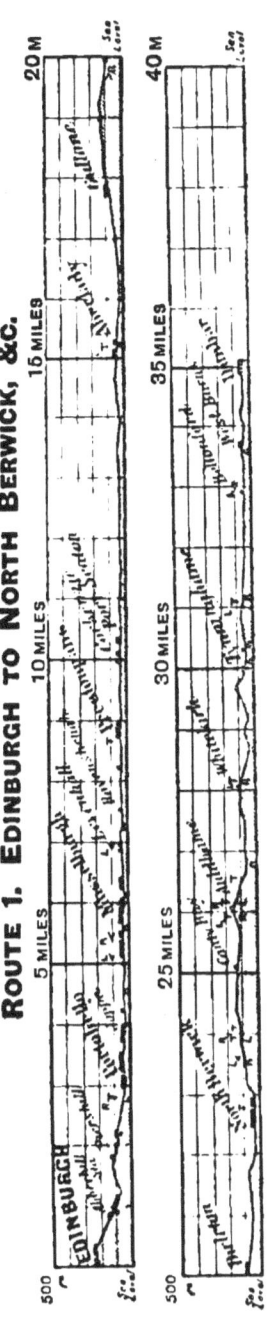

Route 2. Edinburgh to Drem, &c.

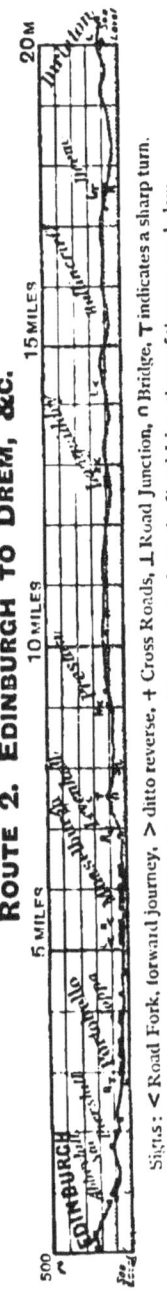

Signs: < Road Fork, forward journey. > ditto reverse. + Cross Roads. ⊥ Road Junction. ∩ Bridge. T indicates a sharp turn.

(The directions R (right) and L (left) for the forward journey are above the Road Line, those of the reverse, below.

3 EDINBURGH TO BERWICK.

Description.—Class I. Magnificent highway throughout. The surface between Edinburgh and Musselburgh is only fair, on account of suburban traffic; the next mile and a half to Levenhall past the Race Course very rough indeed, but after Tranent the road is very fine right on to Cockburnspath, though a little rough about Dunbar. Be careful entering East Linton from both sides, as the road is narrow at the turn. The remaining section to Berwick is good. The direct road, Beltonford to Broxburn, avoiding Dunbar, is very variable, usually rough. The old-fashioned paving in Haddington is simply execrable.

Gradients.—Very favourable on the whole, except the ascent from Levenhall, 1 in 24; ascent at Cockburnspath 1 in 15, and the highly dangerous Tower Bridge, descent on both sides 1 in 13.

Milestones.—Measured from New Waverley Hotel, Edinburgh (Old G.P.O.), and from Berwick Town Hall, only fairly accurate. Between Cockburnspath and Burnmouth they are unreliable.

Measurements.

Edinburgh,* G.P.O.									
3¼	Portobello,* Town Hall.								
5⅝	2⅜	Musselburgh * Bridge.							
9¾	6½	4⅛	Tranent,* P.O.						
16¾	13⅜	11	6⅞	Haddington,* Town Hall.					
22¼	19	16⅝	12½	5⅝	East Linton * Bridge.				
27¾	24½	22⅛	18	11⅛	5½	Dunbar,* High St.			
36¼	32¾	30⅜	26¼	19⅜	13¼	8¼	Cockburnspath.		
49⅝	46⅜	44	39⅞	33	27⅜	21⅞	13⅜	Ayton.*	
57¾	54½	52⅛	48	41⅛	35½	30	21¼	8⅛	Berwick,* Town Hall.

Principal Objects of Interest.—1¾m., Piershill Barracks. 5½m., MUSSELBURGH; Old Bridge, Pinkie House and Battlefield, 1547. 6m., Race Course. 9m., To N., Preston Tower; Battle, 1745. 16½m., Fergusson's Monument. HADDINGTON; Abbey; monument on hill to N. is the Hopetoun Monument. DUNBAR; Castle ruins. 29¾m., Battlefield. 36½m., to N., Pease Bridge and Fast Castle. 46½m., to N., Coldingham Priory. 51¾m., Burnmouth at bottom of cliffs; BERWICK; Walls; and Bridge, built in 1624.

Hotels or Inns at places marked * and at Levenhall, Grant's House, and Houndwood.

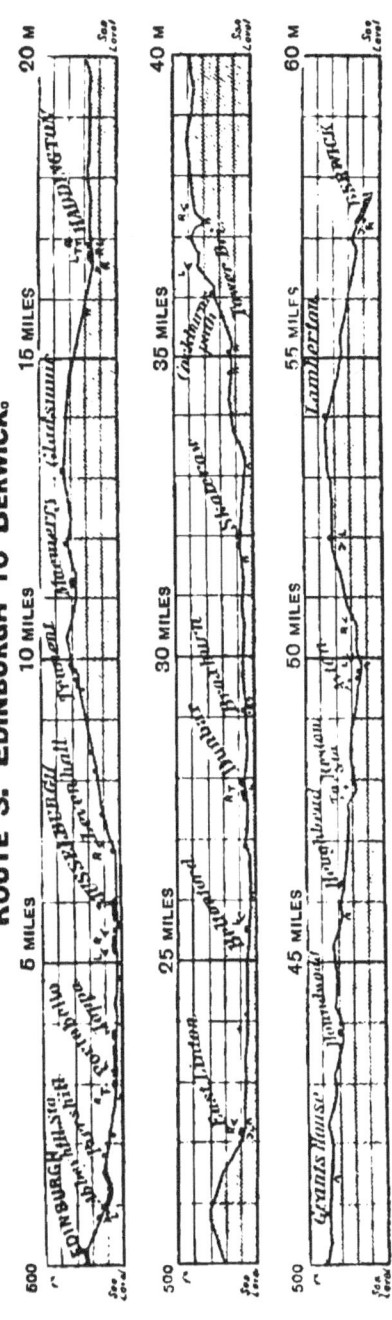

Signs: < Road Fork, forward journey. > ditto reverse. + Cross Roads. ⊥ Road Junction. ∩ Bridge. ⊤ indicates a sharp turn

The directions R (right) and L (left) for the forward journey are above the Road Line, those of the reverse, below

4 EDINBURGH TO COLDSTREAM.

Description.—Class I. The first 4 miles are rather rough and steep, but thereafter the road, with the exception of some loose parts about the summit, is of exceedingly good surface to Carfraemill Inn. The next section is very hilly and rough, until the road from Lauder joins in, when the surface improves, and continues very good on to Coldstream.

Gradients.—Little France Hill 1 in 14-20; Dalkeith Bri. descent 1 in 25; ascent 1 in 16; long ascent 1 in 24-26. Pathhead Hill 1 in 19. Soutra Hill 1 in 19-23; descent 1 in 21-25. From Carfraemill to Whiteburn, grades of 1 in 15-23-25-21, from thence Roweston Hill 1 in 16, and at 46m. 1 in 17.

Milestones.—Measured from Crosscauseway, Edinburgh, correct to Soutra, then only a few till near Coldstream.

Measurements.

Edinburgh,* G.P.O.						
6¾	Dalkeith,* High St.					
11⅞	5⅛	Pathhead,* P.O.				
15¼	8½	3⅜	Blackshiels Inn.			
22½	15¾	10⅝	7¼	Carfraemill Inn.		
37⅞	31⅛	26	22⅝	15⅜	Greenlaw,* County Ho.	
48	41¼	36⅛	32¾	25½	10⅛	Coldstream,* Market Pl.

Principal Objects of Interest.—3¼m., Craigmillar Castle ruins. 6¾m., Dalkeith Palace. 26¾m., Thirlestane Castle; GREENLAW; County Hall. 40m., Roweston Chapel. Fine view of the Lothians from Soutra.

Hotels or Inns at places marked * and at Whiteburn.

---

5 EDINBURGH TO KELSO.

Description.—Class II. See above to Carfraemill. This Route to Whiteburn is very much better than the direct road. From thence the road is good but very hilly.

Gradients.—See above to Carfraemill, thence descent to Leader Bridge 1 in 23; ascent 1 in 20-25. Thirlestane Mill 1 in 21. Deanbrae 1 in 17. Ascent at 37¼m. 1 in 19, at 38¼m. 1 in 20-22. Nenthorn Hill 1 in 16-23; at 41m. 1 in 24.

Measurements.

Edinburgh,* G.P.O.					
6¾	Dalkeith,* High St.				
22½	15¾	Carfraemill.			
26½	19¾	4	Lauder,* Town House.		
35¾	29	13¼	9¼	Gordon.*	
44⅛	37⅜	21⅝	17⅝	8⅜	Kelso,* Square.

Milestones.—Measured from Crosscauseway to Soutra,—

(*Continued next page.*)

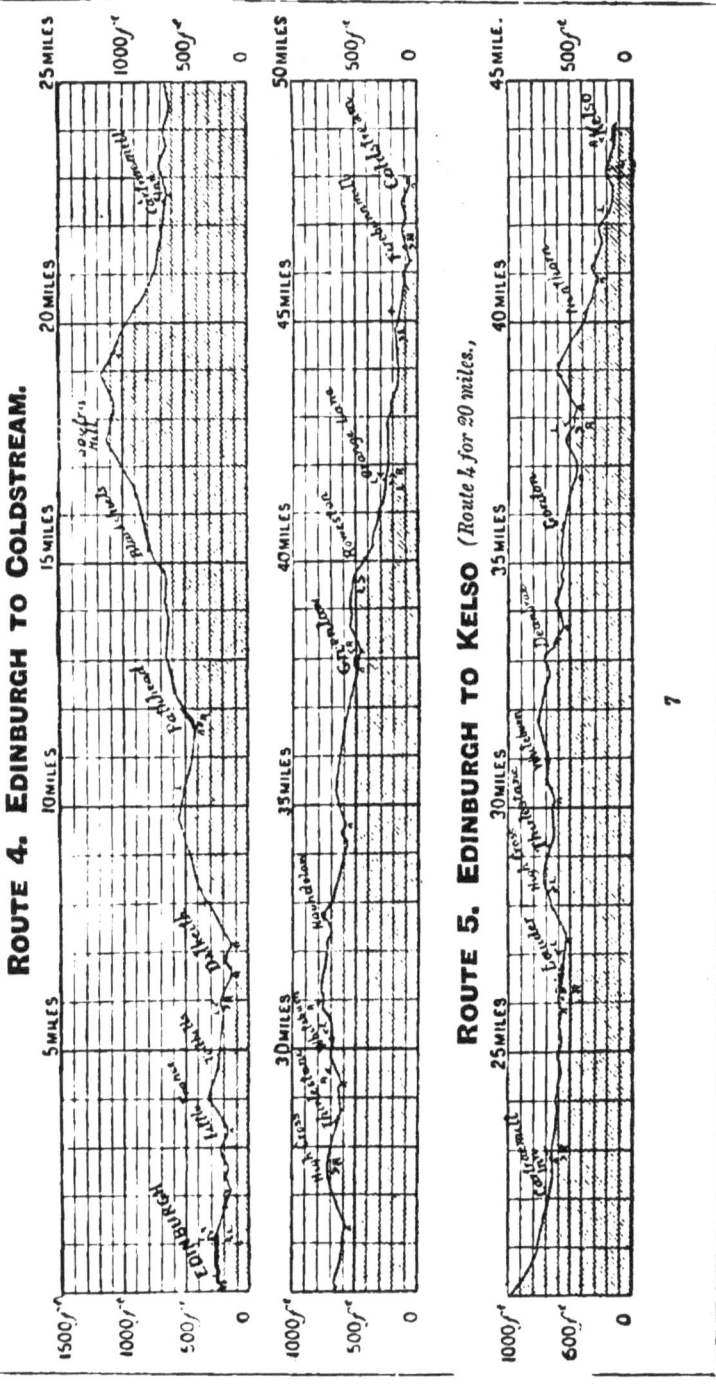

(*Route 5 continued.*)

correct; then none till beyond Carfraemill, when they are measured from Kelso by a disused road from Whiteburn. The milestones from Kelso are inaccurate.

Principal Objects of Interest.—DALKEITH; Palace. Newbattle Abbey. LAUDER; Castle, Church. KELSO; Floors Castle, Abbey, Roxburgh Castle ruins.

Hotels or Inns at places marked * and at Pathhead, Blackshiels, and Whiteburn.

6 EDINBURGH TO JEDBURGH, &c.

Description.—Class I. To Carfraemill Inn, Route 4. From thence on to Earlston the road is very smooth, with a few slight hills. The next section to near Jedburgh is very good but more hilly, from thence to Camptown is not quite so good, and the last part to the summit is very rough and stony. As a through road to Newcastle this Route is not recommended. (The more direct road from Lauder southwards is very hilly, but has a good surface.)

Gradients.—See Route 4 to Carfraemill. Descent to Drygrange 1 in 20-18. Ascent Lilliard's Edge 1 in 13; descent 1 in 17-23. From Jedburgh to Carter there are two ascents of 1 in 12, and one descent of 1 in 13, also Camptown Hill 1 in 14-16, and Carter Fell 1 in 16-18. By the Old Road south of Lauder in parts 1 in 13-16.

Milestones.—Measured from Crosscauseway, Edinr., correct to Soutra, thence *via* Oxton and old road south of Lauder, irregular. Afterwards correct from Jedburgh.

Measurements.

Edinburgh,* G.P.O.								
6¾	Dalkeith,* High St.							
26½	19¾	Lauder,* Town House.						
33½	26¾	7	Earlston.*					
38	31¼	11½	4½	St. Boswells * Station.				
47¾	41	21¼	14¼	9¾	Jedburgh,* Market.			
58½	51¾	32	25	20½	10¾	Carter Boundary.		
73½	66¾	47	40	35½	25¾	15	Otterburn.	
104¼	97½	77¾	70¾	66¼	56½	45¾	30¾	Newcastle, Bigg Mark't.

Principal Objects of Interest.—3¼m., Craigmillar Castle. 6¾m., Dalkeith Palace. EARLSTON; Rhymer's Tower. 41¾m., Lilliard's Edge; Battle, 1545. JEDBURGH; Abbey.

Hotels or Inns at places marked * and at Pathhead, Blackshiels, Carfraemill, and Ancrum.

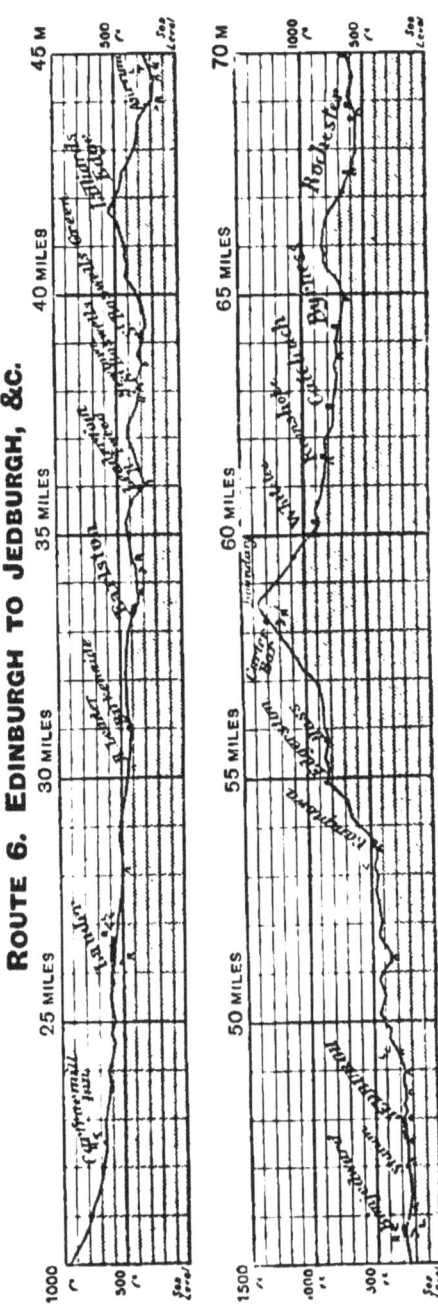

ROUTE 6. EDINBURGH TO JEDBURGH, &C.

Signs: < Road Fork, forward journey, > ditto reverse, + Cross Roads, ⊥ Road Junction, ∩ Bridge T indicates a sharp turn. The directions R (right) and L (left) for the forward journey are above the line, those of the reverse, below.

7 EDINBURGH TO HAWICK.

Description.—The first 10 miles are rather lumpy in parts, but afterwards the road is very fine to summit, on which there are usually patches of stones. The descent along the Gala water is not quite so good—sometimes rather lumpy—to Galashiels. From thence to Selkirk is very fine; but the section to Hawick, though of very good surface, is somewhat trying. Class I.

Travellers up Ettrick and Yarrow keep to right at 38¼m., and join the road from Selkirk ¾ of a mile further on.

Gradients.—At 6m., 1 in 21; 6¼m., 1 in 22; 8m., 1 in 25, thence easier to summit. Ascent at 38½m., 1 in 24; past Selkirk, 1 in 23-19; at 43¾m. and 44½m., 1 in 19. The descent to Hawick is 1 in 24, followed by 1 in 16.

Milestones.—Measured from Crosscauseway, Edinr., correct to Galashiels, where those from Selkirk are met; the milestones after Selkirk are from Edinr. *via* Clovenfords.

Measurements.

Edinburgh,* G.P.O.								
4¼	Gilmerton * Inn.							
6½	2¼	Eskbank * Inn.						
16¾	12½	10¼	Heriot * Station.					
25¼	21	18¾	8½	Stow,* Town Hall.				
33	28¾	26½	16¼	7¾	Galashiels,* Market Pl.			
39	34¾	32½	22¼	13¾	6	Selkirk,* Town Hall.		
44¼	40	37¾	27½	19	11¼	5¼	Ashkirk Bridge.	
50¾	46½	44¼	34	25½	17¾	11¾	6½	Hawick,* Tn. Hall.

Principal Objects of Interest.—6m., Melville Castle. 6½m., to East, Newbattle Abbey. 9m., Dalhousie Castle to West. 12m., Borthwick Castle. 34¾m., Abbotsford, across Tweed. 39m., Selkirk. 50¾m., Hawick.

Hotels or Inns at places marked *.

8 EDINBURGH TO PEEBLES.

Description.—Class II. A hilly road, of very good surface to Leadburn. The surface is loose about the summit and for a mile down, but thereafter it is very fine to Eddleston. The last few miles to Peebles are poor.

Gradients.—From Liberton Dams, 1 in 16; Burdiehouse, 1 in 21; Penicuik, 1 in 20-27; at 14m. 1 in 21.

Milestones.—Measured from Crosscauseway, — correct, but the first milestone from Peebles is 1⅛.

(*Continued next page.*)

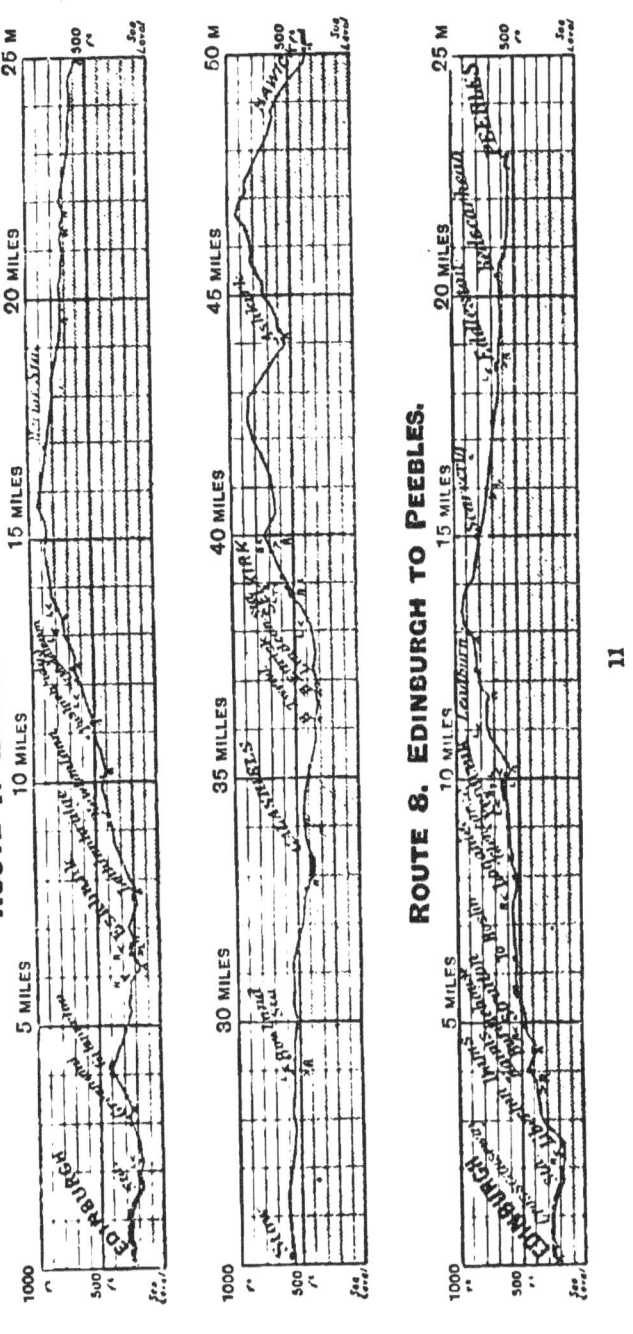

(*Route 8 continued.*)

Measurements.

Edinburgh,* G.P.O.						
5	Straiton * Inn.					
8¼	3¼	Glencorse.				
10	5	1¾	Penicuik,* Square.			
13	8	4¾	3	Leadburn * Inn.		
18½	13½	10¼	8½	5½	Eddleston.	
22⅞	17⅞	14⅝	12⅞	9⅞	4⅜	Peebles * Cross.

Caledonian Sta., Edin., to Penicuik, *via* Fairmilehead, 9⅝m.

Principal Objects of Interest.—4½m., Burdiehouse. 5m., Straiton Oil Works. 6¼m., Fork to Roslin. 8¼m., Glencorse Barracks. 12¼m., Wellington Reformatory. 23m., PEEBLES, Neidpath Castle, River Tweed, &c.

Hotels or Inns at places marked * and at Loganlee.

---

9 EDINBURGH TO MOFFAT.

Description.—Class II. Good surface, but hilly, to Leadburn, thence very good to Knock, poor into Broughton, good to Crook, and then gradually getting loose; but the descent to Moffat is good. The only bad part is at the summit, about a mile long. Some travellers prefer the road *via* Abington.

Gradients.—See previous route to Leadburn, thence nothing difficult to Broughton, with the exception of a very short hill at 18¾m., 1 in 21, with a sharp turn at the top and bottom. The descent to Moffat is an average grade of 1 in 29 for the first half, 1 in 25 for the second, with a maximum of 1 in 20 for a short distance.

Milestones.—To Leadburn as previous route, thence deficient until Romanno Bridge, after which they are correct. This set, however, is measured from Grassmarket, Edinburgh, *via* Howgate. The 20th and onwards is 20⅜ from G.P.O.

Measurements.

Edinburgh,* G.P.O.							
5	Straiton * Inn.						
10	5	Penicuik,* Square.					
13	8	3	Leadburn * Inn.				
19¾	14¾	9¾	6¾	Romanno * Bridge.			
28½	23½	18½	15½	8¾	Broughton.*		
35½	30½	25½	22½	15¾,	7	Crook * Inn.	
52	47	42	39	32¼	23½	16½	Moffat,* High St.

Principal Objects of Interest.—To Leadburn, see Route 9. 30m., to East, Drummelzier Castle. 47m., Devil's Beef Tub (Punch Bowl), 500 ft. below road. 52m., MOFFAT; Spa; and many interesting places in neighbourhood.

Hotels or Inns at places marked * and at Loganlee.

ROUTE 9. EDINBURGH TO MOFFAT. *Route 8 for 10 miles.*

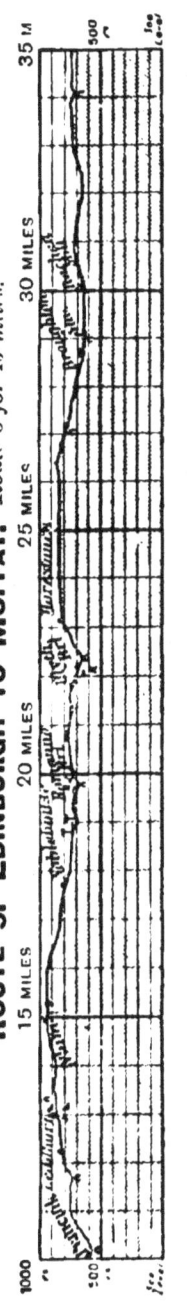
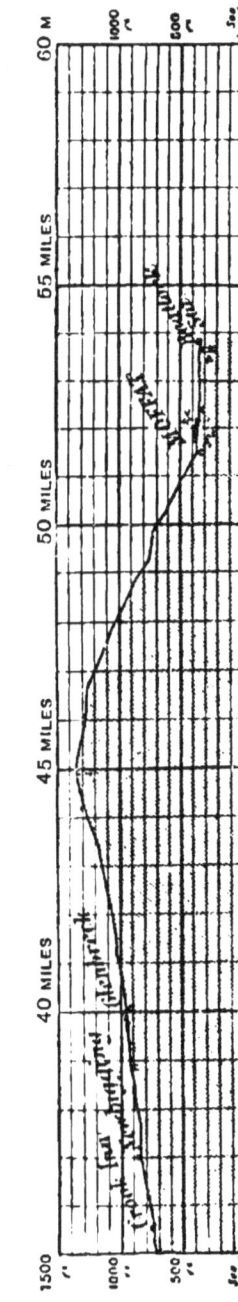

Signs: < Road Fork, forward journey, > ditto reverse, + Cross Roads, ⊥ Road Junction, ∩ Bridge, T indicates a sharp turn.

The directions R (right) and L (left) for the forward journey are above the Road Line, those of the reverse, below.

10 EDINBURGH TO ABINGTON.

Description.—Class II. The better road to Carlops is *via* Glencorse (see Route 9), thence the surface is good. Travellers from the West End travel *via* Hillend, but this road has rather severe hills, although the surface is quite good. From Carlops onwards is good; through Dolphinton it is rather rough, but nearing Biggar the road improves, and on to Lamington is exceedingly smooth. From thence to Clyde Bridge is very rough in parts, but from this point to Abington is exceedingly good.

Gradients.—Glencorse road, see Route 9. *Via* Hillend, from Morningside Station 1 in 26. Descent from Fairmilehead 1 in 19. Ascent from Hillend 1 in 22. Ascent from Flotterstane Bridge 1 in 14-29-14. No further difficult hills.

Milestones.—Measured from Tollcross, *via* Hillend, irregularly placed. Those to Penicuik are measured from Crosscauseway.

Measurements.

Edinburgh,* G.P.O.							
5	Straiton * Inn.						
9½	4½	Penicuik * (Shottstown).					
15	10	5½	Carlops.*				
17⅝	12⅝	8⅛	2⅝	West Linton.*			
22	17	12½	7	4⅜	Dolphinton.*		
29	24	19½	14	11⅜	7	Biggar.*	
41⅛	36⅛	31⅝	26⅛	23½	19⅛	12⅛	Abington.*

Edinburgh,* Caledonian Station.				
4½	Hillend.			
13¾	9¼	Carlops.*		
27¾	23¼	14	Biggar.*	
39⅞	35⅜	26⅛	12⅛	Abington.*

From Edinr., Caledonian Station, *via* Penicuik, 40⅞m.

Principal Objects of Interest.—*Via* Glencorse, Route 9. *Via* Hillend,—7¾m., Rullion Green Battlefield. 13½m., Habbie's Howe (Dell). BIGGAR; Church; Mote. 35m., Lamington Tower.

Tinto Hill is very prominent near Biggar.

Hotels or Inns at places marked * and at Loganlee or Nine Mile Burn.

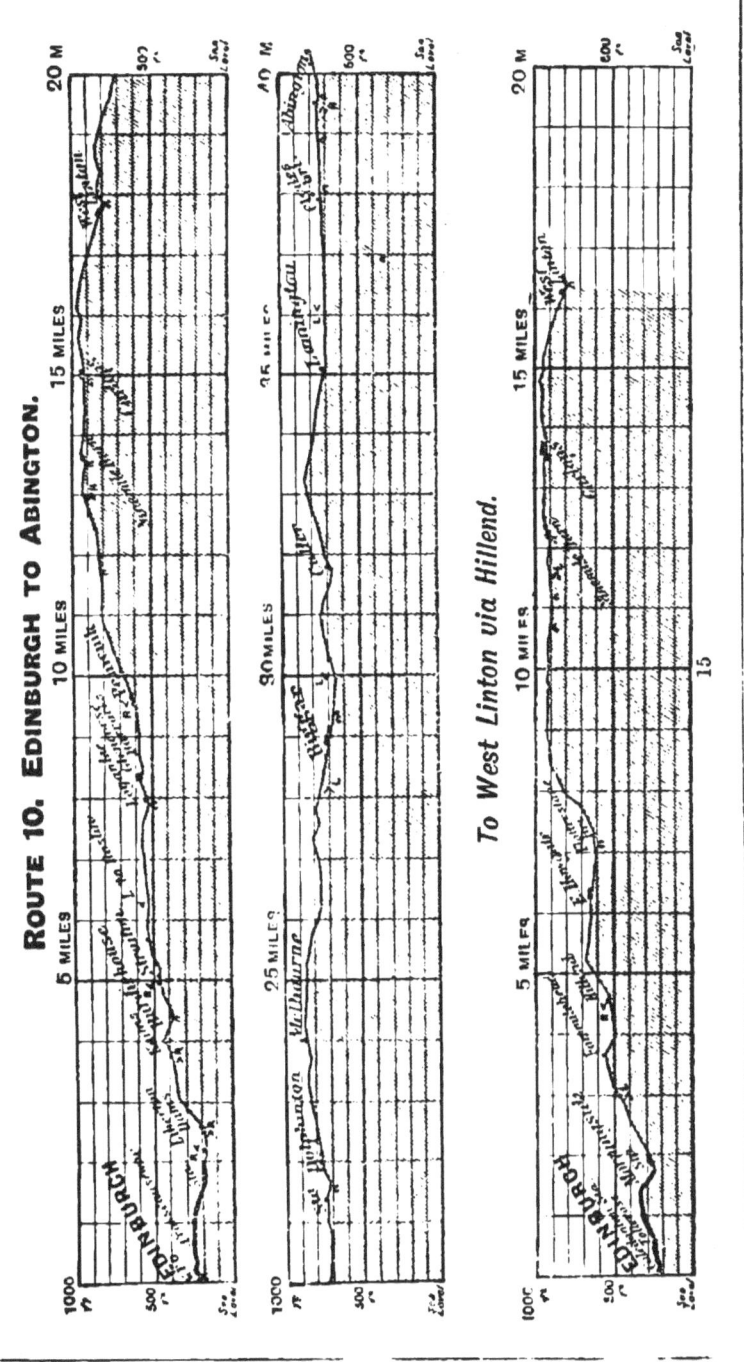

11 EDINBURGH TO LANARK.

Description.—Class III. This is a most trying and monotonous journey. The newer road, *via* Midcalder, see below, is much better. The first eight miles are very undulating, but quite good, then the road gets narrow and steep for a short distance, improving again until the branch to Kirknewton joins, after which it degenerates, and again becomes steep and loose—indeed it is a very bad road—until nearing Carnwath, when it again becomes good.

Gradients.—From Slateford, 1 in 28-16; at 8m., 1 in 13; at 12m., 1 in 13; and other short hills of 1 in 17-19-23. Descent to Lanark 1 in 20.

Milestones.—Measured from Tron Church, Edinburgh,—correctly placed.

Measurements.

Edinburgh,* G.P.O.					
6¼	Currie.*				
7⅝	1⅜	Balerno * Station.			
14	7¾	6⅜	Cairns Castle.		
25¾	19½	18⅛	11¾	Carnwath.*	
32⅝	26⅜	25	18⅝	6⅞	Lanark,* Cross.

Principal Objects of Interest.—Dreary moorland road. LANARK; Falls of Clyde, Cartland Crags.

Hotels or Inns at places marked * and at Carstairs Junction.

---

12 EDINBURGH TO LANARK.

Description.—Good road, but lumpy, to Midcalder, thereafter good to West Calder. It then deteriorates considerably, and becomes loose about the summit, but improves again near Wilsontown, and from thence to Lanark is very good.

Gradients.—The principal gradients are Forth Hill 1 in 23, and at Cleghorn Station 1 in 18.

Measurements.

Edinburgh,* G.P.O.				
12½	Midcalder.*			
17¼	4¾	West Calder.*		
24⅜	11⅞	7⅛	Wilsontown.	
33⅜	20⅞	16⅛	9	Lanark * Cross.

Milestones.—Measured from West Port, Edinburgh, and from Lanark Municipal Boundary,—correctly placed.

(*Continued next page.*)

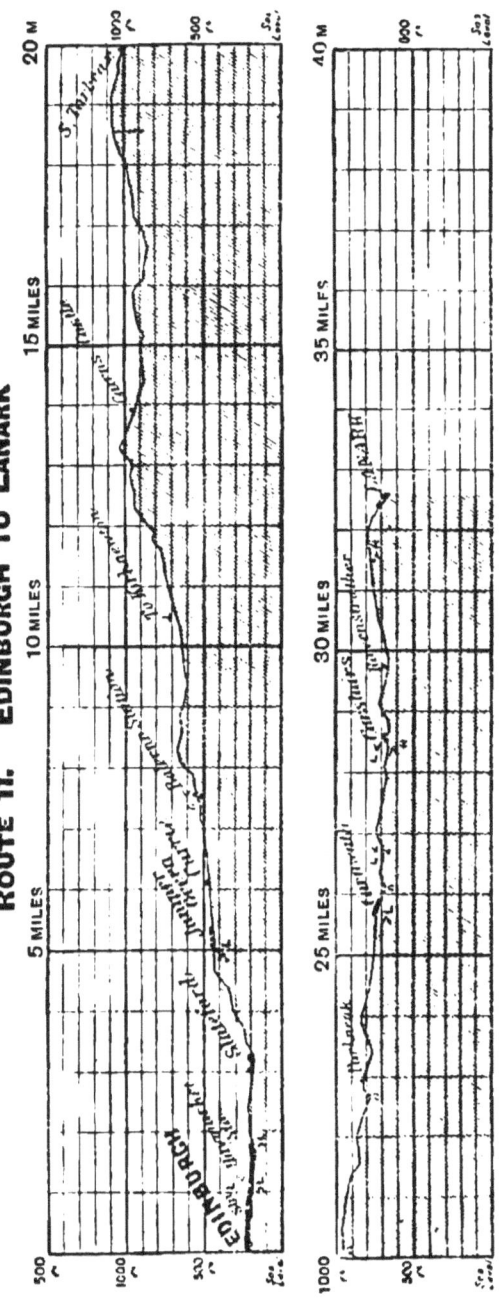

ROUTE 11. EDINBURGH TO LANARK

Signs < Road Fork, forward journey > ditto reverse. + Cross Roads, ⊥ Road Junction, ∩ Bridge, ⊤ indicates a sharp turn. The directions R (right) and L (left) for the forward journey are above the Road Line, those of the reverse, below.

(*Route 12 continued.*)
Principal Objects of Interest.—7¾m., Dalmahoy House. MIDCALDER; Calder House. Wilsontown; Ironworks. LANARK, as Route 11.

Hotels or Inns at places marked * and at East Calder and Forth.

13 EDINBURGH TO STRATHAVON.

Description.—Class II. This is a good road to Midcalder, though rather lumpy, and continues good until a few miles after West Calder, when it becomes very stony and loose, through disuse. Nearing Newmains the surface improves, and is quite good on to Strathavon.

Gradients.—Descent and ascent at Midcalder 1 in 26; maximum to summit, 1 in 29. Descent at Overton 1 in 22-14-17; ascent from Garrion Bridge 1 in 17-20.

Milestones.—Measured from West Port, Edinburgh,—tolerably correct.

Measurements.

Edinburgh,* G.P.O.
12¼ Midcalder.*
17¼ 4¾ West Calder.*
30¾ 18¼ 13½ Newmains.*
38¾ 26¼ 21¾ 7¾ Stonehouse.*
42½ 30 25¼ 11¾ 3¾ Strathavon,* Green.

Principal Objects of Interest.—7¾m., Dalmahoy House. MIDCALDER; Calder House; through moorland to Newmains in coal and iron district. STRATHAVON; Castle ruins; Falls.

Hotels or Inns at places marked * and at East Calder.

14 EDINBURGH TO HAMILTON.

Description.—Class I. A fairly good road throughout. The first few miles are good but lumpy, thereafter to Midcalder is better; very smooth to Whitburn; not so good about Shotts; and from thence to Hamilton, a good road.

This is really the Old Glasgow Road, but is seldom used for through traffic.

Gradients.—The steepest are 1 in 25 at Salsburgh and Newarthill, and 1 in 21 descending to the Clyde.

Milestones.—Are generally correctly placed. They are measured from Edinburgh, West Port, and from Glasgow Suburbs in Lanarkshire. Those to Hamilton are measured from the Glasgow set.

(*Continued next page.*)

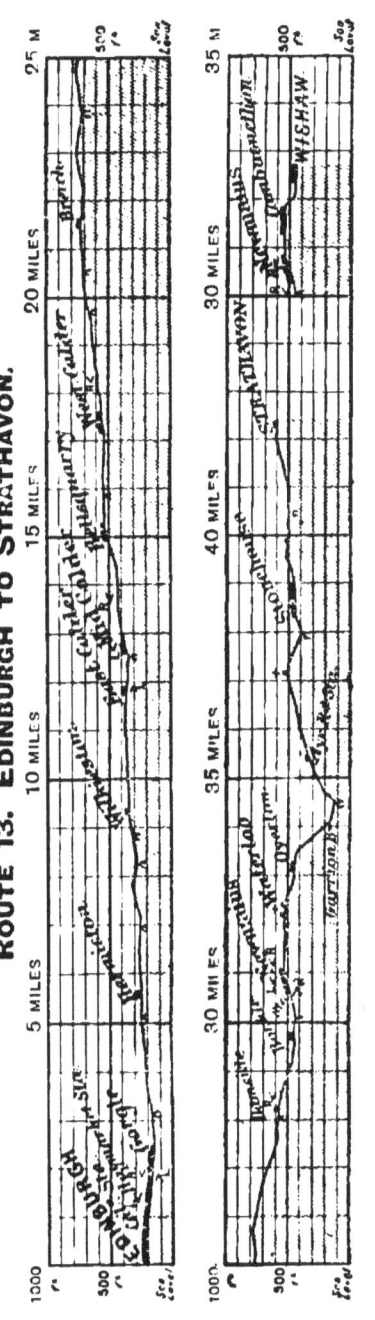

(*Route 14 continued.*)

Measurements.

Edinburgh * G.P.O.							
12½	Midcalder.*						
17¼	4¾	West Calder.*					
18¾	6¼	1½	Blackburn.*				
21⅛	8⅝	3⅞	2⅜	Whitburn.*			
30¾	18¼	13½	12	9⅝	Newhouse.		
34½	22	17¼	15	13⅜	3¾	Motherwell.*	
37⅛	24⅝	19⅞	18⅜	16	6⅜	2⅝	Hamilton.*

Principal Objects of Interest.—7¾m. Dalmahoy House. MIDCALDER; Calder House. HAMILTON; Palace; Cadzow Castle ruins.

Hotels or Inns at places marked * and at East Calder, Livingstone, Harthill, and Shotts.

---

15 EDINBURGH TO STIRLING.

Description.—Class I. A very fine road to Kirkliston, then not quite so good as far as Linlithgow. From thence to Larbert and Plean is exceedingly good, but from this point the road is much poorer into Stirling. The road is paved, and rough, through Linlithgow and Falkirk.

Gradients.—Descent to Linlithgow 1 in 23; short dip at Laurieston 1 in 12, and 1 in 14.

Milestones.—Measured from Caledonian Station, Edinburgh, to near Plean, where they are reckoned from Stirling Burgh Hall.

Measurements.

Edinburgh,* G.P.O.						
9	Kirkliston.*					
11¼	2¼	Winchburgh.				
16⅞	7⅞	5⅝	Linlithgow,* Cross.			
24⅜	15⅜	13⅛	7½	Falkirk,* Town Clock.		
27⅛	18⅛	15⅞	10¼	2¾	Larbert.*	
35½	26½	24¼	18⅝	11⅛	8⅜	Stirling,* King St.

Principal Objects of Interest.—4m., Convalescent Home. 11m., Niddry Castle. LINLITHGOW; Palace and Church. 23¾m., Roman Wall. 25¾m., Carron Iron Works. 33m., Bannockburn, Battlefield, 1314; Sauchieburn, Battlefield, 1488. St. Ninians; Church Steeple. STIRLING; Castle, Cemetery, King's Park, Wallace Monument, Cambuskenneth Abbey.

Hotels or Inns at places marked * and at Corstorphine, Laurieston, Polmont, Plean, and Bannockburn.

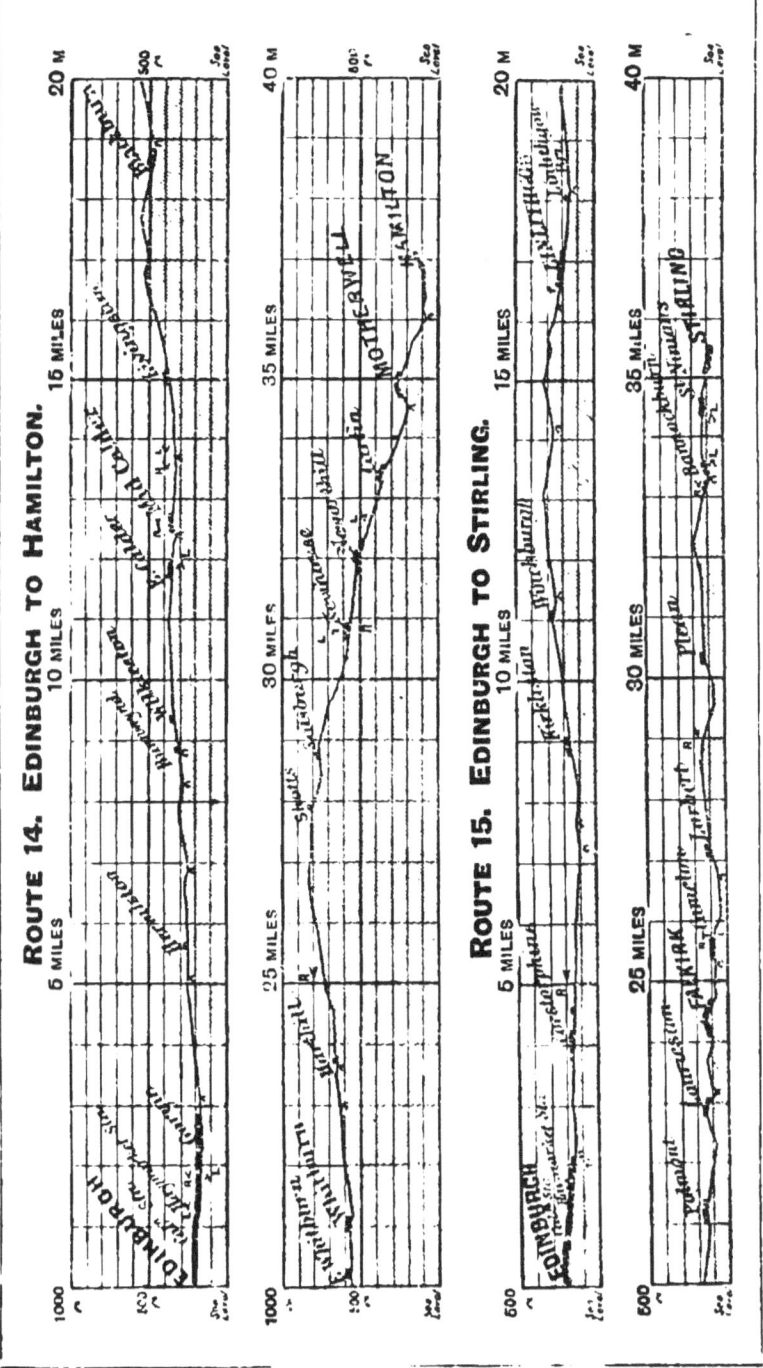

16 EDINBURGH TO CRIEFF.

Description.—Class I. & II. The section to Queensferry is very good, but cut up with coaching traffic. The descent to Hawes Inn, with the abrupt turn at the foot, is rather dangerous. Ferry to North Queensferry. From there to Dunfermline the road is hilly but quite good, it then becomes much looser over the hills through dreary country to near Rumbling Bridge, where it is very rough. From this point it improves, and is a good road up Glendevon, and right on to Crieff.

Gradients.—Hags Hill 1 in 20; Hawes Brae 1 in 13; North Queensferry Hill 1 in 26, descent 1 in 22; at 11½m. 1 in 11, descent 1 in 23; ascent near St. Margaret's Stone 1 in 15; ascent past Dunfermline 1 in 19; Gateside Hill 1 in 15; Dunduff Hill 1 in 23; descent to Hillend 1 in 22; descent and ascent at Mossendgreen 1 in 20 and 1 in 14; ascent to Rumbling Bridge Hotel 1 in 21; to Yetts 1 in 19; descent Gleneagles 1 in 22-27; at 41¾m., descent 1 in 22, ascent 1 in 24; short descent beyond Muthill 1 in 21; Crieff 1 in 12.

Milestones.—Only a few after Dunfermline. To Queensferry they are measured from Caledonian Station, Edinburgh, and thereafter from North Queensferry Inn as far as Dunfermline. Those between Yetts and Bishop's Bridge are measured from Crieff Bridge, thereafter measured from Stirling.

Measurements.

Edinburgh,* G.P.O.								
8¾	Hawes Inn,* Queensferry.							
9¾	1	North Queensferry.*						
16½	7¾	6¾	Dunfermline,* Town Hall.					
26½	17¾	16¾	10	Rumbling Bridge.*				
28	19¼	18¼	11½	1½	Yetts of Muckhart.			
36⅜	27⅝	26⅝	19⅞	9⅞	8⅜	Loaninghead.		
43¼	34½	33½	26¾	16¾	15¼	6⅞	Muthill.*	
46⅝	37⅞	36⅞	30⅛	20⅛	18⅝	10¼	3⅜	Crieff,* James Sq.

Principal Objects of Interest.—3⅝m., Cramond on R. 5½m., Dalmeny House. QUEENSFERRY; Forth Bridge. 13½m., Queen Margaret's Stone. DUNFERMLINE; Abbey. 26½m., Rumbling Bridge and Cauldron Linn. 42m., Culdees Castle. 44m., Drummond Castle. CRIEFF; Falls of Barvick, Turret; Ochtertyre. The scenery at Rumbling Bridge and in Glendevon is very picturesque.

Hotels or Inns at places marked * and at Cramond Bridge and Glendevon.

ROUTE 16. EDINBURGH TO CRIEFF.

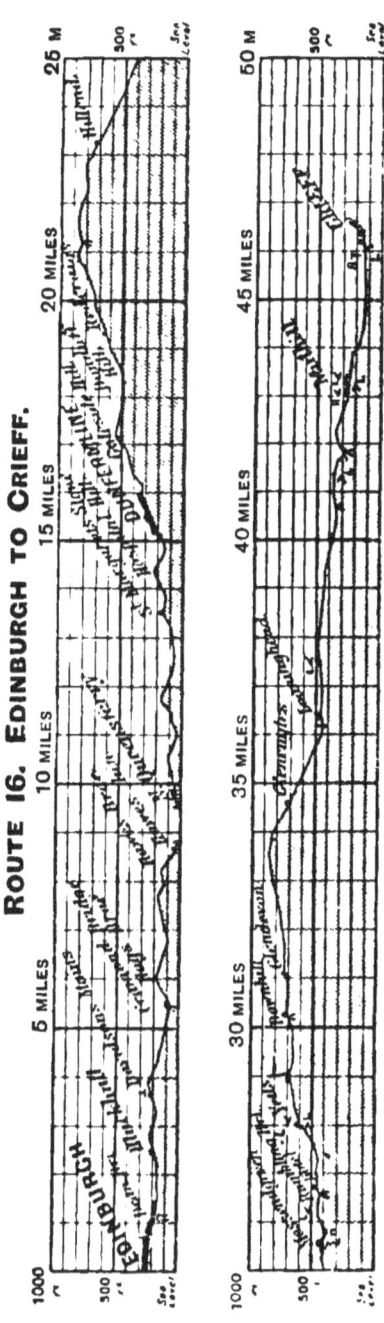

Signs: < Road Fork, forward journey, > ditto reverse, + Cross Roads, ⊥ Road Junction, ∩ Bridge, ⊤ indicates a sharp turn

The directions R (right) and L (left) for the forward journey are above the Road Line, those of the reverse, below.

17 EDINBURGH TO PERTH.

Description.—Class I. Ferry Granton to Burntisland. Very fine road, with splendid stretches of level. The surface throughout is very good, except in the upper part of Glenfarg.

Via North Queensferry see previous Route to that place, thence very good road. Ferry at Queensferry.

Gradients.—Burntisland Hill 1 in 22-14 ; 11m., 1 in 19-25 ; ascent Moncreiffe Hill 1 in 16-22 ; descent 1 in 25. On Queensferry Road, at 13m., 1 in 22-25.

Milestones.—On the Burntisland and Cowdenbeath section, irregular. At Cowdenbeath the regular milestones, measured from N. Queensferry, are met, and continue correct to Perth (the last M.S. is 1½ miles from Perth Cross).

Measurements.

Edinburgh,* G.P.O.							
3	Granton,* Pier.						
8	5	Burntisland,* Pier.					
14¾	11¾	6¾	Cowdenbeath.*				
22¾	19¾	14¾	8	Kinross,* P.O.			
24½	21½	16½	9¾	1¾	Milnathort.*		
36¼	33¼	28¼	21½	13½	11¾	Bridge of Earn.*	
40¼	37¼	32¼	25½	17½	15¾	4	Perth,* Cross.

via Queensferry.

10⅞	Inverkeithing.*	
26	15⅛	Kinross.*

Principal Objects of Interest.—20¼m., Gairney Bridge Memorial. KINROSS ; Loch Leven and Castle ; St. Serf's Island. MILNATHORT ; Burleigh Castle ruins. 33¼m., Rocking Stone. 36⅜m., Old Bridge. 36½m., Moncreiffe House. PERTH ; North Inch ; St. John's Church ; County Buildings ; Glover's Cottage ; Kinnoull Hill ; Scone Palace.

Hotels or Inns at places marked * and at Stewart's Arms, Blairadam, Glenfarg, Bein, and Aberargie. And at Cramond Bridge, N. & S. Queensferry, &c., *via* Queensferry.

18 EDINBURGH TO DUNDEE.

Description.—Class I. A very fine but undulating road nearly all the way. The surface is rather rough through the paved "Lang Toun"—for three miles—and after New Inn. Ferries: Granton to Burntisland, Newport to Dundee.

Gradients.—Pathhead Hill 1 in 12-18 ; past New Inn 1 in 18 ; Newport Hill 1 in 13.

Milestones.—Measured from Burntisland Pier, practically correct. The 1st M.S. from Newport is ⅜m. from the pier.

(*Continued next page.*)

ROUTE 17. EDINBURGH TO PERTH.

Via Queensferry (to Cowdenbeath).

(Route 18 continued.)

Measurements.

Edinburgh,* G.P.O.								
3	Granton,* Pier.							
8	5	Burntisland,* Pier.						
11	8	3	Kinghorn.*					
14	11	6	3	Kirkcaldy,* Town Hall.				
23	20	15	12	9	New Inn.*			
31¾	28¾	23¾	20¾	17¾	8¾	Cupar,* Town Hall.		
42⅞	39⅞	34⅞	31⅞	28⅞	19⅞	11⅛	Newport,* Pier.	
44¾	41¾	36¾	33¾	30¾	21¾	13	1⅞	Dundee,* Town Ho.

Principal Objects of Interest.—9¾m. King Alexander's Cliff. KINGHORN; Tower. 12½m. Seafield Castle ruins. KIRKCALDY; Church Tower, Burgh School, Balwearie Tower. 29¼m. to N., Springfield Asylum, Crawford Priory. CUPAR; Duncan Institute, Parish Kirk. 34m. to S., Dura Den. 34⅜m. Dairsie Church, and Castle. Newport; Mars Training Ship.

Hotels or Inns at places marked * and at St. Michaels.

---

19 FIFE COAST ROUTE.

Description.—Class II. With the exception of the bad part through Pathhead, the road is exceedingly good the whole way. If travelling *via* Elie, add 1 mile.

Gradients.—Pathhead Hill 1 in 12; 2m., 1 in 19; 23½m., 1 in 20; 31¾m., 1 in 22; 35m., 1 in 21-25.

Milestones.—Measured from Burntisland Pier, correct to Crail. Thence measured from St. Andrews old Town Hall, and on to Leuchars.

Measurements.

Kirkcaldy,* Town Hall.									
2	Dysart.*								
9	7	Leven.*							
11¾	9¾	2¾	Largo,* (Lundin Mill Bridge).						
22¼	20¼	13¼	10½	Anstruther * Bridge.					
26½	24½	17½	14¾	4¼	Crail.*				
36⅜	34⅜	27⅜	24⅝	14⅛	9⅞	St. Andrews.*			
42⅛	40⅛	33⅛	30⅜	19⅞	15⅝	5¾	Leuchars * Church.		
47¾	45¾	38¾	36	25½	21¼	11⅜	5⅝	Tayport,* Pier.	
18	16	9	6¼	5¼	9½	19⅝	25⅛	29¾	*Elie.**

Principal Objects of Interest.—1m. Ravenscraig Castle ruins. 5⅜m. Macduff's Castle. 11¼m. Standing Stones; LARGO; "Robinson Crusoe's" Birthplace. CRAIL; Town Hall. ST. ANDREWS; Castle, University, Cathedral, Links. 39⅜m. Guard Bridge. LEUCHARS; Church.

Hotels or Inns at places marked * and at Colinsburgh and St. Michaels.

Route 18. Edinburgh to Dundee.

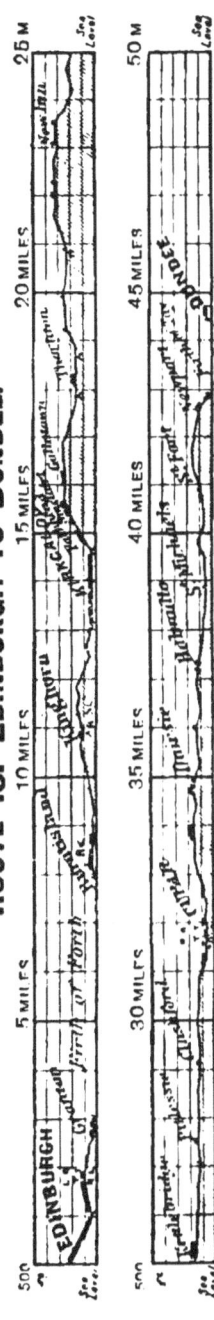

Route 19. Fife Coast Route.

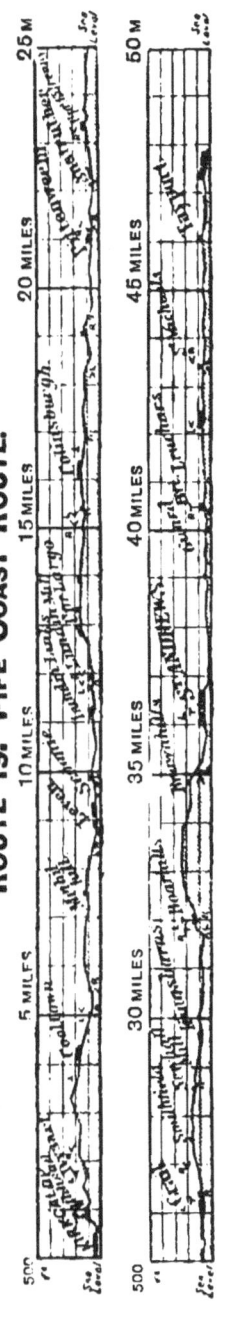

20 EDINBURGH TO LASSWADE.

Description.—Class III. A very hilly road, but of good surface. There is a very dangerous turn on the hill descending to Lasswade from Bonnyrigg.

Gradients.—At 2½m. 1 in 11-14; 4m. 1 in 14; 6¼m. 1 in 13; 8¾m. 1 in 12.

Milestones.—Measured from Edinr., Buccleuch Church.

Measurements.—Edinburgh,* G.P.O.

6⅛	Lasswade* Bridge.		
7	⅞	Bonnyrigg.*	
9¼	3⅛	2¼	Newtonloan.

Principal Objects of Interest.—8½m. Dalhousie Castle.

21 LINLITHGOW TO QUEENSFERRY.

Description.—Class II. The surface throughout is good. There are a number of curious and very confusing turns.

Gradients.—At 9m. 1 in 18.

Measurements.—Linlithgow,* Cross.

9⅛	Queensferry,* Town Hall.	
9⅝	½	Hawes Inn.

Principal Objects of Interest.—Hopetoun House.

22 BO'NESS TO BATHGATE.

Description.—Class III. A very hilly road with several dangerous hills. The surface, however, is fair.

Gradients.—At ¼m. 1 in 10; 1¼m. 1 in 17; 2m. 1 in 17; 4¾m. 1 in 14; 7¼m. 1 in 11.

Milestones.—Measured from Linlithgow, West Port.

Measurements.—Bo'ness,* Town Hall.

3¾	Linlithgow,* Cross.		
7½	4⅝	Torphichen.	
10⅜	7½	2⅞	Bathgate,* Station.

Principal Objects of Interest.—LINLITHGOW; Palace.

CONTOUR ROAD BOOK OF SCOTLAND.   29

FALKIRK TO DENNY, &c.   23

Description.—Class II. Smooth and level to Denny; thereafter steep, but with fair surface.
Gradients.—At 7m. 1 in 19; 7½m. 1 in 18.
Measurements.—Falkirk,* Town Clock.
    5¼ Denny,* Church.
   10¾ 5½ Carronbridge P.O.

FALKIRK TO ALLOA.   24

Description.—Class II. A good and fairly level road after Carron Ironworks. Ferry to Alloa (½m.).
Measurements.—Falkirk,* Town Clock.
    2 Carron P.O.
    9¼ 7¼ Alloa,* P.O.

FALKIRK TO BO'NESS, &c.   25

Description.—Class II. A very good and level road, but the continuation towards Queensferry, after Bo'ness, is steep.
Gradients.—At 10m. 1 in 11-20.
    Measurements.
Falkirk,* Town Clock.
 3 Grangemouth.*
 8½ 5½ Bo'ness,* Town Hall.
 18⅝ 15¾ 10¼ Queensferry,* Town Hall.

TRANENT TO GIFFORD.   26

1000
5 MILES   10 MILES
800   500
                                                           Level

Description.—Class III. A fair road, undulating but good surface.

   Hotels or Inns at places marked *.

Gradients.—At 5¾m. 1 in 17 ; 8½m. and 9½m. 1 in 20.
Measurements.—Tranent,* P.O.
                5¾   East Salton.
                9¾ 4   Gifford,* P.O.
Principal Objects of Interest.—4½m. Salton Hall. Gifford ; Castle.

27   ABERLADY TO GIFFORD.

Description.—Class III. Good surface, but very hilly.
Gradients.—At 3m. 1 in 18; 4½m. 1 in 15; 6¼m. 1 in 16; 6¾m. 1 in 14; 7¼m. 1 in 15; 9m. 1 in 18.
Measurements.—Aberlady.*
                5¼   Haddington,* Town Hall.
                9½ 4¼ Gifford,* P.O.
Principal Objects of Interest.—HADDINGTON ; Abbey. Gifford ; Castle.

28   DUNS TO COLDSTREAM.

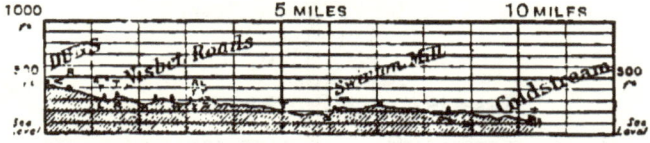

Description.—Class III. The surface is fair ; there are a number of abrupt turns.
Gradients.—¾m. 1 in 15 ; 3½m. 1 in 17.
Measurements.—Duns,* Town Hall.
                6½   Swintonmill.
               10¾ 4¼ Coldstream,* Market.

29   KELSO TO YETHOLM.

Description.—Class II. A hilly road, but of fair surface.
Gradients.—At ½m. and 3¾m. 1 in 15 ; 4½m. 1 in 23 ; 5½m. 1 in 21.
Milestones.—Measured from Kelso Square,—correct
Measurements.—Kelso,* Square.
                7¾   Yetholm,* P.O.
Principal Objects of Interest.—Kirk Yetholm is occupied by the descendants of the gypsies.

KELSO TO HOUNAM, &c.   30

Description.—Class II. The surface is fair, but the road has some stiff hills.

Gradients.—At ½m. 1 in 15; 3¼m. 1 in 21; 4m. 1 in 19; 6½m. 1 in 16; 8¾m. 1 in 16; 10m. 1 in 16.

Milestones.—Measured from Kelso Square,—correct.

Measurements.—Kelso,* Square.
        7¾ (Morebattle.*)
        11¾ ... Hounam.

KELSO TO EARLSTON.   31

Description.—Class III. A very hilly road, but with fair surface throughout.

Gradients.—At 3m. 1 in 19; 4¾m. 1 in 21; 6¾m. 1 in 13; 10½m. 1 in 18.

Milestones.—Measured from Kelso Square,—correct.

Measurements.—Kelso,* Square.
        6 Smailholm.
        12 6 Earlston.*

Principal Objects of Interest.—1½m. Floors Castle. Smailholm; Tower. EARLSTON; Rhymers Tower.

KELSO TO CORNHILL.   32

Description.—Class II. After the steep hill at Maxwellheugh the road is good, but somewhat undulating.

Gradients.—At ½m. 1 in 15.

Milestones.—Measured from Maxwellheugh,—correct.

Measurements.—Kelso,* Square.
        2¾ Sproustn.
        7¾ 5 Wark.
        10¼ 7¾ 2¾ Cornhill.*

Principal Objects of Interest.—Wark; Castle and Battlefield.

Hotels or Inns at places marked *.

33 BERWICK TO LAUDER, &c.

Description.—Class II. A good road as far as Gavinton, thence very hilly and somewhat rough to Westruther, after which the surface improves. From Lauder to Stow is a rough and very steep road. For Duns keep to R. at 13⅝m., and join this road at 17¾m.—⅛m. longer.

Gradients.—At 18¾m. 1 in 22; 29½m. 1 in 21; 32¼m. 1 in 25-20; 34m. 1 in 22, 1 in 15; 38m. 1 in 27-13, 9-12.

Milestones.—Measured from Duns, except near Berwick.

Measurements.

Berwick,* Town Hall.
5 Paxton.*
(15¼ 10¼ *Duns,* Town Hall*).
25⅝ 20⅝ 10½ Westruther Church.
33¼ 28¼ 17⅛ 7⅝ Lauder,* Town House.
38½ 33½ 23⅜ 12⅜ 5¼ Stow,* Town Hall.

Principal Objects of Interest.—4½m., Paxton House. DUNS; Castle, Spa, Duns Law. Moorland Road to Westruther. LAUDER; Thirlestane Castle.

Hotels or Inns at places marked * and at Whiteburn.

34 BERWICK TO DUNS.

Description.—Class II. A very fair but hilly road all the way. This joins the previous Route at 13⅜m.

Gradients.—1½m. 1/20; 2¾m. 1/24; 13¾m. 1/22; 14¼m. 1/24.

Milestones.—Measured from Duns, except near Berwick.

Measurements.

Berwick,* Town Hall.
8¾ Chirnside* Church.
15¼ 6½ Duns,* Town Hall.

Principal Objects of Interest.—2½m., Battlefield, 1333. CHIRNSIDE; Ninewells Old Tree. 12m., Wedderburn Castle. DUNS; as above.

Hotels or Inns at places marked *.

35 EYEMOUTH TO GREENLAW.

Description.—Class III. On the whole the surface is fair, but the hills are very stiff.

Gradients.—At 2½m. 1 in 14; 7¾m. 1 in 14-17; 17¾m. 1 in 15-25; 20¾m. 1 in 17-22, 10-12.

Milestones.—Measured from Duns Town Hall.

Measurements.

Eyemouth.*
2⅝ Ayton.*
7½ 4⅞ Chirnside.*
13⅝ 11¼ 6⅜ Duns,* Town Hall.
21¼ 18⅝ 13¾ 7⅝ Greenlaw,* County Hall.

Principal Objects of Interest.—Ayton; Red Hall. CHIRNSIDE and DUNS as above.

Hotel or Inns at places marked *.

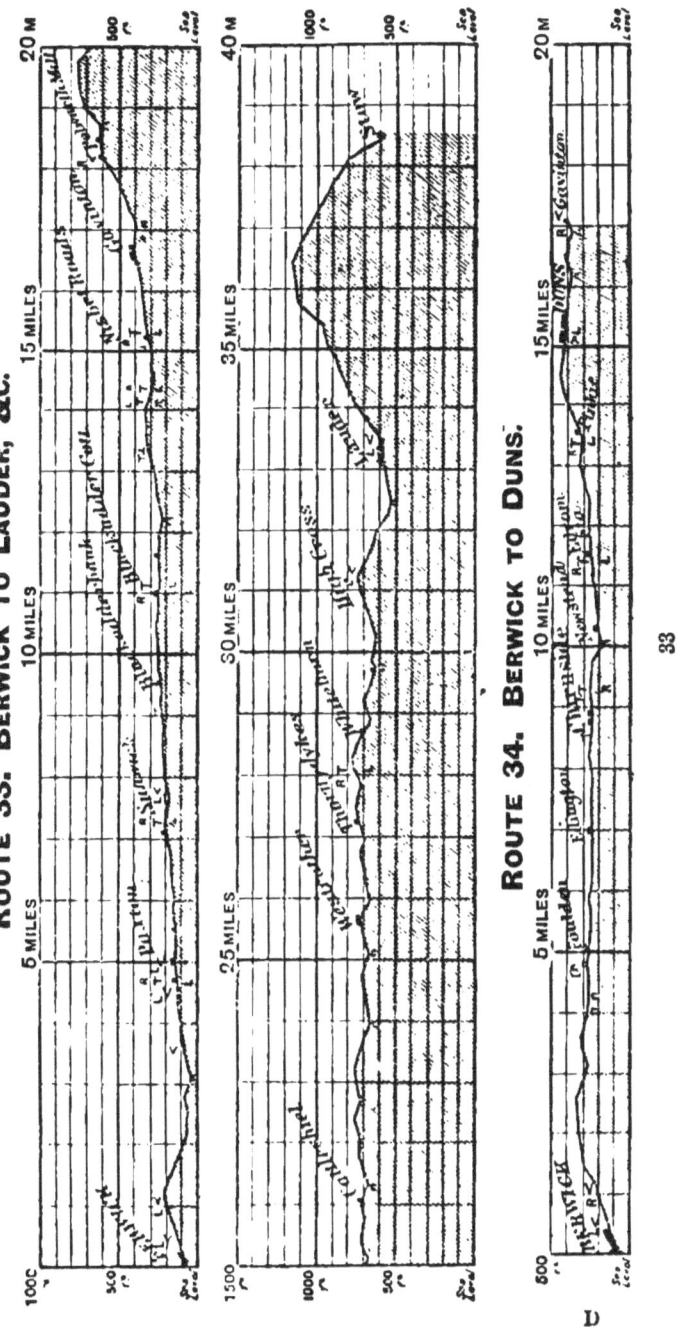

36 KELSO TO BERWICK.

Description.—Class I. A very fine smooth road, with easy undulations. This is the best road.

Gradients.—At 6¼m. 1 in 24 (Turn); 8¼m. 1 in 20.

Milestones.—Measured from Kelso, and Berwick Bridge.

Measurements.

Kelso,* Square.				
8¾	Coldstream.*			
13⅜	4⅝	Twizell Bridge.		
23	14¼	9⅝	Tweedmouth.*	
23½	14¾	10⅛	½	Berwick,* Town Hall.

Principal Objects of Interest.—Hendersidc Park. Twizell Bridge and Castle. 16⅝m., Norham Castle. BERWICK; Bridge and ancient Walls. The scenery is very pretty.

Hotels or Inns at places marked * and at Cornhill.

37 KELSO TO BERWICK.

Description.—Class II. The road has a good surface, but is hilly. Special attention to the proper road will need to be taken at the turns.

Gradients.—4¼m. 1 in 23; 20½m. 1 in 25.

Milestones.—Measured from Kelso Square, and Berwick Town Hall,—not very correct.

Measurements.

Kelso,* Square.				
5¾	Eccles.			
8¼	2½	Leitholm.		
11¾	6	3½	Swinton.*	
23⅝	17⅞	15⅜	11⅞	Berwick,* Town Hall.

Principal Objects of Interest.—Ednam; Thomson's Birthplace.

Hotels or Inns at places marked *.

38 HAWICK TO KELSO.

Description.—Class I. A very fine but undulating road all the way. Care should be taken at turn descending through Maxwellheugh.

Gradients.—Short hills of 1 in 17-25 to Kalemouth, thence at 16½m. and 18m. 1 in 19; 20¾m. 1 in 15 (dangerous).

Measurements.

Hawick,* Town Hall.					
5	Denholm.*				
12¼	7¼	Jedfoot Bridge Station.			
14	9	1¾	Crailing.		
21	16	8¾	7	Kelso,* Square.	
13¾	8¾	2½	4½	11¼	Jedburgh,* Market.

Milestones.—Measured from Hawick, fork of Edinburgh Road, and from Maxwellheugh. Those in centre are from Jedburgh Market.

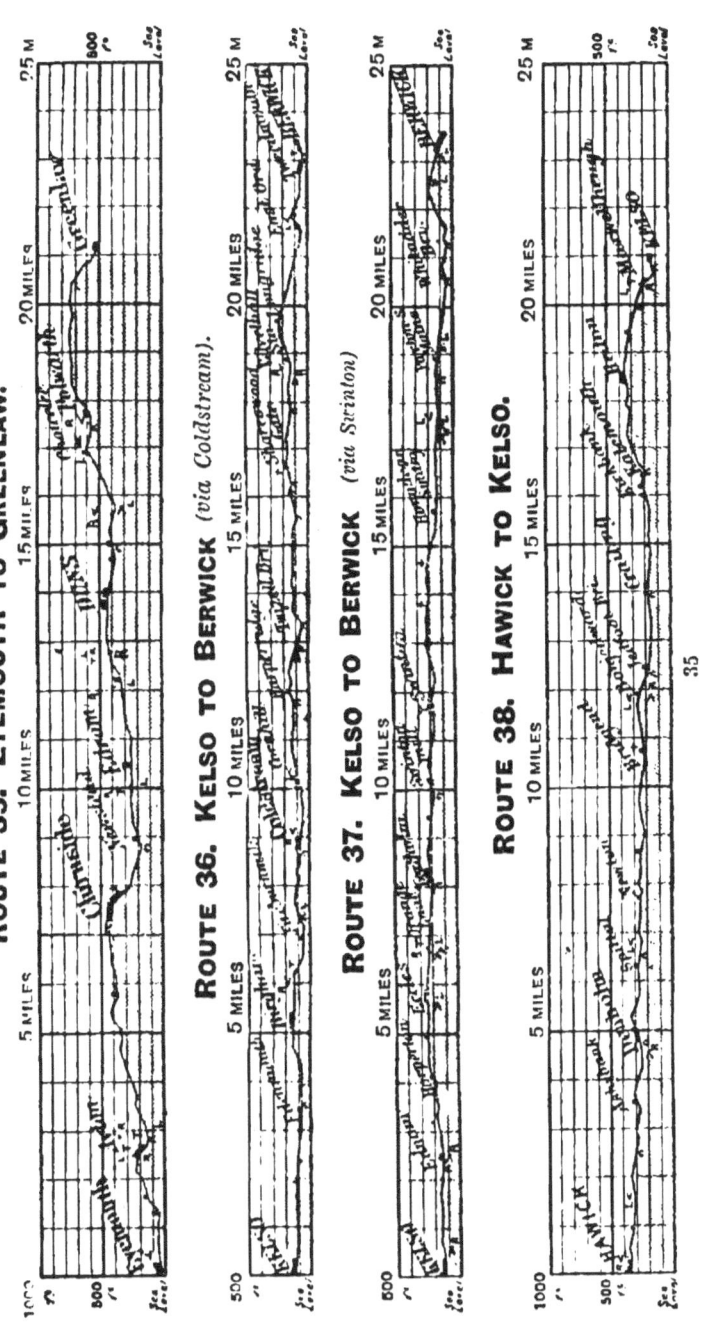

(*Route 38 continued.*)

Principal Objects of Interest.—Denholm; Minto House. 10¾m., Mounteviot House and Waterloo Monument. 12¼m., Roman Road. KELSO; Abbey, &c.

Hotels or Inns at places marked *.

39 HAWICK TO CARTER, &C.

Description.—Class II. The first few miles are good, but thereafter it is a steep and hilly road, very stony on the higher parts. The hills into Bonchester are dangerous.

Gradients.—The first ascent is, in parts, between 1 in 14 and 1 in 19. The descent to Bonchester is 1 in 16, ending 1 in 11, rising again 1 in 14-20, and falling again 1 in 15, thence at 12¾m. 1 in 19; 14½m. 1 in 17.

Milestones.—Measured from fork of Edinburgh road in Hawick,—fairly correct.

Measurements.

Hawick,* Town Hall.					
7⅜	Bonchester Bridge.				
10¼	2⅞	Chesters.			
15¾	8⅜	5½	Carter Boundary.		
30¾	23⅜	20½	15	Otterbourne.*	
61½	54⅛	51¼	45¾	30¾	Newcastle,* Bigg Market.

Principal Objects of Interest.—After Chesters the road is very bleak.

Hotels or Inns at places marked *.

40 HAWICK TO NEWCASTLETON.

Description.—Class III. For the first 4 miles the road is very good, but thereafter, as far as Hermitage, it is rough and loose, especially on the steeper parts. Thereafter the road is fair, but undulating, to Newcastleton.

Gradients.—At 5m. 1 in 12 to 1 in 18; 9½m. 1 in 18-13-20. Descent past Whitterhope mostly 1 in 22-27.

Milestones.—Measured from Edin. 50th milestone, correct, and from Jedburgh-Canobie milestones near Newcastleton.

Measurements.

Hawick,* Town Hall.			
7¼	Shankend Station.		
15¼	8	Hermitage School.	
20⅜	12⅛	5⅛	Newcastleton,* Square.

Principal Objects of Interest.—4¼m. Stobs Castle. 9½m. Catrail. 9⅝m. Robert's Linn. 14¾m. Hermitage Castle. NEWCASTLETON; Cross. Rather monotonous scenery.

Hotels or Inns at places marked *. None on road.

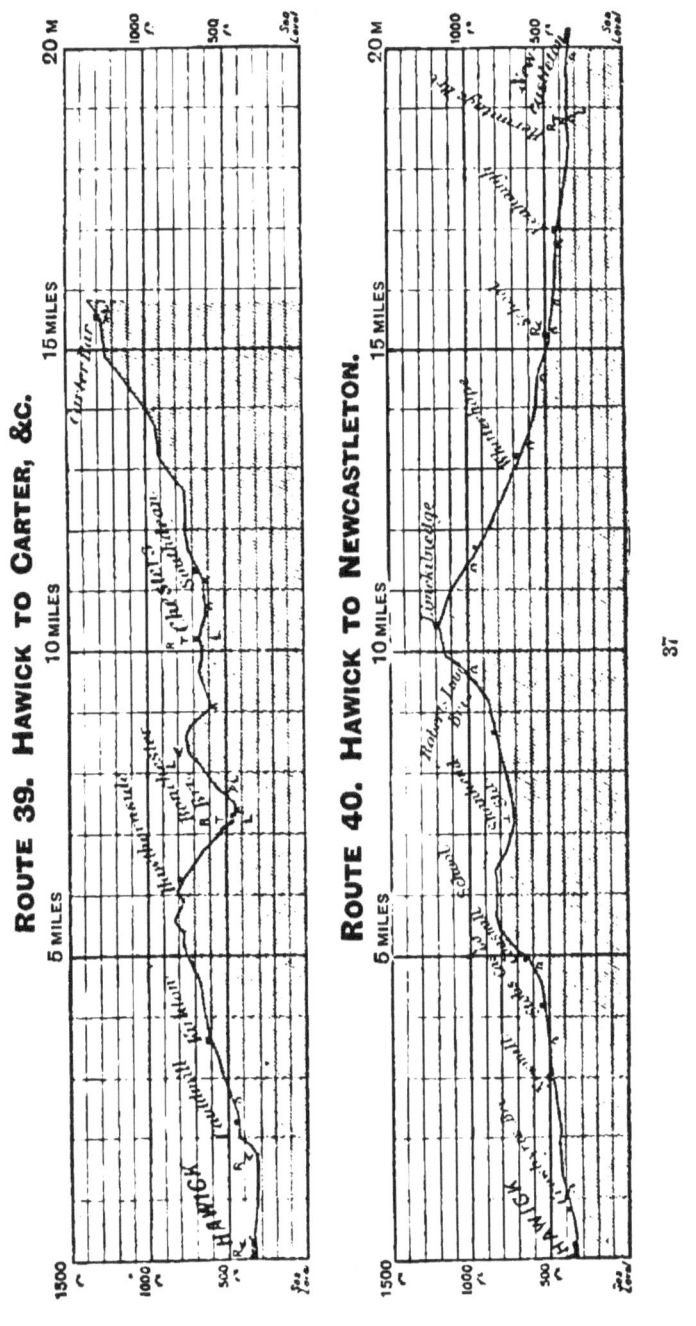

41   HAWICK TO CARLISLE.

Description.—Class I. A magnificent road the whole way to Carlisle. Leaving Hawick, the road is a little rough, but thereafter it is very smooth with easy hills right up to the summit. The descent is gradual, with several slight undulations to Langholm, after which the road is very good till near Carlisle, when it becomes lumpy through heavy traffic.

Gradients.—1 in 25 is the maximum grade to Langholm, then at 24¼m. 1 in 19; and 24¾m. 1 in 24. Stanwix Hill is about 1 in 16.

Milestones.—Measured from Edinr., Crosscauseway, *via* Clovenfords,—correct to Scots Dyke; thence measured from Carlisle Market.

Measurements.

    Hawick,* Town Hall.
   9   Teviothead.
  23   14   Langholm,* Town Hall.
  29   20   6   Canobie.*
  35   26   12   6   Longtown.*
  43¼   34¼   20¼   14¼   8¼   Carlisle,* Market Place.

Principal Objects of Interest.—3½m. Branxholm Tower, 9m., Caerlanrig Chapel. 27¾m., Gilnockie Tower. 31⅝m., Scots Dyke. CARLISLE; Cathedral, Prison. Pretty scenery between Langholm and Canobie.

Hotels or Inns at places marked *; none at Mosspaul.

42   HAWICK TO ST. MARY'S LOCH.

Description.—Class III. For the first 5 miles the road is fair, but thereafter as far as Tushielaw it is a very hilly, soft, and bad road. Thence the road is a very loose one, specially rough on the steep descent to Tibbie Shiels.

Gradients.—At 2¾m. 1 in 18. Ascent past Greenbank 1 in 16-19-13-18-12. Descent 1 in 19-22; 13m. 1 in 18-20. The dangerous descent to St. Mary's Loch commences 1 in 25, and is 1 in 10 at the steepest part.

Milestones.—Measured from the 50th Edinburgh milestone in Hawick,—correct.

Measurements.

    Hawick,* Town Hall.
  15¾   Tushielaw * Inn.
  21¾   6   St. Mary's Loch; Tibbie Shiels.*

Principal Objects of Interest.—3¼m. Harden Castle, to N. 16m., Tushielaw Tower. The road winds among the hills and is rather monotonous.

Hotels or Inns at places marked *.

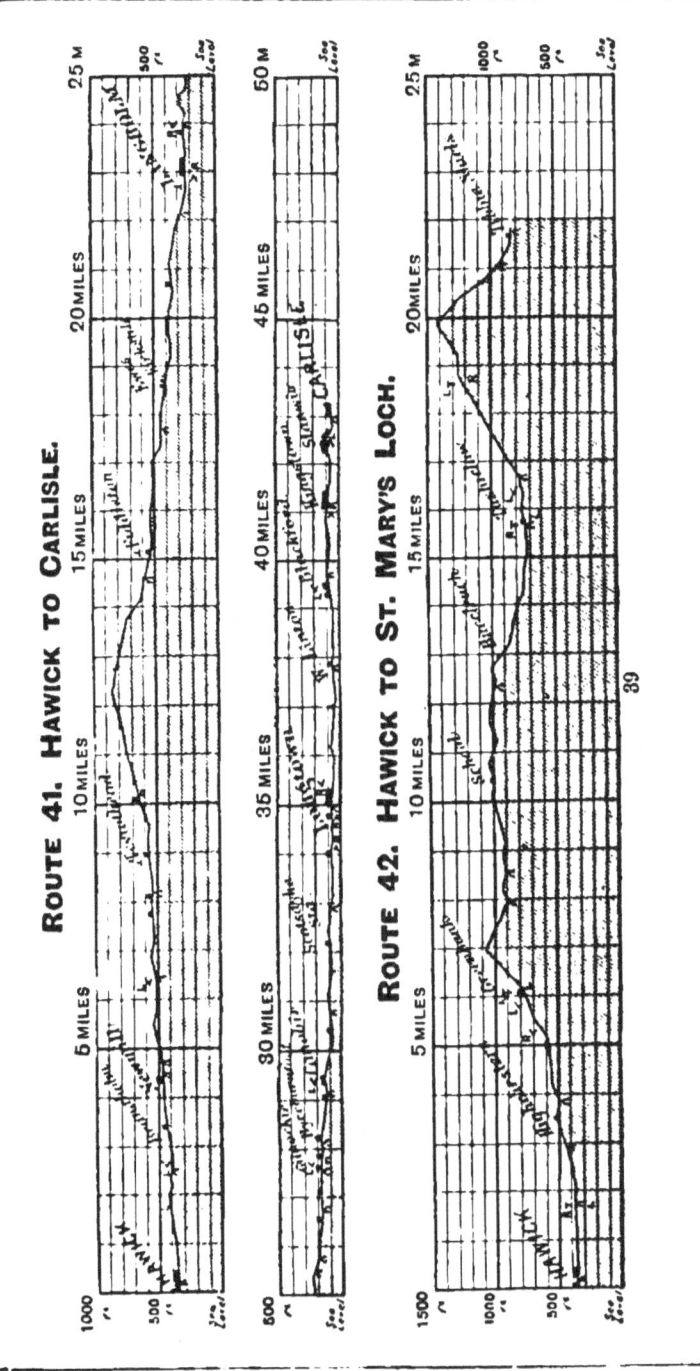

43 JEDBURGH TO ANNAN.

Description.—Class III. For the first 10 miles the surface is fair, although the road is somewhat steep, but thereafter it is very rough and stony as far as Saughtree Station. Thence the road, though of good surface, is undulating with short steep hills, improving about Canobie.

Gradients.—At 2m. 1 in 16-24; 4½m. 1 in 23; 5¾m. 1 in 13; 11½m. 1 in 11-16-22-16; 13¾m. 1 in 16; 16m. 1 in 10-14. Then numerous short hills, and care should be taken descending 30¼m. 1 in 19; 31¼m. 1 in 19-16; 31¾m. 1 in 15; 34¼m. 1 in 12; 36m. 1 in 12 (dangerous). 45½m. 1 in 21.

Milestones.—Measured from Jedburgh,—fairly correct to Canobie.

Measurements.

Jedburgh,* Market.						
7⅝	Bonchester.					
17¼	9⅝	Saughtree Station.				
26¼	18⅝	9	Newcastleton,* Square.			
36¼	28⅝	19	10	Canobie,* Church.		
45½	37⅞	28¼	19¼	9¼	Kirkpatrick.	
51¾	44⅛	34½	25½	15½	6¼	Annan,* Cross.

Principal Objects of Interest.—A very monotonous journey over moorland to Newcastleton.

Hotels or Inns at places marked *.

---

44 SELKIRK TO ETTRICK, &c.

Description.—Class II. A good road on the whole, but undulating. The surface to Ramseycleuch is very fair, but thereafter it is rough to the County Boundary. The road past Ettrick Church is good for about 6 miles up from Ramseycleuch, then degenerates into a cart track.

Gradients.—At ½m. 1 in 15; descent 1 in 23-18. Thereafter a number of short hills between 1 in 18 and 1 in 23.

Milestones.—Measured from Selkirk Town Hall,—correct to Tushielaw; thence to County Boundary measured from Peebles.

Measurements.

Selkirk,* Town Hall.				
7	Ettrick Bridge.			
15	8	Tushielaw* Inn.		
17¾	10¾	2¾	Ramseycleuch.	
43½	36½	28½	25¾	Langholm,* Town Hall.

Ettrick Church is ¾m. beyond Ramseycleuch.

Principal Objects of Interest.—4⅜m. Oakwood Tower. Tushielaw, Tower; 17m. Thirlestane Castle. A very pretty road up the Ettrick Water.

Hotels or Inns at places marked *.

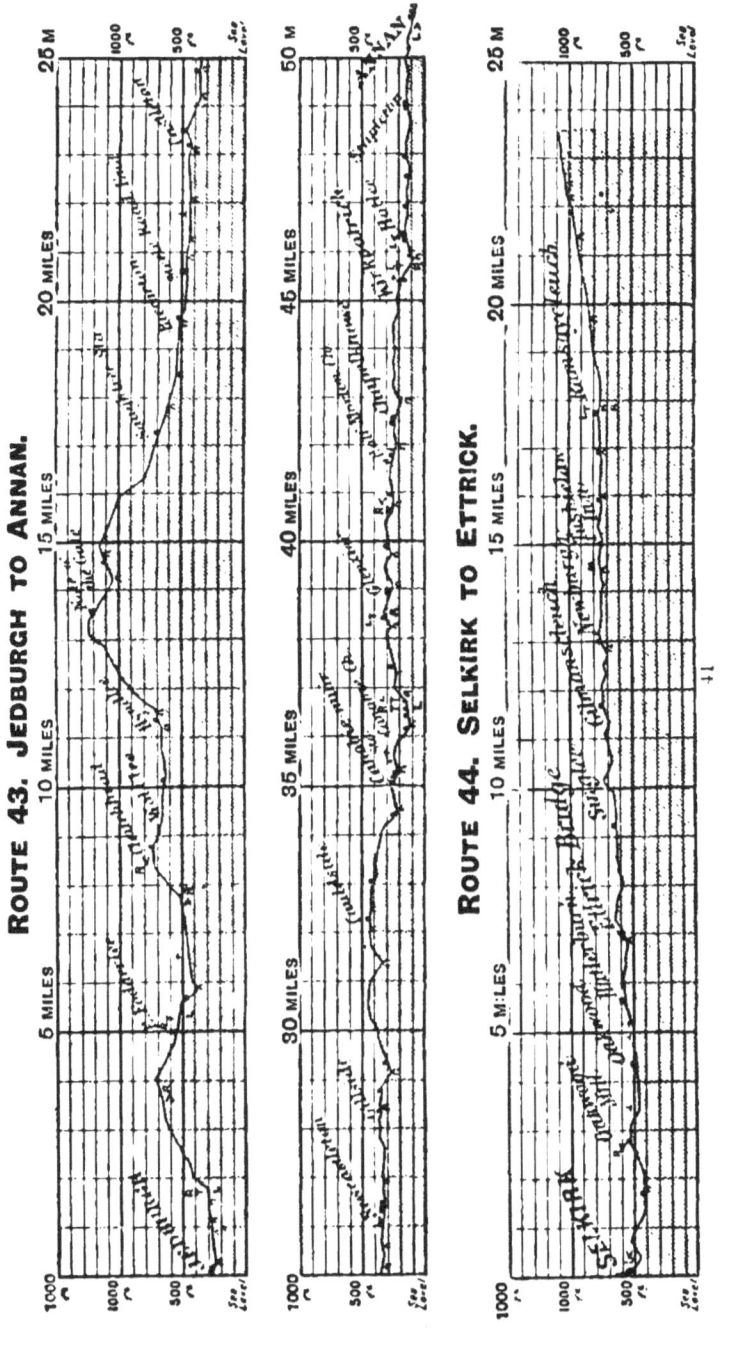

45 SELKIRK TO MOFFAT.

Description.—Class II. & III. After the steep descent at Selkirk, the road is good and undulating to Tibbie Shiels, thereafter becoming loose and soft. The descent past Birkhill is at first very rough and dangerous, but the road gradually improves in quality, though very hilly, and latterly becomes fairly good, to Moffat. On the whole the road is a heavy one, especially on the Dumfriesshire side.

Gradients.—The ascent at 22½m. is mostly 1 in 26. The descent begins 1 in 11 (dangerous) to 1 in 17. At 26¾m. 1 in 15; 31½m. 1 in 20; 31¾m. and 32¾m. 1 in 18; 33m. 1 in 15.

Milestones.—Measured from Selkirk Town Hall,—tolerably correct; and from Moffat, High Street,—correct.

Measurements.

Selkirk,* Town Hall.						
8¾	Yarrow Church.					
12¾	4	Gordon Arms* Inn.				
18	9¼	5¼	Rodono* Hotel.			
19	10¼	6¼	1	Tibbie Shiels* Inn.		
23	14¼	10¼	5	4	Birkhill.*	
34⅛	25⅜	21⅜	16⅛	15⅛	11⅛	Moffat,* High St.

Principal Objects of Interest.—2m. Philiphaugh Battlefield, 1645. 4m. Newark Castle, ruins. 19m. Hogg's Monument. 24½m. Grey Mare's Tail Fall, and Loch Skene. 28½m. Bodesbeck. At first the road is well wooded, but afterwards is rather bleak in parts. The scenery along St. Mary's Loch is charming.

Hotels or Inns at places marked *.

---

46 GALASHIELS TO KELSO.

Description.—Class II. A very fine road to Melrose, thence only fair to St. Boswells (with rough and dangerous hills at Bogleburn); after which it is good and undulating all the way to Kelso.

Gradients.—At 4¾m. 1 in 22; descent to Bogleburn 1 in 12, both sides (dangerous). At 6¼m. 1 in 14; 8¾m. 1 in 15-18.

Milestones.—Measured from Edinburgh, Crosscauseway, to St. Boswells, thereafter measured from Kelso Square,—fairly correct.

Measurements.

Galashiels,* Market.			
4	Melrose,* Cross.		
6¾	2¾	St. Boswells* Station.	
17⅞	13⅞	11⅛	Kelso,* Square.

Hotels or Inns at places marked *.

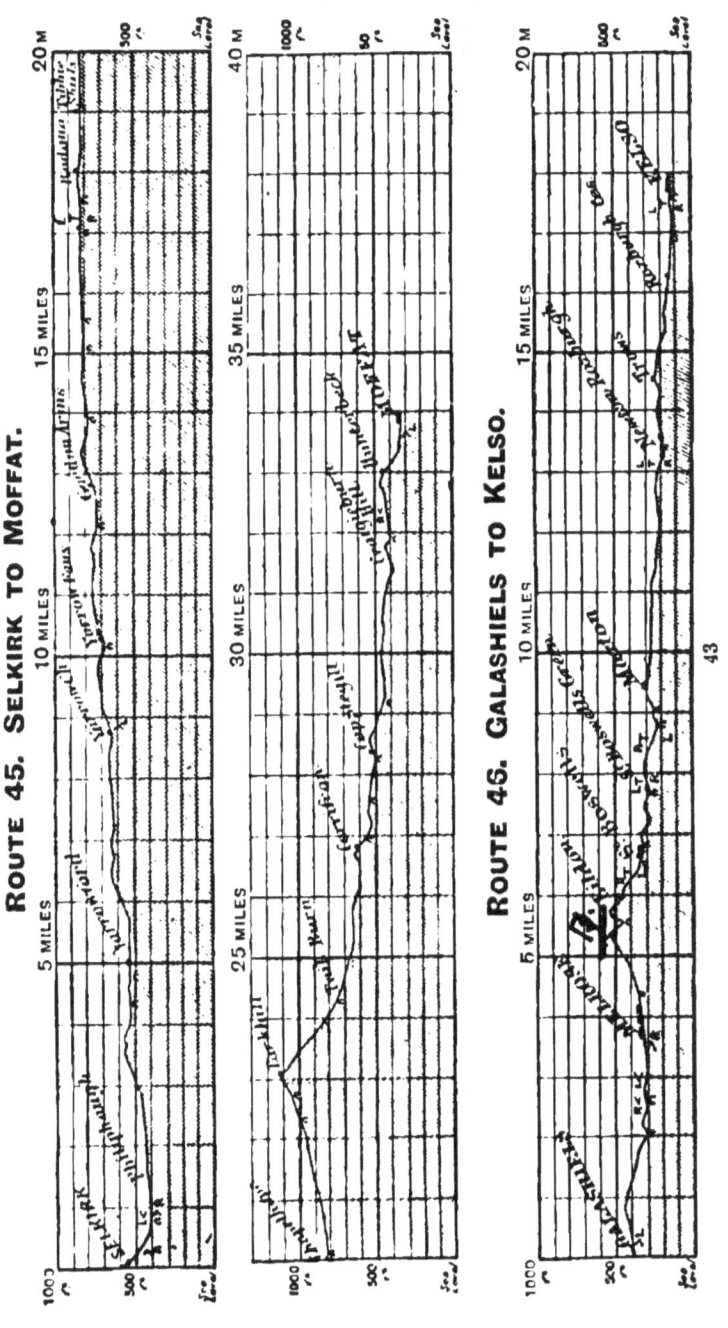

(Route 46 continued.)

Principal Objects of Interest.—MELROSE; Abbey, Eildon Hills. St. BOSWELLS; Dryburgh Abbey. 16½m. Site Roxburgh Castle. KELSO; Abbey, Floors Castle.

47 PEEBLES TO GALASHIELS.

Description.—Class II. With the exception of several stiff hills, the road is very fine but, undulating, all the way.

Gradients.—At 13m. 1 in 20-15; 14½m. 1 in 20; 16m. 1 in 24; 17m. 1 in 22.

Milestones.—Measured from Peebles Cross, and from Victoria Buildings, Galashiels.

Measurements.

Peebles,* Cross.
6½ Innerleithen,* Bridge.
8¼ 1¾ Walkerburn.
18¼ 11¾ 10 Galashiels,* Market.

Principal Objects of Interest.—2⅜m. Horsburgh Castle, ruins. 14m. (across Tweed) Ashiestiel.

Hotels or Inns at places marked * and at Clovenfords.

48 PEEBLES TO TUSHIELAW.

Description.—Class II. A very fine undulating road down Tweedside to Traquair, thence steep and rough to Gordon Arms. Thereafter it is of poor surface and stony, to Tushielaw. There is a road from Peebles to Traquair along the south bank of the Tweed, Class III., ¼m. shorter,—a fair road, but not so easy as that on the north bank.

Gradients.—From Traquair the ruling gradient is 1 in 24, with 1 in 17 near summit. The descent is easy, with 1 in 18-24 at 14¾m. At 20m. 1 in 21.

Milestones.—Measured from Peebles Cross,—correct.

Measurements.

Peebles,* Cross.
7⅝ Traquair Village.
14¾ 7⅛ Gordon Arms * Inn.
21¼ 13⅝ 6½ Tushielaw * Inn.

Principal Objects of Interest.—2⅜m. Horsburgh Castle, ruins. 7⅝m. Traquair House. 14¾m. Gordon Arms Inn After Gordon Arms the road is rather dreary.

Hotels or Inns at places marked * and at Innerleithen.

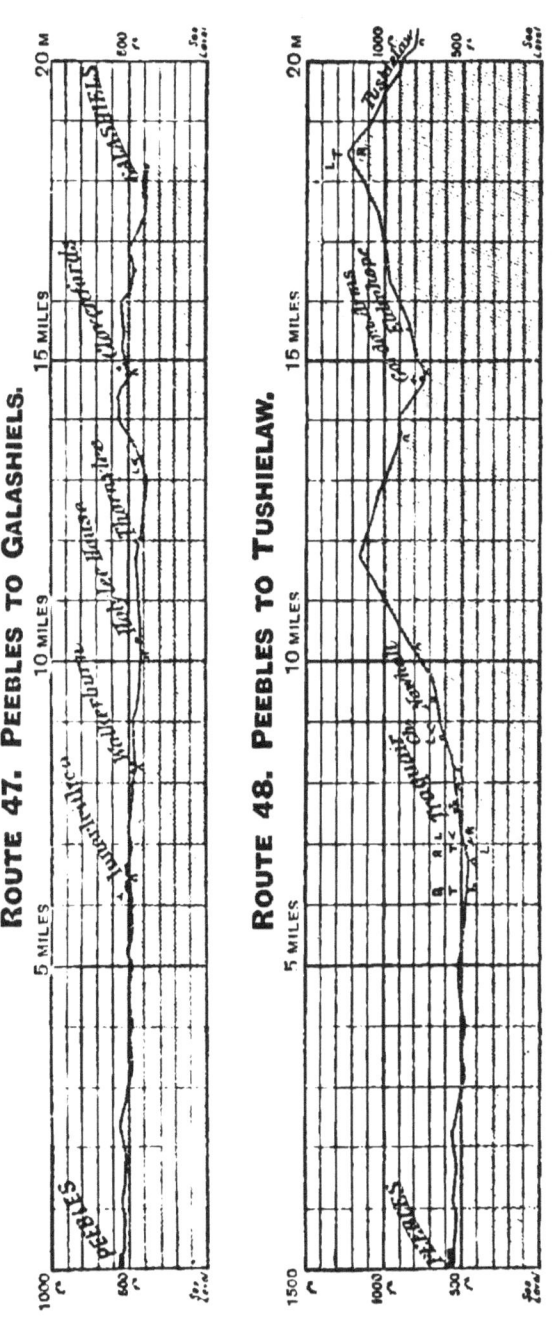

Signs: < Road Fork, forward journey, > ditto reverse, + Cross Roads, ⊥ Road Junction, ⌒ Bridge, T indicates a sharp turn. The directions R (right) and L (left) for the forward journey are above the Road Line, those of the reverse, below.

49 PEEBLES TO SYMINGTON.

Description.—Class II.-III.-I. The first 7 miles are very good, after which the road, as far as Biggar, is hilly, but of fair surface. The next stage to Symington is very good, and the road continues a fine smooth highway to Lanark, by the Abington-Stirling road, joined at 20m. (9m. from Abington).

Gradients.—The ascent from Peebles is 1 in 21. At 7½m. 1 in 25; 9¼m. 1 in 20; 9¾m. 1 in 13; 10¼m. 1 in 12.

Milestones.—Measured from Peebles Cross to Lyne, thereafter from Edinburgh *via* Eddleston,—each set correct. After Symington, measured from Stirling.

Measurements.

Peebles, * Cross.					
5¾	Stobo Church.				
11¼	5½	Broughton.			
16¼	10½	5	Biggar,* Fountain.		
20	14¼	8¾	3¾	Symington * Station.	
28⅞	23⅛	17⅝	12⅝	8⅞	Lanark,* Cross.

Principal Objects of Interest.—Neidpath Castle. Biggar; Church, Mote. Lanark, as below.

Hotels or Inns at places marked *.

50 ABINGTON TO CUMBERNAULD.

Description.—Class I. A magnificent broad, smooth road, with easy grades to Newmains. The road thereafter becomes hilly, with several rough parts in the mining villages through which it passes. Route 125 is joined at Cumbernauld, from which place the road is very fair on to Stirling.

Gradients.—No grades above 1 in 25 until after Newmains. At 27m. 1 in 24; 27½m. 1 in 22; 27¾m. 1 in 21; 32½m. 1 in 21; 34m. 1 in 24; 37¾m. 1 in 25. Descent to Cumbernauld 1 in 14 (dangerous).

Milestones.—Measured from Stirling,—correct.

Measurements.

Abington.*					
17¼	Lanark,* Cross.				
22¾	5½	Carluke,* Market.			
33½	16¼	10¾	(Airdrie).*		
40⅜	23⅛	17⅝	6⅞	Cumbernauld.*	
52⅞	35⅝	30⅛	19⅜	12½	Stirling,* King Street.

(*Continued next page.*)

Route 49. Peebles to Symington, &c.

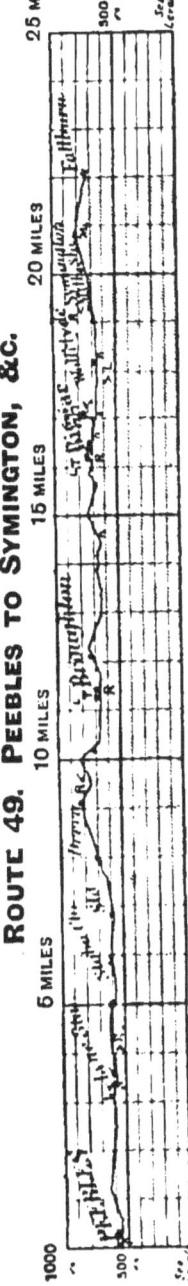

Route 50. Abington to Cumbernauld.

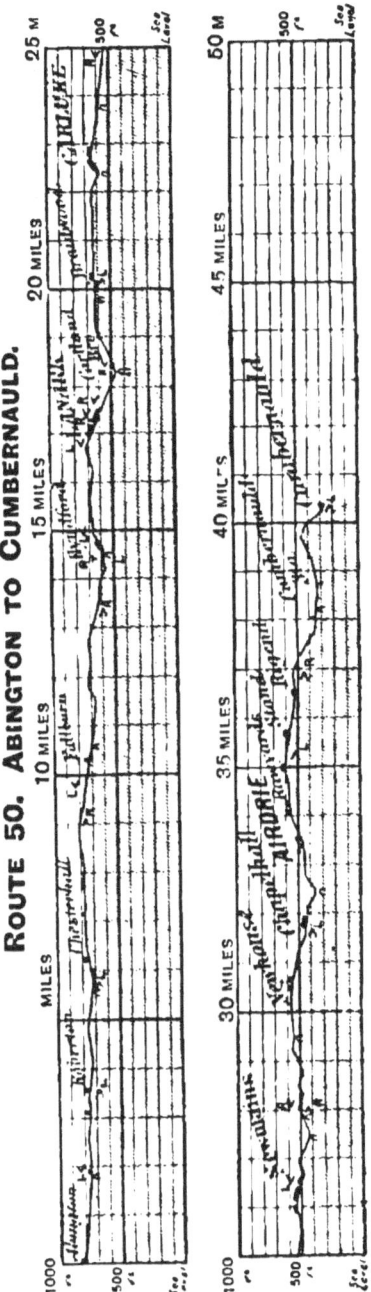

(*Route 50 continued.*)

Principal Objects of Interest.—7¼m. Fatlips Castle and Tinto Hill. LANARK; Falls of Clyde, Cartland Crags. The next stage is through the coal and iron district—not very pleasant travelling—to near Cumbernauld.

Hotels or Inns at places marked *, and at Roberton, Braidwood, Chapelhall, and Rawyards.

---

51 ABINGTON TO CARLISLE.

Description.—Class I. This road presents an almost perfect surface the whole way, and excepting a few patches of stones here and there, is generally in the best of condition in wet or dry weather. Generally speaking the higher parts of the road are in less perfect order than the rest, but there is really little difference. Nearing Carlisle, however, the road becomes lumpy owing to the heavy traffic.

Gradients.—The majority of the gradients on this road are 1 in 27, but 1 in 21 at 36¼m., 1 in 25 at 38¼m., and Stanwix Hill about 1 in 16, will be found the only slopes of note. The road is beautifully engineered.

Milestones.—Measured from Glasgow, through Ecclefechan,—correct.

Measurements.

Abington.*							
3¼	Crawford.*						
18¾	15½	Beattock Station.					
25⅝	22⅜	6⅞	Johnston Bridge, P.O.				
32¾	29½	14	7⅛	Lockerbie,* Town Hall.			
38¾	35½	20	13⅛	6	Ecclefechan.*		
48	44¾	29¼	22⅜	15¼	9¼	Gretna Green.*	
57½	54¼	38¾	31⅞	24¾	18¾	9½	Carlisle,* Market Place.

Principal Objects of Interest.—18m. Garpol Glen. 29¼m. Jardine Hall. ECCLEFECHAN; Carlyle's Birthplace and Grave. 42½m. Merkland Cross. GRETNA GREEN; Inn, Tollhouse, etc. 49m. Sark Bridge, boundary England and Scotland. CARLISLE; Cathedral, Prison.

Hotels or Inns at places marked * and at (Moffat), Kirtlebridge, and Kirkpatrick. Beattock Hotel closed.

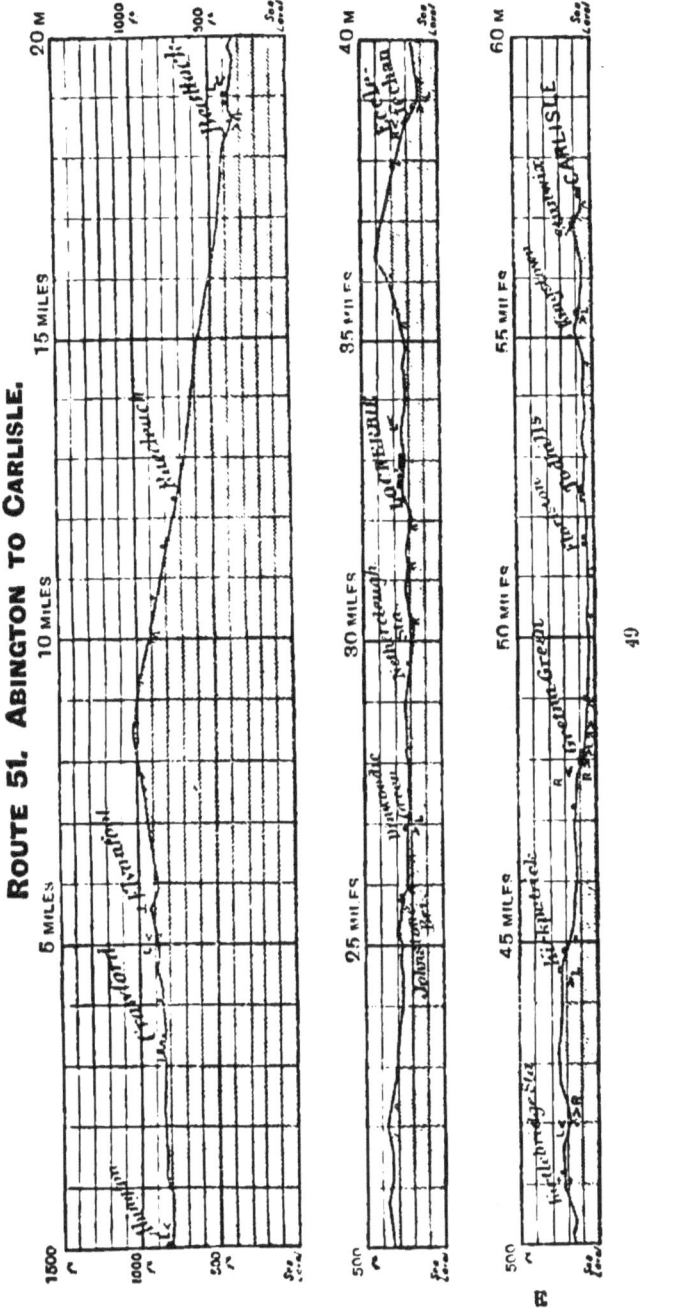

Route 51. Abington to Carlisle.

52 ABINGTON TO THORNHILL.

Description.—Class II. A very fair and easy road of good surface all the way to Thornhill. Travellers to Penpont save ⅜m. by keeping to R. at 22¼m., joining next Route at the Bridge at ⅜m.

Gradients.—The descent in the Dalveen Pass is 1 in 22 at 13½m., thence 1 in 24 and 25. At 19½m. 1 in 23.

Milestones.—Measured from the Dumfries Mid-steeple,—correct.

Measurements.

Abington.*				
6⅛	Elvanfoot.			
17⅛	11	Durisdeer Mill.		
21⅜	15¼	4¼	Carronbridge.*	
23	16⅞	5⅞	1⅝	Thornhill.*

Principal Objects of Interest.—Dalveen Pass, Covenanter's Monument. DURISDEER (off road); Church and Monument. 19½m. Enoch Castle.

Hotels or Inns at places marked * and at Crawford.

53 THORNHILL TO NEWTON STEWART.

Description.—Class II. The road is very fair, but hilly to Moniaive, thereafter it is a little rough till near New Galloway; it is then good for a few miles, but soon becomes a very bad road until near Talnotry, when the surface improves a little; there are several steep inclines until the Portpatrick road is joined. The direct road to Moniaive through Tynron has a precipitous hill.

Gradients.—At 4¼m. 1 in 20; 5¼m. 1 in 25; 17m. 1 in 20; 18m. 1 in 18; 18½m. 1 in 16; 19¼m. 1 in 16. After New Galloway, 24½m. 1 in 23, thereafter several short hills, 1 in 22.

Milestones.—After New Galloway measured from Dumfries,—correctly placed (see Route 71).

Measurements.

Thornhill.*						
2⅛	Penpont.*					
8⅜	6¼	Moniaive * Bridge.				
22	19⅞	13⅝	Ken Bridge.			
22⅝	20½	14¼	⅝	(New Galloway).*		
29⅜	27¼	21	7⅜	6¾	Bridge of Dee.	
41⅛	39	32¾	19⅛	18½	11¾	Newton Stewart,* Town Hall.

Principal Objects of Interest.—½m. Old Monument. MONIAIVE; Renwick's Monument. Balmaclellan; Mote, 27m. King's Stone. 34m. Murray's Monument. 36½m. Rocking stone. 39¾m. Battlefield. NEWTON STEWART; Academy, Monument Earl of Galloway.

Hotels or Inns at places marked * and at Balmaclellan.

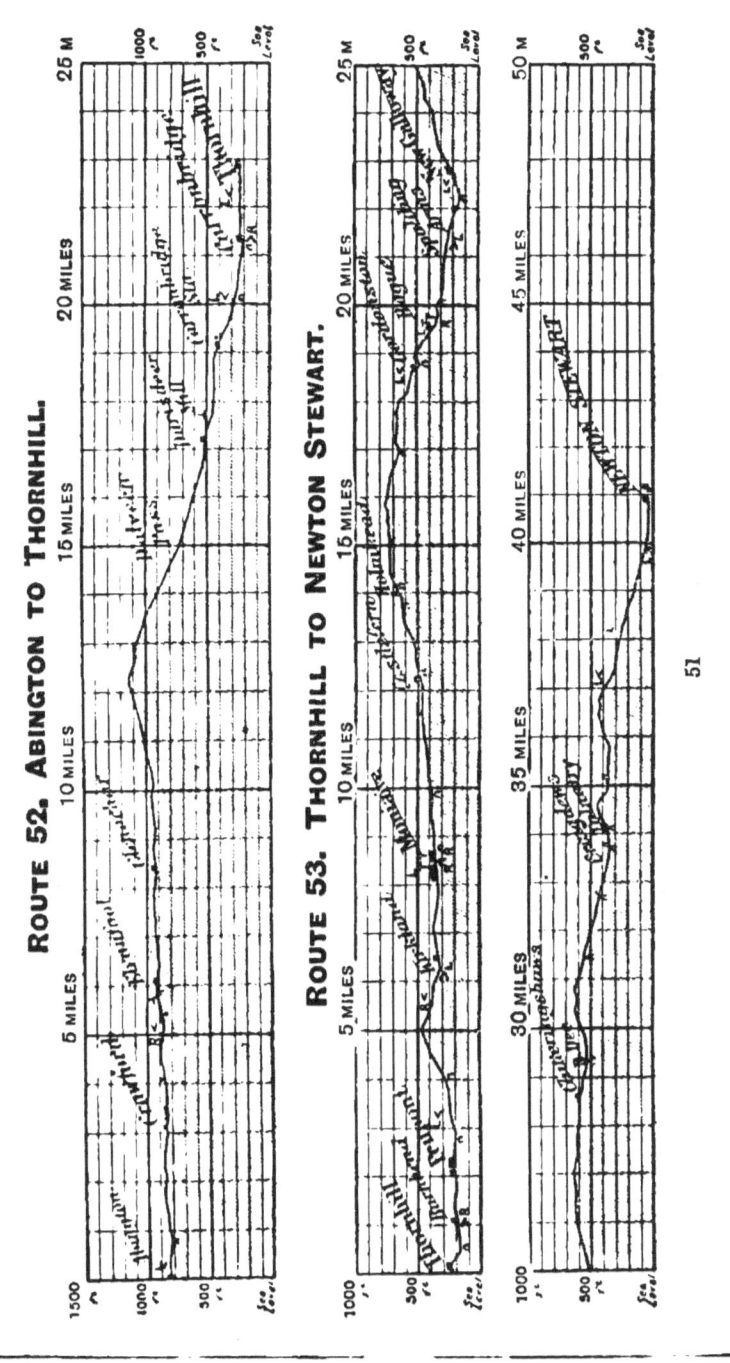

54 SELKIRK TO ST. BOSWELLS.

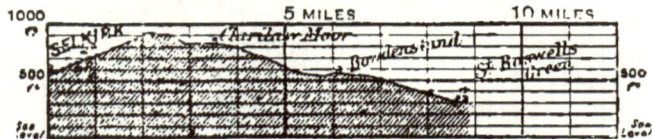

Description.—Class II. Fair surface, but long hills.
Gradients.—At 1m. 1 in 22-27.
Measurements.—Selkirk,* Town Hall.
        8¾ St. Boswells Green.
    10   1¼ St. Boswells* Station.

55 SELKIRK TO MELROSE.

Description.—Class III. After the steep descent from Selkirk, the road is fair but undulating.
Gradients.—At ½m. 1 in 22-24.
Measurements.—Selkirk,* Town Hall.
        7¾ Melrose,* Cross.
Principal Objects of Interest.—4½m. Abbotsford. MELROSE; Abbey. Eildon Hills.

56 SELKIRK TO WALKERBURN, &C.

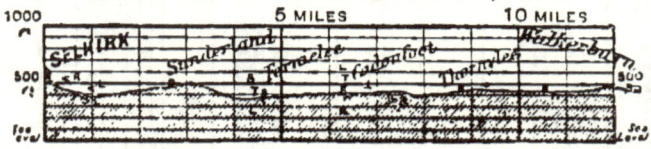

Description.—Class II. Good surface, but hilly at first.
Gradients.—At ½m. 1 in 13-18.
Milestones.—Measured at first from Edinburgh *via* Clovenfords; afterwards from Peebles Cross.
Measurements.—Selkirk,* Town Hall.
        12¼ Walkerburn.
    20¾ 8½ Peebles,* Cross.
Principal Objects of Interest.—2¾m. Sunderland Hall. 6½m. Ashiestiel (across Tweed).

Hotels or Inns at places marked *.

ANNAN TO LOCKERBIE. 57

Description.—Class II. A good road but slightly hilly.

Gradients.—At 2½m. 1 in 24; 4m. 1 in 22.

Milestones.—Measured from Annan Bridge, fairly correct.

Measurements.—Annan,* Cross.
            4¾   Hoddam Bridge.
           10½ 6¼ Lockerbie,* Town Hall.

Principal Objects of Interest.—4½m. Hoddam Castle and "Repentance" Tower.

ANNAN TO LONGTOWN. 58

Description.—Class II. The road has a very fine surface.

Gradients.—At 9½m. 1 in 19.

Milestones.—At first, as Route 62. After Gretna, measured from Carlisle *via* Longtown.

Measurements.—Annan,* Cross.
           8¼   Gretna * Green.
          12⅔ 4¼ Longtown.*

Principal Objects of Interest.—Gretna Green; Inn, Tollhouse, &c.

DUMFRIES TO LOCKERBIE. 59

Description.—Class II. The surface generally is good, except on the Torthorwald Hills.

Gradients.—At 3½m. 1 in 14; 4½m. 1 in 23; 6½m. 1 in 24.

Milestones.—Measured from Dumfries, Kings Arms Hotel,—correct.

Measurements.—Dumfries,* Mid-steeple.
           4¼   Torthorwald.
           8¼ 4¾ Lochmaben,* Town Hall.
          12¾ 8½ 4½ Lockerbie,* Town Hall.

Principal Objects of Interest.—Torthorwald Castle. LOCHMABEN; Castle.

Hotels or Inns at places marked *.

60 LANGHOLM TO ESKDALEMUIR.

Description.—Class III. The surface of the road as far as Bentpath is good, but thereafter rather poor, besides being rough on the steep hills over to Eskdalemuir. After that there are no bad hills, but the road is rather loose.

Gradients.—At ¾m. 1 in 20 ; 1¾m. 1 in 17 ; 2½m. 1 in 24 ; 9m. 1 in 15-17 ; 11¼m. 1 in 10.

Milestones.—Measured from Langholm Town Hall to County Boundary,—correct.

Measurements.

Langholm,* Town Hall.
5¾ Bentpath.*
13½ 7¾ Eskdalemuir Church.
25¾ 20 12¼ Ramseycleuch.

Principal Objects of Interest.—1¾m. Peden's Well. 5¾m. Telford's Birthplace. 13½m. Eskdalemuir Camp. The road up the Esk is a very pretty one at first, but rather uninteresting beyond Eskdalemuir.

Hotels or Inns at places marked.*

61 LANGHOLM TO LOCKERBIE.

Description.—Class III. This road is a very steep and hilly one, with loose surface, nearly the whole way. On account of the adverse gradients the road is avoided as much as possible. The best road to Langholm from the West is round by Canobie.

Gradients.—Care should be taken on most of the hills although they are not absolutely dangerous. At ¾m. 1 in 16 ; 2m. 1 in 18 ; 3¾m. 1 in 17 ; 5¼m. 1 in 16-23 ; 7½m. 1 in 17-21 ; 7¾m. 1 in 19 ; 8¾m. 1 in 21 ; 10½m. 1 in 23 ; 11¾m. 1 in 18-21 ; 12¾m. 1 in 14-16-12 ; 13¼m. 1 in 22 ; 13½m. 1 in 18 ; 14m. 1 in 21-15-20-18 ; 14¾m. 1 in 20 ; 15¼m. 1 in 22 ; 15½m. 1 in 13-15 ; 16¼m. 1 in 19 ; 17½m. 1 in 19-16.

Measurements.

Langholm,* Town Hall.
7¾ Fallford.
13⅞ 6⅛ Bankshill.
18 10¼ 4⅛ Lockerbie,* Town Hall.

Principal Objects of Interest.—1m. Wauchope Castle. Until near Tundergarth the road is a monotonous one. 15m. to S., Birrenswark Camps.

Hotels or Inns at places marked *, and Callisterhall.

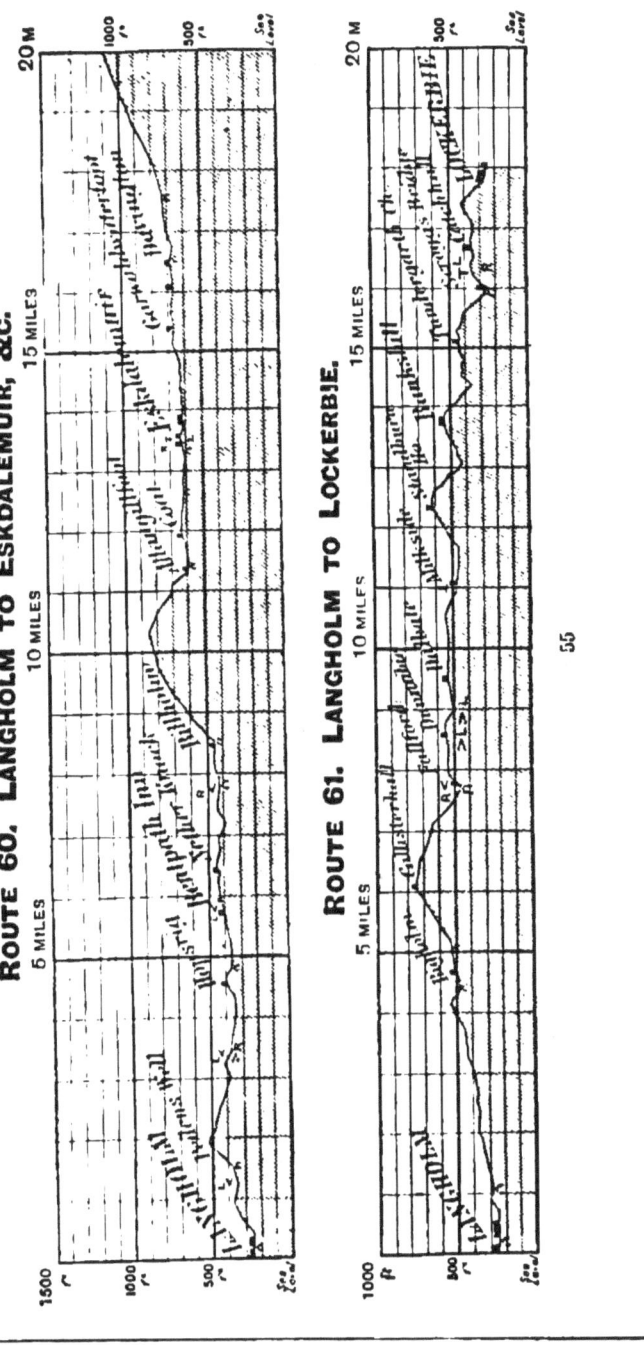

62 DUMFRIES TO CARLISLE.

Description.—Class I. The surface of the road is very fine almost the whole way to Carlisle, and the gradients are remarkably easy. Nearing Carlisle the road becomes very lumpy with the heavy traffic over it, and the descent at Stanwix is rather steep. The next route to Annan, though shorter and a good road, is not quite so easy as this.

Gradients.—Stanwix Hill is about 1 in 16.

Milestones.—Measured from Greyfriars Church Dumfries, to Collin; thereafter to the Border (where the milestones measured from Glasgow are met), they are seemingly measured from Carlisle, Market Place.

Measurements.

Dumfries,* Mid-steeple.						
3⅝	Collin.					
9⅞	6¼	Clarencefield.*				
13¼	9⅝	3⅜	Cummertrees.			
16¾	13⅛	6⅞	3½	Annan,* Cross.		
23	19⅜	13⅛	9¾	6¼	Rigg.	
34⅛	30½	24¼	20⅞	17⅜	11⅛	Carlisle,* Market Place.

Principal Objects of Interest.—9½m. Comlongan Castle. 10¾m. Ruthwell Cross. (25m. Gretna Green). 25½m. Sark Bridge, the boundary Scotland and England. CARLISLE; Cathedral, Prison.

Hotels or Inns at places marked *.

63 DUMFRIES TO ANNAN.

Description.—Class II. This road has a good surface, but is more hilly than the previous Route. It is however more direct.

Gradients.—Ruling gradient 1 in 28, but at 6¾m. 1 in 22.

Milestones.—To Collin measured from Dumfries, Greyfriars Church; thereafter seemingly from Carlisle, Market.

Measurements.

Dumfries,* Mid-steeple.				
3⅝	Collin.			
9	5⅜	Carrutherstown.		
15½	11⅞	6½	Annan,* Cross.	
32⅞	29¼	23⅞	17⅜	Carlisle,* Market Place.

Hotels or Inns at places marked *.

64 ANNAN TO MOFFAT.

Description.—Class III. The road is of good surface, but hilly, as far as Lochmaben; thereafter it is rather loose to Beattock. The better road is by Lockerbie.

Route 62. Dumfries to Carlisle.

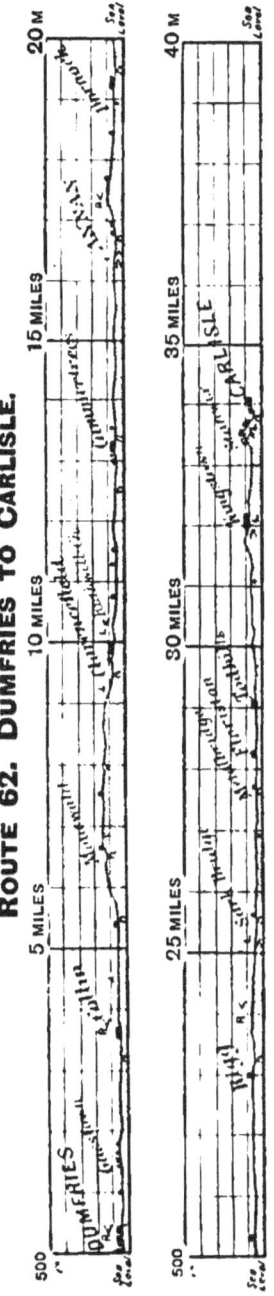

Route 63. Dumfries to Annan.

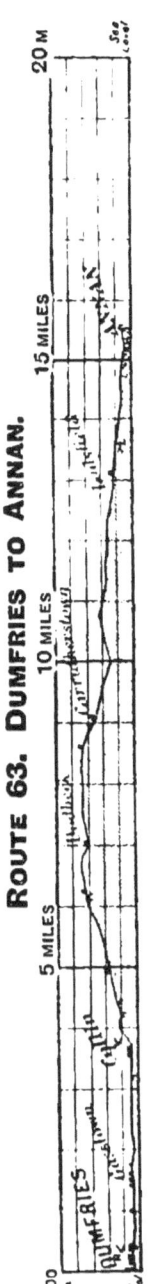

Signs: < Road Fork, forward journey. > ditto reverse. + Cross Roads. ⊥ Road Junction. ∩ Bridge ⊤ indicates a sharp turn. The directions R (right) and L (left) for the forward journey are above the line, those of the reverse, below.

Gradients.—At 18¾m. 1 in 23.

Milestones.—Seemingly measured from Carlisle, Market.

Measurements.

Annan,* Cross.					
7	Dalton.				
12⅞	5⅞	Lochmaben * Town Hall.			
15½	8½	2⅝	Templand.		
25¾	18¾	12⅞	10¼	Beattock Station.	
27⅝	20⅝	14¾	12⅛	1⅞	Moffat,* High Street.

Principal Objects of Interest.—4m. "Repentance Tower." LOCHMABEN; Castle. 26½m. Lochhouse Tower.

Hotels or Inns at places marked *.

65 DUMFRIES TO MOFFAT.

Description.—Class I. This is a fine road of very good surface almost the whole way, but there are some stiff hills to be faced. Near Dumfries the road is rather lumpy, and about St. Anns it is apt to be loose.

Gradients.—The rise from Amisfield is 1 in 26-27; descent to Ae Bridge 1 in 17-22. Thereafter the only steep part is beyond St. Anns Bridge 1 in 22.

Milestones.—Measured from Edinburgh,—correct; (the first is 1⅛m. from Mid-steeple).

Measurements.

Dumfries,* Mid-steeple.					
4½	Amisfield.				
8¾	4¼	Parkgate.			
13¼	8¾	4½	St. Ann's.		
19⅛	14⅝	10⅜	5⅞	Beattock Station.	
21	16½	12¼	7¾	1⅞	Moffat,* High Street.

Principal Objects of Interest.—Locharbriggs; Quarries. Amisfield, Tower. 19⅞m. Lochhouse Tower. MOFFAT; Spa, &c.

Hotels or Inns at places marked *; none at Beattock.

66 DUMFRIES TO PENPONT, &c.

Description.—Class I-III. The first 5 miles are very smooth to Isle Toll, but thereafter the road is hilly almost the whole way to Penpont. The ascent then becomes more regular, but rather steep, past Drumlanrig on to the Nith, where the main Dumfries-Sanquhar road is joined, which, though undulating at this part, is very smooth.

Gradients.—At 5m. 1 in 24; 5¼m. 1 in 20; 7¾m. 1 in 17; 9½m. 1 in 19-21. After Penpont the gradient is 1 in 22, then 1 in 15 followed by 1 in 18; the descent 1 in 18 and 23; 18½m. 1 in 21; descent to bridge over the Nith 1 in 24.

Milestones.—Measured from Dumfries, Mid-steeple,—correct.

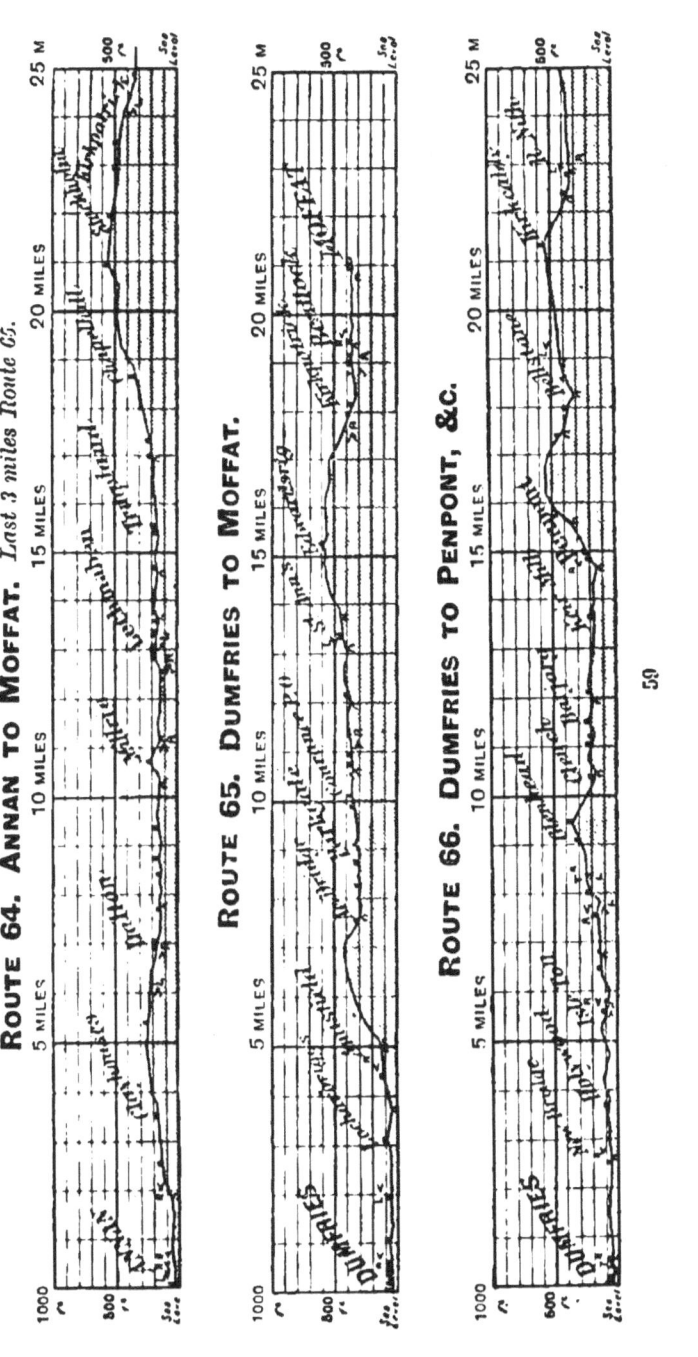

Measurements.

Dumfries,* Mid-steeple.		
14⅞	Penpont.*	
27⅜	12½	Sanquhar,* Town Hall.

Principal Objects of Interest.—1¼m. Lincluden Abbey. 6m. Ellisland. 6½m. Friar's Carse. 11½m. Barjarg Tower. 20m. Drumlanrig Castle. 24m. Elliock House. The road is very pretty.

Hotels or Inns at places marked *.

67 DUMFRIES TO NEW CUMNOCK.

Description.—Class I. A magnificent broad smooth road with easy hills to Enterkinfoot; thence the road is somewhat undulating but of very fine surface to Kirkconnel. From there to New Cumnock is a succession of short and steep hills exceedingly wearisome and trying. This part is Class III.

Gradients.—At 5m. 1 in 24; 5¼m. 1 in 20; beyond Carronbridge 1 in 16. From Kirkconnel the ascent begins with 1 in 26, and onwards there are grades from 1 in 14 to 23; the descent to Afton is 1 in 23.

Milestones.—Measured from Dumfries, Mid-steeple, correct to the county boundary, after which they are measured from Ayr.

Measurements.

Dumfries,* Mid-steeple.						
8	Auldgirth Bridge.*					
14⅜	6⅜	Thornhill.*				
16	8	1⅝	Carronbridge.*			
26⅝	18⅝	12¼	10⅝	Sanquhar,* Town Hall.		
30	22	15⅝	14	3⅜	Kirkconnel,* Station.	
38	30	23⅝	22	11⅜	8	New Cumnock,* Church.

Principal Objects of Interest.—1¼m. Lincluden Abbey. 6m. Ellisland. 6½m. Friar's Carse. 12m. Closeburn Castle. THORNHILL; site of Tibbers Castle. 17¾m. Drumlanrig Cas. 24¾m. Elliock House. SANQUHAR; Castle ruin, Monument. The scenery on the route is remarkably fine.

Hotels or Inns at places marked *.

68 ABINGTON TO SANQUHAR.

Description.—Class II. A fair road but with deep ruts as far as the Smelting Mill, thence better to the summit. The descent is abrupt and very steep, and towards the foot of the hill is very rough. The rest of the road is good, but undulating.

Gradients.—Past the Mill, 1 in 18-19. After Leadhills to summit, 1 in 21-15-22-20; the descent begins abruptly 1 in 15 and continues with varying grades till at 10¾m.—the steep and dangerous part—1 in 12, after which the road is easy. The descent at 14¼m. is 1 in 15.

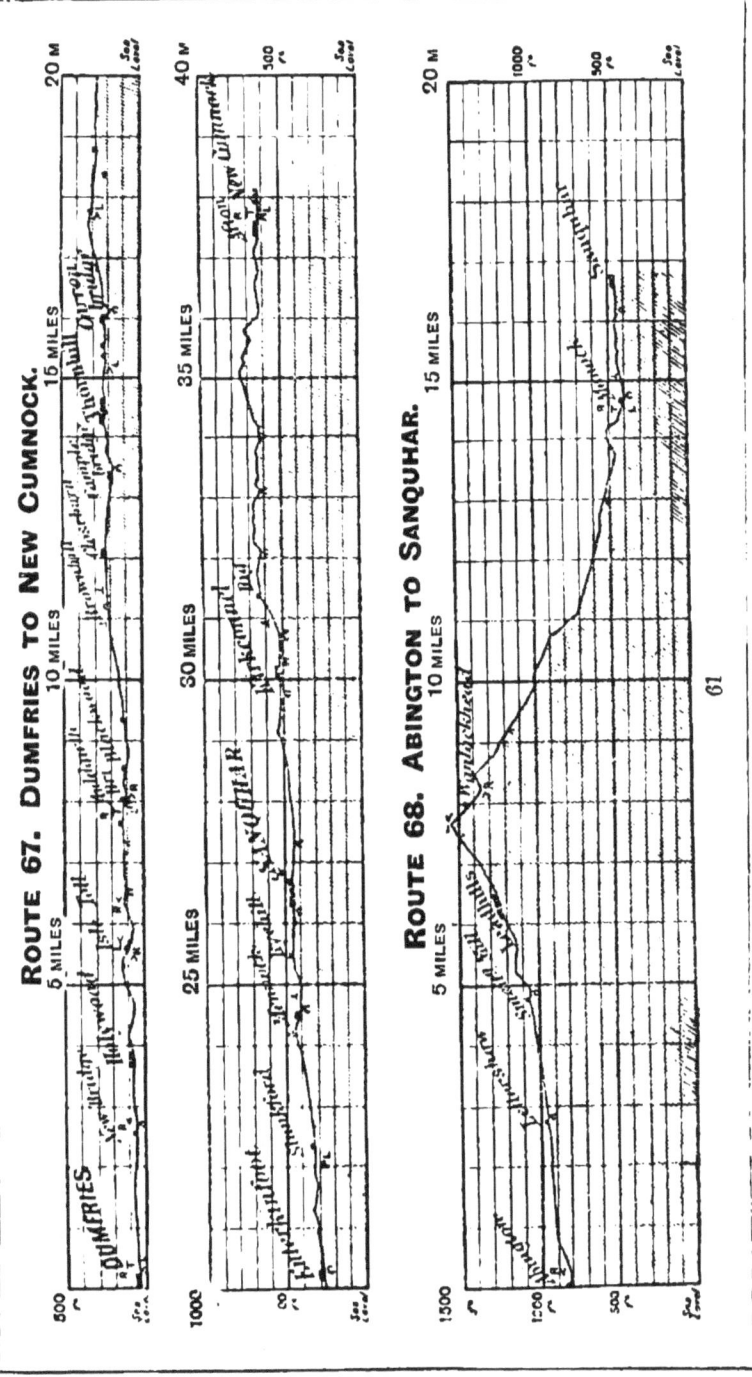

Measurements.

Abington.*		
6¼	Leadhills,* Hotel.	
16¾	10½	Sanquhar,* Town Hall.

Principal Objects of Interest.—Leadhills; Smelting Mill; Enterkin Pass, to S.E. Wanlockhead the highest village in Britain.

Hotels or Inns at places marked *.

69 DUMFRIES TO MONIAIVE.

Description.—Class I and II. The first 5 miles are very smooth, thereafter it is a fair but hilly road all the way.

Gradients.—At 5m. 1 in 24; 5¼m. 1 in 20; 9m. 1 in 21.

Milestones.—Measured from Dumfries, Mid-steeple; after Dunscore, measured *via* Corsehead,—correct.

Measurements.

Dumfries,* Mid-steeple.		
10	Dunscore.*	
17⅜	7⅜	Moniaive,* Bridge.

Principal Objects of Interest.—1¼m. Lincluden Abbey. 6m. Ellisland. MONIAIVE; Renwick's Monument.

Hotels or Inns at places marked *.

70 DUMFRIES TO NEWTON STEWART.

Description.—Class I. A very fine, smooth, and beautifully engineered road the whole way. It is, however, somewhat hilly.

Gradients.—To Castle Douglas, none above 1 in 25. Castle Douglas to Newton Stewart; Tyrebank Hill 1 in 23, at 12m. 1 in 23; descent to Gatehouse, 1 in 20-17. At 27m. 1 in 25.

Milestones.—Correctly placed, but not measured from a particular point, though at one time no doubt measured from Carlisle. The first M.S. is ⅝m. from Dumfries Bridge.

Measurements.

Dumfries,* Mid-steeple.						
9⅝	Crocketford.*					
18¼	8⅝	Castle Douglas,* Town Clock.				
24⅛	14½	5⅞	Ringford.*			
33	23⅜	14¾	8⅞	Gatehouse,* P.O..		
45	35⅜	26¾	20⅞	12	Creetown.*	
51½	41⅞	33¼	27⅜	18½	6½	Newton Stewart,* Town Hall.

Principal Objects of Interest.—CASTLE DOUGLAS; Threave Castle, Carlingwark Loch. GATEHOUSE; Cally House, Anwoth Kirk. 18m. Cardoness Castle. 21¼m. Dirk Hatteraick's Cave. 23¼m. Carsluith Castle. CREETOWN; Granite Quarries. 32¼m. Battlefield. NEWTON STEWART; Academy, Earl of Galloway's Monument.

Hotels or Inns at places marked *, and at Springholm.

Route 69. Dumfries to Moniaive.

Route 70. Dumfries to Newton Stewart.

71 DUMFRIES TO NEW GALLOWAY.

Description.—Class I & II. A very fine smooth road to Crocketford, then undulating but fair to New Galloway.

Gradients.—Nothing above 1 in 25 to Crocketford, then at 14½m. 1 in 24, and at 23m. 1 in 25.

Milestones.—To Crocketford as Route 70. Thereafter correctly placed, but the 10th M.S. is 11m. from Dumfries.

Measurements.

Dumfries,* Mid-steeple.				
9⅝	Crocketford.*			
15	5¾	Corsock Bridge.*		
24⅜	14¾	9⅝	Ken Bridge.	
25¼	15⅝	10¼	⅞	New Galloway,* Town Hall.

Principal Objects of Interest.—The road is very pretty near Dumfries, at Corsock Bridge, and nearing N. Galloway.

Hotels or Inns at places marked *.

72 DUMFRIES TO KIRKCUDBRIGHT.

Description.—Class II. This is a beautiful road of fine surface as far as Dalbeattie, but thereafter it is hilly and has only tolerable surface. The usual road is *via* Castle Douglas.

Gradients.—Two slightly dangerous hills,—at 3¾m. 1 in 16, and 14¾m. 1 in 18. The gradient at 16¾m. is 1 in 20; 18½m. 1 in 24; 19m. 1 in 20; 21½m. 1 in 25; and final descent 1 in 25, increasing to 1 in 20.

Milestones.—Measured from Dumfries Bridge,—correct.

Measurements.

Dumfries,* Mid-steeple.		
13⅝	Dalbeattie,* Town Hall.	
27¼	13⅝	Kirkcudbright,* Town Hall.

Principal Objects of Interest.—DALBEATTIE; Quarries.

Hotels or Inns at places marked *.

73 DUMFRIES TO NEW ABBEY & DALBEATTIE.

Description.—Class III. A fair road on the whole, but the first part is decidedly the best.

Gradients.—At 4½m. 1 in 12-15 (dangerous); 7m. and 7¾m. 1 in 20; 16¼m. 1 in 23; 17¼m. 1 in 13; 18m. 1 in 21; 19m. 1 in 17; 20¾m. 1 in 23; 22¾m. 1 in 21.

Milestones.—Measured from Dumfries, Mid-steeple,—fairly correct.

Measurements.

Dumfries,* Mid-steeple.			
7¼	New Abbey.*		
16	8¾	Caulkerbush.	
25½	18¼	9½	Dalbeattie,* Town Hall.

Principal Objects of Interest.—7¼m. Sweetheart Abbey, Waterloo Monument.

Hotels or Inns at places marked.*

ROUTE 71. DUMFRIES TO NEW GALLOWAY.

ROUTE 72. DUMFRIES TO KIRKCUDBRIGHT.

ROUTE 73. DUMFRIES TO NEW ABBEY AND DALBEATTIE.

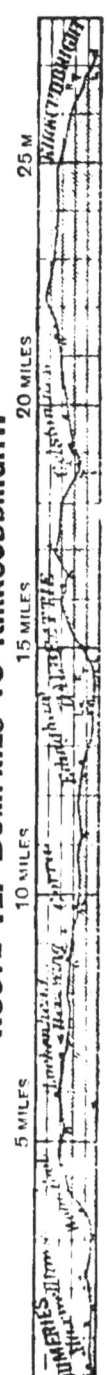

74 DALBEATTIE TO KIRKCUDBRIGHT *(via Coast)*.

Description.—Class III. A very fair road as far as Auchencairn, thereafter more or less hilly all the way.

Gradients.—At Auchencairn 1 in 17; 9m. 1 in 22; 9½m. 1 in 25; 15m. 1 in 20. (Short cut to Kirkcudbright 1 in 14).

Milestones.—Continue those from Dumfries,—correct.

Measurements.

Dalbeattie,* Town Hall.
3½ Palnackie.*
7⅝ 4⅛ Auchencairn.*
18⅝ 15⅛ 11 Kirkcudbright,* Town Hall.

A short cut at 15¾m. leads to Kirkcudbright, 1¾m.

75 CASTLE DOUGLAS TO DALRY.

Description.—Class II. A good but hilly road.

Gradients.—6m. 1/24; 9m. 1/20; 12¼m. 1/24; 12½m. 1/23.

Milestones.—Measured from Castle Douglas Town Clock.

Measurements.

Castle Douglas,* Town Clock.
6¾ Parton.
13½ 6¾ Ken Bridge.
16 9¼ 2½ Dalry * (St John's Town of).

Principal Objects of Interest.—A very pretty road.

76 CASTLE DOUGLAS TO LOCHENBRECK, &c.

Description.—Class II. The road has a good surface to Laurieston, but poor to Lochenbreck. Thereafter it is very rough and stony till near Gatehouse.

Gradients.—3m. 1/21; 7m. 1/17-20; 12¾m. 1/16-20-24-15.

Measurements.

Castle Douglas,* Town Clock.
6¼ Laurieston.*
8¾ 2½ Lochenbreck.*
16 9¾ 7¼ Gatehouse,* P.O.

Principal Objects of Interest.—2¾m. Glenlochar Abbey. 8¾m. Lochenbreck Spa. This road first traverses cultivated country, but after Lochenbreck lies through wild moorland.

77 KIRKCUDBRIGHT TO NEW GALLOWAY.

Description.—Class III. Hilly road, but fair surface.

Gradients.—Short hills about 1 in 15; at 15m. 1 in 17.

Measurements.

Kirkcudbright,* Town Hall.
4¾ Ringford.*
9⅝ 4⅞ Laurieston.*
18¾ 14 9⅛ New Galloway.*
19⅝ 14⅞ 10 ⅞ Ken Bridge.

Principal Objects of Interest.—Moorland road generally, but pretty scenery along Loch Ken.

*Hotels or Inns at places marked.**

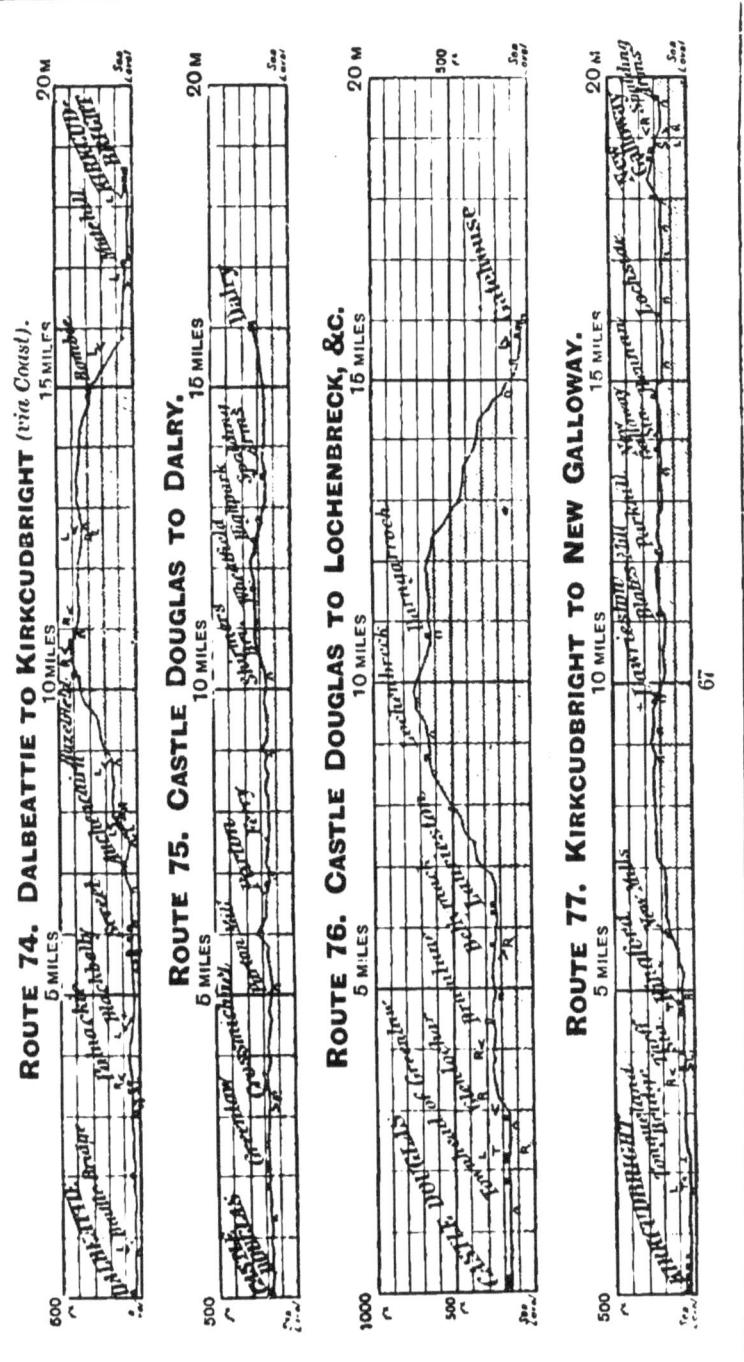

78 DALBEATTIE TO CORSOCK.

Description.—Class III. The road has a fair surface, but is somewhat hilly.

Gradients.—At 3¼m. 1 in 10.

Milestones.—Measured from Dalbeattie Quay,—correct.

Measurements.—Dalbeattie,* Town Hall.
           3¼ Haugh of Urr.
           11¾ 8½ Corsock Bridge.*

Principal Objects of Interest.—2½m. Mote of Urr. Pretty scenery at Corsock Bridge.

79 CASTLE DOUGLAS TO AUCHENCAIRN.

Description.—Class II. A fairly level road of very good surface.

Milestones.—Measured from Palnackie,—correct.

Measurements.—Castle Douglas,* Town Clock.
           8¼ Auchencairn.*

80 CASTLE DOUGLAS TO KIRKCUDBRIGHT.

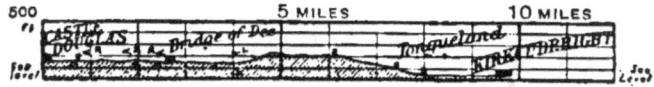

Description.—Class II. The road has a very fine surface, but is undulating between Bridge of Dee and Tongueland.

Milestones.—Continuation of those from Dumfries.

Measurements.—Castle Douglas,* Town Clock.
           7¾ Tongueland.
           9¾ 2¼ Kirkcudbright,* Town Hall.

Principal Objects of Interest.—2½m. Old Bridge of Dee. 6¾m. Queen Mary's Bridge. Tongueland; Abbey, Bridge. KIRKCUDBRIGHT; St. Mary's Isle. Pretty scenery near Tongueland.

Hotels or Inns at places marked *.

KIRKCUDBRIGHT TO DUNDRENNAN, &c. 81

Description.—Class III. The road is good for 2 miles, but then becomes rough, with some stiff hills, joining Route 74, 1 mile beyond Dundrennan.

Gradients.—At 2½m. 1 in 15; 4¾m. 1 in 22; 5¼m. 1 in 19; 5¾m. 1 in 20; 7m. 1 in 16-18.

Measurements.—Kirkcudbright,* Town Hall.
    6¼ Dundrennan.*
    11   4¾ Auchencairn.

Principal Objects of Interest.—¾m. St. Mary's Isle, Dundrennan; Abbey, "Port Mary."

KIRKCUDBRIGHT TO GATEHOUSE. 82

Description.—Class II. The road has a fine surface, but the hills are long; there is a steep descent to Gatehouse.

Gradients.—Not above 1 in 25, till 8¼m. 1 in 20-17.

Measurements.—Kirkcudbright,* Town Hall.
    8¾ Gatehouse,* P.O.

Principal Objects of Interest.—GATEHOUSE; Cally House, Anwoth Kirk.

WIGTOWN TO KIRKCOWAN, &c. 83

Description.—Class III. A hilly road to Spittal; thence easier to Kirkcowan.

Gradients.—At ½m. 1 in 14 (dangerous).

Measurements.—Wigtown, County Buildings.
    5¾ Spittal.
    8¼   2¾ Kirkcowan,* P.O.
    17¾ 12   9½ Glenluce.*

Hotels or Inns at places marked *.

84 NEWTON STEWART TO WHITHORN.

Description.—Class II. The road has a fair surface all the way, but is very hilly.

Gradients.—At 3½m. 1 in 21; 6¾m. 1 in 17; 7½m. 1 in 20; 10¾m. 1 in 18-25. Through Whithorn 1 in 21; 18m. 1 in 23.

Milestones.—Measured from Wigtown, County Buildings.

Measurements.

Newton Stewart,* Town Hall.
7 Wigtown,* County Buildings.
17⅜ 10⅜ Whithorn,* Town Hall.
21⅝ 14⅝ 3¾ Isle of Whithorn.*

Principal Objects of Interest.—WIGTOWN; Martyr's Monument. 13⅝m. Sorbie Tower. WHITHORN; Priory Ch.

85 NEWTON STEWART TO PORT WILLIAM.

Description.—Class II. Fair surface, but undulating.

Gradients.—At 13½m. 1 in 22; 13¾m. 1 in 23; 17m. 1 in 16.

Measurements.

Newton Stewart,* Town Hall.
10¾ Whauphill Station.
17⅛ 6⅜ Port William.*

86 NEWTON STEWART TO STRANRAER.

Description.—Class I. The surface is rather poor.

Gradients.—At 1m. 1 in 24; through Glenluce 1 in 18.

Milestones.—Continuation of those from Dumfries.

Measurements.

Newton Stewart,* Town Hall.
15½ Glenluce.*
25¼ 9¾ Stranraer,* Court House.

Principal Objects of Interest.—Glenluce; Abbey. 22m. Castle Kennedy and Inch Castle.

87 ISLE OF WHITHORN TO GLENLUCE.

Description.—Class III. For the most part the surface is very good, but apt to be soft.

Gradients.—8m. 1/16; 17½m. 1/13; 23¾m. 1/22; 24½m. 1/18.

Measurements.

Isle of Whithorn.*
10¾ Port William.*
24½ 13¾ Glenluce.*

Principal Objects of Interest.—2¾m. to St. Ninian's Cave.

88 STRANRAER TO DRUMMORE.

Description.—Class II. This is a good undulating road all the way. To the Mull of Galloway is fair but hilly.

Gradients.—No hills of any length above 1 in 22.

Milestones.—Continue those from Girvan to Sandmill Bridge, where those from Glenluce are joined—correct.

Hotels or Inns at places marked.* At Kirkinner on Routes 84 & 85; and Kirkcowan (off road) on Route 86.

ROUTE 84. NEWTON STEWART TO WHITHORN.

ROUTE 85. NEWTON STEWART TO PORT WILLIAM.

ROUTE 86. NEWTON STEWART TO STRANRAER.

ROUTE 87. ISLE OF WHITHORN TO GLENLUCE.

ROUTE 88. STRANRAER TO DRUMMORE.

71

Measurements.

Stranraer,* Court House.			
7¾	Sandhead, Hall.		
10¾	3	Ardwell * Inn.	
17¼	9⅝	6⅝	Drummore,* P.O.

Principal Objects of Interest.—The Port Logan Fishery and the scenery of the Mull of Galloway.

89 GIRVAN TO PORTPATRICK.

Description.—Class II. With the exception of the hill over Bennane Head,—beyond Lendalfoot,—and the upper part of Glen App, the road is very smooth, and in splendid condition, to Stranraer. Thence to Portpatrick the surface is fair. In some places the road lies close to the sea, and is therefore liable to be washed out. *Via* Inch 1¼m. longer.

Gradients.—At 8½m. 1 in 25; at 9½m. 1 in 23-24-19-21. Ascent beyond Ballantrae begins 1 in 20, but is not above 1 in 23 to summit. The descent of Glen App is 1 in 17-16 (dangerous), then 1 in 20-19, thereafter a few parts 1 in 25. At 33½m. 1 in 23; 34¼m. 1 in 20-22; 36¾m. 1 in 20; 37¾m. 1 in 20-22.

Milestones.—From Girvan (Old Parish Church) to Stranraer,—correct. Thence continue those from N'ton Stewart.

Measurements.

Girvan,* Town Steeple.					
6½	Lendalfoot.				
12¾	6¼	Ballantrae,* Clock.			
24¼	17¾	11½	Cairnryan.*		
30¼	23¾	17½	6	Stranraer,* Court House.	
38¼	31¾	25½	14	8	Portpatrick.*

Principal Objects of Interest.—2¾m. Ardmillan House. 4½m. Kennedy's Pass. 6½m. Carleton Tower. 10m. Bennane Cave. 12m. Ardstinchar Castle. Glen App; fine woods. Innermessan; Mote. STRANRAER; Castle. PORTPATRICK; Dunskey Castle, and magnificent cliff scenery.

90 GIRVAN TO BALLANTRAE *(Inland)*.

Description.—Class II. The road is good but steep to Daljarrock, thence very undulating to Ballantrae. The post road—a few hundred yards longer—turns off at 13m. and joins Coast road 1½m. from Ballantrae.

Gradients.—Ascent from Girvan 1 in 24-22; descent 1 in 23. At 5¼m. 1 in 23; 7¾m. 1 in 18; 13m. 1 in 19.

Milestones.—From Girvan (Old Parish Church)—correct.

Measurements.

Girvan,* Town Steeple.		
11¼	Colmonell.*	
16½	5¼	Ballantrae,* Clock.

Principal Objects of Interest.—Colmonell; Craigneil Cas. 13m. Knockdolian Castle and Mote. 16⅝m. Ardstinchar Cas.

*Hotels or Inns at places marked *.*

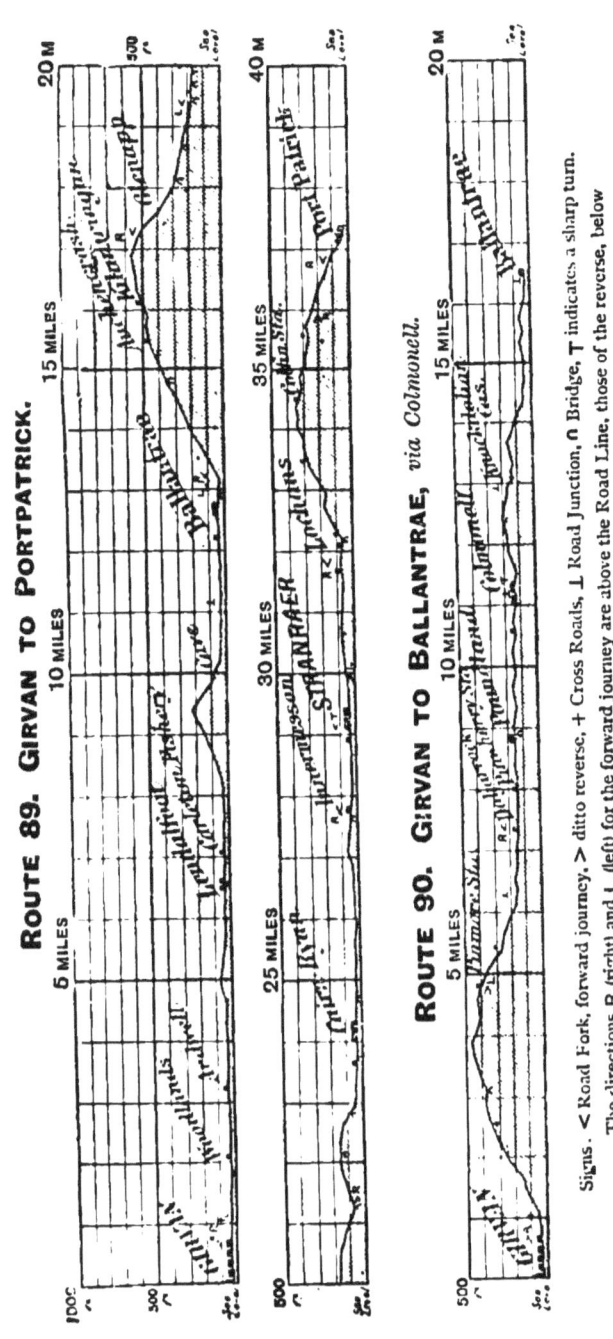

Signs. < Road Fork, forward journey. > ditto reverse. + Cross Roads. ⊥ Road Junction. ∩ Bridge. ⊤ indicates a sharp turn. The directions R (right) and L (left) for the forward journey are above the Road Line, those of the reverse, below

91   GIRVAN TO NEWTON STEWART.

Description.—Class II. A good but steep road to Pinwherry, thence fair but very undulating before Barhill. Thereafter the road has a good surface but is hilly to Bargrennan, when it becomes very easy to Newton Stewart. (Route 97).

Gradients.—Ascent from Girvan mostly 1 in 24-22; descent 1 in 23; at 5½m. 1 in 23; 7¾m. 1 in 18; 14m. 1 in 19-25.

Milestones.—Measured from Girvan, site of Old Parish Church,—correct.

Measurements.
Girvan,* Town Steeple.
8   Pinwherry Station.
12½   4½   Barhill.*
21½   13½   9   Bargrennan.*
30¼   22¼   17¾   8¾   Newton Stewart,* Town Hall.

Principal Objects of Interest.—4½m. British Camp. 5¾m. Pinmore House. 8½m. Pinwherry Castle. Near Bargrennan; Loch Trool. Remainder as Route 97.

Hotels or Inns at places marked *.

92   GIRVAN TO NEWTON STEWART.

Description.—Class III. As above to Barhill, thence an exceedingly hilly road of rather soft surface to Newton Stewart. The previous Route is less fatiguing.

Gradients.—As above to Barhill, thence short but steep hills.

Measurements.
Girvan,* Town Steeple.
12½   Barhill.*
22½   9¾   Knowe.*
30   17½   7¾   Newton Stewart.* Town Hall.

Principal Objects of Interest.—As above to Barhill, thence a moorland road to Newton Stewart.

Hotels or Inns at places marked *.

93   GIRVAN TO DALMELLINGTON.

Description.—Class II. & III. A very good undulating road to Straiton, thence steep, and rough.

Gradients.—At 13¾m. 1 in 18; 15m. 1 in 12-22; 19½m. 1 in 19.

Milestones.—Measured from N. end of Girvan,—correct.

Measurements.
Girvan,* Town Steeple.
14⅝   Straiton.*
21¼   6⅝   Dalmellington.*

The distance to Maybole by this road is 14m.

Hotels or Inns at places marked *, and at Dailly (off road).

ROUTE 91. GIRVAN TO NEWTON STEWART. *Route 92 for 10 miles.*

ROUTE 92. GIRVAN TO NEWTON STEWART. *After Barrgrennan see Route 97.*

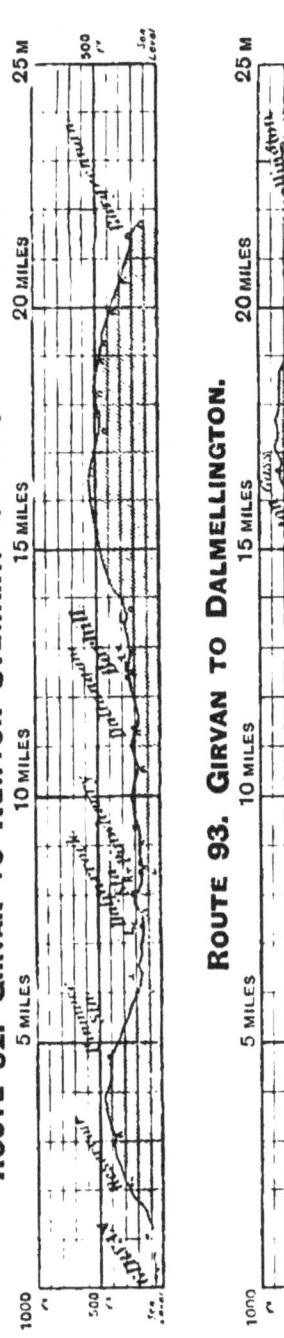

ROUTE 93. GIRVAN TO DALMELLINGTON.

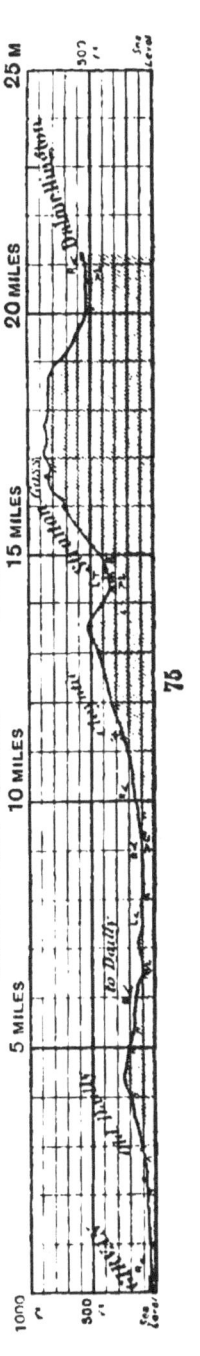

94 AYR TO GIRVAN.

Description.—Class I. The road is a magnificent one, with smooth surface the whole way.

Gradients.—At 16m., 1 in 19-22-18.

Milestones.—Measured from Ayr Town Hall as far as Maybole, thence measured from Maybole Castle.

Measurements.

Ayr,* Town Hall.
5½ Minnyshant.
9⅛ 3⅝ Maybole,* Castle.
13⅝ 8⅛ 4½ Kirkoswald.
21⅜ 15⅞ 12¼ 7¾ Girvan,* Town Steeple.

Principal Objects of Interest.—MAYBOLE; Castle, Tolbooth. 11¼m., Crossraguel Abbey, ruin. 16⅝m., to N., Turnberry Castle, ruin.

95 AYR TO GIRVAN *(Coast Road)*.

Description.—Class III. A rather hilly and soft road.

Gradients.—At 4m., 1 in 24; 5½m., 1 in 15; 9¾m., 1 in 14 (dangerous). 11m., 1 in 15; 12¾m., 1 in 23; 14¾m., 1 in 16; 15m., 1 in 19; 17¼m., 1 in 16.

Milestones.—Measured from Ayr Town Hall,—correct.

Measurements.

Ayr,* Town Hall.
7¾ Dunure Mains.
15½ 7¾ Maidens.
22¼ 14½ 6¾ Girvan,* Town Steeple.
Maybole is 2⅝m. distant at 11¼m.

Principal Objects of Interest.—4½m., Heads of Ayr. 6⅝m. and 7¾m., to Dunure Castle. 14½m., Culzean Castle. 16¼m., Turnberry Castle, ruin.

Hotels or Inns at places marked,* None on the road.

96 AYR TO GIRVAN

(via Alloway, Maybole, and Dailly Station).

Description.—Class II. As far as Brig o' Doon very fine; thence to Maybole, only fair and rather steep. Thereafter to Girvan fair, but very hilly.

Gradients.—3½m. 1 in 24-23. Near Maybole 1 in 19. At 10½m. 1 in 20; 17½m. 1 in 16. and several short steep hills.

Milestones.—Measured from Ayr Town Hall to Maybole; thence from points outside Maybole and Girvan,—correct.

Measurements.

2¼ Alloway.*
8½ 6¼ Maybole,* Castle.
21⅝ 19⅜ 13⅛ Girvan,* Town Steeple.

Route 94. Ayr to Girvan.

Route 95. Ayr to Girvan *(Coast Road).*

Route 96. Ayr to Girvan *(via Brig o' Doon and Dailly Station).*

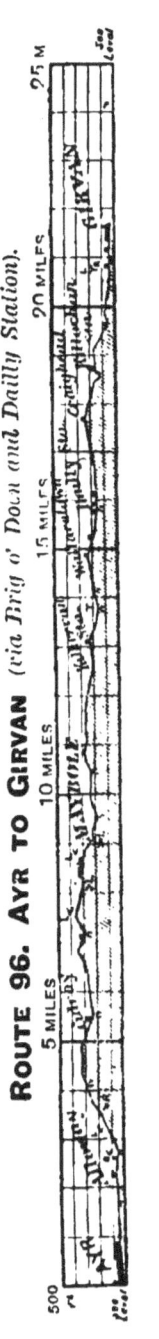

Signs. < Road Fork, forward journey. > ditto reverse. + Cross Roads. ⊥ Road Junction. ∩ Bridge. ⊤ indicates a sharp turn. The directions R (right) and L (left) for the forward journey are above the Road Line, those of the reverse, below.

(*Route 96 continued.*)

Principal Objects of Interest.—ALLOWAY; Burns' Cottage, Monument, Kirk, and Brig o' Doon. MAYBOLE; Tolbooth, Castle.

Hotels or Inns at places marked,* and at (Dailly.)

97 AYR TO NEWTON STEWART.

Description.—Class II. The first 10 miles of this road are very smooth and with easy grades; on to Straiton is still good but with steeper hills. The next few miles are good until the ascent commences, when the surface degenerates and is very poor until nearing Bargrennan,—18 miles of very rough road. From here to Newton Stewart is a beautiful road with easy grades and very good surface.

Gradients.—At 10m. 1 in 22; 11½m. 1 in 25; at 17¾m. the ascent begins with 1 in 14 and 1 in 12, followed by 1 in 18, 21, and 24. The gradient then varies between 1 in 20 and 24 up to the summit, when the descent commences with 1 in 24, increasing to 1 in 20. Immediately after Rowantree Toll there is a grade of 1 in 20, but this decreases to 1 in 25 which is not again exceeded to Bargrennan.

Milestones.—Measured from Ayr Town Hall,—correct.

Measurements.

Ayr,* Town Hall.
5¼ Minnyshant.
10   4¾ Kirkmichael.
14½ 9   4½ Straiton.*
35¾ 30¼ 25¾ 21¼ Bargrennan.*
44¾ 38¾ 34¼ 29¾ 8¾ Newton Stewart,* Town Hall.

Principal Objects of Interest.—6½m. Cassillis House, then after Straiton a very dreary wild road to near Bargrennan. 34¼m., to W., Loch Trool. 40¾m. Penninghame House. 41m. Churchyard, and Castle Stewart, ruins. NEWTON STEWART; Academy, Earl of Galloway's Monument.

Hotels or Inns at places marked *.

N.B.—This road was constructed to supersede that from Maybole *via* the Nick of the Balloch, which has 2 miles of 1 in 14, as well as grades of 1 in 11; it is almost disused.

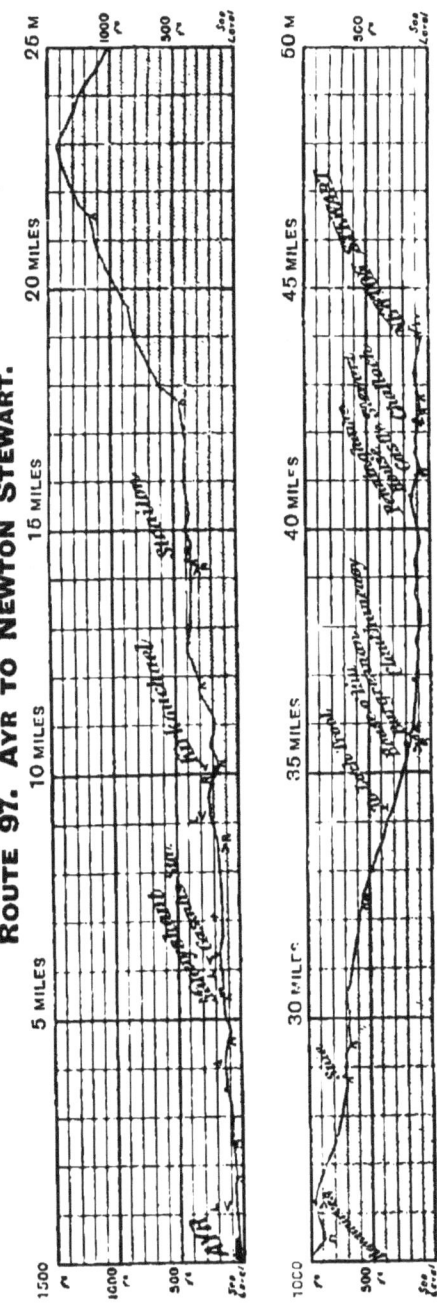

Signs < Road Fork, forward journey, > ditto reverse, + Cross Roads, ⊥ Road Junction, ∩ Bridge, ⊤ indicates a sharp turn. The directions **R** (right) and **L** (left) for the forward journey are above the Road line, those of the reverse, below.

79

98 AYR TO NEW GALLOWAY.

Description.—Class II. While the road has a very good surface, the steepness of the hills makes it very trying—especially on the outward journey—as far as Patna Station. From here as far as Dalmellington the road is level with fair surface; it is good up to the summit with a very steady gradient, but the next 5 miles are a series of steep and very trying undulations. From Carsphairn the road is very stony for some miles, after which it is very good all the way to New Galloway. There is a direct but steep road to New Galloway, straight on at 34¼m.

Gradients.—At 2¼m. 1 in 19; Whitehill 1 in 14-21; 4¼m. 1 in 19; 4¾m. 1 in 24; 5½m. 1 in 23; 7¼m. 1 in 19; easy grades past Dalmellington to summit. At 20m. 1 in 20; 24½m. 1 in 21. From Carsphairn the ascent is easy, and the descent mostly 1 in 25, except at 31½m., 1 in 17.

Milestones.—In Ayrshire measured from Ayr Town Hall; in Kirkcudbright from Carsphairn.

Measurements.

Ayr,* Town Hall.						
10⅛	Patna * Station.					
15½	5⅜	Dalmellington.*				
25½	15⅜	10	Carsphairn.*			
34⅞	24¾	19⅜	9⅜	Dalry * (St. John's Town of).		
37⅜	27¼	21⅞	11⅞	2½	Ken Bridge.	
38¼	28⅛	22¾	12¾	3⅜	⅞	New Galloway,* Town Hall.

Routes from Thornhill, Dumfries, Castle Douglas, Kirkcudbright, and Newton Stewart, meet at Ken Bridge.

Principal Objects of Interest.—Iron Works near Dalmellington. 19m. View of Loch Doon and Castle. Carsphairn; is in the midst of the Covenanters' District. Thereafter some pretty scenery along the banks of the Ken.

Hotels or Inns at places marked *.

ROUTE 98. AYR TO NEW GALLOWAY.

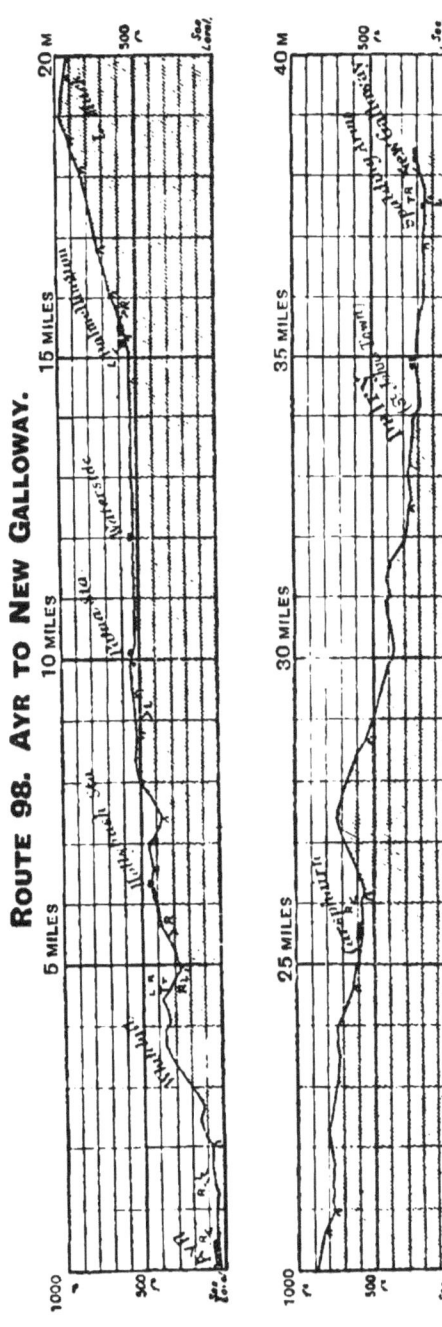

Signs: < Road Fork. forward journey, > ditto reverse, + Cross Roads, ⊥ Road Junction, ∩ Bridge, T indicates a sharp turn.

The directions R (right) and L (left) for the forward journey are above the Road Line, those of the reverse, below.

99 AYR TO CARSTAIRS.

Description.—Class II. Undulating but very good road to Cumnock, thence hilly and somewhat rough to Muirkirk, after which it is very fair past Douglas to Carstairs. The road is rather rough about Rigside.

Gradients.—At 3½m. 1 in 21; 6½m. 1 in 25; 7½m. 1 in 23; 16m. 1 in 19; 17m. 1 in 18; 18¼m. 1 in 23; 38m. 1 in 17; 39m. 1 in 16; 40¼m. and 42½m. 1 in 22; 43m. 1 in 20; 45m. 1 in 22; 46¾m. 1 in 14.

Milestones.—Measured from Ayr Town Hall to Cumnock, then from Cumnock Church to Wellwood. Here those from Ayr *via* Mauchline continue to the County Boundary, when the numbers and positions of those from Cumnock are resumed. After Douglas they are irregular.

Measurements.

Ayr,* Town Hall.					
11½	Ochiltree.*				
15¾	4¼	Cumnock,* Church.			
29⅝	18⅛	13⅞	Muirkirk.*		
35¾	24¼	20	6⅛	Douglas.*	
48⅜	36⅞	32⅝	18¾	12⅝	Carstairs, Church.

Principal Objects of Interest.—CUMNOCK; Peden's Grave, Dumfries Ho. 17¾m. Lugar Ironworks. Aird's Moss Skirmish, 1686. 22¼m. Cameron's Monument. Thence dreary moorland road past reservoirs. Douglas; Church and Monuments, Castle.

Hotels or Inns at places marked,* at Coylton, and Carstairs Junction.

100 AYR TO MUIRKIRK.

Description.—Class II. A very good but hilly road to Mauchline; thence very steep grades for some miles, after which it is a fair road to Muirkirk, though rough about Sorn.

Gradients.—At 4m. 1 in 22; 5¾m. 1 in 19; 6¾m. 1 in 21; 8¼m. 1 in 19; 10m. 1 in 19; 11½m. 1 in 18-13; 12m. 1 in 18; 13¼m. 1 in 16; 13¾m. 1 in 24; 14¼m. 1 in 10; Sorn Hill 1 in 11-13.

Milestones.—Measured from Ayr, Town Hall,—correct.

Measurements.

Ayr,* Town Hall.			
11	Mauchline.*		
15	4	Sorn Village.	
24½	13½	9½	Muirkirk.*

Principal Objects of Interest.—Beautiful scenery where this road touches the Water of Ayr. MAUCHLINE; is in th midst of scenes and references in Burn's Poems. 14½m Sorn Castle.

Hotels or Inn at places marked *.

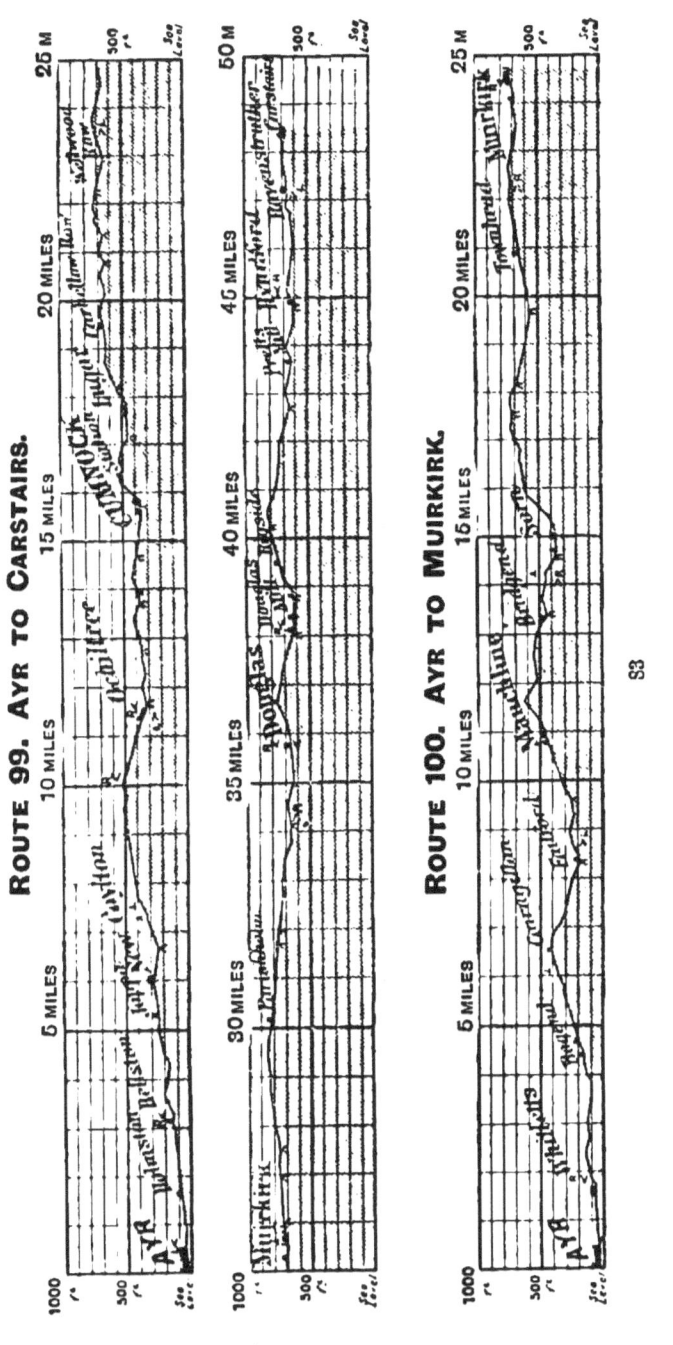

ROUTE 99. AYR TO CARSTAIRS.

ROUTE 100. AYR TO MUIRKIRK.

101 AYR TO HAMILTON.

Description.—Class II. A hilly road to Galston, good to Darvel, thence hilly and rough to near Strathavon, after which it is good, but steep to Hamilton. The best road to Galston is *via* Kilmarnock.

Gradients.—At 4¼m. 1 in 20; 4¾m. 1 in 21; 6m. 1 in 17; 6¾m. 1 in 15; 13m. 1 in 20; 13¾m. 1 in 18; 17½m. 1 in 17; 20¼ and 21½m. 1 in 23-22; 30½m. 1 in 17-21; descent to Hamilton 1 in 16-18-15.

Milestones.—Measured from Ayr Town Hall, to Galston, thence from Kilmarnock Cross to County Boundary, after which as far as Strathavon they are from Edinburgh, West Port. After Strathavon measured from Hamilton.

Measurements.

Ayr,* Town Hall.					
14¾	Galston.*				
17⅜	2⅝	Newmilns.*			
19	4¼	1⅝	Darvel.		
30	15¼	12⅝	11	Strathavon,* Green.	
37½	22¾	20⅛	18½	7½	Hamilton.*

Principal Objects of Interest.—15¼m. Loudon Castle; 17½m. "Patie's Mill." 24¼m., ½m. to N., Drumclog Battlefield, 1679. STRATHAVON; Castle ruin, Falls. HAMILTON; Palace, Cadzow Castle, ruin.

Hotels or Inns at places marked *.

---

102 AYR TO DALRY *(Ayrshire)*.

Description.—Class I. A beautiful smooth road with no hills worth speaking of to Kilwinning; thence undulating, but with very good surface.

Gradients.—None above 1 in 25.

Milestones.—Measured from Ayr Town Hall, correct to Kilwinning.

Measurements.

Ayr,* Town Hall.					
2¾	Prestwick,* School.				
3⅞	1⅛	Monkton.*			
11½	8¾	7⅝	Irvine.*		
14½	11¾	10⅝	3	Kilwinning,* Cross.	
19	16¼	15⅛	7½	4½	Dalry,* Church.

Principal Objects of Interest.—The road is low lying most of the way; it is less uninteresting near Kilwinning.

Hotels or Inns at places marked*, and at Loans.

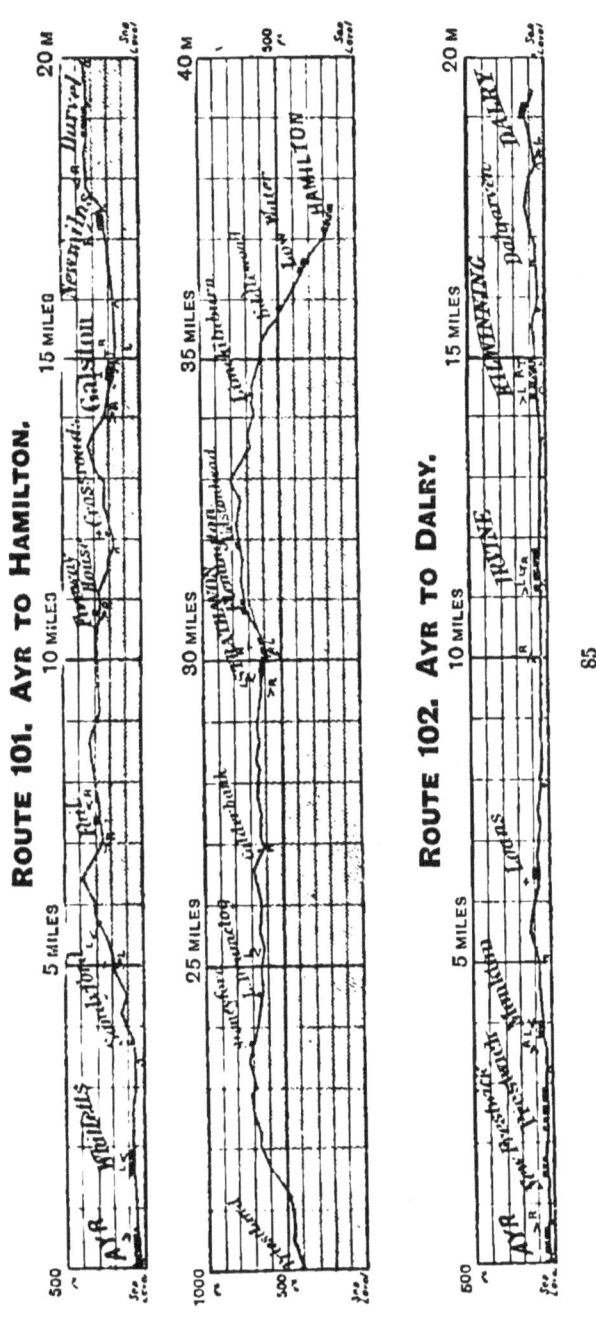

103 CUMNOCK TO GALSTON, &c.

Description.—Class II. A very hilly road of rather poor surface most of the way. To Glasgow, better go by Kilmarnock.

Gradients.—At 1¾m. 1 in 19; 4¾m. 1 in 11; 5¼m. 1 in 10; 6¾m. 1 in 14; 12m. 1 in 14; 13¼m. 1 in 17-12-17; 15¾m. 1 in 17; 18¼m. 1 in 21; 18¾m. 1 in 22.

Milestones.—Measured from Galston,—nearly correct.

Measurements.

Cumnock,* Church.				
5	Sorn Church.			
12⅝	7⅝	Galston.*		
17½	12½	4⅞	Waterside.	
33¾	28¾	21⅛	16¼	Glasgow*, Jamaica Street.

Principal Objects of Interest.—5m., Sorn Castle. 13m., Loudon Castle.

Hotels or Inns at places marked *, and at Malletsheugh, Newton Mearns, and Giffnock.

104 KILMARNOCK TO NEW CUMNOCK.

Description.—Class II. A very good and smooth undulating road to Cumnock; thence only fair surface.

Gradients.—At 3m. 1 in 21; 4¼m. 1 in 13; 10¼m. 1 in 20; 10¾m. 1 in 20; 12m. 1 in 20; 13m. 1 in 19; 13¼m. 1 in 20; 15¾m. 1 in 24; 17¾m. 1 in 17.

Milestones.—Measured from Kilmarnock Cross to Cumnock, thereafter from Ayr, Town Hall,—each set correct.

Measurements.

Kilmarnock,* Cross.			
8¾	Mauchline.*		
15⅜	6⅝	Cumnock,* Church.	
21	12¼	5⅝	New Cumnock,* Church.

Principal Objects of Interest.—8¼m., Mossgiel. MAUCHLINE; in this district are the scenes of many of Burn's Poems. 10¼m., Ballochmyle Viaduct. CUMNOCK; Peden's Grave, Dumfries House.

Hotels or Inns at places marked *.

105 PAISLEY TO GREENOCK.

Description.—Class II. This road has a fair surface, but is lumpy near the towns through which it passes.

Measurements.

Paisley,* Cross.					
3½	Johnstone,* Square.				
7	3½	Bridge of Weir.*			
10½	7	3½	Kilmalcolm.*		
14¾	11¼	7¾	4¼	Port Glasgow,* Town Hall.	
17⅝	14⅛	10⅝	7⅛	2⅞	Greenock,* Town Hall.

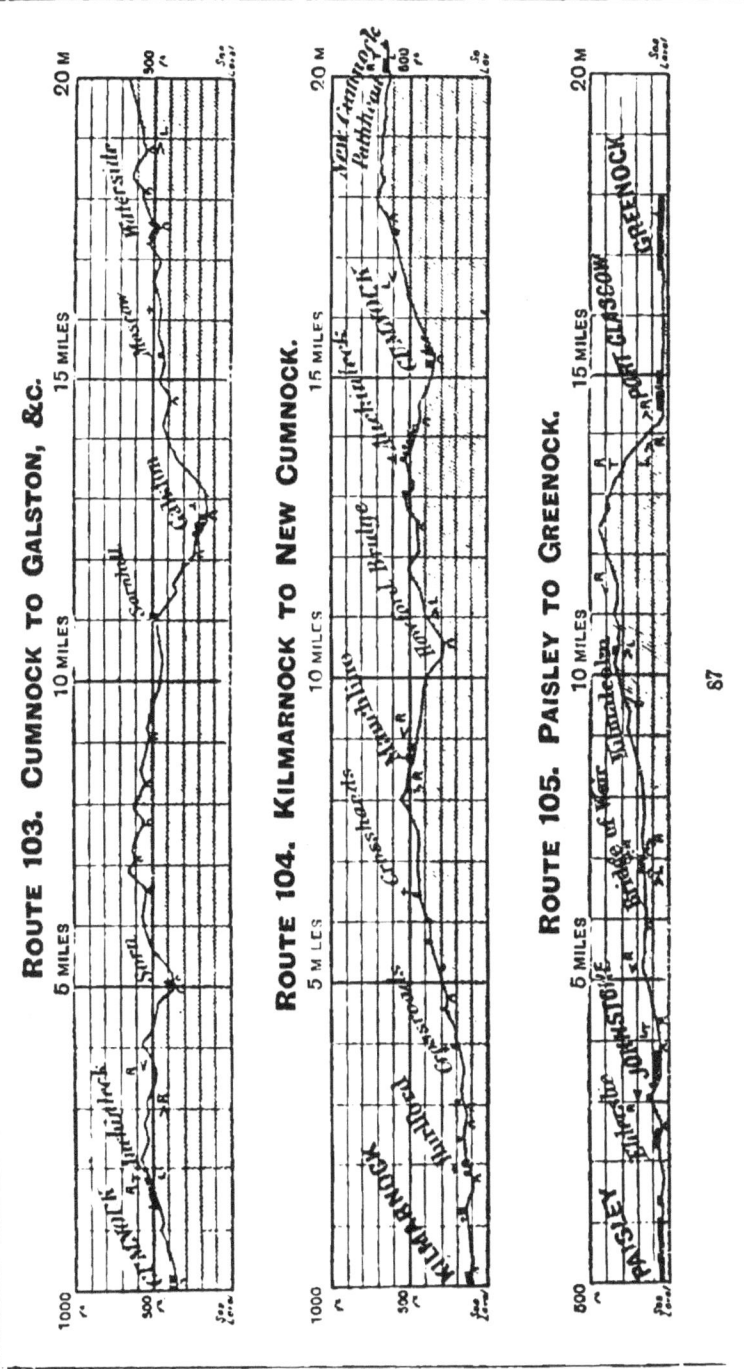

Gradients.—Descent to Port Glasgow 1 in 22-15-10-17-13.

Principal Objects of Interest.—ELDERSLIE; Wallace's tree. BRIDGE OF WEIR; Orphan Homes. 10½m. Hydropathic. 14¼m., Newark Castle, ruin.

Hotels or Inns at places marked * and at Elderslie.

106 HAMILTON TO FENWICK.

Description.—Class II. & III. As far as Eaglesham the road is good but undulating; thereafter it is poor and hilly.

Gradients.—9¾m. 1 in 17; 12¼m. 1 in 17-21; 13¼m. 1 in 24; 14m. 1 in 20; 14¼m. 1 in 20; 14½m. 1 in 14; 16¼m. 1 in 21.

Milestones.—Measured from Hamilton.

Measurements.

Hamilton.*					
3	Blantyre.*				
6½	3½	East Kilbride.*			
10⅞	7⅞	4⅜	Eaglesham.*		
19⅞	16⅞	13⅜	9	Fenwick.*	
24¼	21¼	17¾	13⅜	4⅜	Kilmarnock,* Cross.

Principal Objects of Interest.—The road passes through colliery district at first; after Eaglesham it is uninteresting.

Hotels or Inns at places marked *.

107 GREENOCK TO IRVINE.

Description.—Class II. Usually an exceedingly good road, but liable to sudden change; it runs for 20 miles along the sea shore, and is sometimes "washed out" in stormy weather. There is a direct road over the hill from Greenock to Inverkip, 3¼m. shorter than by the Cloch Lighthouse. Gradient mostly 1 in 20.

Gradients.—Very slight, except at Largs, 1 in 20.

Milestones.—Measured *via* the direct road to Inverkip, and through West Kilbride,—correctly placed.

Measurements.

Greenock,* Town Hall.							
3¼	Gourock,* Station.						
11	7¾	Wemyss Bay,* Pier.					
17½	14¼	6½	Largs.*				
20½	17¼	9½	3	Fairlie.*			
30½	27¼	19½	13	10	Saltcoats.*		
34½	31¼	23½	17	14	4	Kilwinning.*	
37½	34¼	26½	20	17	7	3	Irvine.*

Principal Objects of Interest.—A most delightful road running close to the water's edge nearly the whole way.

Hotels or Inns at places marked * and at Inverkip, Skelmorlie, West Kilbride, Ardrossan, and Stevenston.

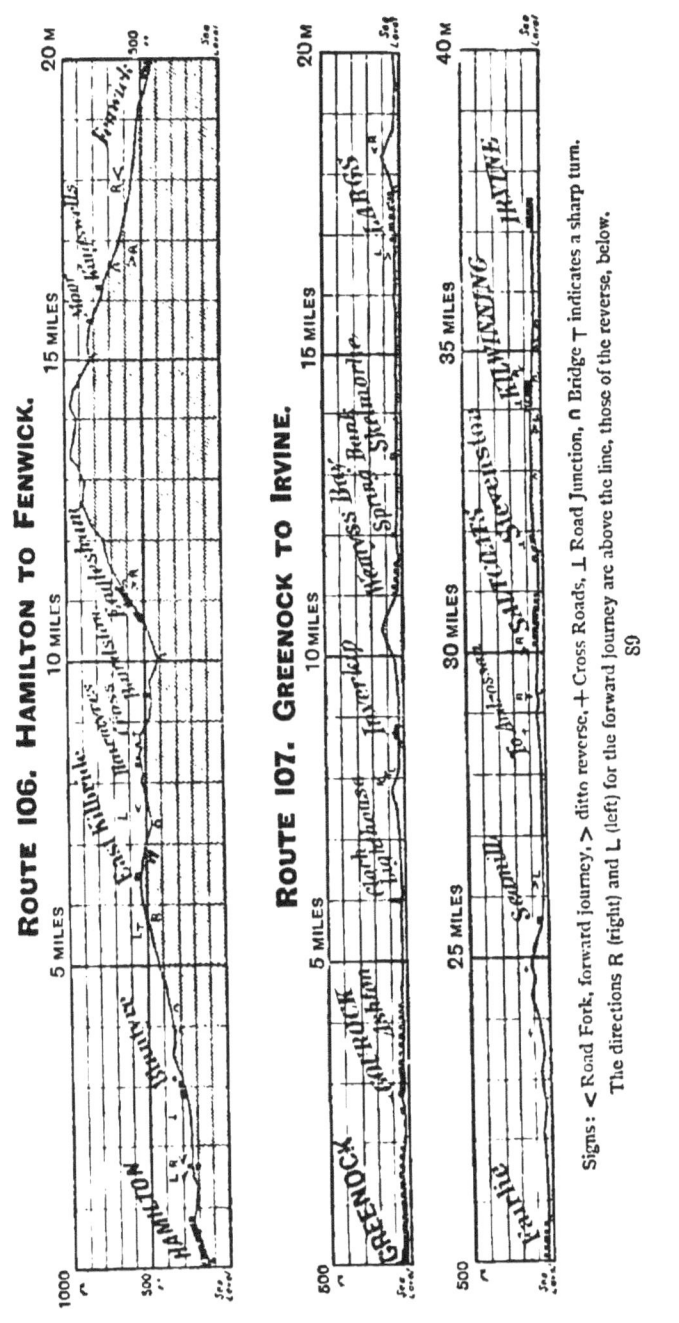

Signs: < Road Fork, forward journey, > ditto reverse, + Cross Roads, ⊥ Road Junction, ∩ Bridge ⊤ indicates a sharp turn. The directions R (right) and L (left) for the forward journey are above the line, those of the reverse, below.

108   IRVINE TO GALSTON.

Description.—Class II. An undulating road with very good surface.

Milestones.—Measured from Kilmarnock Cross,—correct.

Measurements.—Irvine.*
- 7½   Kilmarnock,* Cross.
- 9   1¾   Hurlford,* P.O.
- 12   4¾   3   Galston.*

Principal Objects of Interest.—KILMARNOCK ; Burns' Memorial. Galston: Loudoun Castle.

109   KILMARNOCK TO TROON.

The dotted line indicates the direct road by Dundonald.

Description.—Class III. The direct road is good as far as Dundonald, but then becomes steep and rather rough until Loans, whence it is good to Troon. A much better and easier road is that by Parkthorn shown on diagram.

Gradients (*direct road*).—At 5½m. 1 in 17-24; 7m. 1 in 16-11-16.

Measurements.—Kilmarnock,* Cross.
- 5¼   Dundonald.
- 9   3¾   Troon.*
- 10¾   ...   Troon* *via* Parkthorn.

Principal Objects of Interest.—2m. Riccarton Castle. Dundonald ; Castle.

110   KILMARNOCK TO LUGTON.

Description.—Class II. A fine smooth road, but slightly hilly after Kilmaurs.

Gradients.—At 3½m. 1 in 23-20; 6m. 1 in 24; 8½m. 1 in 17-19.

Milestones.—Measured from Kilmarnock Cross, to Stewarton ; thereafter from Glasgow.

Measurements.—Kilmarnock,* Cross.
- 5¾   Stewarton.*
- 8¼   2½   Dunlop.
- 10¾   4¾   2½   Lugton,* Station.
- 25¾   19¾   17¼   15   Glasgow,* Jamaica St.

ARDROSSAN TO AUCHENTIBER, &c. 111

Description.—Class II. A good road with easy gradients.
Measurements.—Ardrossan.*
      1½ Saltcoats.*
      5½ 4 Kilwinning,* Cross.
      10¼ 8¾ 4¾ Auchentiber.
      20¾ 28¾ 24¾ 19¾ Glasgow,* Jamaica St.
Principal Objects of Interest.—KILWINNING; Abbey ruins, Cross. Eglinton; Castle.

DALRY TO WEST KILBRIDE. 112

Description.—Class II. Good surface, but rather hilly.
Gradients.—At 3m. 1 in 13; 4½m. 1 in 15; 5m. 1 in 19.
Measurements.—Dalry* Church.
      6½ West Kilbride* Church.

PAISLEY TO EAST KILBRIDE. 113

Description.—Class II. The road has an excellent surface, but is somewhat hilly after Thornliebank.
Gradients.—At 8½m. 1 in 23-18; 9m. 1 in 21.
Measurements.—Paisley,* Cross.
      2¾ Hurlet.
      5¾ 2½ Thornliebank.*
      8 5¼ 2¾ Busby.*
      12 9¼ 6¾ 4 East Kilbride.*

BARRHEAD TO RENFREW. 114

Description.—Class II. A fine smooth road, except through Paisley.
Milestones.—Measured from Renfrew Cross.
Measurements.—Barrhead.*
      3 Paisley,* Cross.
      6¼ 3¼ Renfrew,* Cross.
Principal Objects of Interest. PAISLEY; Abbey.

115   GLASGOW TO GREENOCK.

Description.—Class I. After quitting the suburbs the road has a very good surface to Port Glasgow, but thereafter is very rough, owing to heavy traffic.

Gradients.—Descent to Langbank 1 in 22.

Milestones.—Correct, but add the Cessnock Dock deviation ¼m. After Bishopton measured from Greenock, T. H.

Measurements.

Glasgow,* Jamaica Street.
    6¼   Renfrew,* Cross.
  11¾   5¾   Bishopton.
  19⅜   13¼   7½   Port Glasgow,* Town Hall.
  22¼   16¼   10⅜   2⅞   Greenock,* Town Hall.

Principal Objects of Interest.—18⅞m. Newark Castle. There are many fine views of the Clyde, and the hills surrounding it.

Hotels or Inns at places marked *.

116   GLASGOW TO DALRY.

Description.—Class I. To Paisley the road is generally very rough, owing to heavy traffic, but thereafter it is very fair, though somewhat hilly.

Gradients.—At 13⅞m., & 14¼m. 1/20; 22¼m. 1/25; 24m. 1/23.

Milestones.—Measured from Royal Exchange, Glasgow, and from Paisley Cross.

Measurements.

Glasgow,* Jamaica Street.
    6⅞   Paisley,* Cross.
  9¼   2⅜   Elderslie.*
  18¼   11¾   9   Beith,* Town Hall.
  23   16¼   13¾   4¼   Dalry,* Church.

Principal Objects of Interest.—4¾m., to S., Crookston Castle, ruins. PAISLEY; Abbey. Elderslie; Wallace's Tree. KILWINNING; Abbey, ruins.

Hotels or Inns at places marked *, Thorn, and Howwood.

117   GLASGOW TO LARGS.

Description.—Class II. As Route 116 for 15m., thence hilly and rather steep road; poor surface after Kilbirnie.

Gradients.—21m. 1 in 18-25; descent to Largs 1 in 13-12-1.

Measurements.

Glasgow,* Jamaica Street.
    6⅞   Paisley,* Cross.
  16¼   9⅜   Lochwinnoch.*
  20½   13¼   4¼   Kilbirnie * Bridge.
  29¼   22¾   13¾   9¼   Largs.*

Principal Objects of Interest.—24m. Supposed site Battle of Largs, 1263.

Hotels or Inns at places marked *, Thorn, and Howwood.

Route 115. Glasgow to Greenock.

Route 116. Glasgow to Dalry.

Route 117. Glasgow to Largs. (Route 116 for 5 miles.)

Route 118. Glasgow to Irvine.

118 GLASGOW TO IRVINE.

Description.—Class I. Generally speaking the surface is fair, but in some parts it is rather rough.

Gradients.—The road is beautifully engineered.

Milestones.—Measured from the commencement of the Pollockshaws road,—correct.

Measurements.

Glasgow,* Jamaica Street.				
7½	Barrhead.*			
10	2½	Neilston *Station.		
15	7½	5	Lugton * Station.	
26	18½	16	11	Irvine.*

Principal Objects of Interest.—5¾m., 1m. to N., Crookston Castle. Past Barrhead are many Printworks, Bleachfields, &c.

Hotels or Inns at places marked *, and at Hurlet.

119 GLASGOW TO AYR.

Description.—Class I. A beautiful surface to Kilmarnock, rough through the town, thence exceedingly good to Ayr.

Gradients.—Hardly perceptible, the maximum is 1 in 32.

Milestones.—Measured from Glasgow Royal Exchange to County Boundary, thereafter from Kilmarnock Cross; after Monkton from Ayr Town Hall.

Measurements.

Glasgow,* Jamaica Street.					
7	Newton Mearns.*				
16¾	9¾	Fenwick.*			
21	14	4¼	Kilmarnock,* Cross.		
28⅞	21⅞	12⅛	7⅞	Monkton.*	
32¾	25¾	16	11¾	3⅞	Ayr,* Town Hall.

Principal Objects of Interest.—KILMARNOCK; Burns' Memorial. AYR; Wallace Tower, Bridges, Burns' Cottage, etc. This is a favourite road, and though there are few objects of special note, it is by no means uninteresting.

Hotels or Inns at places marked *, Malletsheugh, and Prestwick.

120 GLASGOW TO STRATHAVON.

Description.—Class II. A very hilly road, but with fair surface to Strathavon.

Gradients.—At 4¾m. 1 in 23-20; 9½m. 1 in 20; 12¼m. 1 in 16; 15¾m. 1 in 21; 28¾m. 1 in 20-24.

Milestones.—Measured from Glasgow Cross—fairly correct.

Measurements.

Glasgow,* Jamaica Street.			
3	Rutherglen.*		
8⅜	5⅜	East Kilbride.*	
16½	13½	8⅛	Strathavon,* Green.

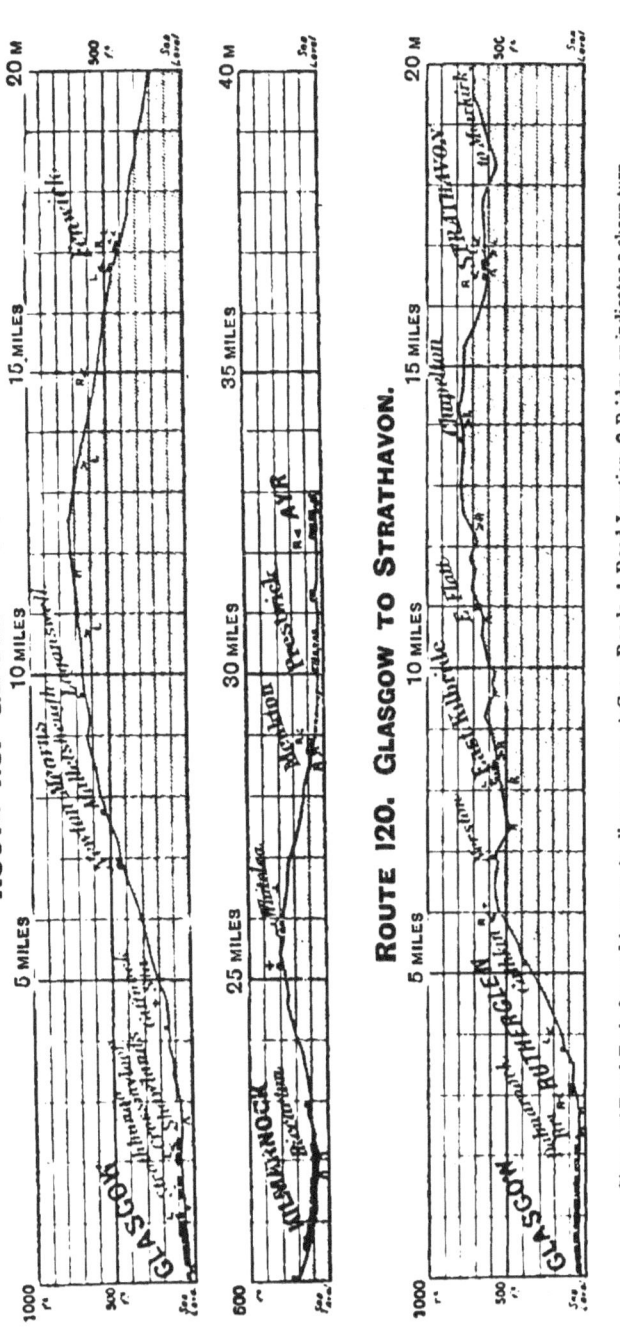

Signs: < Road Fork, forward journey, > ditto reverse, + Cross Roads, ⌐ Road Junction, ∩ Bridge, T indicates a sharp turn. The directions R (right) and L (left) for the forward journey are above the Road Line, those of the reverse, below.

Principal Objects of Interest.—Some fine views of the Vale of Clyde are obtained from this road. STRATHAVON; Castle ruins, Waterfall.

Hotels or Inns at places marked*.

121 GLASGOW TO ABINGTON.

Description.—Class I. The first ten miles are lumpy with suburban traffic, but thereafter the road is a splendid highway of very fine surface, though often with patches of metal in the higher parts. The road is good in all weathers.

Gradients.—To Bothwell Bridge, both sides 1 in 19; 28m. 1 in 18; 29m. 1 in 18; 35½m. 1 in 23.

Milestones.—Perfectly correct after Hamilton,—measured from Glasgow Cross.

Measurements.

Glasgow,* Jamaica Street.						
9¼	Bothwell.*					
11½	2¼	Hamilton.*				
15	5¾	3½	Larkhall.*			
23	13¾	11½	8	Leshmahagow,* Toll.		
28⅝	19⅜	17⅛	13⅝	5⅝	Douglas Mill.	
37½	28¼	26	22½	14½	8⅞	Abington * Hotel.

Principal Objects of Interest.—BOTHWELL; Castle, ruin. Bothwell Bridge, Battle, 1679. HAMILTON; Palace, Cadzow Castle, ruin. Moorland after Douglas Mill.

Hotels or Inns at places marked.*

122 GLASGOW TO LANARK.

Description.—Class I. This road though rather undulating has a magnificent surface. As far as Bothwell the suburban traffic makes the road lumpy, but thereafter it is very good but hilly.

Gradients.—To Bothwell Bridge 1 in 19, both sides; at 13½m., & 17¾m., & 22¼m. 1 in 20; at 23m. 1 in 13; at 24¾m. 1 in 10 (dangerous).

Milestones.—Measured from Glasgow Cross; correct after Hamilton.

Measurements.

Glasgow,* Jamaica Street.					
9¼	Bothwell.*				
11½	2¼	Hamilton.*			
17⅝	8⅜	6⅛	Dalserf.		
20¾	11½	9¼	3⅛	Crossford.*	
25½	16¼	14	7⅞	4¾	Lanark,* Cross.

Principal Objects of Interest.—BOTHWELL; Castle, ruin, Bridge. HAMILTON; Palace, Cadzow Castle, ruin. 20½m. to W., Craignethan Castle, ruin. 23m. Stonebyres Fall. LANARK; Cartland Crags, Falls of Clyde.

Hotels or Inns at places marked *, and at Kirkfieldbank.

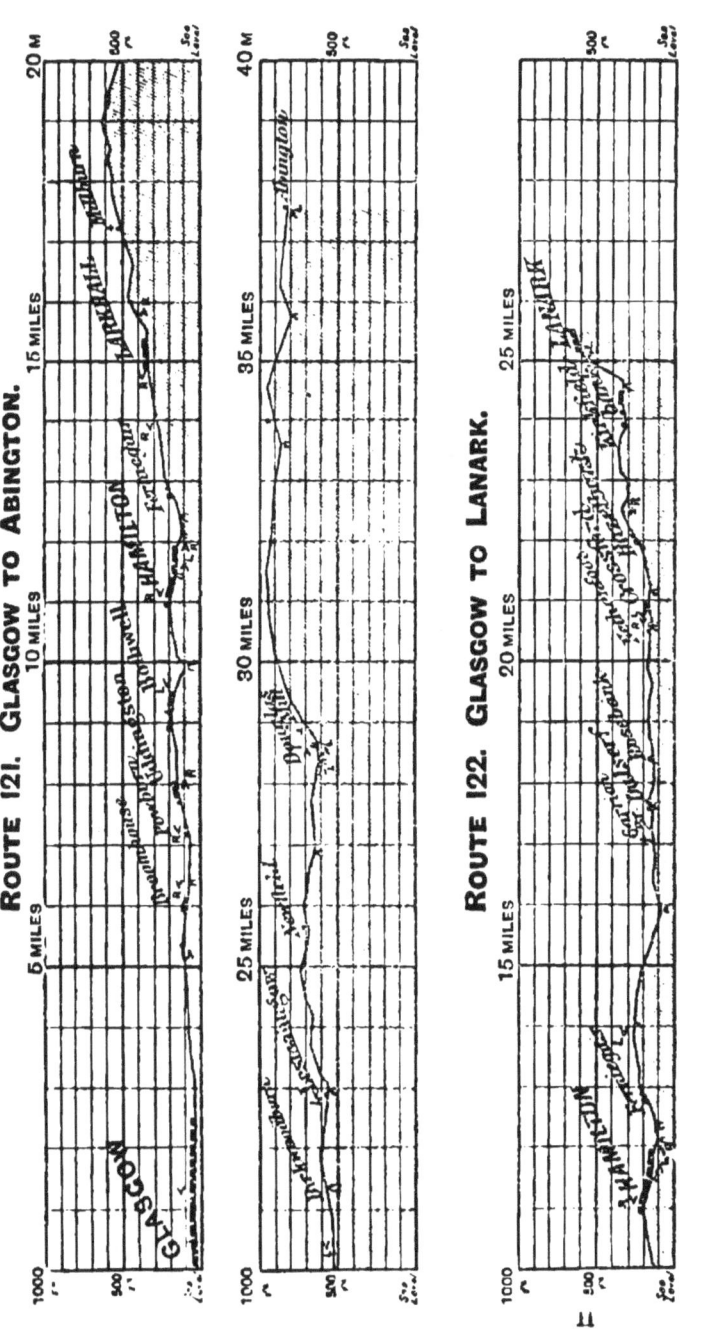

123 GLASGOW TO PEEBLES.

Description.—Class I. & II. A well-made, good, but hilly road, rather rough in the coal and iron district through which it passes. After Carluke the surface is better, but the road is more or less hilly till within 8m. of Peebles.

Gradients.—At 10¾m. 1 in 17; 11m. 1 in 16; 14m. 1 in 18; 21¼m. 1 in 18; 24¼m. 1 in 19; 26¾m. 1 in 18; 27m. 1 in 17; 33½m. 1 in 23; 34m. 1 in 18-21-24; 35¼m. 1 in 15; 38m. 1 in 18-21; 38¾m. 1 in 20-16; 41½m. 1 in 12; 50m. 1 in 21.

Milestones.—These are indifferently placed, except from Carluke to Elsrickle, and for some miles approaching Peebles.

Measurements.

Glasgow,* Jamaica Street.

9¾	Bellshill.*						
12¼	2½	Motherwell.*					
15⅝	5⅞	3⅜	Wishaw.*				
20⅜	10⅝	8⅛	4¾	Carluke,* Market.			
29½	19¾	17¼	13⅞	9⅛	Carnwath,* Cross.		
35½	25¾	23¼	19⅞	15⅛	6	Elsrickle.	
50½	40¾	38¼	34⅞	30⅛	21	15	Peebles,* Cross.

Principal Objects of Interest.—20m. of the Coal and Iron district, afterwards uninteresting till near Peebles.

Hotels or Inns at places marked *, and at Carstairs Jun.

---

124 GLASGOW TO EDINBURGH.

Description.—Class I. Until Airdrie is passed this road is much cut up with suburban traffic, but from there it is an exceedingly good and smooth road right in to Edinburgh. This is the most direct route to Edinburgh, but many prefer the more interesting road by Falkirk, 46¾m. The road by Shotts, 44⅜m., is seldom used for through traffic.

Gradients.—The only stiff hill is through Airdrie, 1 in 22.

Milestones.—These are measured from Glasgow suburbs, and from Caledonian Station, Edinburgh,—correct.

Measurements.

Glasgow,* Jamaica Street.

4	Shettleston.*							
9¼	5¼	Coatbridge.*						
11¼	7¼	2	Airdrie,* Cross.					
23	19	13¾	11¾	Armadale.*				
25⅝	21⅝	16⅛	14⅛	2⅝	Bathgate,* Station.			
31⅜	27⅜	22⅛	20⅛	8⅜	6	Uphall.*		
32¾	28¾	23½	21½	9¾	7⅜	1⅜	Broxburn.*	
44⅛	40⅛	34⅞	32⅞	21⅛	18¾	12¾	11⅜	Edinburgh,* G.P.O.

Principal Objects of Interest.—Ironworks about Coatbridge and Airdrie, shale oil works at Uphall, Broxburn.

Hotels or Inns at places marked *, and at Corstorphine.

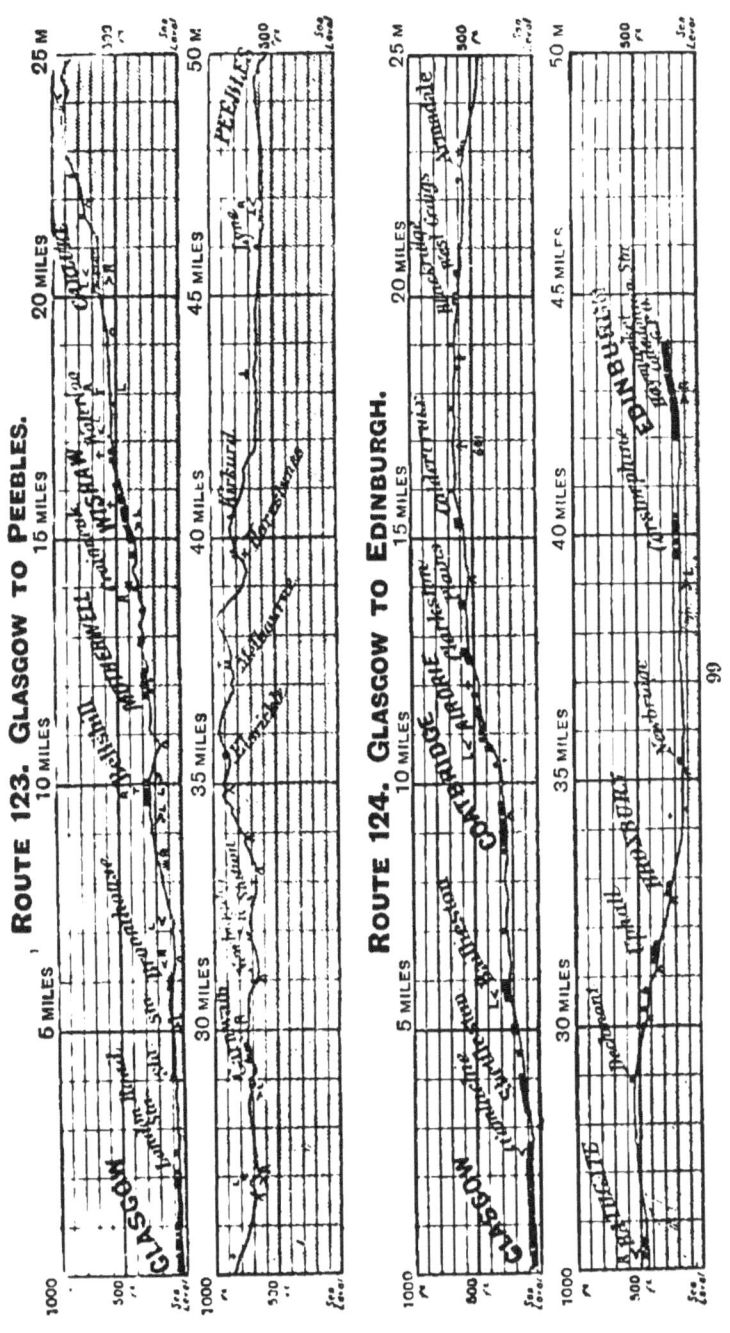

125 GLASGOW TO STIRLING.

Description.—Class I. This road is a fine broad highway throughout, but with only tolerable surface. Care should be taken passing through St. Ninians.

Gradients.—None of any extent, except at 14¾m. 1 in 23.

Milestones.—Measured from Glasgow Cross, and from Stirling, Burgh Hall,—correct.

Measurements.

Glasgow,* Jamaica Street.					
8⅜	Moodiesburn.				
14	5⅝	Cumbernauld.*			
17⅝	9¼	3⅝	Dennyloanhead.*		
19⅜	11	5⅜	1¾	Denny,* Church.	
26½	18⅛	12½	8⅞	7⅛	Stirling,* King Street.

Principal Objects of Interest.—16m. Roman Wall. 24½m. Bannockburn Battlefield, 1314.

Hotels or Inns at places marked *, Steps, and Mollinburn.

126 GLASGOW TO KILSYTH & FALKIRK.

Description.—Class II. Surface fair, but a rather hilly road to Dennyloanhead; thereafter good to Falkirk. The road avoids the main parts of Kirkintilloch and Kilsyth.

Gradients.—At Bonnybridge, 1 in 19.

Milestones.—Variable for 14m., thence from Edin. correct.

Measurements.

Glasgow,* Jamaica Street.				
8¼	Kirkintilloch.*			
13⅛	4⅞	Kilsyth.*		
19¼	11	6⅛	Dennyloanhead.*	
24⅜	16⅛	11¼	5⅛	Falkirk,* Town Clock.

Principal Objects of Interest.—6⅝m. Roman Wall. 10m. Covenanter's Tombstone. KILSYTH; Battlefield. A very pretty road running along the foot of the Campsie Fells.

Hotels or Inns at places marked *, Bishopbriggs and Bonnybridge.

127 GLASGOW TO KIPPEN.

Description.—Class II. As far as Lennoxtown the road is good; thereafter very rough, and steep over the hill. After passing Fintry the road improves in quality.

Gradients.—From 11m. 1/16-11-15-23; descent 1/19-24-16-11. Dangerous turns at 11⅜m. and 17m. 1/12.

Milestones.—Measured from Glasgow, Barony Church, to Fintry; thereafter measured from Stirling.

Measurements.

Glasgow,* Jamaica Street.				
10¼	Lennoxtown.*			
18	7¾	Fintry.*		
25	14¾	7	Kippen.*	
26	15¾	8	1	Kippen Station.

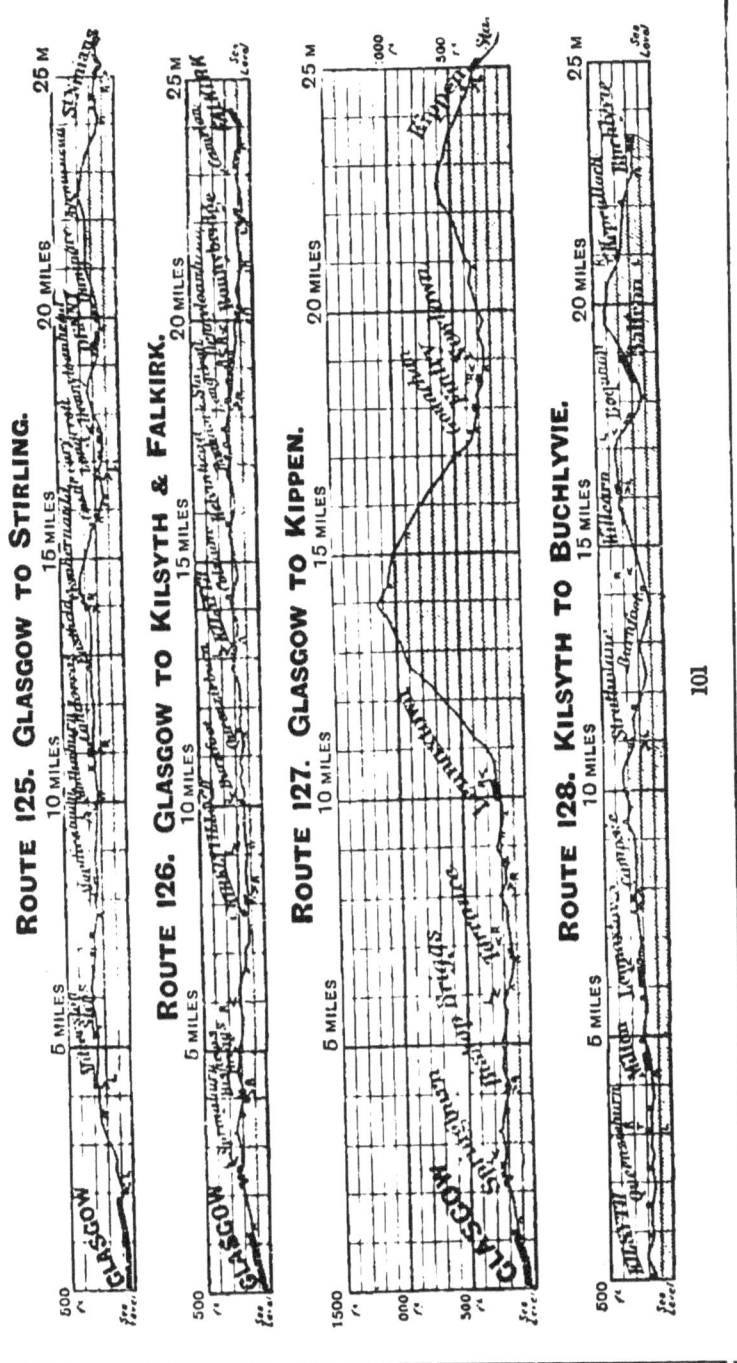

Principal Objects of Interest.—12½m. Campsie Glen. 18m. Loup of Fintry (fall). Moorland on the higher parts.

Hotels or Inns at places marked *, and at Bishopbriggs.

128 KILSYTH TO BUCHLYVIE.

Description.—Class II. A very good road the whole way with comparatively easy hills.

Gradients.—At 14½m. 1 in 18; 17m. 1 in 22; 19m. 1 in 21-16.

Milestones.—After Strathblane, measured from Royal Exchange, Glasgow.

Measurements.

Kilsyth.*					
6¼	Lennoxtown.*				
11	4¾	Strathblane.*			
16¼	10	5¼	Killearn.*		
18⅝	12⅜	7⅝	2⅜	Balfron.*	
23½	19¼	12½	7¼	4⅞	Buchlyvie.*

Principal Objects of Interest.—7¾m. Campsie Glen, very pretty. Killearn; Buchanan's Monument.

129 GLASGOW TO ABERFOYLE, &c.

Description.—Class II. The first few miles are rough; thereafter the road is good but hilly to Strathblane, when it becomes almost level—with splendid surface—right on to Aberfoyle. The Trossachs section is a toll-road, well kept, but very steep: cyclists are prohibited by the proprietors.

Gradients.—Past Milngavie 1 in 19-14; descent 1 in 19-16-(dangerous turn)-20. Trossachs section nearly all 1 in 12 both sides, with dangerous turns.

Milestones.—Measured from Glasgow, Royal Exchange, and from Aberfoyle Hotel,—correct.

Measurements.

Glasgow,* Jamaica Street.						
3	Maryhill.*					
7¼	4¼	Milngavie.*				
11¼	8¼	4	Strathblane.*			
20	17	12¾	8¾	Stirling-Dumbarton Road.		
27½	24½	20¼	16¼	7½	Aberfoyle * Hotel.	
34¼	31¼	27	23	14¼	6¾	Trossachs Pier.

Aberfoyle Hotel to Trossachs Hotel, 6¼m.

Principal Objects of Interest.—9m. Craigmaddie Cas., ruin. 13¼m. Duntreath Cas. Aberfoyle; Churchyard, Bailie's "Coulter," etc. Fine views on the Trossachs section.

Hotels or Inns at places marked * (and Trossachs Hotel).

130 GLASGOW TO DRYMEN.

Description.—Class III. The first 6 miles are comparatively easy, after which it is very hilly, but with a fair surface.

Gradients.—Frequent lengthy grades of 1 in 15 to 1 in 22.

Milestones.—Measured from Glasgow, Royal Exchange.

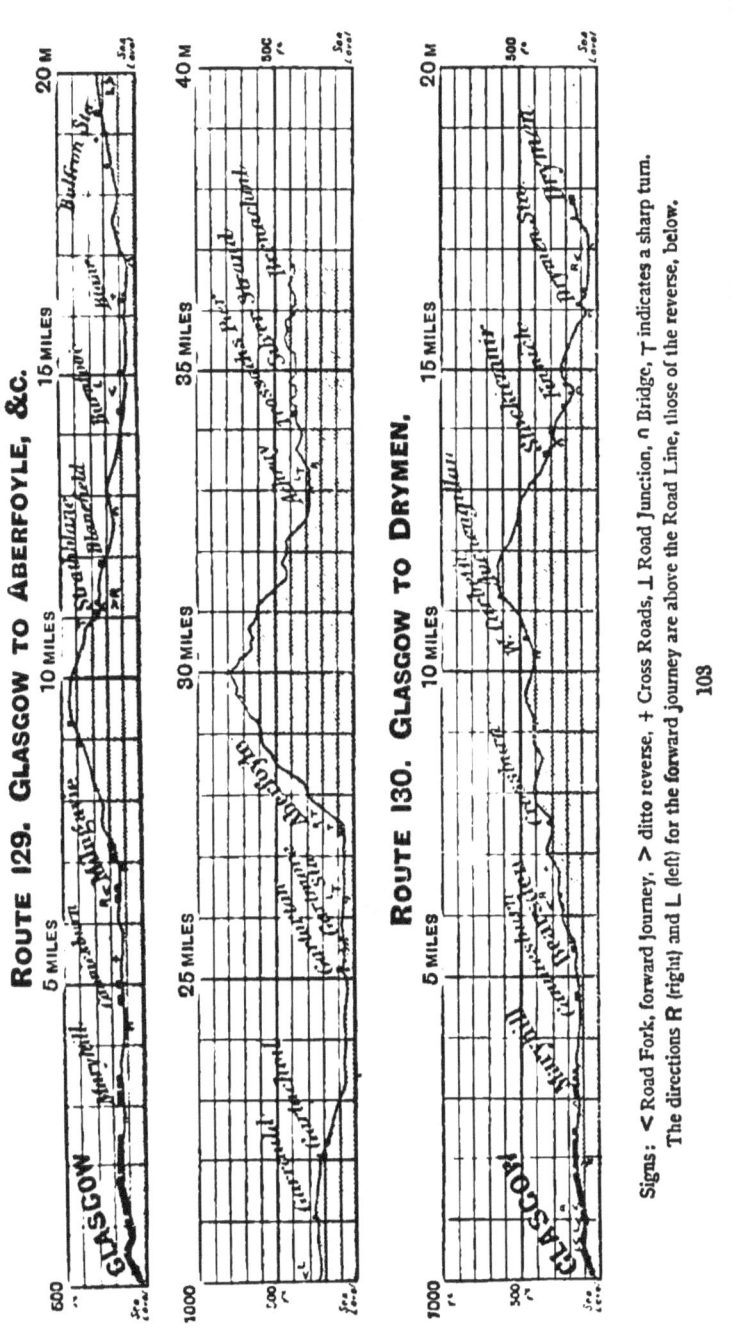

ROUTE 129. GLASGOW TO ABERFOYLE, &c.

ROUTE 130. GLASGOW TO DRYMEN.

Signs: < Road Fork, (forward journey, > ditto reverse, + Cross Roads, ⊥ Road Junction, ⌒ Bridge, ⊤ indicates a sharp turn. The directions R (right) and L (left) for the forward journey are above the Road Line, those of the reverse, below.

Measurements.

Glasgow*, Jamaica Street.			
3	Maryhill.*		
5½	2½	Bearsden.*	
17¾	14¾	12¼	Drymen.*

Principal Objects of Interest.—3m. Forth and Clyde Canal. 5½m. Roman Wall. Drymen; Buchanan Castle.

---

131 GLASGOW TO ARROCHAR.

Description.—Class I & II. After clearing the suburbs the road is very smooth with a fine surface all the way, specially good along Loch Lomond.

Gradients.—All very easy, none steep.

Milestones.—Measured from Glasgow, Royal Exchange; after Dumbarton from Dumbarton Cross.

Measurements.

Glasgow,* Jamaica Street.							
6¾	Clydebank.*						
9½	2¾	Old Kilpatrick.*					
14⅜	7⅝	4⅞	Dumbarton,* Cross.				
17⅝	10⅞	8⅛	3¼	Alexandria.*			
26⅝	19⅞	17⅛	12¼	9	Luss.*		
35	28¼	25½	20⅝	17⅜	8⅜	Tarbet* Hotel.	
36½	29¾	27	22⅛	18⅞	9⅞	1½	Arrochar* Hotel.

Principal Objects of Interest.—Shipbuilding yards along the Clyde to Clydebank, and at Dumbarton. 11⅜m. Dunglass Castle, ruin. DUMBARTON; Castle. 16½m. Smollett's Monument. 29m. Inverbeg—Ferry to Rowardennan for Ben Lomond. Very pretty road along Loch Lomond.

Hotels or Inns at places marked*, and at Renton, (Balloch), and Inverbeg.

---

132 TARBET TO KILLIN.

Description.—Class II. This is a beautiful and perfectly smooth road to Inverarnan, but thereafter it is rather rough and steep through Glenfalloch to Crianlarich. Thence to Killin the road is soft and rather heavy travelling.

Gradients.—12¼m. and 16½m. 1 in 16; these are the steepest parts, all the rest is about 1 in 24.

Milestones.—Measured from Dumbarton Cross. and in Perthshire from Killin Church.

Measurements.

Tarbet,* Hotel.				
8¼	Ardlui.*			
16¾	8½	Crianlarich,* Hotel.		
24¼	16	7½	Luib,* Hotel.	
30⅝	22⅜	13⅞	6⅜	Killin,* P.O.

Principal Objects of Interest.—7m. Pulpit Rock. 12¼m. Falls. Scenery monotonous along Glendochart. 30m. Falls of Dochart. Killin; Finlarig Castle, Glen Lochay.

Hotels or Inns at places marked,* none at Inverarnan.

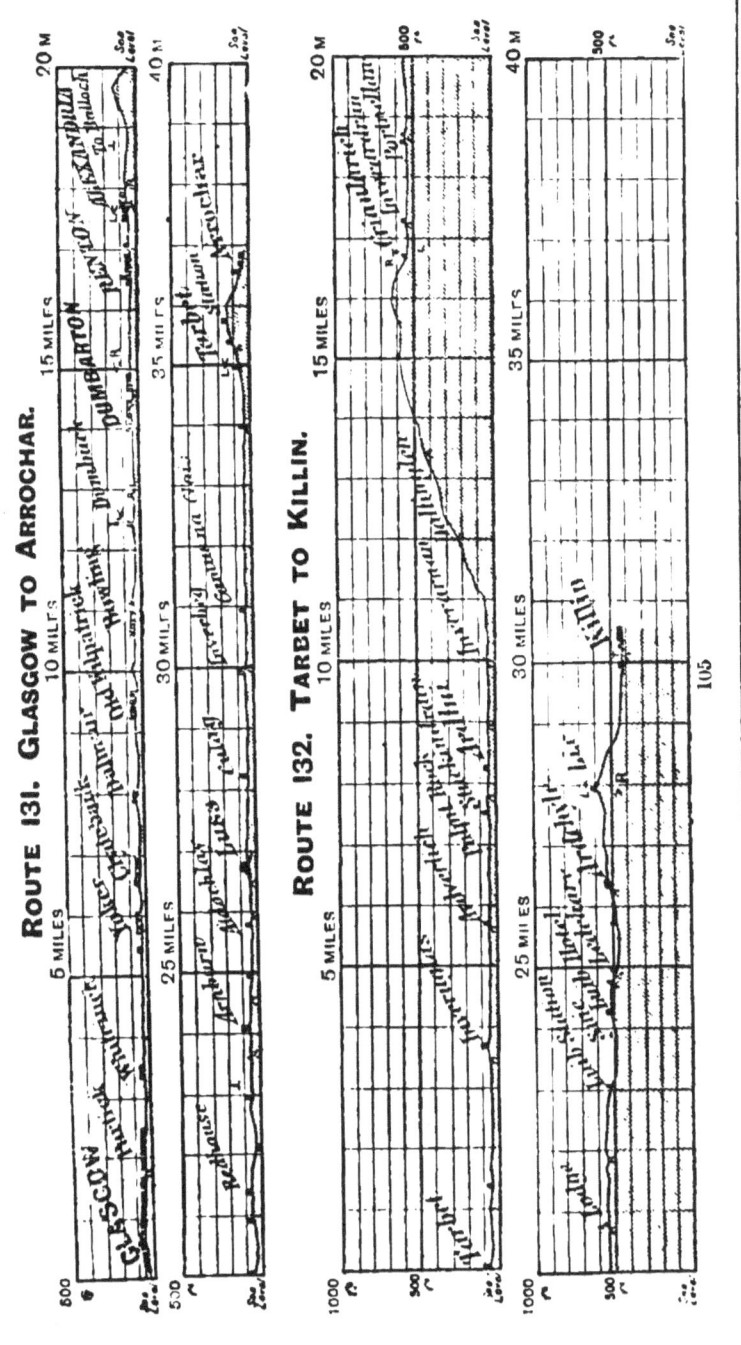

133 GLASGOW TO EAGLESHAM.

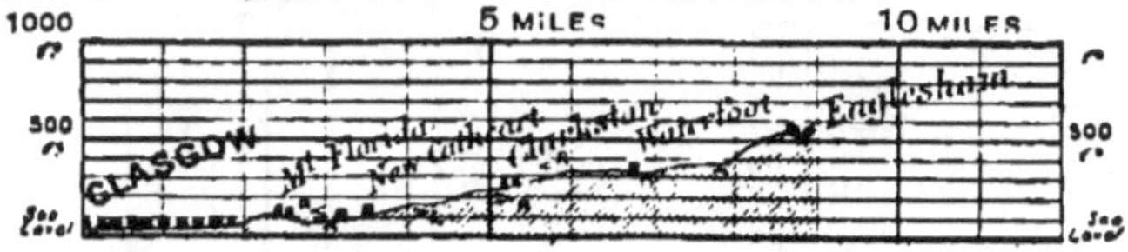

Description.—Class II. A fine smooth road with comparatively easy slopes, until just before Eaglesham.

Gradients.—At 7m. 1 in 20; 8m. 1 in 14.

Measurements.—Glasgow,* Jamaica Street.
3¼ Cathcart.
8⅞ 5⅝ 3⅜ Eaglesham.*

Principal Objects of Interest.—Cathcart; Cas., Langside.

134 GLASGOW TO HAMILTON *via Cambuslang.*

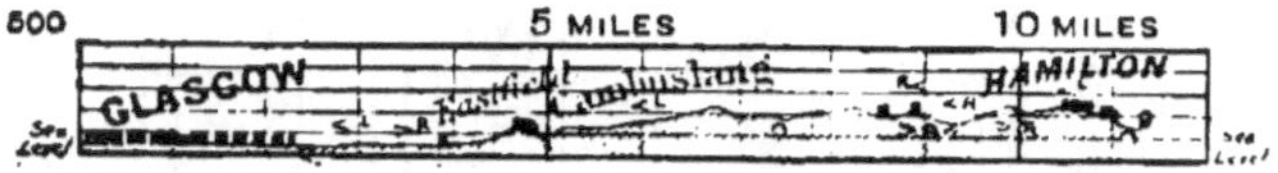

Description.—Class I. A fine undulating road, but rather cut up with heavy traffic at several points, and not so good as the road by Bothwell.

Milestones.—Measured from Glasgow Cross,—correct.

Measurements.—Glasgow,* Jamaica Street.
4¾ Cambuslang.*
11¼ 6½ Hamilton.*

Principal Objects of Interest.—Blantyre; Livingstone's Birthplace. HAMILTON; Palace. Cadzow Castle.

135 GLASGOW TO HOLYTOWN, &c.

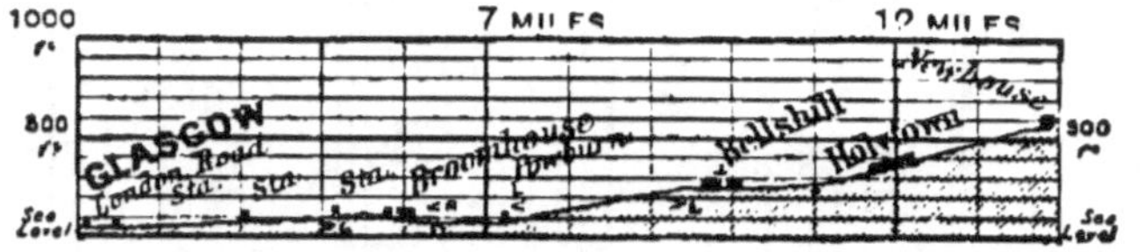

Description.—Class I. The Old Edinburgh road *via* Shotts, but seldom used for through traffic. The surface is good but apt to be lumpy; the hills are very easy.

Milestones.—Measured from Glasgow Suburbs by Old road.

Measurements.—Glasgow,* Jamaica Street.
6 Broomhouse.
9¾ 3¾ Bellshill.*
12 6 2¼ Holytown.*
13⅞ 7⅞ 4⅛ 1⅞ Newhouse.

Principal Objects of Interest.—Collieries, &c., about Holytown.

Hotels or Inns at places marked *.

DENNYLOANHEAD TO KINCARDINE. 136

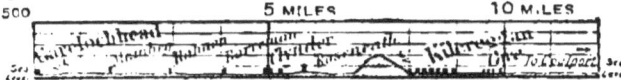

Description.—Class II. A fair road. Ferry to Kincardine (¼m.). Measurements.—Dennyloanhead *; 3½m. Larbert*; 10m. Kincardine * Principal Objects of Interest.—Kincardine; Tulliallan Castle.

GARELOCHHEAD TO KILCREGGAN, &c. 137

Description.—Class II. A fine level road, but with a steep rise and dangerous descent before Kilcreggan. Thence good to Coulport.
Gradients.—At 7m. 1 in 14; 8m. 1 in 12 (very dangerous).
Measurements.—Garelochhead.*
        5   Clynder.*
        8   3   Kilcreggan * Pier.
       15 16   7   5   Coulport Ferry.
Principal Objects of Interest.—5½m. Roseneath Castle.

DUNOON TO TOWARD, &c. 138

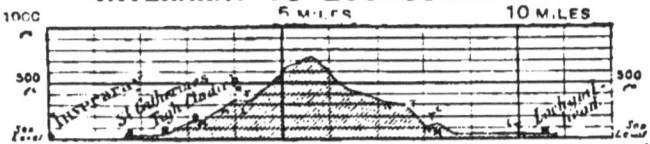

Description.—Class II. A fine smooth road, hilly after Toward, with a most dangerous descent to Loch Striven.
Gradients.—At 10m. 1 in 14.
Milestones.—Measured from Dunoon.
Measurements.—Dunoon Pier.
        4   Inellan Pier.
       6¼ 2¼ (Toward Pier).
     13¾ 9½ 7¼ Inverchaolin Church.
Principal Objects of Interest.—Toward; Castle.

INVERARAY TO LOCHGOILHEAD. 139

Description.—Class III. Ferry to St. Catherines (1½m.). Thence a very bad road—rough and dangerously steep.
Gradients.—At 3½m. 1/19; 4½m. 1/10; 6m. 1/13; 8m. 1/10.
Measurements.—Inveraray * Pier.
       1¾ St. Catherines Pier.
     10¾ 9½ Lochgoilhead Pier.

140 DUMBARTON TO ARROCHAR.

Description.—Class II. This is a fine smooth road along the shores of the Gareloch and Loch Long. There is a slight hill over to Cardross, and a very dangerous hill—Whistlefield—beyond Garelochhead.

Gradients.—At 2m.1 in 17; 2¼m.1 in 18; 16¼m.1 in 17-12-15; 18m.1 in 20-24-12.

Milestones.—Measured from Dumbarton Cross.

Measurements.

Dumbarton,* Cross.
8¼ Helensburgh,* Pier.
15⅝ 7⅜ Garelochhead.*
25⅜ 17⅛ 9¾ Arrochar,* Hotel.

Principal Objects of Interest.—A very pleasant road with fine views of the mountains up Loch Long. There are many handsome villas on the Gareloch.

Hotels or Inns at places marked,* and at Row, Shandon, and Whistlefield.

---

141 INVERARAY TO ARROCHAR.

Description.—Class II. & III. As far as Cairndow this is a fine smooth road, but thereafter through Glen Kinglas and Glen Croe it is very bad with stony surface, which does not improve till quite near Arrochar. There are several dangerous parts.

Gradients.—At 10¼m.1 in 10-12 (dangerous); 11¼m.1 in 21; 12m.1 in 17; 13¾m.1 in 10-11-12 (dangerous); 15½m.1 in 15-9-8-10-15 (very dangerous turn); 18¼m.1 in 15-11.

Milestones.—Measured from Inveraray Cross.

Measurements.

Inveraray,* Cross.
9¾ Cairndow,* Inn.
22¼ 12½ Arrochar,* Hotel.
23¾ 14 1½ Tarbet,* Hotel.

Principal Objects of Interest.—A pleasant road along Loch Fyne to Cairndow, thence wild scenery through Glen Croe. 15¼m., "Rest and be Thankful" Stone.

Hotels or Inns at places marked *.

---

142 INVERARAY TO TIGHNABRUAICH.

Description.—Class II. & III. A splendid road to Cairndow, rough to St. Catherines, fair to Strachur, after which it is a bad road with some rather dangerous hills.

Gradients.—10⅝m.1/10-12 (dangerous); 10¾m.1/15; 12½m. 1/21; 13½m. 1/17; 23m. 1/12-22-25; 25m. 1/15; 35½m. 1/10-9 (dangerous); 36½ & 45¾m. 1/16; 37m.1/23; 37½ & 46½m.1/14; 38½m. 1/15-19-14; 39½ & 41¼m. 1/20; 41¾m. 1/15-11-9; 44m. 1/14-25-14; 45¾m.1/16-21. (Short hills omitted.)

Milestones.—Measured from Inveraray Cross, to Cairndow; after St. Catherines they are measured by a cart road from the Glen Croe Milestones.

ROUTE 140. DUMBARTON TO ARROCHAR.

ROUTE 141. INVERARAY TO ARROCHAR.

ROUTE 142. INVERARAY TO TIGHNABRUAICH.

Measurements.

Inveraray,* Cross.						
9¾	Cairndow,* Inn.					
15¾	6	St. Catherine's,* Pier.				
20⅝	10⅝	4⅝	Strachur,* Pier.			
35½	25¾	19¾	15⅜	Otter Ferry.		
39¼	29½	23½	18⅞	3¾	Kilfinnan.	
47¾	38	32	27⅜	12¼	8½	Tighnabruaich,* P.O.

Principal Objects of Interest.—Moorland after Otter. Powder Works at Kames.

Hotels or Inns at places marked *.

143 INVERARAY TO ROTHESAY.

Description.—Class II. Ferry to St. Catherines, 1⅝m. As far as Strachur the road is level and good, but thereafter the surface is wretched, and on the higher parts in a fearful state, to Glendaruel, when the surface improves. Ferry at Colintraive, ¼m. Thence the road is good.

Gradients.—At 9¼m. 1 in 12·22; at 11m. mostly 1 in 15; steepest 1 in 10; at 13½m. 1 in 15-13-11-18; 16m. 1 in 13-17-11; 27¾m. 1 in 12; 28¼m. 1 in 17; 28½m. 1 in 15.

Measurements.

Inveraray,* Cross.						
1⅝	St. Catherines,* Pier.					
6⅜	4¾	Strachur,* Pier.				
21⅛	19½	14¾	Glendaruel,* Inn.			
29¼	27⅝	22⅞	8⅜	Colintraive,* Pier.		
35¾	34⅛	29¾	14⅝	6½	Port Bannatyne,* Pier.	
37⅞	36¼	31½	16¾	8⅝	2⅛	Rothesay,* Pier.

Principal Objects of Interest.—The scenery in Glendaruel is very fine.

Hotels or Inns at places marked *.

144 INVERARAY TO TARBERT.

Description.—Class II. This is a very fair but undulating road to Lochgilphead; thence a fine level road with rise over the shoulder of a hill near Tarbert.

Gradients.—3m. 1 in 22; 3¼m. 1 in 16; 4m. 1 in 20-25-16; 12½m. 1 in 20.

Milestones.—Measured from Inveraray Pier to Lochgilphead, thereafter from Campbeltown.

Measurements.

Inveraray,* Cross.						
8	Furnace.					
10⅝	2⅝	Crarae,* Pier.				
17	9	6⅜	Lochgair,* Inn.			
24⅜	16⅜	13¾	7⅜	Lochgilphead,* Market.		
26½	18½	15⅞	9½	2⅛	Ardrishaig,* Pier.	
38	30	27⅜	21	13⅝	11½	Tarbert * Hotel.

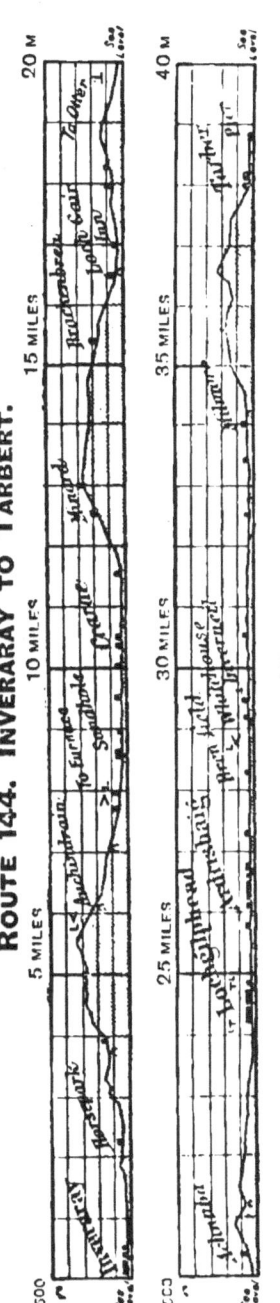

Principal Objects of Interest.—3¾m., Old Bridge. Crarae: Quarries. There are few objects of special interest, but the road is a pleasant one.

Hotels or Inns at places marked *.

145 DUNOON TO OTTER.

Description.—Class III. As far as Clachaig the road is fair, but thereafter it is rough to Glendaruel, when it becomes little better than a cart road over to Otter.

Gradients.—At 5¼m. 1 in 11-13; 10¼m. 1 in 16-12; 12m. 1 in 11-9; 12¾m. 1 in 9; 13¾m. 1 in 15-19-18. From 17m. mostly 1 in 8; and after 19½m. 1 in 9-8-15.

Milestones.—Measured from Dunoon Pier,—correct.

Measurements.

Dunoon,* Pier.				
6¼	Clachaig,* Inn.			
11¾	5½	Craigandave.		
16½	10¼	4¾	Glendaruel Bridge.	
22	15¾	10¼	5½	Otter Ferry.

Principal Objects of Interest.—5¾m., Old Powder Works. 11m., Loch Striven; fine scenery here, and at Glendaruel.

Hotels or Inns at places marked *.

146 DUNOON TO INVERARAY.

Description.—Class III. A fair road all the way, but undulating and rather soft along Loch Eck.

Gradients.—Descent at Strachur, 1 in 17.

Measurements.

Dunoon,* Pier.				
9	Inverchapel Pier.			
15⅜	6⅜	Locheckhead Pier.		
20¼	11¼	4⅞	Strachur,* Pier.	
25½	16½	10⅛	5¼	Inveraray,* Cross.

Principal Objects of Interest.—Pretty scenery along Loch Eck.

Hotels or Inns at places marked *.

147 DUNOON TO ARDENTINNY, &C.

Description.—Class II. & III. As far as Ardentinny the road is very fine and level along the water side, but thereafter it is rough and bad.

Gradients.—At 17 and 18½m. 1 in 8; very dangerous.

Measurements.

Dunoon,* Pier.					
1¼	Kirn,* Pier.				
7⅝	6⅜	Kilmun,* Pier.			
13¾	12½	6⅛	Ardentinny,* Pier.		
18¾	17½	11⅛	5	Whistlefield.*	
26⅛	24⅞	18½	12⅜	7⅜	Strachur,* Pier.

Hotels or Inns at places marked *.

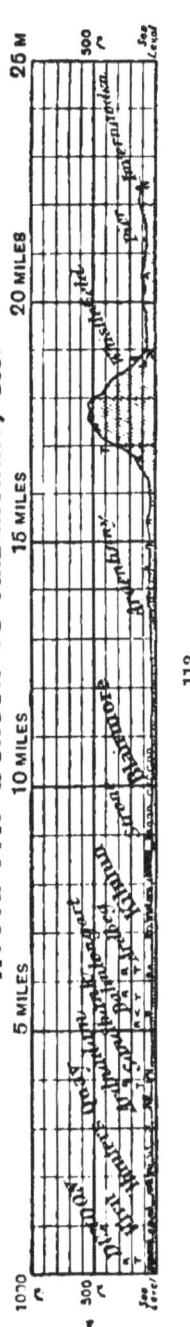

148 CAMPBELTOWN TO TARBERT.

Description.—Class II. This is a fine undulating road all the way, but at several points it leaves the coast line and becomes rather loose and steep.

Gradients.—At 5¼m. and 11¾m. 1 in 21; 12½m. 1 in 17-21; 13½m. 1 in 27-17-22; 19m. 1 in 15; 24¾m. 1 in 17; 25¼m. 1 in 12; 25¾m. 1 in 23; 27m. 1 in 10; 27½m. 1 in 10; 28¾m. 1 in 20; 30¾m. 1 in 19; 31½m. 1 in 13 (dangerous turn); 31¾m. 1 in 19; 36m. 1 in 16; 36¼m. 1 in 13-16 (dangerous turn).

Milestones.—Measured from Campbeltown Cross.

Measurements.

Campbeltown,* Cross.						
9⅝	Bellochantuy.*					
12½	2⅞	Glenbarr.*				
18⅞	9¼	6⅜	Tayinloan,* Inn.			
26⅞	17¼	14⅜	8	Clachan.		
31⅝	22	19⅜	12¾	4¾	Whitehouse.	
37¾	28⅛	25¼	18⅞	10⅞	6⅛	Tarbert,* Hotel.

Principal Objects of Interest.—4¼m. Kilkenzie Kirk. Glenbarr; "Abbey." The Island of Gigha is a prominent feature. The scenery is very varied.

Hotels or Inns at places marked *.

149 CAMPBELTOWN TO TARBERT (*E. Coast*).

Description.—Class III. The first few miles are fair, but the road soon degenerates, and even although in some parts the surface is good the hills are very steep and dangerous.

Gradients.—The following are the more important, mostly with dangerous turns:—4¼m. 1/13; 8m. 1/10; 10m. 1/9; 10½m. 1/10; 11¾m. 1/7; 12¾m. 1/9 (2 turns); 14m. 1/12; 18¾m. 1/8; 19⅜m. 1/8; 21¾m. 1/12; 29¾m. 1/14; 31¾m. 1/14.

Milestones.—Measured from Campbeltown Cross to Saddell, where there is an error; thence correct.

Measurements.

Campbeltown,* Cross.				
10	Saddell.			
14¼	4¼	Dippen,* Bridge.		
28⅛	18⅛	13⅞	Claonaig,* Inn.	
38⅜	28⅜	24⅛	10¼	Tarbert,* Hotel.

Carradale Pier is 1½m. distant at 14⅝m.

Principal Objects of Interest.—Saddell: Castle, and Abbey. The road dips into several pretty glens, and there are fine views of Arran.

Hotels or Inns at places marked *.

150 TARBERT TO KILBERRY.

Description.—Class III. At first this is a fair road, but the surface soon becomes very soft and loose.

Gradients.—Mostly about 1/17; but the following require caution:—4¾m. 1/10; 5½m. 1/11; 12¼m. 1/13; 13m. 1/16.

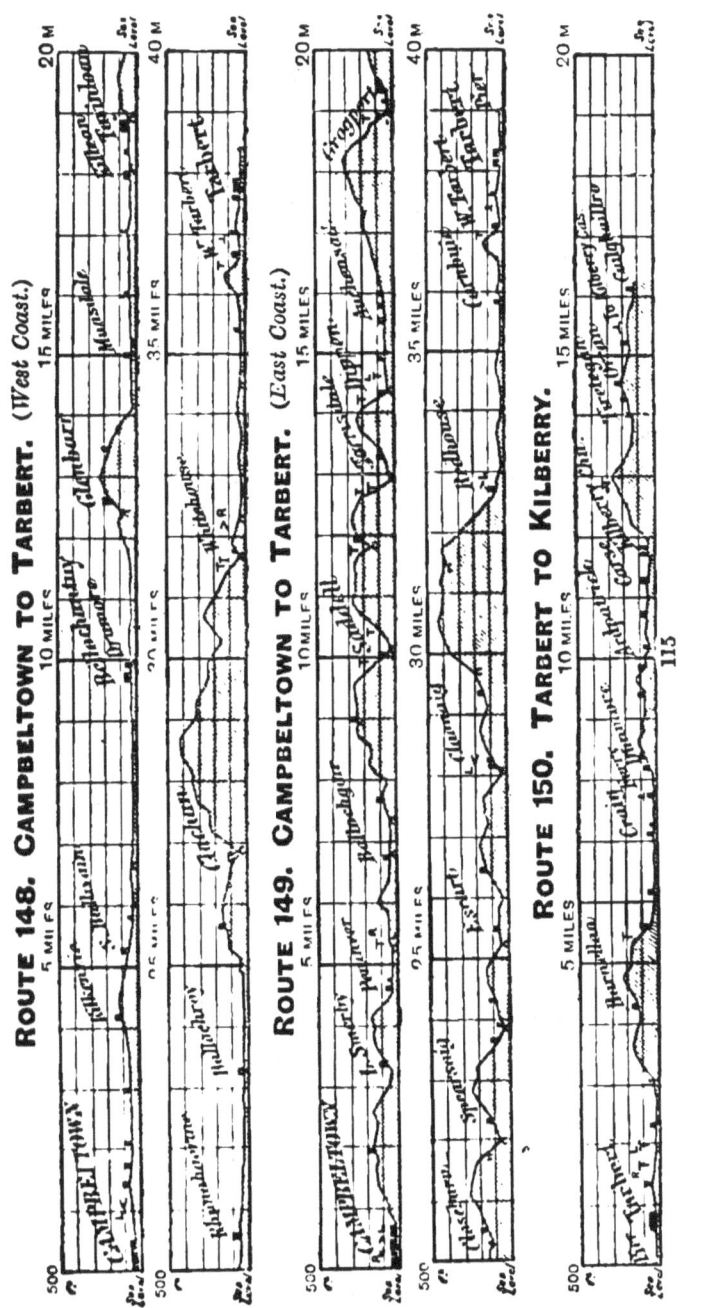

Measurements.

Tarbert,* Hotel.
9⅜ Ardpatrick, P.O.
15 5⅝ Kilberry.

151 ARDRISHAIG TO KILBERRY.

Description.—Class III. As far as Inverneil the road is smooth and level, but thereafter it is rough.

Gradients.—At 2½m. 1 in 15-27; thence mostly 1 in 19. The descent is 1 in 22-17-15-20; 9m.1 in 17; 11¾m.1 in 15; 14m.1 in 15-17-22; 16¾m.1 in 18; 17½m.1 in 21.

Milestones.—Measured from those at Ardrishaig.

Measurements.

Ardrishaig,* Pier.
7¾ Achahoish,* Inn.
12 4¼ Ormsary.
18 10¼ 6 Kilberry.

152 ARDRISHAIG TO KEILLS.

Description.—Class II. & III. A fine road to Bellanoch; thence rather poor to Tayvallich, and rough to Keills.

Gradients.—At 7m.1 in 13; 9½m.1 in 10-15-17; 13½m.1 in 9-17; 14m.1 in 10.

Measurements.

Ardrishaig,* Pier.
4 Cairnbaan,* Inn.
7 3 Bellanoch (*to Crinan** 1¾m.).
13¼ 9¼ 6¼ Tayvallich,* Church.
17¾ 13¾ 10¾ 4½ Keills, P.O.

Principal Objects of Interest.—The scenery at Loch Sween is very pretty.

153 INVERARAY TO DALMALLY.

Description.—Class II. & III. As far as Cladich the road is rather soft and loose, but with a comparatively easy grade on the Inveraray side; thereafter it is a steep, loose, and very hilly road to Dalmally—very slow travelling.

Gradients.—1 in 22 out of Inveraray; at 1¾m.1 in 25. Descending to Cladich 1 in 24-17-14-10; at 9¾m.1 in 17; 10½m. 1 in 13-18; 12¾m. 1 in 14; 13¼m. 1 in 12-25-11; 14¼m. 1 in 22; 14¾m.1 in 18; 15¼m.1 in 22.

Milestones.—Measured from Inveraray Cross,—correct.

Measurements.

Inveraray,* Cross.
9⅜ Cladich.
15¼ 6⅞ Dalmally,* Hotel.

Principal Objects of Interest.—The road is very pretty alongside the policies of Inveraray Castle; thereafter it is somewhat dreary, with, however, many fine views.

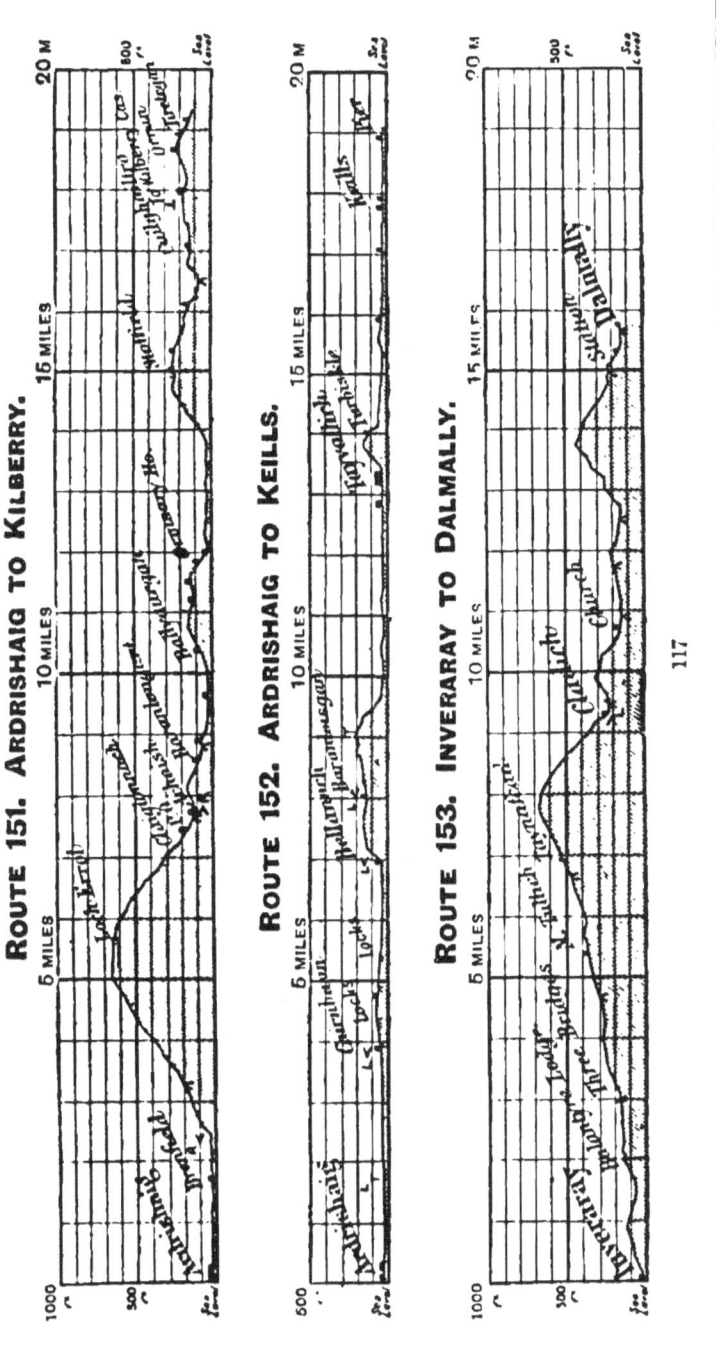

154   Oban to Easdale.

Description.—Class II. & III. The road is steep at first, but with a good surface to Kilninver; thereafter it is soft with several dangerous hills.

Gradients.—Out of Oban 1 in 23; descending to Glenfeochan 1 in 21-14. Thence at 8½m. 1 in 11; and 15½m. 1 in 13 (both dangerous).

Measurements.

Oban,* Argyll Square.
  8½   Kilninver.
 12   3¾   Clachan,* Inn.
 16¼   8   4¼   Easdale,* Pier.

Principal Objects of Interest.—Fine views of Loch Linnhe. Easdale; Slate Quarries.

Hotels or Inns at places marked *, and at (Glenfeochan).

155   Oban to Ardrishaig.

Description.—Class II. On the whole the surface is fair, but there are a number of long hills, and the level parts along the shore are not as smooth as could be desired. The best parts are from Oban to Kilninver, and from Kilmartin to Ardrishaig. The road is rough near Kintraw.

Gradients.—Out of Oban 1 in 23; descending to Glenfeochan 1 in 21-14. At 8½m. 1 in 19; 11m. 1 in 17; 14m. 1 in 21; 15½m. 1 in 20-17; 21¾m. 1 in 21 (dangerous turn); 22¾m. 1 in 14; 24m. 1 in 18-10-14; 25½m. 1 in 16; 26¾m. 1 in 21; 27¾m. 1 in 15.

Milestones.—Measured from Oban, to Kilmelfort; thereafter from Campbeltown, but a deviation near Salachary causes a discrepancy.

Measurements.

Oban,* Argyll Square.
  8½   Kilninver.
 15½   7¼   Kilmelfort.*
 23¾   15¼   8¼   Kintraw.
 29⅜   21⅛   13¾   5⅝   Kilmartin.*
 39⅛   30⅞   23⅝   15⅜   9¾   Ardrishaig,* Pier.

Principal Objects of Interest.—13¾m. Pass of Melfort; the road passes through several pretty glens.

Hotels or Inns at places marked *, at (Glenfeochan), (Ford), (Glassary), and (Cairnbaan).

157   Oban to Crianlarich.

Description.—Class II. The first 8 miles of the road are good. It soon becomes soft and loose—especially in the Pass of Brander—but improves nearing Dalmally. Thence to Tyndrum is a fearful road—grass and loose stones—but the rest is good, though apt to be soft.

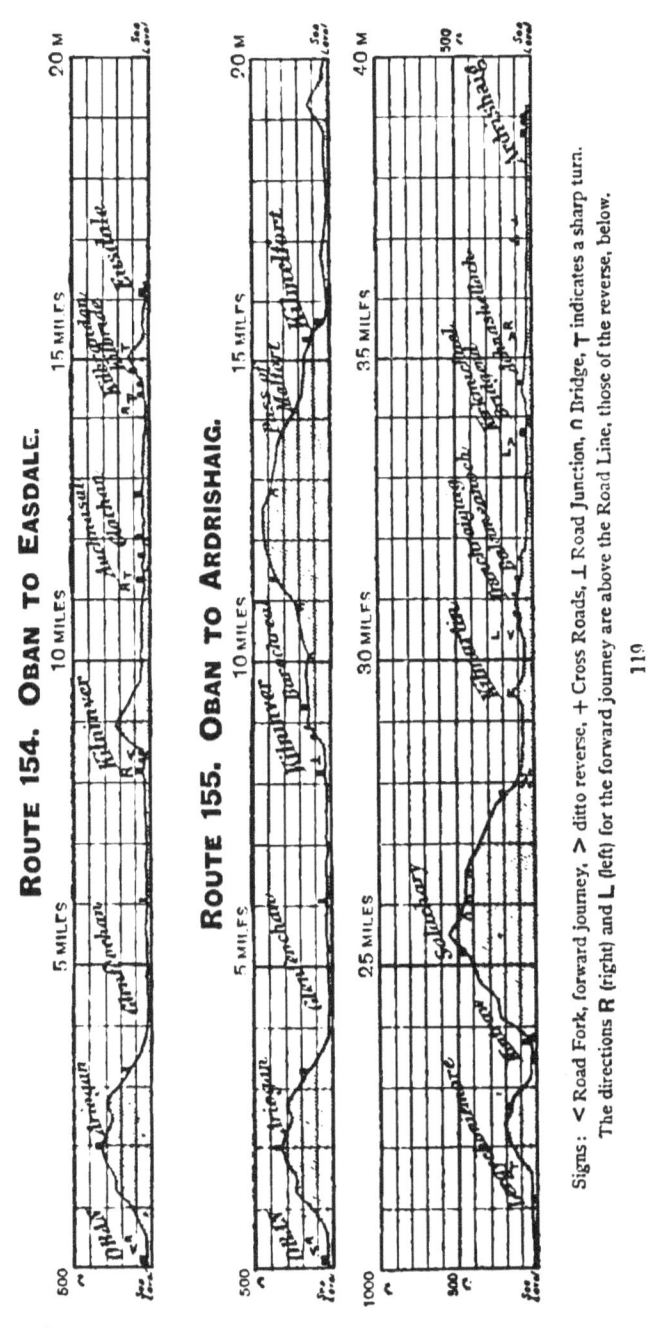

Signs: < Road Fork, forward journey, > ditto reverse, + Cross Roads, ⊥ Road Junction, ∩ Bridge, ⊤ indicates a sharp turn. The directions R (right) and L (left) for the forward journey are above the Road Line, those of the reverse, below.

Gradients.—At ¾m.1/13; 2m.1/21; 8½m.1/24-14; 9½m. 1/19; 11½m., 13¾m., & 15¼m.1/18; 21¾m.1/17; 28¾m.1/20-10-17; 29½m.1/16; 30¼m. & 33¼m.1/17; 34m.1/13-24; 38¾m.1/17.

Milestones.—In Argyllshire, measured from Inveraray Cross *via* Dalmally: in Perthshire, from Killin Church.

Measurements.

Oban,* Argyll Square.					
5½	Connel Ferry,* Station.				
12⅜	6⅞	Taynuilt,* Hotel.			
26	20½	13⅝	Dalmally,* Hotel.		
37¾	22¼	25⅜	11¾	Tyndrum,* Hotel.	
42½	37	30⅛	16½	4¾	Crianlarich,* Hotel.

Principal Objects of Interest.—3m. Dunstaffnage Castle. 5m. Connel Falls. 15m. Battlefield. 18½m. Falls of Cruachan, and Pass of Brander. 21¾m. Loch Awe, and Kilchurn Castle. The scenery on this road is very fine.

Hotels or Inns at places marked *, and Loch Awe Station.

158 CONNEL FERRY TO BALLACHULISH.

Description.—Class II. The road at first though comparatively level, is very loose and stony. From near Appin to Ballachulish is more undulating, but with better surface. Ferries:—Connel ¼m., Shian ⅛m.

Gradients.—10¼ & 17½m.1/21; and other short steep hills.

Milestones.—From Oban Pier, omitting length of ferries.

Measurements.

Connel,* South Ferry Pier (5m. from Oban, Argyll Square).		
8⅞	Appin, P.O. (*to Port Appin Pier*	
17½	8⅝	Duror,* Inn.
22½	13⅝	5 Ballachulish,* Ferry.

Principal Objects of Interest.—There are fine views of the Morvern Hills. Ledaig; "Beregonium," and Barcaldine Cas. Appin; Castle Stalker. Ballachulish; Quarries.

Hotels or Inns at places marked *, and at N. Connel, (Port Appin), and Ballachulish Pier.

159 ROUND BENDERLOCH.

Description.—Class III. A soft, loose, and bad road, very bad between the two Lochs. GRADIENTS.—At 7½m. 1/17-11-21; 10⅜m.1/13-10. MEASUREMENTS.—N. Connel Inn to:—Free Ch. (Loch Creran), 4⅝m.; Barcaldine Ho. Lodge, 6⅞m.; Ardchattan Ch., 14¼m.; back to N. Connel Inn, 17¼m.

To Appin P.O. *via* Cregan Ferry (⅛m.), 11⅝m.
To Appin P.O. *via* Creran Bridge, 17¼m.
To Taynuilt Hotel *via* Bonawe Ferry (¼m.), 10¼m.

Principal Objects of Interest.—Ledaig; as Route 158. 7½m. Glen Salach. 12¼m. Ardchattan Priory, ruin. Very pretty scenery.

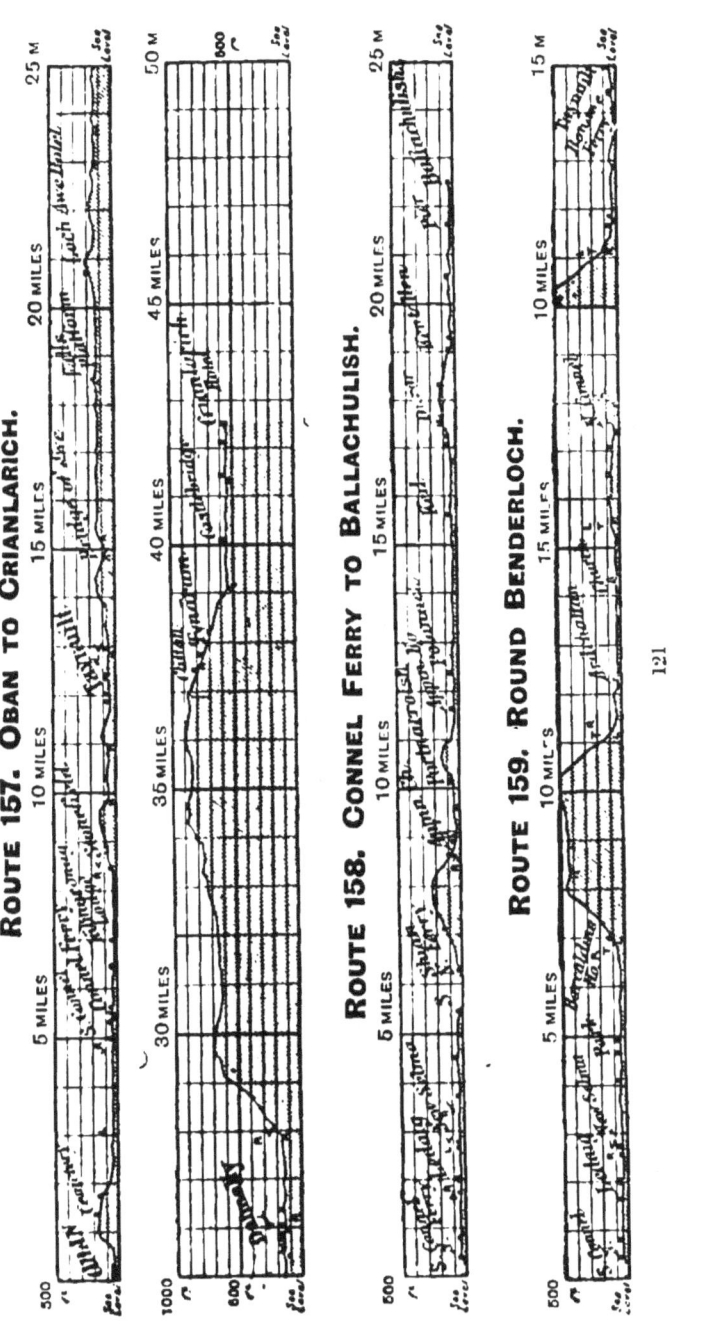

160 CAMPBELTOWN TO SOUTHEND.

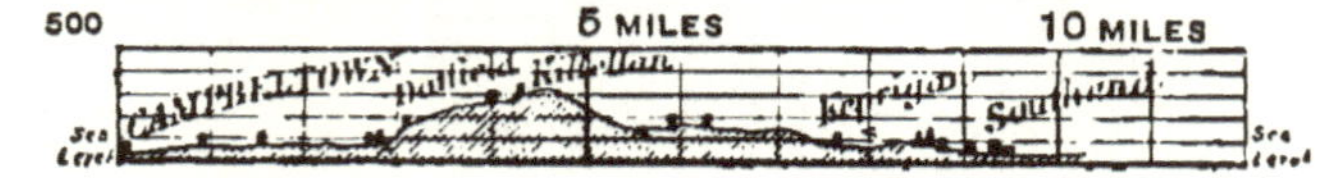

Description.—Class II. The road has a good surface and the hills are comparatively easy.

Gradients.—At 3m. and 5m. 1 in 17.

Milestones.—Measured from Campbeltown Cross, correct.

Measurements.—Campbeltown,* Cross.
$9\frac{3}{8}$ Southend Inn.*

Principal Objects of Interest.—Fine coast scenery of the Mull of Kintyre.

---

161 PORT APPIN TO GLEN CRERAN.

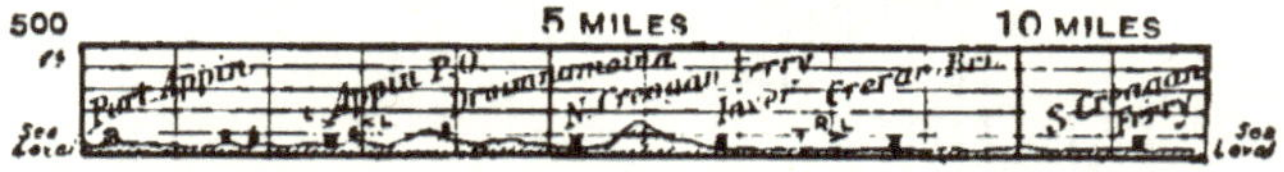

Description.—Class III. The road is hilly but has a fair surface as far as Creagan Ferry, when it becomes very poor. The road continues up Glen Creran for several miles beyond Creran Bridge. To Connel Ferry; see Route 159.

Gradients.—At 3m. 1 in 19; $5\frac{3}{4}$m. 1 in 12; $6\frac{1}{4}$m. 1 in 12-18. There are other short steep hills of 1 in 18.

Measurements.—Port Appin * Pier.

$2\frac{5}{8}$	Appin P.O.		
$7\frac{3}{4}$	$5\frac{1}{8}$	Creran Bridge.	
$8\frac{5}{8}$	6	$\frac{7}{8}$	Fasnacloich P.O.

---

162 TAYNUILT TO CLADICH.

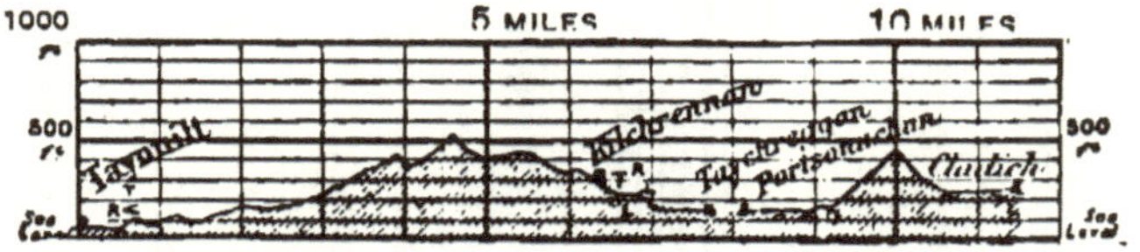

Description.—Class III. A very bad road. The gradients are steep, and the surface is very rough and stony almost the whole way. Ferry at Port Sonachan ($\frac{3}{8}$m.).

Gradients.—At $\frac{1}{2}$m. 1 in 17 (dangerous); $1\frac{3}{4}$m. 1 in 22; 3m. 1 in 14; 4m. 1 in 16; $4\frac{1}{2}$m. 1 in 15-21; $5\frac{3}{4}$m. 1 in 22; $6\frac{1}{4}$m. 1 in 18; 7m. 1 in 23; $9\frac{1}{2}$m. 1 in 13; $10\frac{1}{4}$m. 1 in 11-23.

Milestones.—Measured from Inveraray,—correct.

Measurements.—Taynuilt,* Hotel.
        7¾   Taychreggan Hotel.*
        8½ ¾ Port Sonachan Hotel.*
      11¾ 3⅜ 3¼ Cladich P.O.

Principal Objects of Interest.—Glen Nant is remarkably pretty. Loch Awe is crossed at Taychreggan.

LOCHETIVEHEAD TO KINGSHOUSE. 163

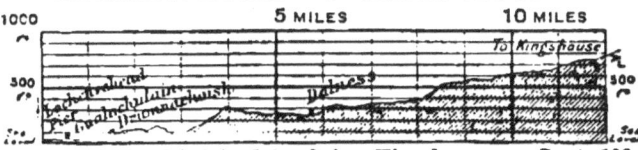

The Glencoe road is joined 1m. before Kingshouse; see Route 166.

Description.—Class III. A very rough bad road with loose surface and a great many short steep hills. Excepting the Coach in the Summer time, there is almost no traffic.

Gradients.—The steepest is 1 in 14.

Measurements.—Lochetivehead Pier.
      13¼ Kingshouse Inn.*

Principal Objects of Interest.—The Glencoe Hills at the head of Loch Etive are very striking. A small steamer sails during the Summer from Achnacloich and Taynuilt to Lochetivehead Pier.

DALMALLY TO BRIDGE OF ORCHY. 164

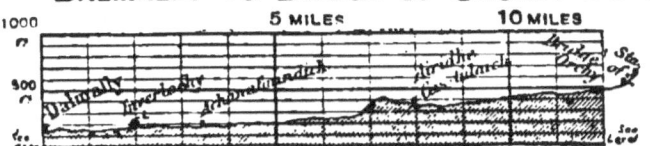

Description.—Class III. The road is soft and loose, and with some short sharp hills makes altogether a bad road.

Gradients.—At 7m. 1 in 15.

Milestones.—Measured from Inverlochy,—correct.

Measurements.—Dalmally Hotel.*
      12⅞ Bridge of Orchy Station; or,
      15⅜ Inveroran Hotel.*

Principal Objects of Interest.—Fine views of Ben Cruachan at first, then rather monotonous till near Bridge of Orchy.

Hotels or Inns at places marked *.

166 Tyndrum to Fort William.

Description.—Class III. & II. This is a bad road. From Tyndrum to Inveroran the surface is poor—in fact, very stony—thereafter the road becomes much worse, and though it improves a little near Kingshouse it is very rough and stony down Glencoe, and has several very nasty turns at 24¾m. As the streams in heavy rains often sweep the road, it is sometimes in parts more like a river-bed. After Clachaig the road is good, though undulating to Ballachulish. Ferry (¼m.) at Ballachulish. Thence to Fort William, undulating at first, is a magnificent road. Ballachulish Pier is ¾m. west of the Ferry.

Gradients.—½m. 1 in 15-20; 2m. 1 in 12; 6½m. 1 in 16-25-12; 11m. 1 in 25-13-17-15-18; 13m. 1 in 20; 13½m. 1 in 18-15; 15m. 1 in 13-18; 15¾m. 1 in 15-12-17; 16½m. 1 in 18; 17½m. 1 in 16; 18¾m. 1 in 17-14; 22m. 1 in 21; 23½m. 1 in 20. The dangerous part is from 24m. to 25½m. beginning 1 in 11; then at 24¾m. 1 in 10 with very dangerous turns, then 1 in 15-12-10-14. After this the grades are comparatively easy.

Milestones.—In Perthshire, measured from Killin Ch. In Argyle, measured southwards from Ballachulish Ferry. Those to Fort William are measured from Spean Bridge.

Measurements.

Tyndrum,* Hotel.						
6½	Bridge of Orchy,* Station.					
9½	3	Inveroran Hotel.*				
19⅜	12⅞	9⅞	Kingshouse,* Inn.			
30½	24	21	11⅛	Bridge of Coe.		
34½	28	25	15⅝	4	Ballachulish,* Ferry.	
47	40½	37½	27⅝	16½	12½	Fort William,* Pier.

Principal Objects of Interest.—Of special objects there are few, but the scenery especially in Glencoe is wild and rugged. At 21¾m. the old road strikes up the hill, then down the "devil's staircase" leading to Fort William. The scene of the massacre of Glencoe is after Clachaig Inn. Ballachulish; Quarries. FORT WILLIAM; Fort ruins, Inverlochy Castle, Ben Nevis, and Glen Nevis.

Hotels or Inns at places marked *, and at Clachaig.

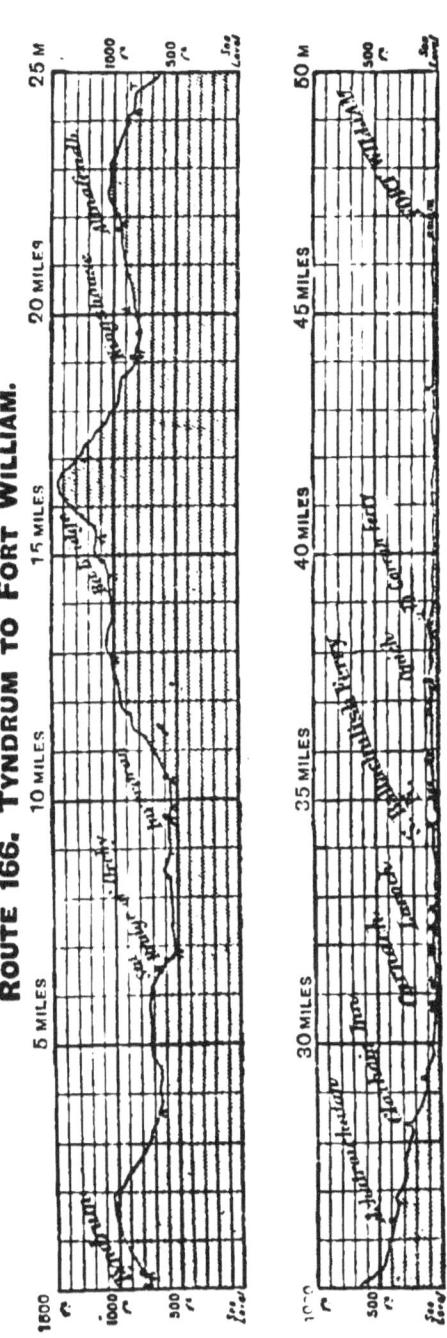

167 STIRLING TO DUMBARTON.

Description.—Class I. For six miles this road is almost level, with magnificent surface, it then becomes undulating, but with fine surface to Drymen. After an easy descent the road is very fair, but hilly to Dumbarton.

Gradients.—Until Drymen is reached there is no gradient above 1 in 28; descent to Drymen Bridge 1 in 21.

Milestones.—The first ten are measured from Stirling, Port Street; but the 11th to the 19th are measured as through Kippen. After Drymen, measured from Dumbarton Cross.

Measurements.

Stirling,* King Street.							
8⅝	Kippen Station.						
14½	5⅞	Buchlyvie.*					
18⅜	9¾	3⅞	Glasgow-Aberfoyle Road.				
21⅞	13¼	7⅜	3½	Drymen.*			
26	17⅜	11½	7⅝	4⅛	Gartocharn.		
30¾	22⅛	16¼	12⅜	9	4¾	Bonhill,* Bridgend.	
34	25⅜	19½	15⅝	12⅛	8	3¼	Dumbarton,* Cross.

Principal Objects of Interest.—⅝m. Kings Knott. 8⅝m. Ford of Frew. 8m. Boquhan. Drymen; Buchanan Castle. DUMBARTON; Castle.

Hotels or Inns at places marked * and at (Kippen).

---

168 STIRLING TO INVERSNAID.

Description.—Class I. & III. Magnificent surface for 6m. when the road becomes undulating, but with good surface. From Thornhill it is very hilly, though with a few level parts at Aberfoyle, and along Loch Ard; after Kinlochard the surface degenerates, and is very bad the rest of the way. The descent to Inversnaid is dangerous.

Gradients.—Short hills of 1 in 18-22 to Kinlochard; then at 24¼m. 1 in 13; 26¾m. 1 in 15; 28m. 1 in 20; 34m. 1 in 12-9 (very dangerous turn).

Milestones.—Continue those from Edinburgh,—correct to Thornhill.

Measurements.

Stirling,* King Street.				
9¾	Thornhill.*			
15¼	5½	Port of Menteith.*		
19½	9¾	4¼	Aberfoyle,* Hotel.	
34½	24¾	19¼	15	Inversnaid,* Hotel.

Principal Objects of Interest.—1½m. Site of old Bridge. 14m. Rednock Castle. 16¼m. Lake of Menteith and Inchmahone Island. Aberfoyle; Bailies "Coulter." 20¾m. Pass of Aberfoyle, and Helen's Rock. Inversnaid; Falls. Round Aberfoyle are many of the scenes in "Rob Roy."

Hotels or Inns at places marked *.

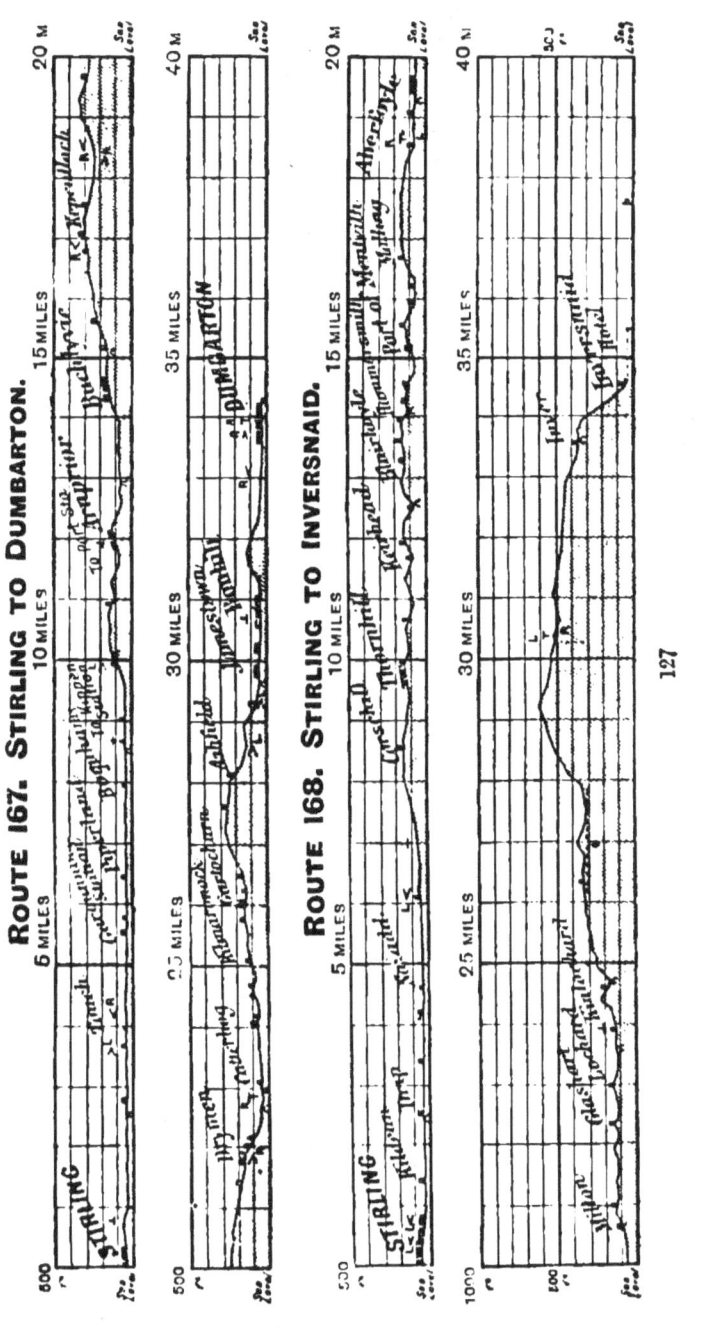

169 STIRLING TO POLMONT, &C.

Description.—Class II. Undulating road to S. Alloa Station; thereafter level and smooth to Beancross, though rough about Airth. To Polmont good, but steep.

Gradients.—At 14m. 1 in 17.

Measurements.

Stirling,* King Street.				
8¼	Airth.			
12⅝	4⅜	(Grangemouth).*		
14¾	6½	3½	Polmont,* P.O.	
19¼	11	8	4½	Linlithgow,* Cross.

Principal Objects of Interest.—8¼m. Airth Castle.

Hotels or Inns at places marked.*

170 STIRLING TO KILLIN.

Description.—Class I. & II. After leaving Stirling the road has a magnificent surface—smooth and level—to Bridge of Teith; thereafter it is undulating, but with fine surface past Callander, rough through the Pass of Leny, then level, followed by considerable undulations past Loch Lubnaig to Kingshouse. After Lochearnhead the road becomes stony up Glen Ogle, and is very rough on the descent to Lix.

Gradients.—Ascent to Doune about 1 in 23; Pass of Leny 1 in 18, and 1 in 14 (short); at 26½m. 1 in 19; 28½m. 1 in 20; ascent Glen Ogle 1 in 23-18-21; descent to Lix 1 in 17-15-24-19-14-18; 35½m. 1 in 23.

Milestones.—Measured from Stirling, Burgh Hall,—correct to Glenoglehead; thereafter from Killin Church.

Measurements.

Stirling,* King Street.					
8¼	Doune,* Woodside Hotel.				
16	7¾	Callander,* P.O.			
24⅝	16⅜	8⅝	Strathyre,* Station.		
29¾	21½	13¾	5⅛	Lochearnhead * Hotel.	
37⅛	28⅞	21⅛	12½	7⅜	Killin,* P.O.

Principal Objects of Interest.—DOUNE; Fine Castle. CALLANDER; Camp, Crags, Tom-ma-Chessaig, Bracklinn Falls. 18¼m. Pass and Falls of Leny. 19¼m. St. Bride's Chapel. Strathyre; Buchanan's Monument. 26¾m. Kingshouse; 2m. to W., Balquhidder and Rob Roy's Grave. 29m. to Falls of Ample. Killin; Falls of Dochart, Finlarig Cas., Glen Lochay. The road passes through fine scenery.

Hotels or Inns at places marked *, and at Kingshouse.

171 CALLANDER TO INVERSNAID.

Description.—Class III. A fine road to Kilmahog; thereafter very hilly—short and steep hills—but with good surface to Trossachs Hotel, after which it is poor to Loch Katrine Pier. Steamer to Stronachlacher, whence the road is rough and soft with a dangerous descent and turn near Inversnaid.

Route 169. Stirling to Polmont, &c.

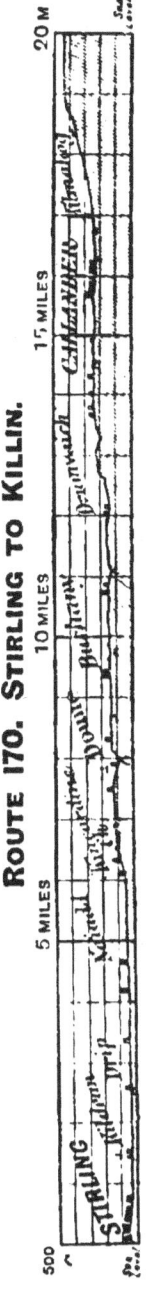

Route 170. Stirling to Killin.

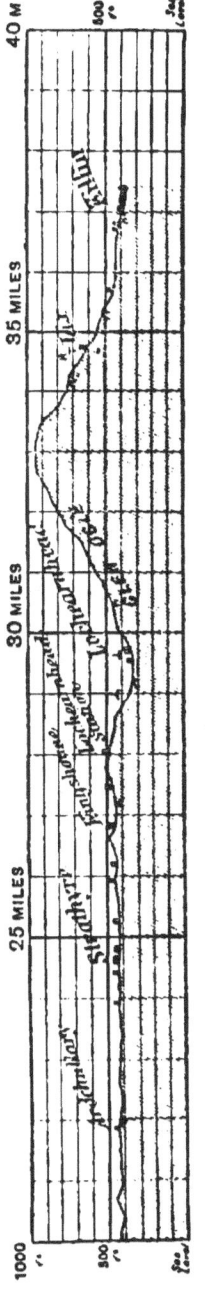

Signs: < Road Fork, (forward journey, > ditto reverse, + Cross Roads, ⊥ Road Junction, ⊓ Bridge, ⊤ Indicates a sharp turn. The directions R (right) and L (left) for the forward journey are above the Road Line, those of the reverse, below.

Gradients.—At 1¼m.1 in 17; 5¼m.1 in 13; 5¾m.1 in 10-13; 6¼m.1 in 14; 8⅜m.1 in 13; 16½m.1 in 13; 20½m.1 in 9.
Milestones.—Continuation of those from Stirling, correct.
Measurements.
Callander,* P.O.
8¼ Trossachs,* Hotel.
9⅞ 1⅝ Trossachs Pier. } Steamer.
16 7¼ 6¾ Stronachlacher,* Pier.
21 12¾ 11⅝ 5 Inversnaid,* Hotel.

Principal Objects of Interest.—1¼m. "Samson's Putting Stone." 2m. Fort. 2¾m. Coilantogle Ford and Waterworks. 0⅜m. Trossachs. Inversnaid; Falls. Very fine scenery.

172   STIRLING TO CRIEFF.

Description.—Class I. To Bridge of Allan the road is rough with heavy traffic, then hilly, but with a fine surface to Greenloaning, poor for some miles, and after passing Muthill it is undulating but smooth into Crieff.

Gradients.—3½m.1 in 20; 7¾m.1 in 22; 14¼m.1 in 20; 19¾m. 1 in 20. Through Crieff about 1 in 12.

Milestones.—Measured from Stirling, Burgh Hall,—correct, except at Dunblane where they follow a short cut.
Measurements.
Stirling,* King Street.
3¼ Bridge of Allan,* P.O.
6 2¾ Dunblane,* Bridge.
12¾ 9⅝ 6¾ Braco.*
19¼ 16 13¼ 6 Muthill.*
22½ 19¼ 16½ 9 3 Crieff,* James Square.

Principal Objects of Interest.—¾m. Old Bridge. 1¼m. Wallace Monument. BRIDGE OF ALLAN; Spa. DUNBLANE; Cathedral. 13½m. Ardoch Roman Camp. 20m. Drummond Castle. CRIEFF; as Route 16.

173   STIRLING TO PERTH.

Description.—Class I. As above to Greenloaning; thereafter the road is undulating, with very fine surface and steadier gradients.

Gradients.—3½m.1 in 20; 7¾m.1 in 22; then 15¼m.1 in 19; 20m.1 in 25; 27¼ and 29m.1 in 22.

Milestones.—As above to Greenloaning; thereafter measured from Perth Cross,—correct.
Measurements.
Stirling,* King Street.
6 2¾ Dunblane,* Bridge.
11¼ 8 5¼ Greenloaning.*
15¾ 12½ 9¾ 4½ Blackford,* P.O.
20 16¾ 14 8½ 4½ Auchterarder,* Church.
34½ 30¾ 28½ 22¾ 18½ 14½ Perth,* Cross.

Principal Objects of Interest.—As above to Dunblane. 25¼m. Gask Ho. 27¾m. Dupplin Cas. PERTH; as Route 17.

Hotels or Inns at places marked *.

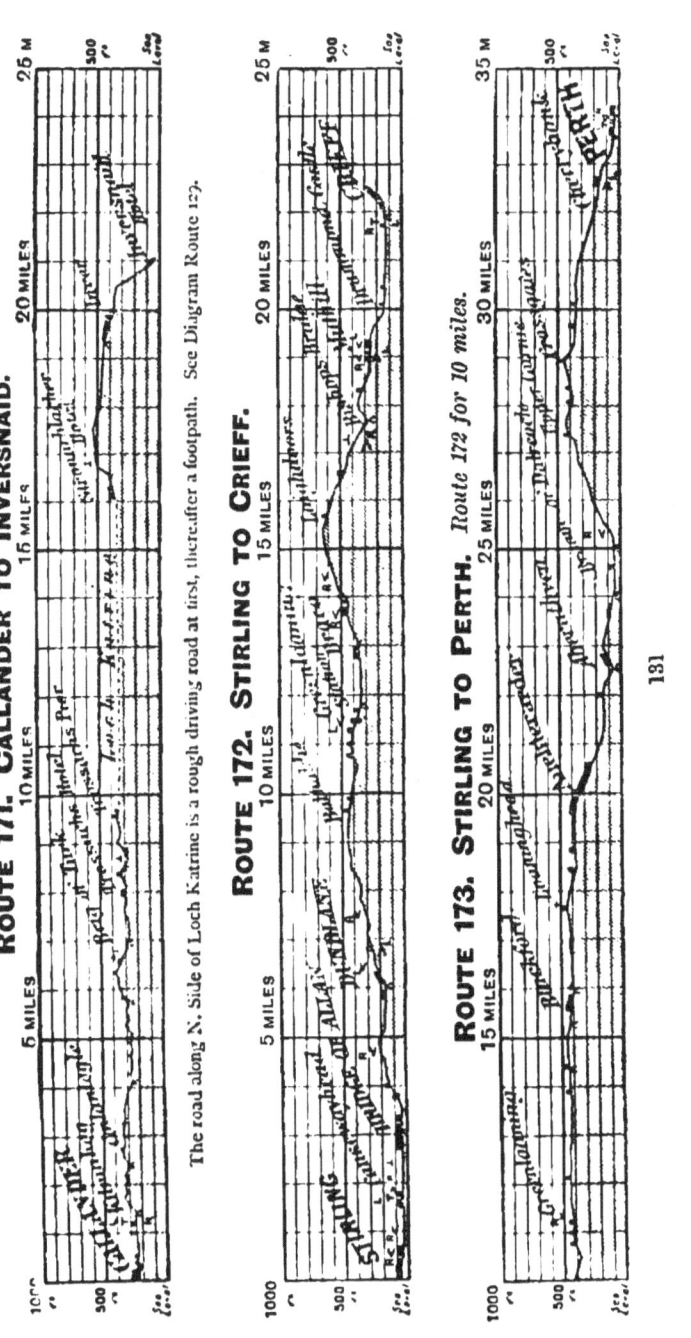

174 STIRLING TO ST. ANDREWS.

Description.—Class II. Rough to Causewayhead, very good to Dollar, then rather poor to near Milnathort. Thereafter the road is better and in parts has a very fine surface.

Gradients.—At 1¾m. 1 in 16; 16m. 1 in 16-17.

Milestones.—Measured from Stirling, Burgh Hall, to Milnathort; thereafter from Cupar Town Hall,—correct.

Measurements.

Stirling,* King Street.								
7	Alva.*							
9	2	Tillycoultry.*						
12⅛	5⅛	3⅛	Dollar.*					
16	9	7	3⅞	Yetts.				
23⅝	16⅝	14⅝	11½	7⅝	Milnathort,* Cross.			
32⅜	25⅜	23⅜	20¼	16¾	8¾	Auchtermuchty.*		
41⅛	34⅛	32⅛	29	25⅛	17½	8¾	Cupar,* Town House.	
50⅞	43⅞	41⅞	38¾	34⅞	27¼	18½	9¾	St. Andrews,* Town Ch.

Principal Objects of Interest.—1¾m. Wallace Monument. DOLLAR; Glen, and Castle Campbell. 36½m. Melville Ho. CUPAR; as Route 18. 44m. Dairsie Church and Castle. 46¾m. Guard Bridge. ST. ANDREWS; as Route 19.

Hotels or Inns where marked *; Strathmiglo, & Collessie.

175 & 176 STIRLING TO DUNFERMLINE.

Description.—Class I. The road is rough to Causewayhead; thence good till near Alloa, where it becomes rough. Thereafter the "High" road (Class II.) to Dunfermline is hilly, but with good surface; the "Low" road (Class I.) has a fine surface with comparatively easy hills.

Gradients.—*High road;* at 13¼m. 1 in 18-21; 14m. 1 in 20; 14½m. 1 in 24; 16½m. 1 in 25; 18m. 1 in 24. *Low road;* 14¼m. maximum 1 in 23; 18m. 1 in 25; 19m. 1 in 20-24; 22¼m. 1 in 15.

Milestones.—Measured from Stirling to New Mills Bridge *via* Tullibody; thence from Dunfermline Crosswynd. Those on the "High" road, which branches off at Kennet, are measured from Dunfermline.

Measurements (*High Road*).

Stirling,* King Street.				
7½	Alloa,* P.O.			
9¼	1¾	Clackmannan,* Free Church.		
18	10½	8¾	Carnock Bridge.	
21¼	13¾	12	3¼	Dunfermline,* Town Hall.

Low Road.

Stirling,* King Street.				
7½	Alloa,* P.O.			
12⅞	5⅜	Kincardine,* Cross.		
19	11½	6⅛	Torryburn.	
23¼	15¾	10⅜	4¼	Dunfermline,* Town Hall.

Principal Objects of Interest.—1¾m. Wallace Monument. 2m. Cambuskenneth Abbey. ALLOA; Tower. Clackmannan; Tower. Kincardine; Tulliallan Castle. 16m., to S., CULROSS; see Route 190. DUNFERMLINE; Abbey.

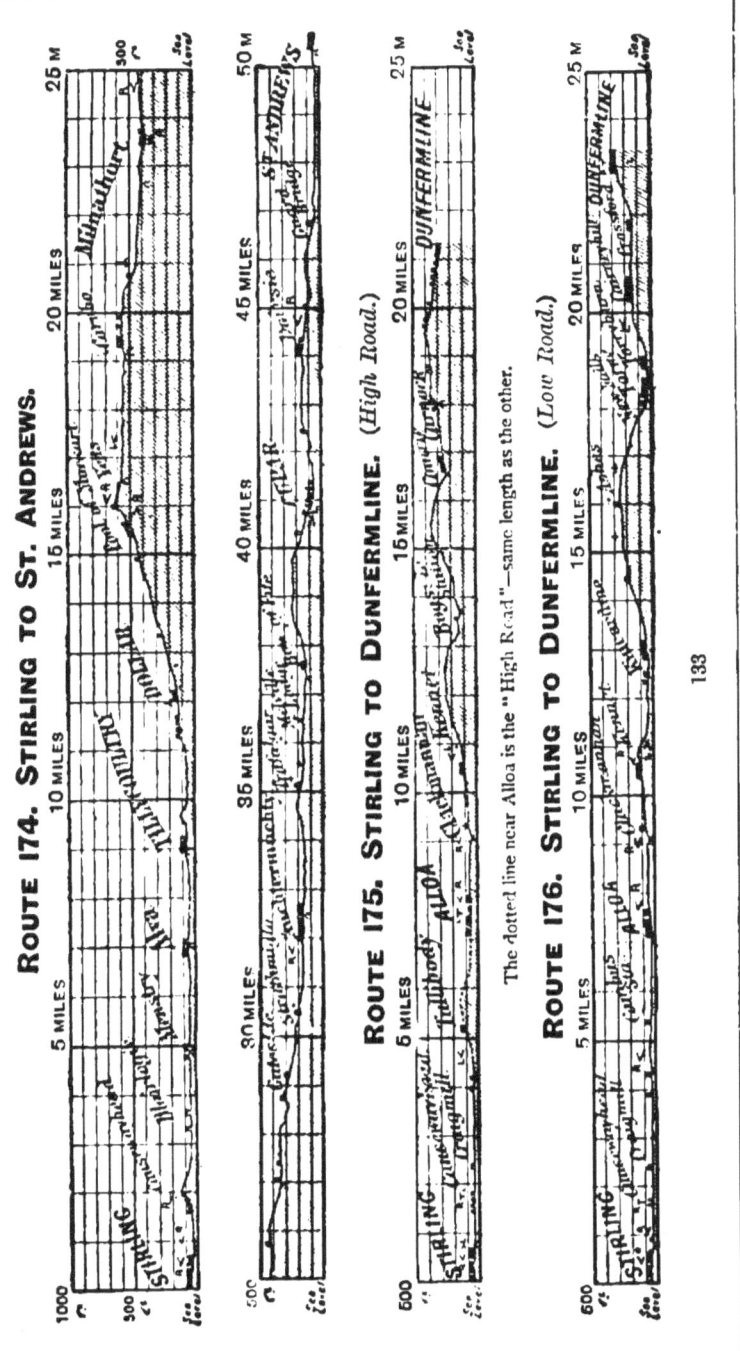

177   STIRLING TO DOUNE.

Description.—Class II. This road is not so good as that by Drip, but is more hilly, as well as being lumpy to Bridge of Allan.

Gradients.—At 5¾m. 1 in 23; 7m. 1 in 23; 7¼m. 1 in 20.

Measurements.—Stirling,* King Street.
     3¼   Bridge of Allan,* P.O.
     8¾   5¼   Doune * Cross; or,
     8¼   5¼   Doune,* Woodside Hotel.

Principal Objects of Interest.—As Route 172 to Bridge of Allan. DOUNE; Castle, Old Bridge.

---

178   CALLANDER TO PORT OF MENTEITH.

Description.—Class III. A good road for 2 miles, then very rough and bad, with gates across, to Hammersmith.

Gradients.—At 2¼m. 1 in 13; 4½m. 1 in 11.

Measurements.—Callander,* P.O.
     6¾   Port of Menteith Inn.*

Principal Objects of Interest.—Port; Rednock Castle, Inchmahone Priory. The Lake of Menteith is very pretty.

---

179   CALLANDER TO KIPPEN.

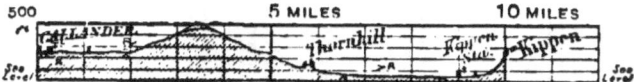

Description.—Class III. A good road for 2 miles, then fair surface, but with several gates across; very good after Thornhill.

Gradients.—At 5m. 1 in 21; 10m. 1 in 18-14.

Measurements.—Callander,* P.O.
     5¾   Thornhill.*
    10   4¼   Kippen.*

Principal Objects of Interest.—Moorland road at first.

Hotels or Inns at places marked '.

CALLANDER TO DOUNE. 180

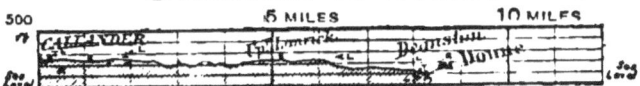

Description.—Class III. The best road is Route 170. This is a fair undulating road. (The road between Doune and Dunblane is Class II., and has a fine surface with easy gradients).

Gradients.—At 6¼m. 1 in 24; 8½m. 1 in 23.

Measurements.—Callander,* P.O.
       8¾ Doune,* Woodside Hotel.
       8¾ Doune,* Cross.
      12¼ 3¾ Dunblane,* Bridge.

Principal Objects of Interest.—5½m. Lanrick Castle. 8¼m. Deanston Mills. DOUNE; Castle. DUNBLANE; Cathedral.

ALLOA TO DOLLAR. 181

Description.—Class II. A very fine undulating road.

Milestones.—Measured from those on the Stirling-Kinross Road near Dollar.

Measurements.—Alloa.*
      4¼ (Tillicoultry).
      7 ... Dollar,* Hotel.

Principal Objects of Interest.—Fine view of the Ochil Hills. DOLLAR; Castle Campbell and Glen, Academy.

DUNFERMLINE TO DOLLAR. 182

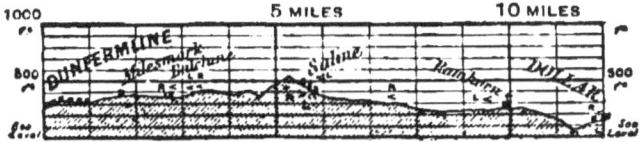

Description.—Class II. The road has a good surface throughout, but there are several stiff hills.

Gradients.—At 5m. 1 in 19-15; 5½m. 1 in 18; 11¼m. 1 in 22.

Milestones.—Measured from Dunfermline, and from Dollar.

Measurements.—Dunfermline,* Town Hall.
       5¾ Saline * Bridge.
      12¼ 6¾ Dollar,* Hotel.

Principal Objects of Interest.—DOLLAR; as above.

183 KIRKCALDY TO AUCHTERTOOL, &C.

Description.—Class III. Although this is the direct road to Dunfermline it is a bad hilly road. Route 191 is best.

Gradients.—At 1½m. & 2m. 1 in 14; 4m. 1 in 19; 4½m. 1 in 15-21; 5½m. 1 in 12; 6m. 1 in 14; 6½m. 1 in 12.

Milestones.—Measured from Dunfermline Crosswynd.

Measurements.—Kirkcaldy,* Town Hall; 4½m. Auchtertool; 6¾m. Stewart's Arms*; 12m. Dunfermline,* Town Hall.

184 NEW INN TO BEIN INN.

Description.—Class II. A good road as far as Edentown; thereafter fair, with rather dangerous descent to Bein Inn.

Gradients.—At 11m. 1 in 19.

Measurements.—Kirkcaldy,* Town Hall.
    9 New Inn.*
  11¾ 2¾ Falkland.*
  15 6 3¾ Strathmiglo.*
  20¼ 11¼ 8½ 5¼ Bein Inn.*
  28¾ 19¾ 17 13¾ 8½ Perth,* Cross.

Principal Objects of Interest.—Falkland; Palace.

185 NEW INN TO NEWBURGH.

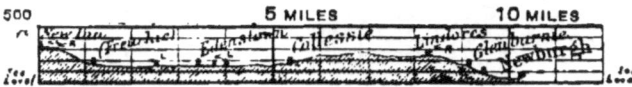

Description.—Class II. A good road with fair surface.

Gradients.—At ½m. 1 in 20.

Measurements.—Kirkcaldy,* Town Hall.
  9 New Inn.*
  14¾ 5¾ Collessie,* Inn.
  19¼ 10¼ 4¾ Newburgh,* Town Hall.

Principal Objects of Interest.—Collessie; Beaton's Tower. 8¼m. Inchrye Abbey. Newburgh; Macduff's Cross, Lindores Abbey.

CUPAR TO LARGO. 186

Description.—Class III. The road has a fair surface, but is very hilly.

Gradients.—At ¾m. 1 in 23; 2¼m. 1 in 20; 4½m. 1 in 13; 6½m. 1 in 22; 7½m. 1 in 12; 8½m., 8¾m., and 9⅜m. 1 in 13.

Measurements.—Cupar,* Town Hall.
                3½ Ceres.
                9½ 6¾ Largo,* Pier.

Principal Objects of Interest.—Largo; see Route 19.

ST. ANDREWS TO ANSTRUTHER. 187

Description.—Class II. A good road throughout, but somewhat steep at several points.

Gradients.—At 1m. 1 in 21; 4¼m. 1 in 15; 6¾m. 1 in 23.

Milestones.—Measured from St. Andrews, Old Town Hall.

Measurements.—St. Andrews,* Town Church.
                5½ Kingsmuir Inn.*
                9¾ 4½ Anstruther,* Bridge.

ST. ANDREWS TO LARGO. 188

Description.—Class III. A fair road, but with very steep hills.

Gradients.—At 1½m. 1 in 15; 2¼m. 1 in 15; 3¼m. 1 in 15; 9½m. 1 in 13-17-24; 11m. 1 in 22; 12m. 1 in 11.

Milestones.—Measured from St. Andrews, Town Church, correct.

Measurements.—St. Andrews,* Town Church.
                6¾ Largoward.
             12 5½ Largo,* Pier.

Principal Objects of Interest.—Largo; see Route 19.

189 ALLOA TO KINROSS.

Description.—Class III. A very fair but undulating road, rather soft in some parts near Crook and towards Kinross.

Gradients.—3½m. 1 in 24; 9¾m. 1 in 14; 10m. 1 in 13-25.

Measurements.

Alloa,* P.O.
7½ Blairingone.
11⅞ 4⅜ Crook * of Devon.
17⅝ 10⅛ 5¾ Kinross,* P.O.

Principal Objects of Interest.—At 6¾m. to Dollar. At 10½m. to Rumbling Bridge. KINROSS; Loch Leven and Castle.

Hotels or Inns at places marked *.

190 BURNTISLAND TO CULROSS.

Description.—Class II. Narrow Lane to Kirkton. Thereafter steep hills to Aberdour, when the road becomes more or less undulating all the way. Good surface throughout.

Gradients.—¼m. 1 in 13; ¾m. 1 in 15; 2¾m. about 1 in 11.

Milestones.—Those from Kinghorn are joined at Kirkton and continue correct to Inverkeithing.

Measurements.

Burntisland,* Pier.
3⅜ Aberdour,* Station.
7¾ 4⅜ Inverkeithing,* Cross.
16 12⅝ 8¼ Torryburn.
18½ 15⅛ 10¾ 2½ Culross,* Town House.

Principal Objects of Interest.—BURNTISLAND; Rossend Castle. Aberdour; Castle, Donibristle, Inchcolm. 9¾m. Rosyth Castle. CULROSS; Abbey, Dunnemarle Castle.

Hotels or Inns at places marked *.

191 KIRKCALDY TO DUNFERMLINE.

Description.—Class II. A very good road with comparatively easy grades all the way. The more direct road by Auchtertool is very hilly and steep.

Gradients.—At 1m. 1 in 24; at 11m. 1 in 18; at 13m. 1 in 24.

Milestones.—Measured from Dunfermline Crosswynd *via* Auchtertool, to Kirkcaldy.

Measurements.

Kirkcaldy,* Town Hall.
7½ Stewart's Arms.*
10 2½ Crossgates,* P.O.
13½ 6 3½ Dunfermline,* Town Hall.

Principal Objects of Interest.—Collieries after Donibristle.

Hotels or Inns at places marked *.

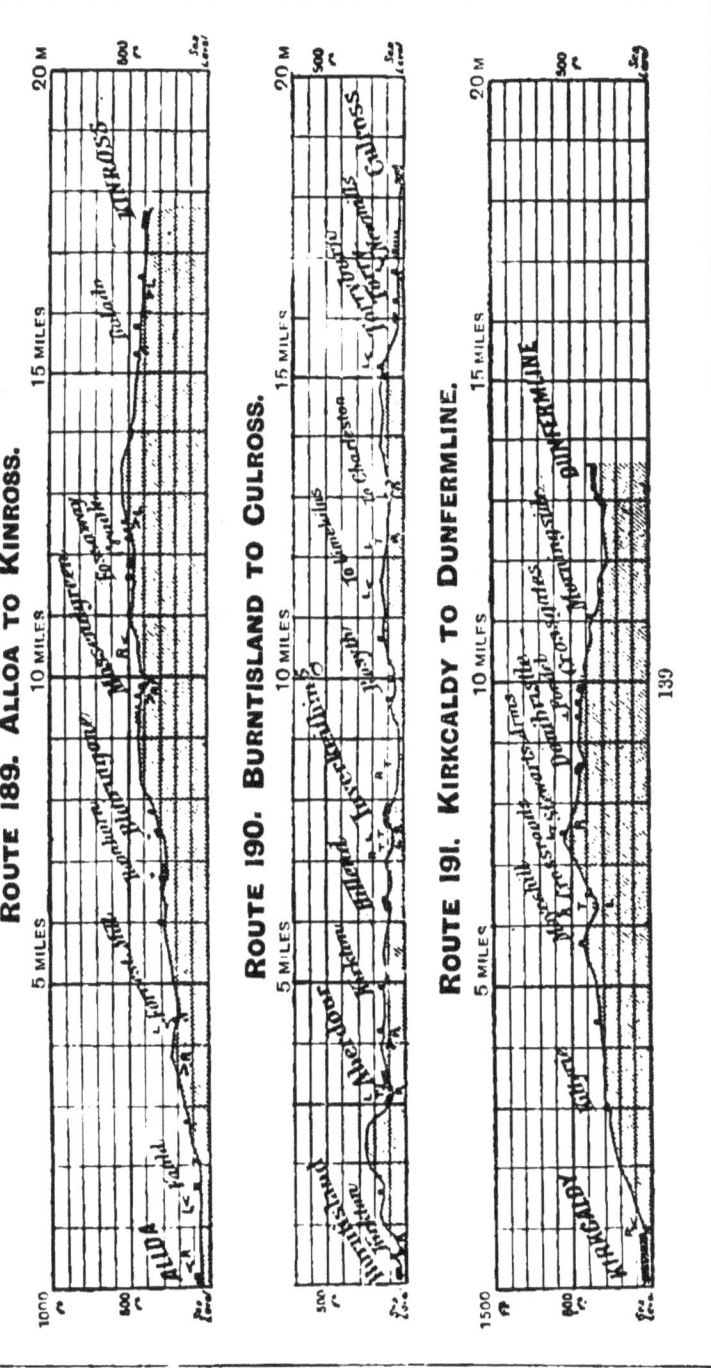

ROUTE 189. ALLOA TO KINROSS.

ROUTE 190. BURNTISLAND TO CULROSS.

ROUTE 191. KIRKCALDY TO DUNFERMLINE.

192 KIRKCALDY TO ST. ANDREWS.

Description.—Class II. After Gallatown this is a fine undulating road to Windygates; thereafter it is scarcely so good till nearing Ceres, when the surface becomes very much better.

Gradients.—8¼m. 1 in 19-25; 11½m. 1 in 20-22; 14m¾. 1 in 24.

Milestones.—Measured from Burntisland Pier, correct to Pratis; after Ceres from St. Andrews, West Port.

Measurements.

Kirkcaldy,* Town Hall.						
7⅜	Windygates.*					
8¾	1⅜	Kennoway.				
(18	10⅝	9¼	Cupar,* Town House).			
16⅜	9	7⅝	...	Ceres.*		
17⅞	10½	9⅛	...	1½	Pitscottie.	
23⅜	16	14⅝	...	7	5½	St. Andrews,* Town Church.

Principal Objects of Interest.—15m. Scotstarvit Tower. 17⅞m. Dura Den. 21⅛m. Magus Muir to S. ST. ANDREWS; as Route 19.

Hotels or Inns at places marked *.

193 NEW INN TO TAYPORT.

Description.—Class II. This is a fine undulating road of very fair surface, a little rough, however, near Kilmany.

Gradients.—12m. 1 in 18.

Measurements.

New Inn.*			
13¾	Kilmany.		
19¼	5½	Newport,* Pier.	
22⅛	8⅜	2⅞	Tayport,* Pier.

Hotels or Inns at places marked *.

194 MILNATHORT TO LARGO.

Description.—Class III. The road, though of fine surface, is very hilly.

Gradients.—2½m. 1 in 24-18; 3m. 1 in 19; 4⅜m. 1 in 15; 6¼m. 1 in 23; 6¾m. 1 in 16-13; 12¾m. 1 in 22; 13m. 1 in 24; 13¾m. 1 in 13.

Measurements.

Milnathort,* Cross.							
4	Kinnesswood.*						
5	1	Scotlandwell.*					
9⅜	5⅜	4⅜	Leslie,* P.O.				
12⅜	8⅜	7⅜	3	Markinch,* P.O.			
16	12	11	6⅝	3⅝	Windygates.*		
(18⅝	14⅝	13⅝	9¼	6¼	2⅝	Leven,* Quay).	
20⅜	16⅜	15⅜	11	8	4⅜	...	Largo, Lundin Mill.

Principal Objects of Interest.—½m. Burleigh Castle. 5m. Scotland "Well." 14⅜m. Balgonie Castle. 14½m. Balfour.

Hotels or Inns at places marked*, and Auchmoorbridge.

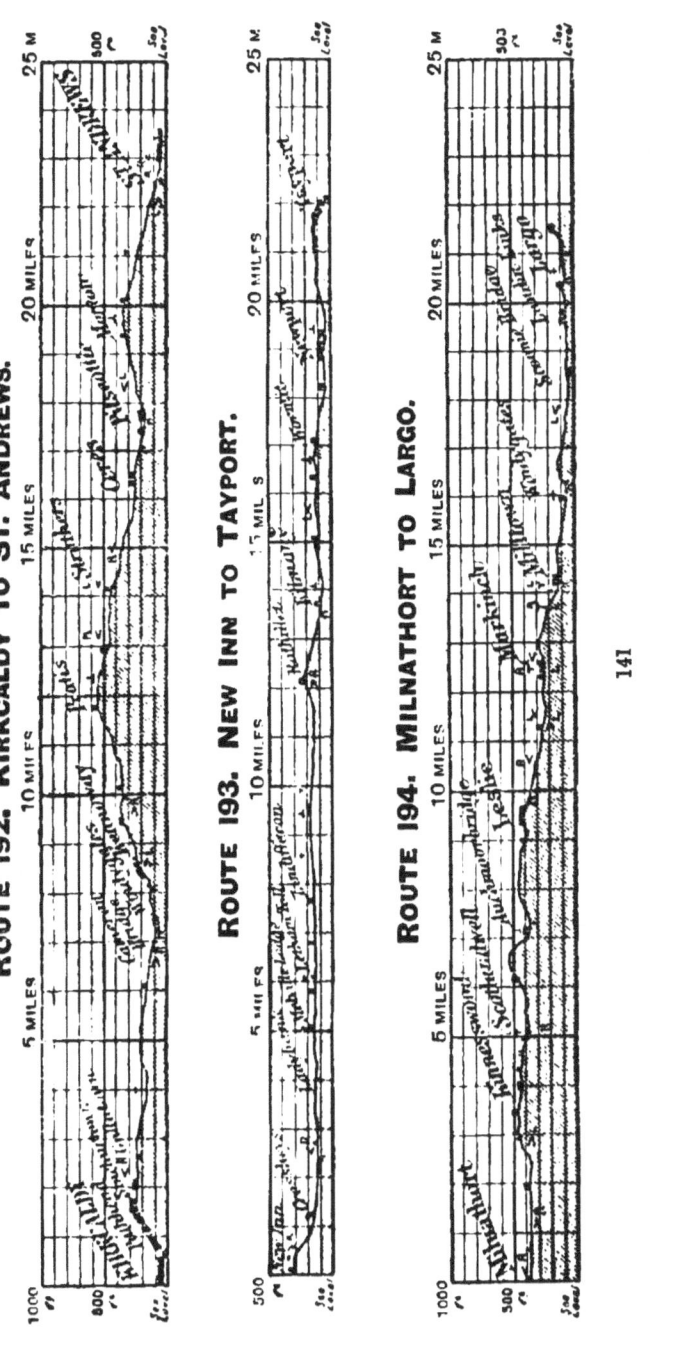

196 PERTH TO CUPAR.

Description.—Class II. Good surface over Moncrieffe Hill, then a magnificent road to Aberargie, almost level. To Lindores is very fair but undulating; thereafter hilly at first, but improving to Cupar.

Gradients.—Moncrieffe Hill, ascent 1 in 25; descent 1 in 22; at 12¾m. 1 in 22; 18½m. 1 in 23; 20m. 1 in 24.

Milestones.—To Aberargie, as Route 17; thereafter in Fife, measured from Cupar Town House,—correct.

Measurements.

Perth,* Cross.
4 Bridge of Earn * Hotel.
8½ 4½ Abernethy.*
11½ 7½ 3 Newburgh,* Town House.
22 18 13½ 10½ Cupar,* Town House.

Principal Objects of Interest.—To Aberargie, as Route 17. Abernethy; Round Tower. NEWBURGH; Macduff's Cross, Lindores Abbey. CUPAR; as Route 19.

Hotels or Inns at places marked,* and at Aberargie.

---

197 CRIEFF TO ABERFELDY, &c.

Description.—Class II. The surface is good to the Sma' Glen, rough to Amulree, good up to near the summit, where it is soft, then very rough on the descent to Aberfeldy. Thereafter the road is good to Coshieville, but speedily degenerates in quality and becomes very loose and stony, with dangerous turn past Foss. To Dalnacardoch, except a short piece at Trinafour, is a fearful road with dangerous turns, almost unfit for traffic.

Gradients.—At 2½m. 1 in 18-20-17-22-17; 8¾m. 1 in 17-25-22; 20½ & 23m. 1 in 14-13-17-13-21; 29½m. 1 in 14; 31¼ & 34m. 1 in 13; 38m. 1 in 13; 40½m. 1 in 11; 42m. 1 in 11; 44½m. 1 in 16.

Milestones.—Measured from Crieff, James Sq., to Aberfeldy—tolerably correct; thereafter from the Inverness milestones at Dalnacardoch.

Measurements.

Crieff,* James Square.
12¼ Amulree.*
23⅛ 10⅞ Aberfeldy,* Crossroads.
28½ 16¼ 5⅜ Coshieville.*
36½ 24¼ 13⅜ 8 Tummel Bridge.*
41½ 29¼ 18⅜ 13 5 Trinafour.
46¼ 34 23⅛ 17¾ 9¾ 4¾ Dalnacardoch.

Principal Objects of Interest.—3m. Monzie Castle. 7m. Sma' Glen and "Ossians Grave." 23m. Falls of Moness. 23⅝m. Wade's Bridge, 1733. 24½m. Menzies Castle. 27¾m. Taymouth Castle to S. 28m. Comrie Castle (ruins).

Hotels or Inns at places marked *, and at Whitebridge.

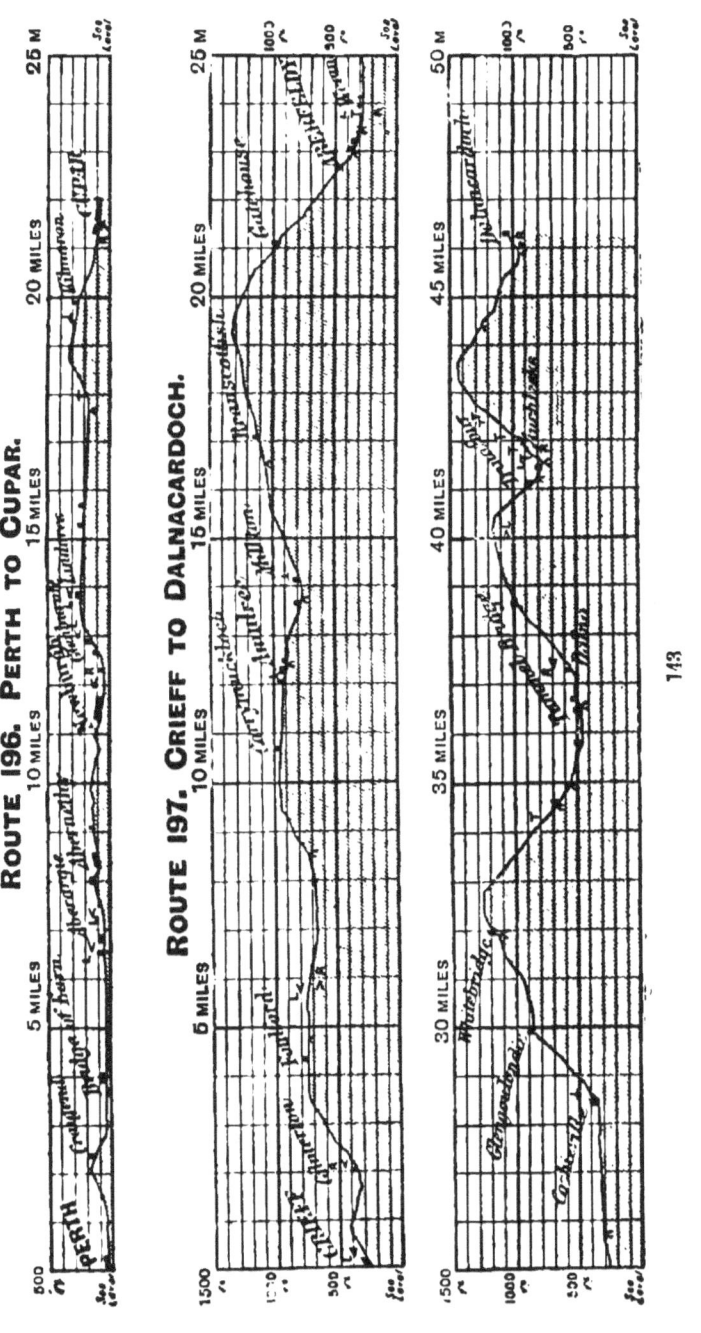

198 AUCHTERARDER TO BRIDGE OF EARN.

Description.—Class III. A very hilly road, but of good surface to Dunning; thereafter easier to Bridge of Earn.

Gradients.—¼m. 1 in 13; 11m. 1 in 17.

Measurements.

Auchterarder,* Church.				
5	Dunning,* Square.			
12	7	Pitkeathly.		
13⅜	8⅜	1⅜	Bridge of Earn * Hotel.	
17⅜	12⅜	5⅜	4	Perth,* Cross.

Principal Objects of Interest.—4¾m. Duncrub. 7⅝m. Invermay, Forteviot ¾m. distant. 12m. Spa.

Hotels or Inns at places marked *.

---

199 PERTH TO LOCHEARNHEAD.

Description.—Class II. As far as Crieff the road is of very fine surface with easy undulations. Thereafter to St. Fillans is usually very smooth, and along Loch Earn level and generally very fine.

Gradients.—Mostly not above 1 in 27; except at 19¾m. 1 in 21.

Milestones.—Measured from Crieff Cross to Perth, and from Crieff, James Square, westwards to Comrie; thereafter a little irregular.

Measurements.

Perth,* Cross.						
6½	Methven,* Bridge.					
17½	11	Crieff,* James Square.				
24	17½	6½	Comrie.*			
29½	23	12	5½	St. Fillans,* P.O.		
36⅝	30⅛	19⅛	12⅝	7⅛	Lochearnhead * Hotel.	
38¼	31¾	20¾	14¼	8¾	1⅝	Lochearnhead Station.

Principal Objects of Interest.—2¾m. Huntingtower. 5¼m. Methven Castle and Battlefield. 11m. Inchaffray Abbey. CRIEFF; Cross, Falls of Turret and Barvick. 18½m. Ochtertyre. 24½m. Melville Monument. 26½m. Dunira. A beautiful road passing through varied scenery. Lochearnhead; Glenogle, Balquhidder, &c.

Hotels or Inns at places marked *.

ROUTE 198. AUCHTERARDER TO BRIDGE OF EARN.

ROUTE 199. PERTH TO LOCHEARNHEAD.

Signs: < Road Fork, forward journey. > ditto reverse. + Cross Roads. ⊥ Road Junction. ∩ Bridge. ⊤ indicates a sharp turn. The directions R (right) and L (left) for the forward journey are above the Road Line, those of the reverse, below.

200   PERTH TO KINGUSSIE.

Description.—Class I. to Dunkeld, II. to Kingussie. The surface is very fine to Strathord Station; thereafter to Dunkeld is good but hilly. To Pitlochry the road is undulating at first, but becomes easier after Dowally, though of poorer surface. Through the Pass of Killiecrankie is steep, but after passing Aldclune the road is level and very good as far as Bruar, where the long ascent of the Grampians commences. From this point the surface gets gradually worse until in some parts it is little else than a loose mass of stones, in others, overgrown with grass. This continues till near Dalwhinnie when the surface improves and shortly after becomes a fine but undulating road to Kingussie.

Gradients.—At $5\frac{1}{4}$m. 1 in 24; $11\frac{3}{4}$m. 1 in 21; $15\frac{1}{4}$m. 1 in 19; 30m. 1 in 18-15; $30\frac{1}{4}$m. 1 in 20; 31m. 1 in 19-14. There are many rough hills after Struan. With the above exceptions the gradients seldom exceed 1 in 27.

Milestones.—Measured from Perth Cross, but not perfectly equidistant, on account of deviations of the road at various points, as far as Perth county boundary. In Inverness-shire they are measured from Inverness.

Measurements.

Perth,* Cross.
$8\frac{3}{4}$ Bankfoot.*
$14\frac{3}{4}$ 6   Dunkeld,* High Street.
$22\frac{1}{2}$ $13\frac{3}{4}$ $7\frac{3}{4}$ Balliuluig Station.
$27\frac{1}{4}$ $18\frac{1}{2}$ $12\frac{1}{2}$ $4\frac{3}{4}$ Pitlochry,* Fountain.
$34\frac{1}{4}$ $25\frac{1}{2}$ $19\frac{1}{2}$ $11\frac{3}{4}$ 7   Blair Athole,* Hotel.
$44\frac{3}{4}$ $36\frac{1}{2}$ $30\frac{1}{4}$ $22\frac{3}{4}$ $17\frac{5}{8}$ $10\frac{3}{4}$ Dalnacardoch.
$57\frac{3}{4}$ 49   43 $35\frac{1}{4}$ $30\frac{1}{2}$ $23\frac{1}{2}$ $12\frac{3}{4}$ Dalwhinnie,* Hotel.
$71\frac{3}{4}$ 63   57 $49\frac{1}{4}$ $44\frac{1}{2}$ $37\frac{1}{2}$ $26\frac{3}{4}$ 14   Kingussie,* Court Ho.

Principal Objects of Interest.—$4\frac{1}{2}$m. Battlefield of Luncarty. 12m. Murthly Castle. DUNKELD; Palace, Craig-y-barns. Birnam Hill and Wood, Falls of Braan, Neil Gow's House. PITLOCHRY; to Falls of Tummel. 30m. to Falls of Tummel and Queen's view; and entrance to old Pass of Killiecrankie. 31m. North entrance to Pass. $31\frac{1}{2}$m. Claverhouse Stone. Blair Athole; Castle, Glen Tilt, Falls of Fender. $37\frac{1}{2}$m. Bruar Falls. Thence a desolate road to about 63m. $66\frac{1}{4}$m. Invernahavon Battlefield, 1386. Kingussie; Ruthven Barracks.

Hotels or Inns at places marked *, and at Birnam, Struan, and Newtonmore. None between Struan and Dalwhinnie—20 miles.

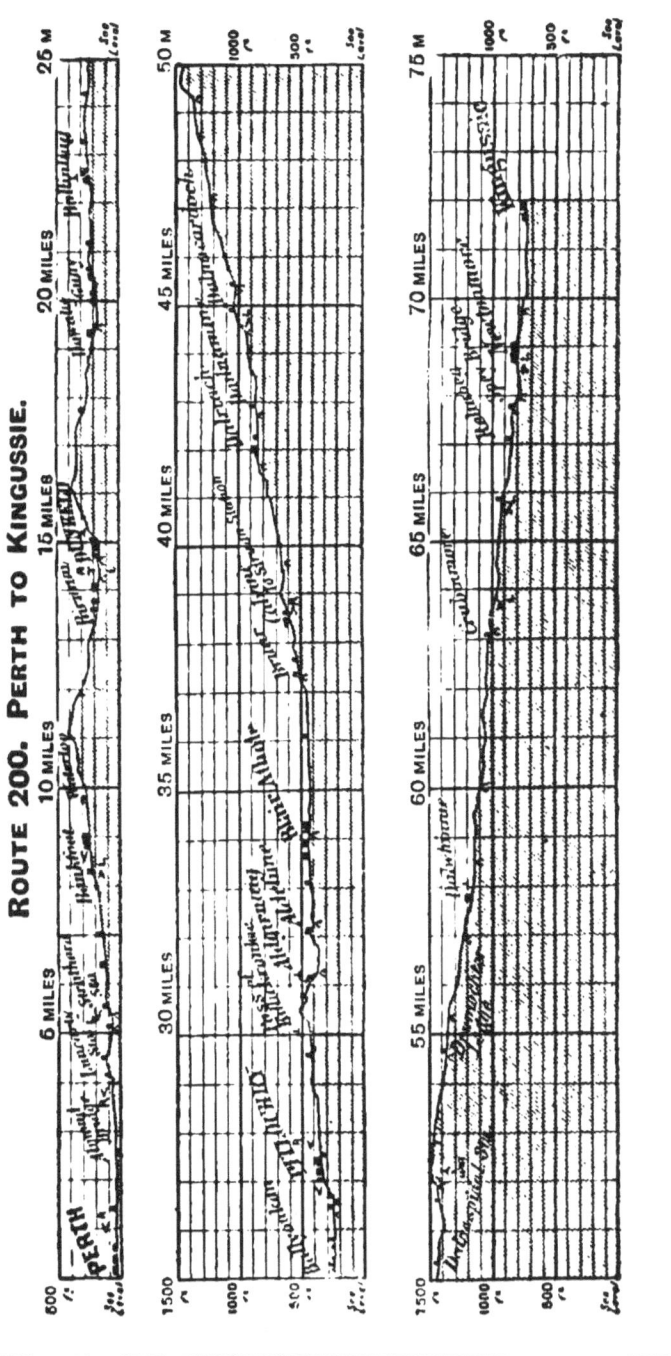

201 PERTH TO BRAEMAR.

Description.—Class I. to Blairgowrie, II. to Bridge of Cally, III. to near Braemar. The road though somewhat undulating has a magnificent surface as far as Blairgowrie; thereafter to Bridge of Cally is good but hilly. From here to Spital the road is very hilly, with fair surface at first, but soft afterwards. It then becomes very bad and rough, with numerous steep hills of varied length, culminating in a nasty double turn on a precipitous incline—the "Devil's Elbow"—which coming from Braemar cannot be taken too carefully. Thereafter the road, though soft and very rough at first, is very good after Altamhait.

Gradients.—Nothing above 1 in 26 to Blairgowrie, thence short hill into Rattray 1 in 14. After Craighall Bridge the ruling gradient is 1 in 25, with a maximum of 1 in 23. At 21½m. 1 in 14 (dangerous turn); 21¾m. 1 in 11; 23¼m. 1 in 13 (dangerous turn at top); 23½m. 1 in 16-13-16; 27¼m. 1 in 14; 27¾m. 1 in 12; 28m. 1 in 23; 29m. 1 in 17; 29¼m. 1 in 20; 29½m. 1 in 19; 29¾m. 1 in 15; 30¾m. 1 in 22; thence various short undulations till the final ascent begins at 38½m. with 1 in 15-17-16-10-14-19, and is 1 in 9 on the exceedingly dangerous double turns; thereafter decreasing to 1 in 12 at the summit. The descent is 1 in 16-15-22-15-20-13-19; and at 42m. 1 in 18.

Milestones.—To Blairgowrie, measured from Perth Bridge,—correct; thereafter measured from Dunkeld.

Measurements.

Perth,* Cross.						
5¾	Guildtown.					
10⅛	4⅜	Cargill Station.				
15⅝	9⅞	5½	Blairgowrie,* Well Meadow.			
21⅜	15⅝	11¼	5¾	Bridge of Cally.*		
34½	28¾	24⅜	18⅞	13⅛	Spital of Glenshee * Hotel.	
49¾	44	39⅝	34⅛	28⅜	15¼	Braemar,* Invercauld Arms.

Principal Objects of Interest.—2½m. Scone Palace. 6¾m. Campsie Linn. 7½m. Stobhall. 11m. Meikleour "Hedges." 14m. Druidsmere. 17¼m. Craighall (Tullyveolan). 35m. Boar Loch. 40½m. Cairnwell Pass, 2,200 ft., highest road in Britain. Braemar; see Route 241.

Hotels or Inns at places marked *, and at Persie.

202 PERTH TO STONEHAVEN.

Description.—Class I. A magnificent road with long slopes at first, but with easy grades to near Coupar Angus when it becomes level. Thence to Forfar is smooth and

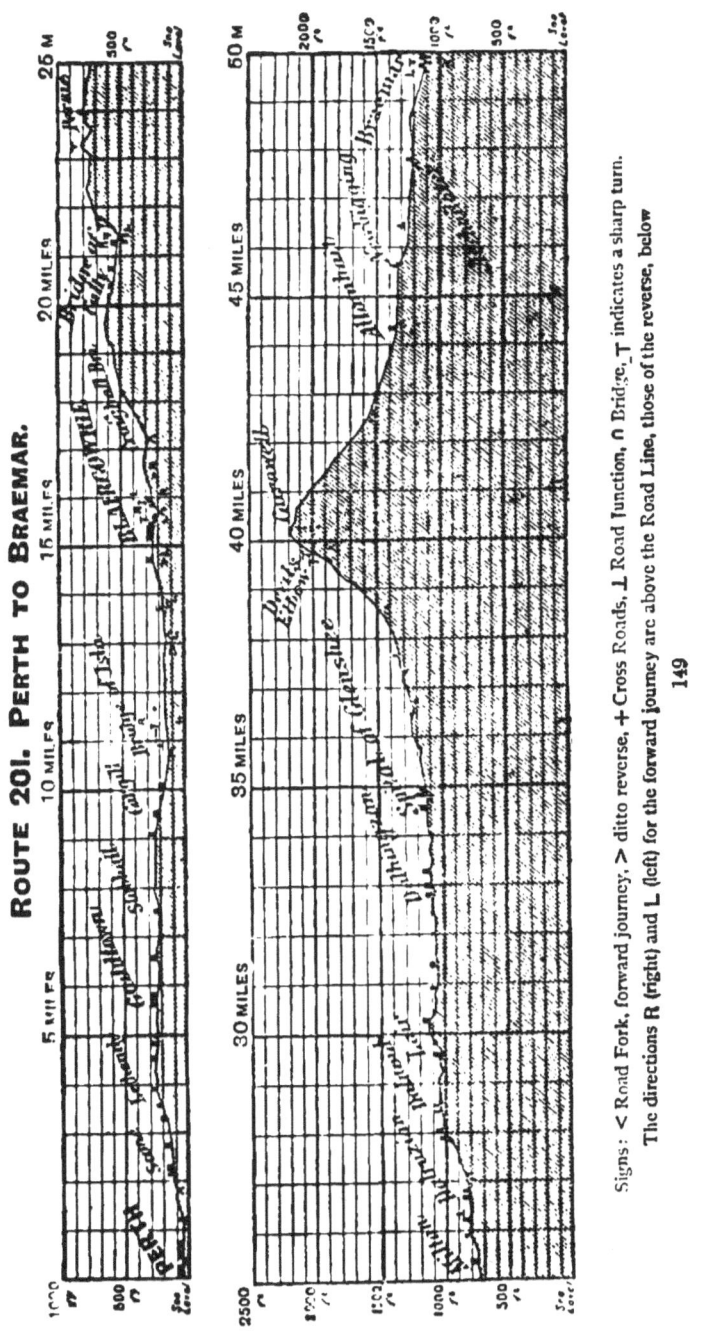

Signs: < Road Fork, forward journey, > ditto reverse, + Cross Roads, ⊥ Road Junction, ∩ Bridge, ⊤ indicates a sharp turn. The directions R (right) and L (left) for the forward journey are above the Road Line, those of the reverse, below

undulating, fair to Brechin, and good past Laurencekirk, ending with long descent to Stonehaven, on which care should be taken towards the foot.

Gradients.—Mostly very easy except 30¼ & 67m. 1 in 24.

Milestones.—Measured from Perth, George Street, to Glamis; thence from Forfar on to the County Boundary, where those from Laurencekirk Town Hall are met. Those to Stonehaven are from the County Buildings at that place.

Measurements.

Perth,* Cross.								
12¾	Coupar Angus,* Cross.							
17⅞	5⅛	Meigle.*						
24½	11¾	6⅝	Glamis.*					
29⅞	17⅛	12	5⅜	Forfar,* Town Hall.				
35¾	23	17⅞	11¼	5⅞	Tannadice * Inn.			
42½	29¾	24⅝	18	12⅝	6¾	Brechin,* Town House.		
53½	40¾	35⅝	29	23⅝	17¾	11	Laurencekirk,* Town Hall.	
67½	54¾	49⅝	43	37⅝	31¾	25	14	Stonehaven,* Market Sq.

Principal Objects of Interest.—COUPAR ANGUS; Abbey. Meigle; Sculptured Stone. Glamis; Castle. FORFAR; Restenneth Priory. BRECHIN; Cathedral, Round Tower, Bridge. 50¼m. Inglismaldie. STONEHAVEN; Dunottar Cas.

Hotels or Inns at places marked *, and at Balbeggie, and (Drumlithie).

---

203 PERTH TO DUNDEE.

Description.—Class I. The surface is very good and level to beyond Inchture when the road becomes more hilly; nearing Dundee the surface is poorer, on account of heavy traffic.

Gradients.—The steepest part is at 14½m. 1 in 25.

Milestones.—Measured from Perth Cross,—correct.

Measurements.

Perth,* Cross.				
6⅜	Glencarse,* Inn.			
13¼	6⅞	Inchture.		
15½	9⅛	2¼	Longforgan,* Church.	
21½	15⅛	8¼	6	Dundee,* Town House.

Principal Objects of Interest.—½m. Kinnoul Hill. 2¾m. Kinfauns Castle. 9⅝m. Megginch Castle. 14⅛m. Rossie Priory. 14¾m. Castle Huntly. The road passes along the famous "Carse of Gowrie," and there are many objects of interest in the immediate vicinity of the road.

Hotels or Inns at places marked * and at (Errol).

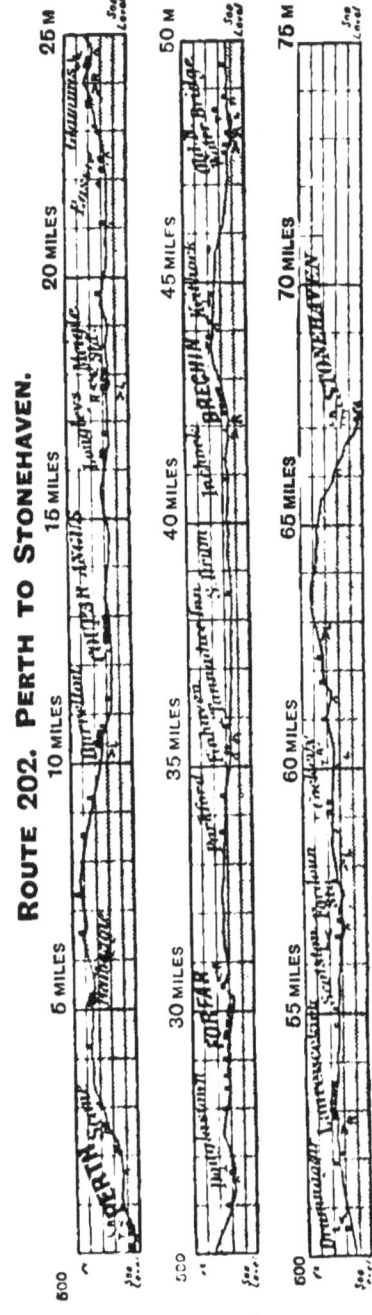
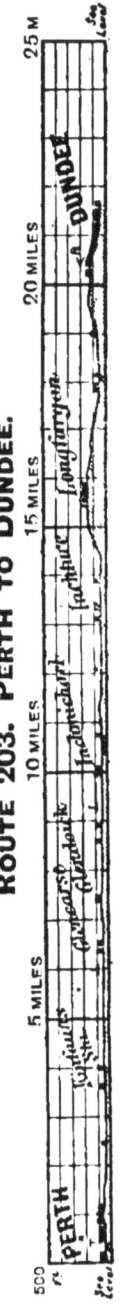

Signs. < Road Fork, forward journey. > ditto reverse. + Cross Roads. ⊥ Road Junction. ⌒ Bridge. ⊤ indicates a sharp turn. The directions R (right) and L (left) for the forward journey are above the Road Line, those of the reverse, below.

204 PERTH TO CAPUTH.

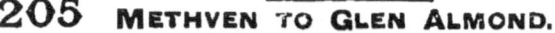

Description.—Class II. A very fine smooth road as far as Strathord Station; thereafter not quite so good.
Gradients.—At 11¾m. 1 in 19.
Milestones.—Measured from Perth Cross,—correct.
Measurements.—Perth,* Cross.

	4½		Luncarty Station.
	7¼	2¾	Stanley,* Square.
	12¼	7¾	5 Caputh,* Church.

Principal Objects of Interest.—4½m. Battlefield of Luncarty. 6½m. Thistlebridge. Stanley; Campsie Linn. Caputh; Murthly Castle.

205 METHVEN TO GLEN ALMOND.

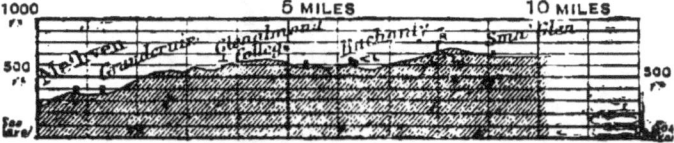

Description.—Class III. A fair, but somewhat hilly road.
Gradients.—At ¼m. 1 in 16; 1¾m. 1 in 24-15; 3m. 1 in 15; 5m. 1 in 24.
Milestones.—Continuation of those from Perth.
Measurements.—Perth,* Cross.

6¼	Methven.'		
12¾	6¾	Buchanty.*	
21	14½	8¾	Amulree*; or,
20½	13¾	7½	Crieff, James Square.

Principal Objects of Interest.—3¾m. Glenalmond College. Very pretty scenery in Glen Almond, and up the Sma' Glen.

206 COMRIE TO GREENLOANING.

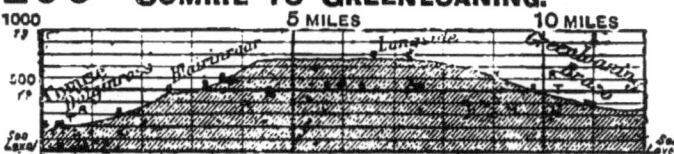

Description.—Class II. The gradients are comparatively easy, but the surface is poor, until near Braco.
Gradients.—At 2½m. 1 in 22-20; 4m. 1 in 23.
Milestones.—Continuation of those from Stirling.
Measurements.—Comrie.*

10¾	Braco.*	
12½	1¾	Greenloaning.*

Principal Objects of Interest.—A rather dreary road. 10½m. Ardoch Roman Camp.

DUNKELD TO AMULREE. 207

Description.—Class II. The road has a fair surface, but is a little stony at several points.

Gradients.—At ½m. 1 in 19.

Milestones.—Measured from Dunkeld, High Street,—correct.

Measurements.—Dunkeld,* High Street.
    3¾   Trochrie.
    9¾ 5¾ Amulree;* or,
  16¾ 13 Aberfeldy,* Square.

Principal Objects of Interest.—2m. Falls of Braan. 2½m. Rumbling Bridge. 3¾m. Trochrie Castle ruin.

DUNKELD TO BLAIRGOWRIE. 208

Description.—Class III. Hilly at first, undulating afterward; the surface is very good nearing Blairgowrie.

Gradients.—At ¾m. 1 in 15; 7½m. 1 in 17.

Milestones.—Measured from Dunkeld, High Street,—correct.

Measurements.—Dunkeld,* High Street.
    4¼   Butterstone.
    7¼ 3 Forneth.
  12¼ 8 5 Blairgowrie,* Well Meadow.

Principal Objects of Interest.—The road is pleasantly wooded, and passes close to a series of charming Lochs.

ABERFELDY TO BALLINLUIG. 209

Description.—Class III. A good, slightly undulating road, but with a very steep hill at the north side of Grandtully Bridge.

Measurements.—Aberfeldy,* Square.
    5   Grandtully,* Hotel.
    9¼ 4¼ Ballinluig P.O.

Principal Objects of Interest.—2¾m. Grandtully Castle. Hotels or Inns at places marked *, and at Logierait.

210 DUNKELD TO ABERFELDY.

Description.—Class II. A remarkably good but very undulating road till quite near Aberfeldy, when it becomes level.

Gradients.—At 1¼m. 1 in 22; 13¼m. 1 in 24; 14¼m. 1 in 25.

Milestones.—Continuation of those from Perth,—correct.

Measurements.

Dunkeld,* High Street.			
5	Dalguise.		
12¼	7¼	Grantully,* Hotel.	
17¼	12¼	5	Aberfeldy,* Square.

Principal Objects of Interest.—1m. Neil Gow's Cottage, Falls of Braan. 14¼m. Grantully Castle. ABERFELDY; Falls of Moness, Wade's Bridge, Weem Rock. The valley of the Tay is well wooded.

Hotels or Inns at places marked *, and at Balnaguard.

---

211 PITLOCHRY TO RANNOCH.

Description.—Class III. The road is very good to the Pass of Killiecrankie, after which it is exceedingly hilly, more or less all the way to Kinloch Rannoch. Along Loch Tummel the road is undulating with short hills. After Kinloch Rannoch the road is poor, and rather soft nearing Rannoch Station. Several of the hills are dangerous.

Gradients.—At 3m. 1 in 17; 3¼m. 1 in 18; 4½m. 1 in 19-21; 5¼m. 1 in 21-13; 6¾m. 1 in 19-23-12-15; 7½m. 1 in 16-23; 16½m. 1 in 24-17; 17¼m. 1 in 17; 17½m. 1 in 19-9 (dangerous turn); 24½m. 1 in 23.

Milestones.—Measured from Pitlochry Fountain, to Rannoch; thereafter from Gaur Bridge.

Measurements.

Pitlochry,* Fountain.						
5½	Fincastle.					
7¼	1¾	Queen's View.				
13⅞	8⅜	6⅝	Tummel Bridge.*			
20⅞	15⅜	13⅝	7	Kinloch Rannoch,* Hotel.		
28¾	23¼	21½	14⅞	7⅞	Killiechonan.	
37½	32	30¼	23⅝	16⅝	8⅜	Rannoch Station.

Principal Objects of Interest.—3⅛m. Killiecrankie Pass. 4m., to Falls of Tummel. 7¼m. Queen's View; Magnificent view of Loch Tummel and Schichallion. 17¾m. Dunalastair.

Hotels or Inns at places marked *, and at Balnald.

---

212 ABERFELDY TO KILLIN.

Description.—Class II. A very good road, but with steep hill descending to Kenmore; thereafter good to Fearnan, poor to Lawers, but improving slightly towards Killin.

Gradients.—At 4½m. 1 in 22; 5¾m. 1 in 16; 17¼m. 1 in 25-21; 17¾m. 1 in 24; 21¼m. 1 in 20-24-21.

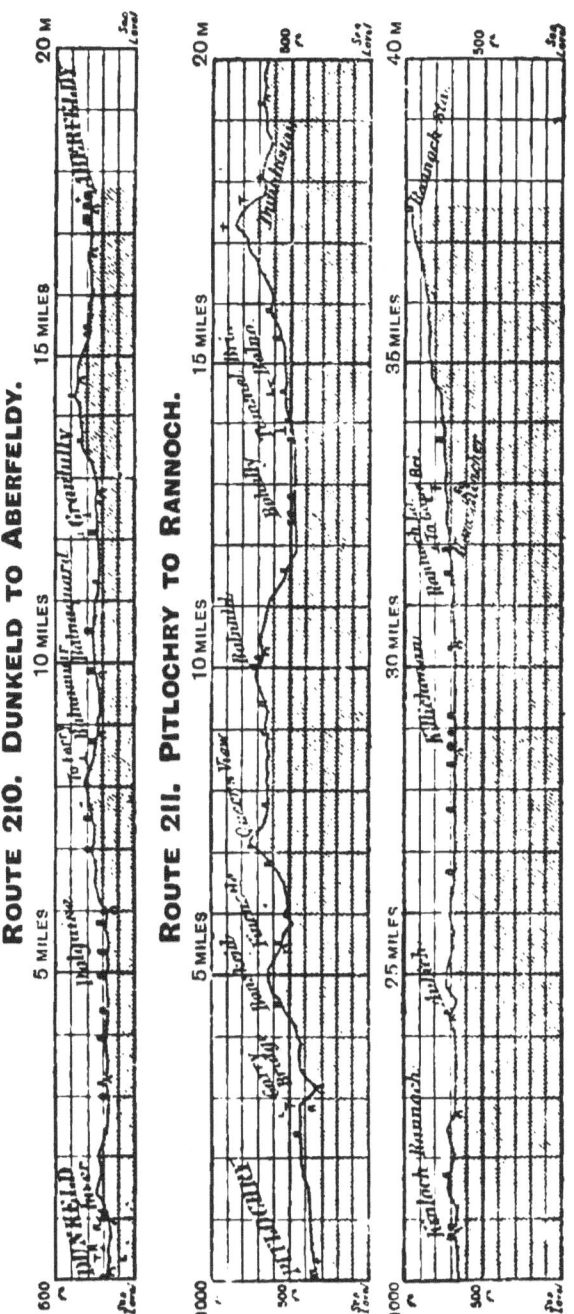

Signs: < Road Fork, forward journey, > ditto reverse, + Cross Roads, ⊥ Road Junction, ∩ Bridge, ⊤ indicates a sharp turn. The directions R (right) and L (left) for the forward journey are above the Road Line, those of the reverse, below.

155

Milestones.—Continuation of those from Perth, to Kenmore; thereafter from Kenmore—doubtful if correct.

Measurements.

Aberfeldy,* Square.				
6¼	Kenmore,* Hotel.			
9⅞	3⅝	Fearnan,* Pier.		
14	7¾	4⅛	Lawers,* Inn.	
22⅝	16⅜	12¾	8⅝	Killin,* P.O.

Principal Objects of Interest.—4¾m. Fort Lodge (Taymouth Castle). 6m. (Acharn Falls, 1⅝m. to West). 14m. for Ben Lawers. Killin; Finlarig Castle, Glen Lochay, Falls of Dochart.

Hotels or Inns at places marked *, also Bridge of Lochay.

213 Aberfeldy to Killin *via Ardeonaig.*

Description.—Class III. As Route 212, to 6m., thereafter level for several miles when the road becomes very hilly almost the whole way to Killin; good surface at first, but poor near Killin. Several gates across the road.

Gradients.—To 6m. as above, then at 8¾m. 1/17-23-16-18-13; 10m. 1/25-19; 12m. 1/19-15; 12¼m. 1/13-15-13; 13½m. 1/20; 14½m. 1/21-16-12-25; 15¾m. 1/16; 16¼m. 1/23; 17½m. 1/22; 17¾m. 1/15; 18¼m. 1/13; 18¾m. 1/20; 20¼m. 1/19-23-16-18-12; 21¾m. 1/15-16; 22m. 1/21.

Milestones.—Measured from Kenmore Hotel,—correct.

Measurements.

Aberfeldy,* Square.				
7⅜	Acharn.			
12⅛	4¾	Ardtalnaig.		
15¼	7⅞	3⅛	Ardeonaig * Bridge.	
22⅜	15	10¼	7⅛	Killin,* P.O.

Principal Objects of Interest.—4¾m. Fort Lodge (Taymouth Castle). 7⅝m. Acharn Falls. Killin; as above.

214 Aberfeldy to Glen Lyon.

Description.—Class III. As Route 197 for 5½m.—a good road—thereafter fair to Fortingal, but poor and hilly, with soft surface, up Glen Lyon. Many travel *via* Fearnan and join this road at 9¼m.—2½m. longer.

Gradients.—At 10 and 10½m. 1/19; 10¾m. 1/18; 13¼m. 1/19.

Measurements.

Aberfeldy,* Square.			
5½	Coshieville,* Inn.		
8½	3	Fortingal.*	
20	14½	11½	Bridge of Balgie.

Principal Objects of Interest.—1m. Weem Rock. 4⅞m., to Comrie Castle. Fortingal; Oak, Garth Castle. Glen Lyon; M'Gregors Leap, Meggernie Castle.

Hotels or Inns at places marked *, Weem, & Innerwick.

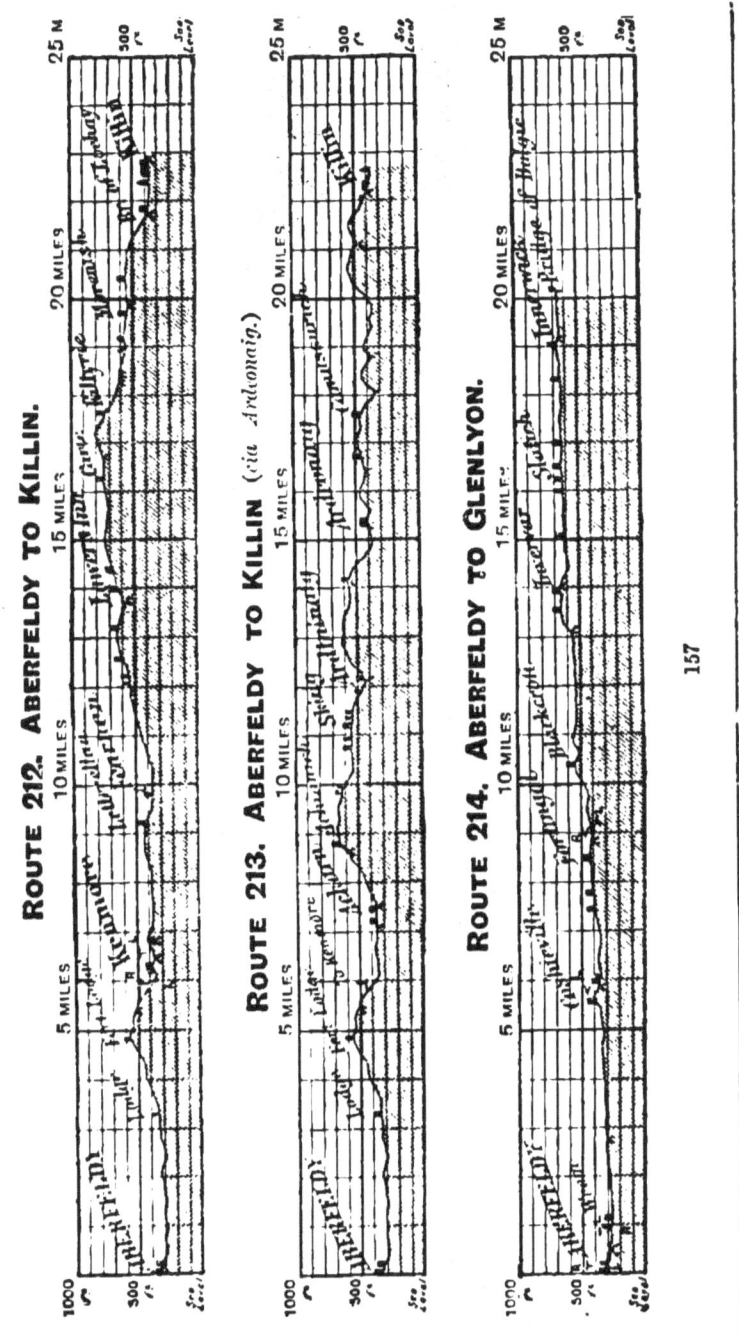

215 STRUAN TO KINLOCH RANNOCH.

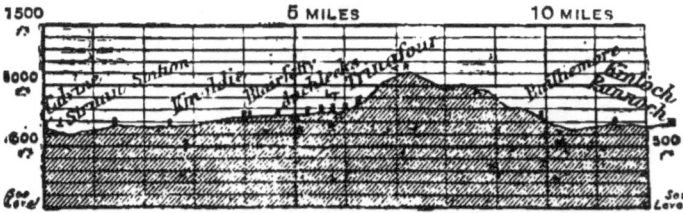

Description.—Class III. A tolerable and undulating road as far as Trinafour; thereafter rough and stony till near Kinloch Rannoch.

Gradients.—At 6½m. 1 in 12-15-11-13; 9m. 1 in 12.

Milestones.—Continuation of those near Kinloch Rannoch.

Measurements.—Struan Station.*
            6   Trinafour.
          12¾ 6¾ Kinloch Rannoch,* Hotel.

Principal Objects of Interest.—Fine view of Strath Tummel and Schichallion.

216 KINLOCH RANNOCH TO ABERFELDY.

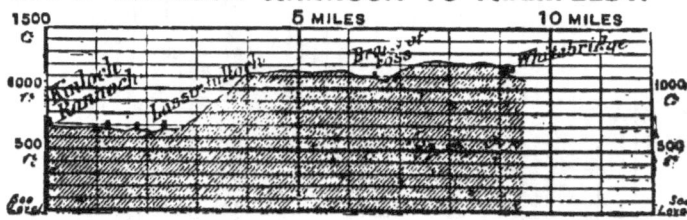

Description.—Class III. A very rough road nearly the whole way to Whitebridge; thereafter as Route 197.

Gradients.—From 2½m. to 4m. 1 in 17-24-12-16-15-16.

Milestones.—Measured from Kinloch Rannoch,—correct.

Measurements.—Kinloch Rannoch,* Hotel.
           9¼   Whitebridge.
         12¼ 3¾ Coshieville.*
         18   8¾ 5¼ Aberfeldy,* Square.

Principal Objects of Interest.—The road crosses the shoulder of Schichallion, and fine views are obtained from the great altitude.

Hotels or Inns at places marked *.

GLAMIS TO NEWTYLE. 217

Description.—Class III. A good undulating road.
Measurements.—Glamis.*
        6¾ Newtyle.*
Principal Objects of Interest.—Kinpurney Tower is on the hilltop above Newtyle.

FETTERCAIRN TO STONEHAVEN. 218

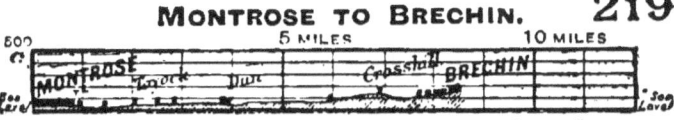

For continuation from Cockcity to Stonehaven; see Route 202.

Description.—Class II. A good road.
Milestones.—From Stonehaven County Buildings.
Measurements.—Fettercairn,* Town Hall.
        6 (Fordoun.*)
        16¾ ... Stonehaven,* Market Square.
Principal Objects of Interest.—1¾m. ruins Kincardine Castle.

MONTROSE TO BRECHIN. 219

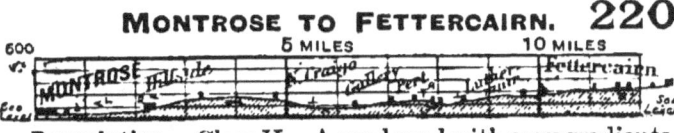

Description.—Class I. A very fine smooth road.
Milestones.—Measured from Brechin Town House.
Measurements.—Montrose,* Town House.
        8¼ Brechin,* Town House.
Principal Objects of Interest.—Brechin; see Route 202.

MONTROSE TO FETTERCAIRN. 220

Description.—Class II. A good road with easy gradients, the first 5 miles are very good.
Milestones.—Measured from Montrose, Town House.
Measurements.—Montrose,* Town House.
        8 Pert P.O.
        12¾   4¾ Fettercairn,* Town Hall.
Principal Objects of Interest.—2¼m. County Asylum. 8⅝m. Inglismaldie.

221 DUNDEE TO BLAIRGOWRIE.

Description.—Class I. Rather rough till after Lochee when the road becomes fine and smooth with easy grades to the summit, then falling rather steeply with a winding descent—Tullybaccart—to Ashley. Thereafter a fine road, but with stiff hills on each side of the River Isla.

Gradients.—At 1¼m. 1 in 25; 10½m. to 12m. 1 in 23-17-15-18-20-18; 15m. 1 in 25; 16m. 1 in 22.

Milestones.—From Dundee Town Ho. *via* Scouringburn.

Measurements.

Dundee,* Town House.				
2	Lochee,* Station.			
5¼	3¼	Muirhead.*		
14⅜	12⅜	9⅛	Coupar Angus,* Cross.	
19	17	13¾	4⅝	Blairgowrie,* Well Meadow.

Principal Objects of Interest.—1½m. Balgay Hill. 3½m. Camperdown House. COUPAR ANGUS; Abbey. BLAIRGOWRIE; Craighall.

Hotels or Inns at places marked *.

222 DUNDEE TO ALYTH.

Description.—Class II. As above to Muirhead; thereafter a hilly but easy road of good surface to Meigle, and fair to Alyth.

Gradients.—At 1¼m. 1 in 25; 14m. 1 in 25; 15¼m. 1 in 20.

Milestones.—As Route 221.

Measurements.

Dundee,* Town House.				
5¼	Muirhead.*			
11¼	6	Newtyle,* Crossroads.		
13½	8¼	2¼	Meigle.*	
17¼	12	6	3¾	Alyth,* Market.

Principal Objects of Interest.—Kinpurnie Tower is very noticeable above Newtyle. Meigle; Sculptured Stone. ALYTH; "Arches," Bamff House.

Hotels or Inns at places marked *, and Alyth Junc. Sta.

223 DUNDEE TO KIRRIEMUIR.

Description.—Class II. A hilly road of fine surface, rough about the summit, poor down Glen Ogilvie, better thereafter, but hilly with a nasty dip just before Kirriemuir.

Gradients.—At ¾m. 1/24-19-20-18; 1¾m. 1/16; 2½m. 1/23; 3m. 1/15-17; 6½m. 1/23-21; 8¼m. 1/15; 9m. 1/19; 11¼m. 1/21-15; 12½m. 1/19; 13m. 1/23; 16¼m. 1/20; 16¾m. 1/12, and 1/11.

Milestones.—From Forfar Cross, and Kirriemuir P.O.

Measurements.

Dundee,* Town House.			
6	Todhills.		
12	6	(Glamis.*)	
16⅞	10⅞	4⅞	Kirriemuir,* Town House.

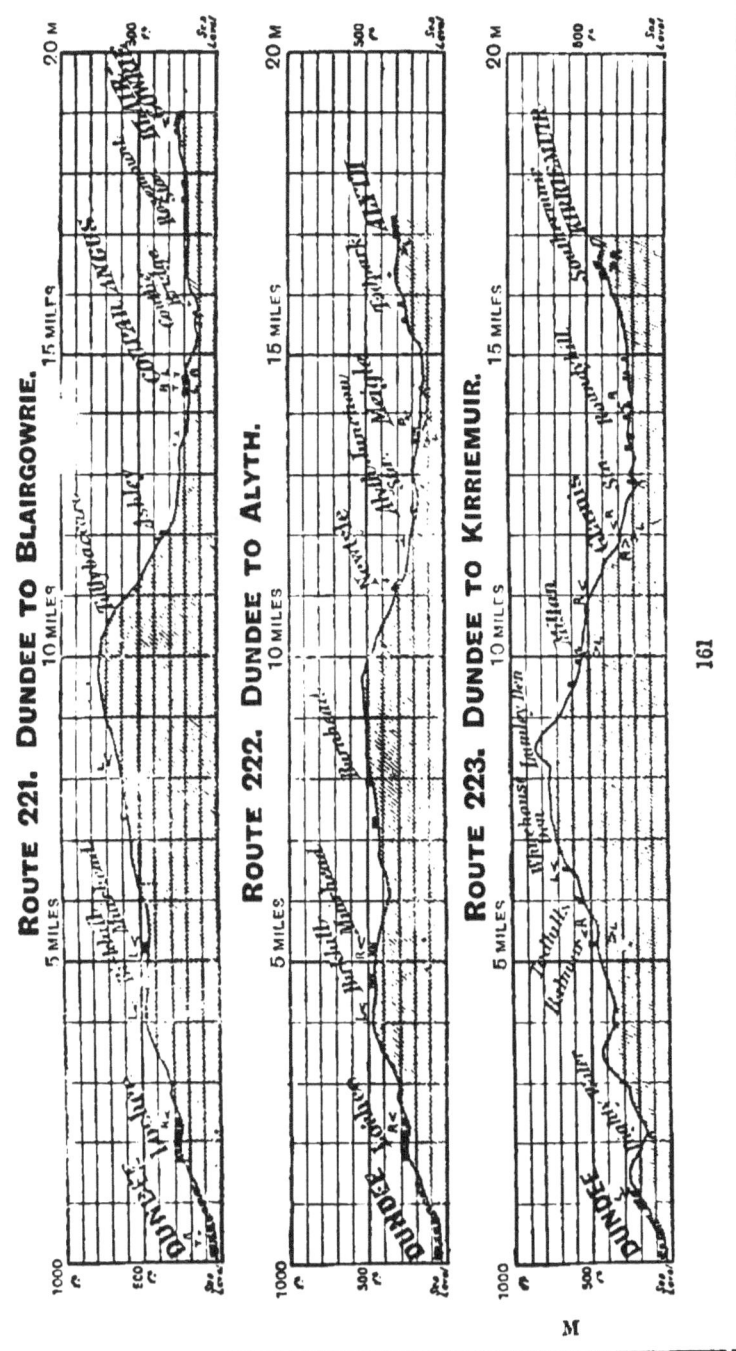

Principal Objects of Interest.—3¼m. Powrie Castle. GLAMIS; Castle. KIRRIEMUIR; "Thrums."

Hotels or Inns at places marked *, and at Glamis Station.

224 DUNDEE TO FORFAR, &c.

Description.—Class I. A hilly road, but of very good surface. Care should be taken at the hill at 6½m. The "Old" road to Brechin—(Class III.)—is very hilly with only tolerable surface.

Gradients.—To 6½m., as Route 223. 7¼m. 1 in 24-22. 9½m. 1 in 20-21-24; 11¼m. 1 in 16; 13½m. 1 in 19. To Brechin mostly 1 in 20, but at 21½m. 1 in 15.

Milestones.—Measured from Forfar Cross,—correct.

Measurements.

Dundee,* Town House.				
6	Todhills.			
14⅝	8⅝	Forfar,* Town Hall.		
19	13	4⅜	Aberlemno P.O.	
25⅜	19⅜	11	6⅜	Brechin,* Town House.

Principal Objects of Interest.—2m. Bleachfields. 3¼m. Powrie Castle. 16¼m. Restenneth Priory. Aberlemno; Sculptured Stones. BRECHIN; as Route 202.

Hotels or Inns at places marked *.

225 DUNDEE TO ABERDEEN.

Description.—Class I. Except near Dundee this is a magnificent road with very fine surface throughout. The undulations are easy to Arbroath; thence nearly all the way to Aberdeen the hills are longer but well engineered.

Gradients.—At 25½m. 1 in 23; 27¼m. 1 in 25; 42½m. 1 in 22; 51m. 1 in 23-21. The Hills at Inverkeilor and Stonehaven should be descended carefully.

Milestones.—Measured *Northwards* from Dundee Town House, Arbroath Cross, Montrose Town House, and North-Water Bridge; *Southwards* from Aberdeen Cross and Stonehaven Bridge.

Measurements.

Dundee,* Town House.							
8⅛	Woodhill,* Inn.						
16⅞	8¾	Arbroath,* Town Hall.					
22½	14⅜	5⅝	Inverkeilor.*				
29½	21⅜	12⅝	7	Montrose,* Town House.			
42⅛	34	25¼	19⅝	12⅝	Bervie,* Cross.		
51¾	43⅝	34⅞	29¼	22¼	9⅝	Stonehaven,* Market Square.	
66½	58⅜	49⅝	44	37	24⅜	14¾	Aberdeen,* Market Street.

Principal Objects of Interest.—Arbroath; Abbey, Caves, St. Vigean's Church. 24½m. Lunan Bay and Redcastle. 36¾m. Den Finella, Kaim of Mathers. 50m. Dunottar Castle. 64½m. Old Bridge of Dee.

Hotels or Inns at places marked *, and at Bourtriebush. Also at (Lunan Bay), (Johnshaven), and (Muchalls).

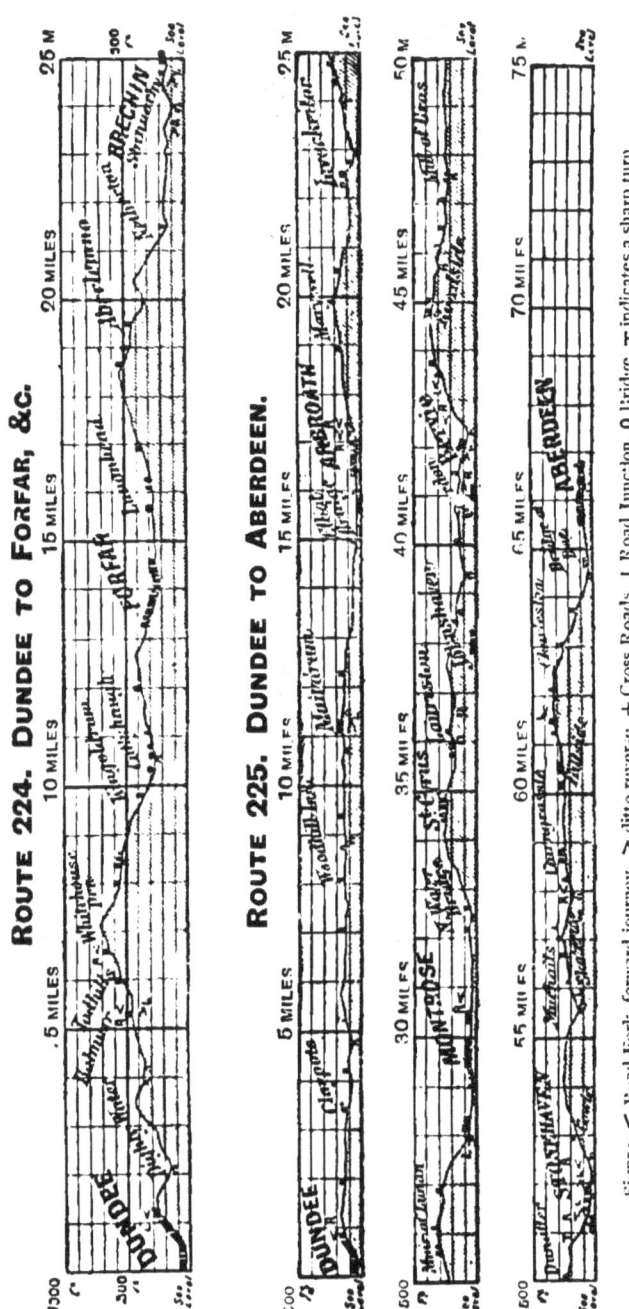

ROUTE 224. DUNDEE TO FORFAR, &C.

ROUTE 225. DUNDEE TO ABERDEEN.

Signs: < Road Fork, forward journey. > ditto reverse. + Cross Roads. ⊥ Road Junction. ∩ Bridge. ⊤ indicates a sharp turn. The directions R (right) and L (left) for the forward journey are above the Road Line, those of the reverse, below.

226 DUNDEE TO BRECHIN *via Aldbar.*

Description.—Class III. & II. A hilly and rather poor road to Aldbar Station; thereafter good surface and easy.

Gradients.—¾m. 1/19-20-22; 1¾m. 1/21-17; 5¼m. 1/19-15-22; 5½m. 1/20; 7m. 1/17; 7¾m. 1/18-22; 8½m. 1/21; 10½m. 1/18-20; 11½m. 1/19; 14¼m. 1/20; 14¾m. 1/18; 15¾m. 1/17; 20½m. 1/18. Thereafter nothing above 1/25.

Milestones.—Measured from outside Dundee; and from Brechin Institute.

Measurements.

Dundee,* Town House.		
15½	Letham.	
25½	10	Brechin,* Town House.

Principal Objects of Interest.—22½m. Aldbar Castle.

Hotels or Inns at places marked *.

227 BLAIRGOWRIE TO PITLOCHRY.

Description.—Class II. & III. The surface is good, and the grades are easy, to Bridge of Cally; but thereafter it is very hilly with tolerable surface to Kirkmichael. Thence to Pitlochry is a very bad road on the higher parts.

Gradients.—At 2m. 1/25-23; 5⅝m. 1/20; 20¼m. 1/19-14; 23m. 1/11; 24m. 1/19.

Milestones.—Measured from Dunkeld,—correct.

Measurements.

Blairgowrie,* Well Meadow.			
5¾	Bridge of Cally* Hotel.		
12⅝	7⅛	Kirkmichael.*	
25¼	19½	12⅝	Pitlochry,* Fountain.

Principal Objects of Interest.—1¾m. Craighall. 8¼m. Blackcraig Castle. Fine view descending to Pitlochry.

Hotels or Inns at places marked *, Strathloch, and Moulin.

228 BLAIRGOWRIE TO KIRRIEMUIR, &c.

Description.—Class III. Steep hills for several miles, then a fine road to Kirriemuir where there is a sharp dip; thereafter a good undulating road to Tannadice.

Gradients.—¼ & 1¼m. 1 in 14; 10¾m. 1 in 20-14 (dangerous); 13¼m. 1 in 24; 14m. 1 in 13; 14⅜m. 1 in 10.

Milestones.—Measured from Kirriemuir P.O.

Measurements.

Blairgowrie,* Well Meadow.			
(5¼	Alyth,* Market).		
14¼	10	Kirriemuir,* Town House.	
22¼	18	8	Tannadice* Inn.

Principal Objects of Interest.—2m. Rattray Cas. 7⅝m. Airlie Cas., 1⅞m. to N. KIRRIEMUIR; "Thrums."

Hotels or Inns at places marked *.

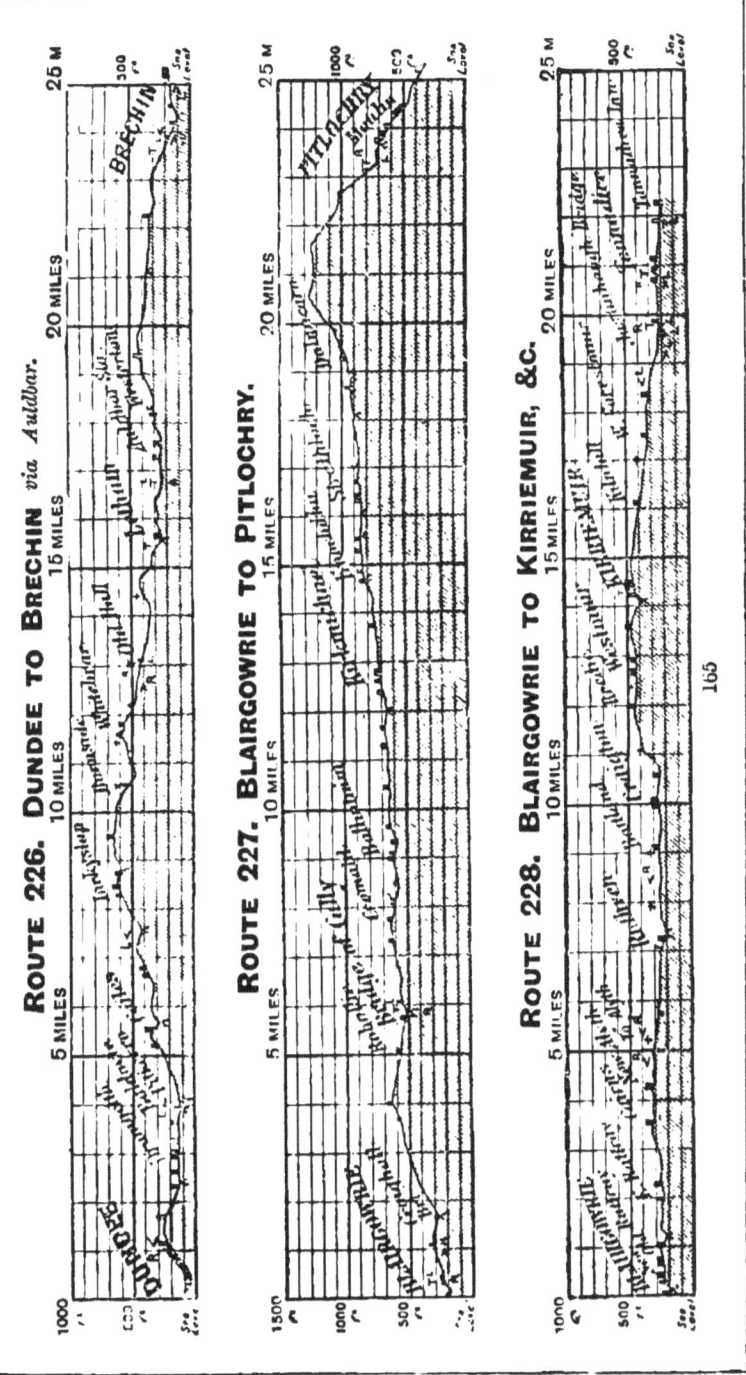

229 COUPAR ANGUS TO DUNKELD.

Description.—Class III. This is a cross country road, fair surface but hilly to Meikleour, good to Dunkeld, but hilly after Caputh.

Gradients.—½m. 1 in 25; 13¼m. 1 in 19; 14¼m. 1 in 25.

Milestones.—Measured from Dunkeld.

Measurements.
Coupar Angus,* Cross.
5   Meikleour.*
10½   5¼   Caputh.*
14¾   9¾   4¾   Dunkeld,* High Street.

Principal Objects of Interest.—4½m. The Hedges. 13¾m. Quarries.

Hotels or Inns at places marked *.

230 KIRRIEMUIR TO GLENISLA, &c.

Description.—Class III. The road is very hilly but with fair surface to Glenisla; thereafter fair to Brewlands Bridge when the road gradually becomes soft and loose, but improves on joining the Glenshee road.

Gradients.—3½m. 1 in 22; 4m. 1 in 21; 4¾m. 1 in 23; 4½m. 1 in 20-17; 6½m. 1 in 22; 6¾m. 1 in 20; 11m. 1 in 17; 11½m. 1 in 18; 12m. 1 in 17-23; 19m. 1 in 25.

Milestones.—To Glenisla, measured from Kirriemuir P.O.,—correct.

Measurements.
Kirriemuir,* Town House.
4   Kingoldrum.
9¾   5¾   Dykend.
13   9   3¼   Glenisla * Hotel.
19¾ 15¾ 9¾   6¾   Lair.
24¾ 20¾ 14¾ 11¾ 5   Spital of Glenshee* Hotel.

Hotels or Inns at places marked *.

231 KIRRIEMUIR TO CLOVA, &c.

Description.—Class III. After the very steep hill in Kirriemuir, the road is level for a short distance; thereafter is hilly almost the whole way to Clova, though with very good surface. To Inchmill; branching off at Dykehead, is a very hilly road, with fair surface.

Gradients.—At ¼m. 1 in 12; 3¾m. 1 in 14; 4¾m. 1 in 15; 7m. 1 in 16; 10½m. 1 in 22; 12m. 1 in 20; 14m. 1 in 22.

Milestones.—Measured from Forfar Cross.

Measurements.
Kirriemuir,* Town House.
5   Dykehead.
14½ 9½   Clova.*
10½ 5½   Inchmill* Inn (Glenprosen).

Principal Objects of Interest.—3½m Cortachy Castle.

Hotels or Inns at places marked *.

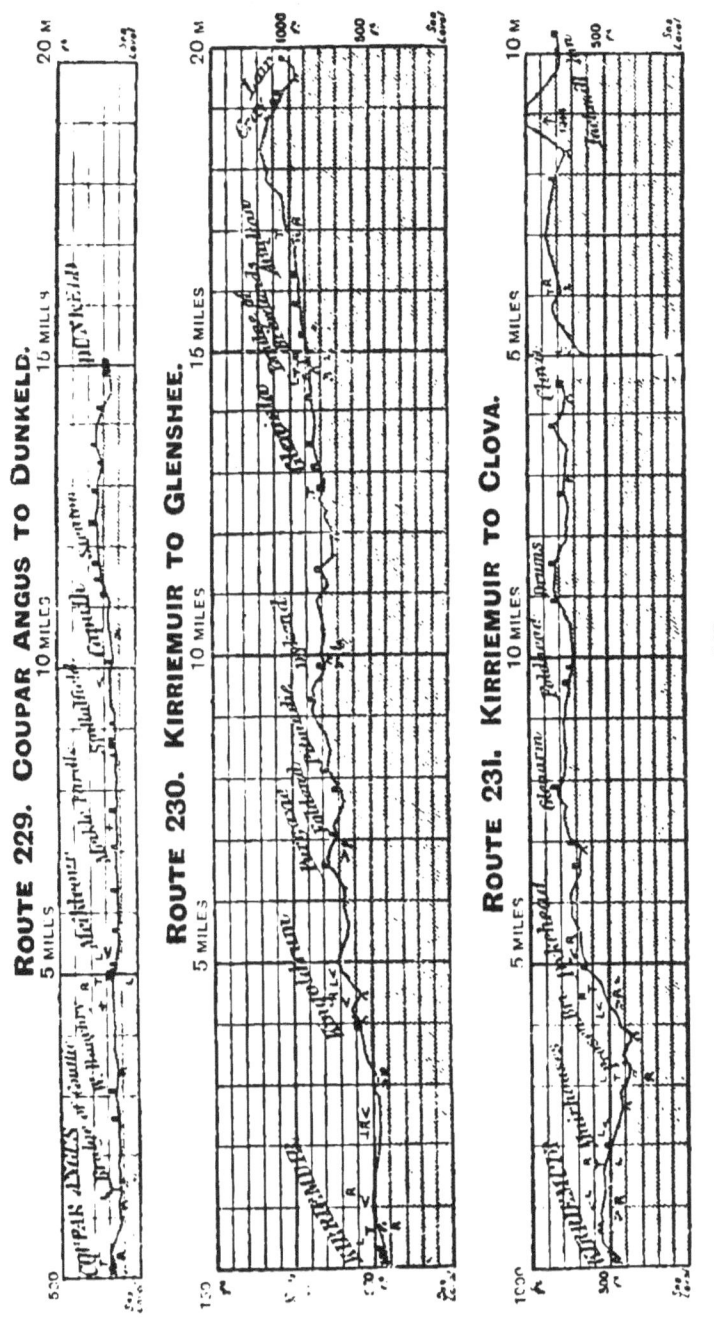

232 FORFAR TO MONTROSE.

Description.—Class II. A very fair road with only slight hills, and nearing Montrose almost level.

Gradients.—Nothing above 1 in 25.

Measurements.

Forfar,* Town Hall.
9⅜ Crossgates.
17⅜ 8 Montrose,* Town House.

Principal Objects of Interest.—1¾m. Restenneth Priory.

Hotels or Inns at places marked *.

---

233 FORFAR TO CARNOUSTIE.

Description.—Class III. The road has a fair surface, but is very hilly. Care should be taken at Craichie Hill.

Gradients.—At 1m. 1 in 24-20; 4m. 1 in 16-12; 4¾m. 1 in 24-16; 9¼m. 1 in 19; 10½m. 1 in 22; 11¾m. 1 in 16; 12m. 1 in 16.

Measurements.

Forfar,* Town Hall.
4 Craichie.
13½ 9½ Carnoustie,* P.O.

Principal Objects of Interest.—10¼m. Panmure House. The Panmure Monument is noticeable on the hilltop.

Hotels or Inns at places marked *.

---

234 ARBROATH TO BRECHIN.

Description.—Class I. & II. A very fine smooth road to Friockheim; thereafter good to Brechin.

Gradients.—14m. 1 in 24.

Milestones.—Measured from Forfar Cross and reckoned on from these after Friockheim.

Measurements.

Arbroath,* Town Hall.
6⅝ Friockheim * Station.
9¼ 2⅝ Crossgates.
14⅝ 7¾ 5⅜ Brechin,* Town House.

Principal Objects of Interest.—12¼m. Kinnaird Castle.

Hotels or Inns at places marked *.

---

235 ARBROATH TO KIRRIEMUIR.

Description.—Class I. A magnificent road of very fine surface, with easy undulations, to Forfar; thereafter very good, but with several stiff hills. Care must be taken at the sharp dip before Kirriemuir.

Gradients.—At 18½m. 1 in 19-18; 20¾m. 1 in 20; 20⅜m. 1 in 12 and 1 in 11.

Milestones.—Measured from Forfar Cross,—correct.

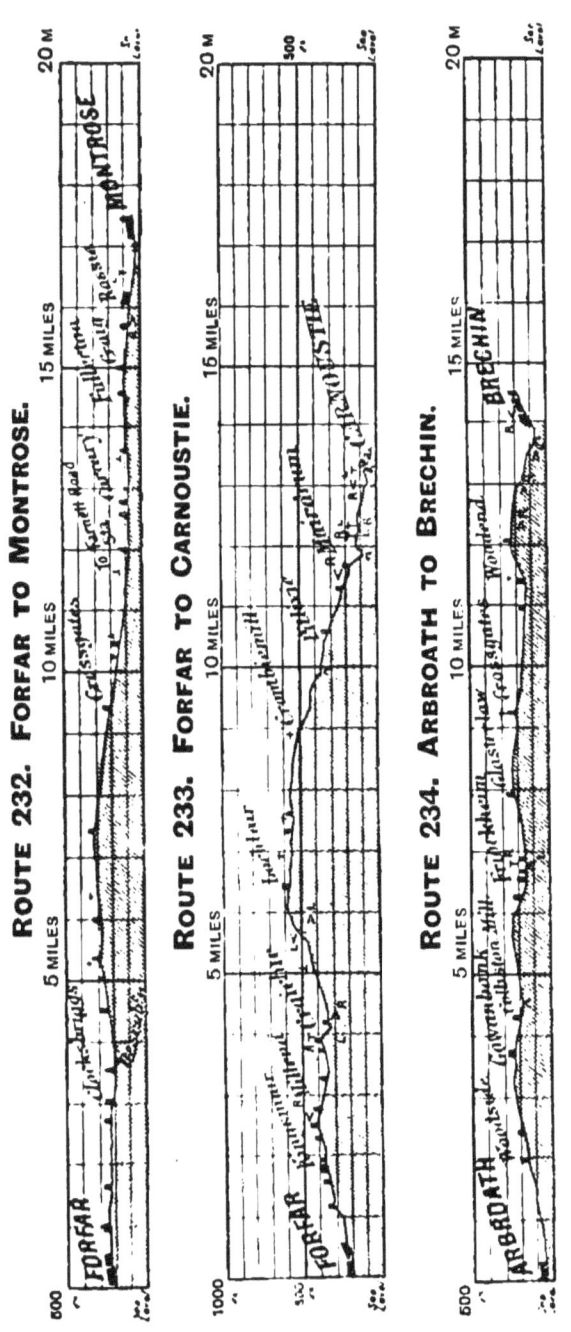

Measurements.

Arbroath,* Town Hall.				
6⅝	Friockheim * Station.			
10	3⅜	Aldbar Station.		
15¼	8⅝	5¼	Forfar,* Town Hall.	
21	14⅜	11	5¾	Kirriemuir,* Town House.

Principal Objects of Interest.—8¼m. Guthrie Castle. FORFAR; Restenneth Priory. KIRRIEMUIR; "Thrums."

Hotels or Inns at places marked *.

236 BRECHIN TO LOCHLEE.

Description.—Class II. & III. A fine but undulating road of very good surface to Gannochy Bridge; thereafter a hilly road with poor surface, and soft in parts.

Measurements.

Brechin,* Town House.				
6	Edzell,* Hotel.			
14¼	8¼	Millden Bridge.		
17	11	2¾	Tarfside.	
21¾	15¾	7½	4¾	Lochlee Church.

Principal Objects of Interest.—2¾m. Battledykes. Edzell; Castle. 8½m. "St. Andrews Tower." Lochlee; Queen's Well. Very fine scenery.

Hotels or Inns at places marked *.

237 EDZELL TO BANCHORY.

Description.—Class II. & III. A fine undulating road to Fettercairn; thereafter poor to Clattering Brig, when the road becomes precipitously steep, with grass and loose stones over the Cairn o' Mount to Bridge of Dye. Thence the road is better, and after Strachan is good.

Gradients.—At 7m. 1 in 18; 8¼ to 10¼m. 1 in 9-8-10-14-8-11; 10¼ to 12¾m. 1 in 11-12-9-17-9-18-20-14-7; 13m. 1 in 10; 13½m. 1 in 25-7-12; 14m. 1 in 13-15; 15¾m. 1 in 15.

Milestones.—Measured from Edzell—*via* Whitestone.

Measurements.

Edzell,* Hotel.			
4⅝	Fettercairn,* Town House.		
18⅞	14¼	Strachan.	
22	17⅜	3⅛	Banchory,* P.O.

Principal Objects of Interest.—A very dreary road over Cairn o' Mount, but very pretty near Bridge of Feugh.

Hotels or Inns at places marked *.

238 MONTROSE TO FORDOUN, &c.

Description.—Class II. & III. The surface of the road is very good to Laurencekirk; thereafter fair, but hilly; rough up Bow Glen, joining Route 237 at Clattering Brig.

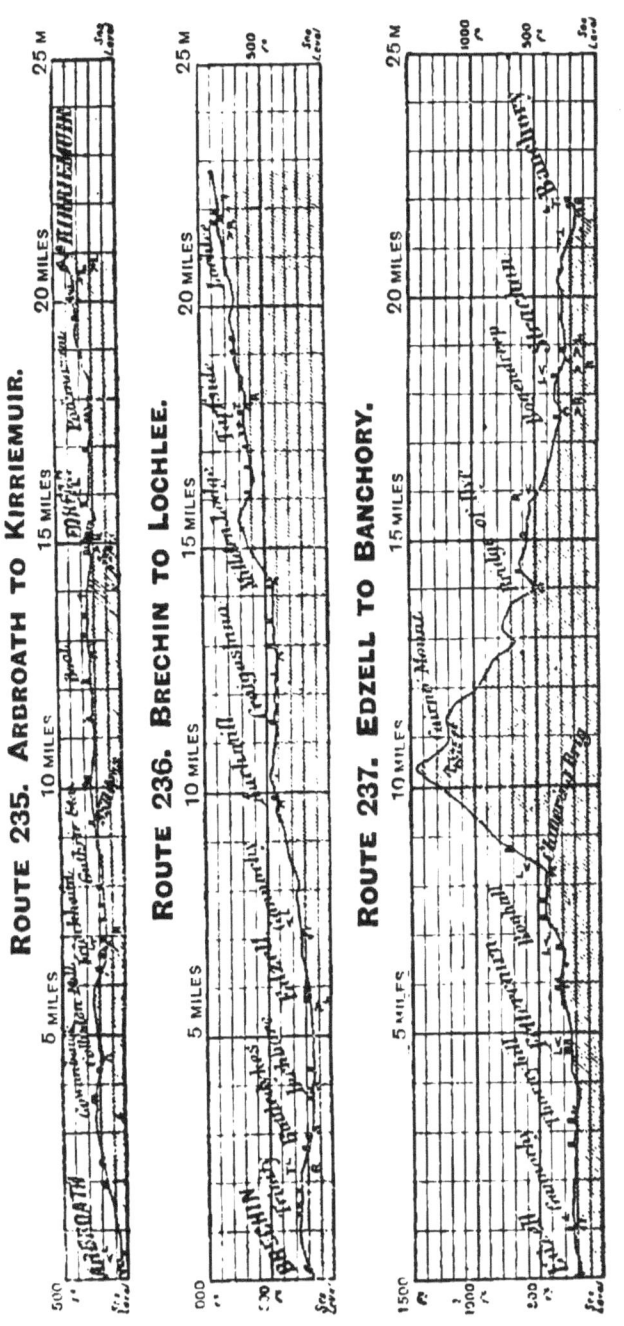

Gradients.—19½m. 1 in 14·11.

Milestones.—Measured from Montrose Town House,—correct.

Measurements.

Montrose,* Town House.				
6	Marykirk,* Cross.			
10¼	4¼	Laurencekirk,* Town Hall.		
15⅛	9⅛	4⅞	Fordoun,* (Auchinblae.*)	
23⅜	17⅜	13⅛	8¼	Fettercairn,* *via* Bow Glen.

Principal Objects of Interest.—2¼m. Hillside Asylum. Bow Glen; Drumtochty Castle. Fine scenery.

Hotels or Inns at places marked *.

239 Stonehaven to Banchory.

Description.—Class II. Except about the summit the road is of good surface, but the long hills are rather trying.

Gradients.—At 1¾m. 1 in 22; 2¾m. and 4¼m. 1 in 20; 8m. 1 in 17; 8½m. 1 in 20; 9¼m. 1 in 23.

Milestones.—Measured from commencement of road in Stonehaven.

Measurements.

Stonehaven,* Market.			
4¾	Rickarton P.O.		
10⅜	5⅝	Blairdryne.	
16⅛	11⅜	5¾	Banchory,* P.O.

Principal Objects of Interest.—A dreary road in the higher parts.

Hotels or Inns at places marked *.

240 Aberdeen to Banchory, *via Durris.*

Description.—Class II. The road has a very fine surface and no hills of any length. It is an undulating and very easy road.

Gradients.—None of any extent.

Milestones.—Measured from Aberdeen, Market Street; but after Balbridie, from Stonehaven.

Measurements.

Aberdeen,* Market Street.			
7⅜	Mill Inn.*		
13⅜	6	Durris.	
18⅞	11⅝	5¾	Banchory,* P.O.

Principal Objects of Interest.—2m. Old Bridge of Dee, scene of Skirmish. 5m. Hydropathic. 5½m. Blair's College. Very pretty scenery, especially at Bridge of Feugh.

Hotels or Inns at places marked *, and at Heathcote.

Route 238. Montrose to Fordoun, &c.

Route 239. Stonehaven to Banchory.

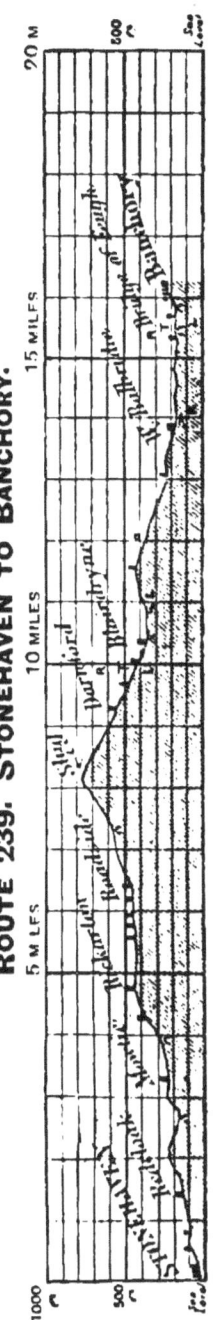

Route 240. Aberdeen to Banchory.

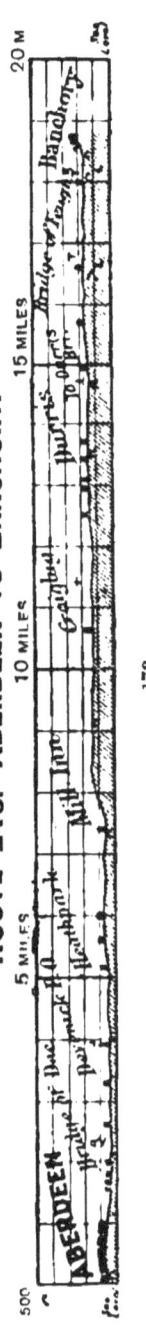

241 ABERDEEN TO BRAEMAR.

Description.—Class I. The surface at first is rather lumpy, but after passing Culter it speedily improves and is very fine to Banchory. Thence to Aboyne is more undulating, but with very fine surface, after which to Ballater, except a short piece near Cambus o' May, is almost perfect. From Ballater is very steep at first and rather stiff to Kyleacreich Inn; thereafter excepting the short hill into Braemar, the surface is splendid with hardly a perceptible slope.

Gradients.—At 40¼m. 1 in 23; 42½m. 1 in 15-20. These are the only hills above 1 in 25.

Milestones.—Measured from Aberdeen, Market Street,—correct to Banchory; thereafter from Banchory.

Measurements.

Aberdeen,* Market Street.

7⅝	Peterculter,* P.O.								
11¼	3⅝	Drumoak.							
18	10⅜	6¾	Banchory,* P.O.						
26	18⅜	14¾	8	Kincardine O' Neil,* P.O.					
30½	22⅞	19¼	12½	4½	Aboyne,* Hotel.				
35	27⅜	23¾	17	9	4½	Dinnet,* Station.			
41¾	34⅛	30½	23¾	15¾	11¼	6¾	Ballater,* Church.		
52	44⅜	40¾	34	26	21½	17	10¼	Inver * Inn.	
58¼	50⅝	47	40¼	32¼	27¾	23¼	16½	6¼	Braemar.*

Principal Objects of Interest.—Very fine scenery almost the whole way. The Banks of the Dee are well wooded on both sides. 10¼m. Drum Castle. 14½m. Crathes Castle. 24m. Potarch Bridge. Aboyne; Aboyne Castle, Glen Tanner. 37⅜m. to N., Vat Burn. Ballater; Glen Muick, Pananich Well. 47¾m. Abergeldie Castle. 49¼m. Balmoral Castle and Crathie Church. 55½m. to Invercauld House. 57⅝m. Braemar Castle. Braemar; Linn of Corriemulzie, Linn o' Dee, Linn of Quoich, Mar Lodge, Lion's Face.

Hotels or Inns at places marked *, and at Bieldside, Bridge of Canny, Potarch Bridge, and Kyleacreich.

Route 241. Aberdeen to Braemar.

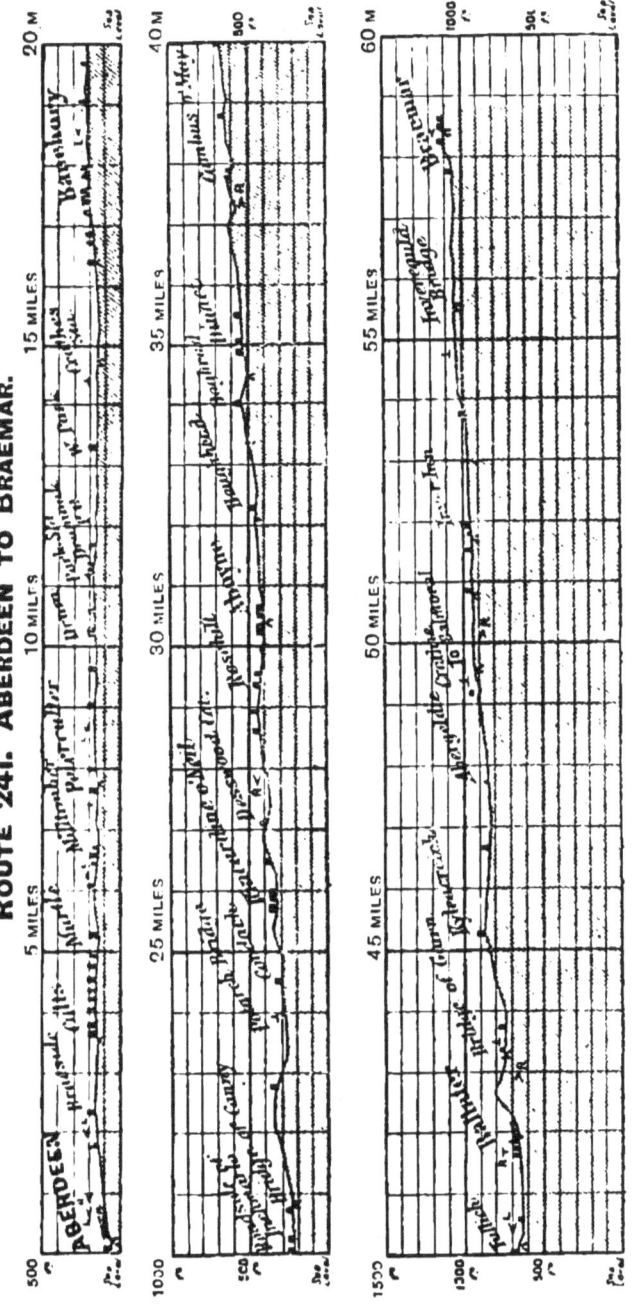

242 ABERDEEN TO LUMPHANAN.

Description.—Class II. From Aberdeen is lumpy at first, but the road soon improves, and is very fair, though undulating, the rest of the way. To Banchory turn off at 17⅝m.

Gradients.—All very easy; at 23½m. 1 in 25.

Milestones.—Start from some point ½m. west of Market Street,—correct.

Measurements.

Aberdeen,* Market Street.						
5½	Countesswells.					
10¼	4¾	Garlogie Bridge.				
14¼	8¾	4	Wicker* Inn.			
(20¼	14¾	10	6	Banchory,* P.O.).		
22¼	16¾	12	8	7¾	Torphins.*	
25¼	19¾	15	11	10¾	3	Lumphanan.

Route 269 is joined at 26¼m.

Principal Objects of Interest.—15¾m. Montrose Trench.

Hotels or Inns at places marked *.

243 ABERDEEN TO TARLAND, &c.

Description.—Class II. From Aberdeen, the road is lumpy at first but soon improves, and is very fair to Echt, when it becomes hilly and the surface degenerates. Nearing Tarland it improves, but soon becomes soft and rough, till it joins the Aberdeen-Braemar road near Cambus o' May. Thence as Route 241.

Gradients.—At 15m. 1 in 24; 18½m. 1 in 25; 19¼m. 1 in 24; 21¼m. 1 in 26; 22¼m. to 23¼m. 1 in 18-21-15-24; 27½m. 1 in 17; 28¾m. 1 in 22; 29¼m. 1 in 25; 31m. 1 in 19.

Milestones.—Measured from a point ½m. West of Market Street,—correct.

Measurements.

Aberdeen,* Market Street.					
10¼	Garlogie Bridge.				
13	2¾	Echt.			
24⅞	14⅝	11⅞	Crossroads.*		
31¼	21	18¼	6⅜	Tarland.*	
42⅛	31⅞	29⅛	17¼	10⅞	Ballater,* Church.

Principal Objects of Interest.—15m. Midmar Castle 36⅝m. "The Vat." Ballater; as Route 241.

Hotels or Inns at places marked *.

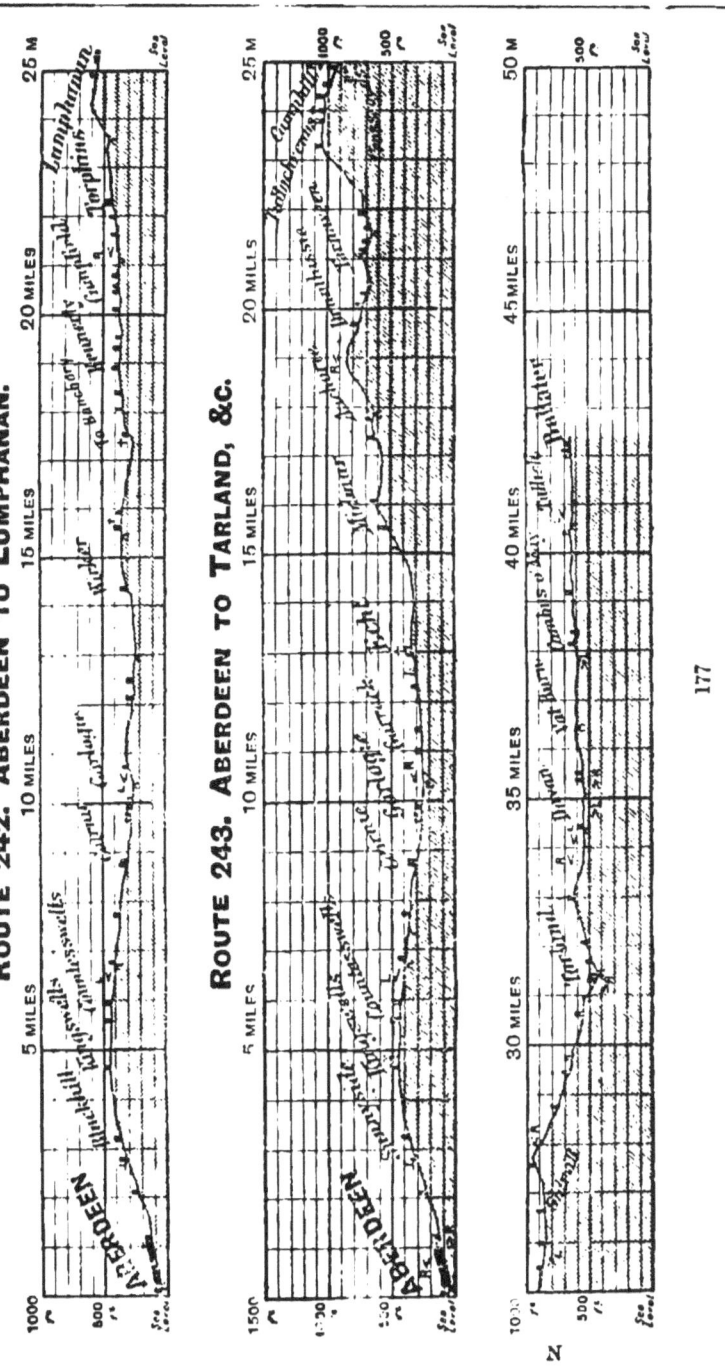

244 ABERDEEN TO STRATHDON.

Description.—Class I. to Alford, thereafter Class II. The road is rough at first through Aberdeen, but soon improves, and is a very fine undulating highway with splendid surface to Alford. Thereafter the road is level with fine surface to Mossat, but then becomes undulating with several stiff hills to Bellabeg, after which—still undulating—it rather degenerates in quality.

Gradients.—At 18¾m. 1 in 18; 19¾m. 1 in 23; 21¾m. 1 in 24; 26¾m. 1 in 25; 36¼m. 1 in 15-25; 37¼m. 1 in 22; 51¾m. 1 in 24-25.

Milestones.—Measured backwards from the Old milestones to Skene, thus starting from a point ½m. west of Market Street,—correct to Bridge of Bucket, where they follow an older road. After Bellabeg,—correct.

Measurements.

Aberdeen,* Market Street.							
8½	Skene.*						
12½	4	Waterton of Echt.*					
20½	12	8	Tillyfourie.				
25¾	17¼	13¼	5¼	Alford,* Hotel.			
35	26½	22½	14½	9¼	Kildrummy Inn.*		
45	36½	32½	24½	19¼	10	Strathdon (Bellabeg).	
53½	45	41	33	27¾	18½	8½	Cockbridge Inn,* (Corgarff).

Principal Objects of Interest.—12½m. Dunecht. Alford; Scene of Skirmish, 1645. 35½m. Kildrummy Castle, ruins. 40½m. Glenbucket Castle, ruins. 44¼m. Colquhonny Castle. 45¼m. Mote of Invernochty. The scenery in many parts of Strathdon is very fine, especially between Glenkindie and Lonach.

Hotels or Inns at places marked *, and at Alford Bridge, Glenkindie, Colquhonny, and Lonach.

245 ABERDEEN TO ELGIN.

Description.—Class I. Until Auchmull is passed the road is very much cut up with heavy traffic; thereafter there is a magnificent surface over the slopes leading to Kintore. Thence to Pitmachie Inn the road is almost level and in splendid condition, after which there is the long, steady, but almost imperceptible ascent of the Foudland Hills with a similar, but slightly steeper descent, to Huntly. To Keith the surface is very good, but the long hills are

ROUTE 244. ABERDEEN TO STRATHDON.

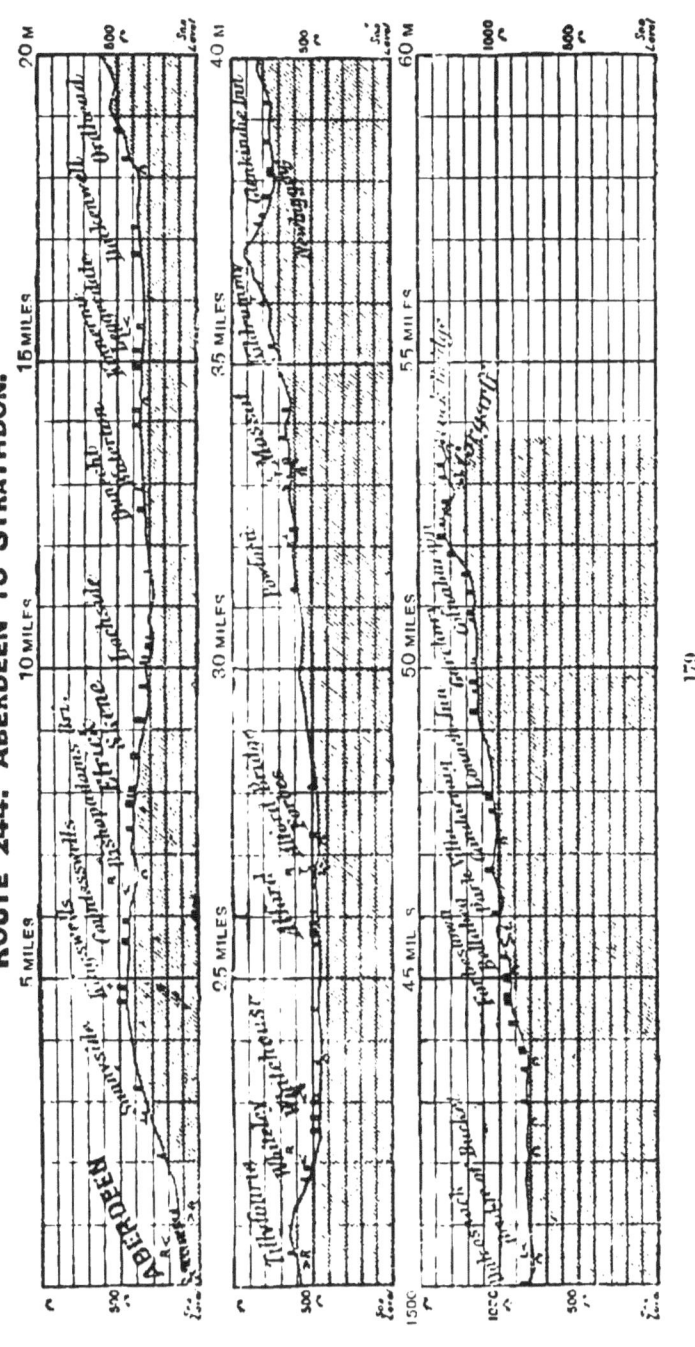

a little trying, though they are not very steep. From Keith to Fochabers is very similar; thereafter to Elgin is a smooth and almost level road. Route 268—3m. longer—is often followed between Pitcaple and Huntly. It runs close to the Railway and does not rise so high as this route.

Gradients.—At 6¾m. 1 in 23; 33m. 1 in 26; 42½m. 1 in 23-25; 43½m. 1 in 23; 49½m. 1 in 27-24; 50m. 1 in 25; 56½m. 1 in 23-19-24.

Milestones.—Measured from a point nearly ½m. from Market Street,—correct to Colpy, whence a new set continues to Huntly. A third set is between Huntly and Keith, and a fourth between Keith and Fochabers, where those measured from Elgin Cross are joined.

Measurements.

Aberdeen,* Market Street.									
2	Woodside.*								
9	7	Blackburn * Inn.							
13	11	4	Kintore,* Station.						
16½	14½	7½	3½	Inverurie,* Square.					
28¾	26¾	19¾	15¾	12¼	Colpy P.O.				
39	37	30	26	22½	10¼	Huntly,* Square.			
49⅝	47⅝	40⅝	36⅝	33⅛	20⅞	10⅝	Keith.*		
57½	55½	48½	44½	41	28¾	18½	7⅞	Fochabers,* Hotel.	
66¼	64¼	59¼	53¼	49¾	37½	27¼	16⅝	8¾	Elgin,* Cross.

Principal Objects of Interest.—Bennachie is very noticeable about Inverurie. 18¼m. Battlefield of Harlaw 1411, to N. 21¼m. Pitcaple Castle. FOCHABERS; Gordon Castle. ELGIN; Cathedral.

Hotels or Inns at places marked *, and at Auchmull, 4-mile house, Inveramsay, Pitcaple, Pitmachie, Fife-Keith.

---

246 ABERDEEN TO BANFF.

Description.—Class I. As above to Auchmull; thereafter to Old Meldrum, a very good and undulating road. The next section to Turriff is rough till nearing Fyvie, when the road becomes level with magnificent surface to Turriff Station, at which care should be taken at the sharp turn. There is a steep hill up to, and past Turriff, after which the road is undulating, with splendid surface.

Gradients.—At 24½m. 1 in 21; 34½ & 35m. 1 in 20; 39½m. 1 in 22 and 21.

Milestones.—Measured from Aberdeen, as Route 245,—correct to Turriff; thence from Banff Bridge.

ROUTE 245. ABERDEEN TO ELGIN.

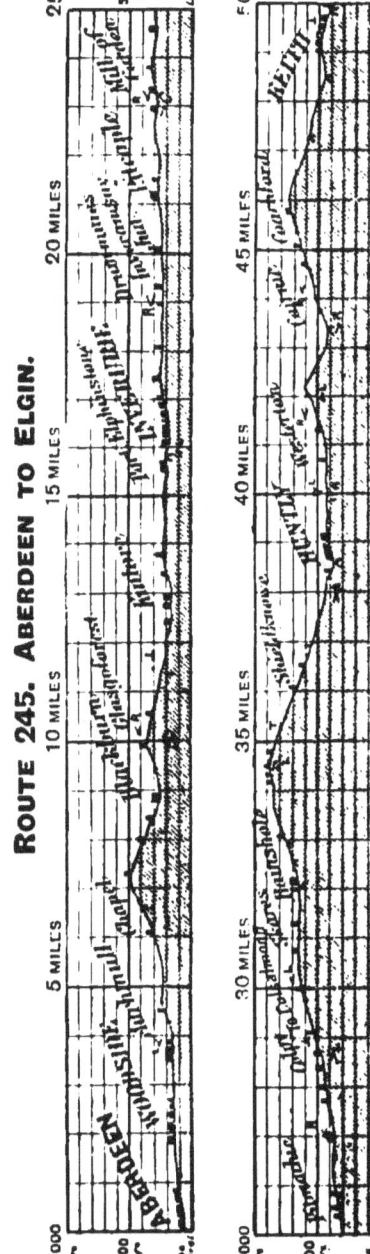

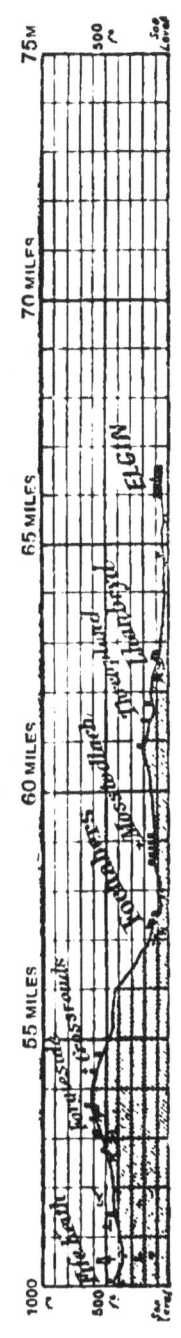

Signs: < Road Fork, forward journey, > ditto reverse, + Cross Roads, ⊥ Road Junction, ∩ Bridge, ⊤ indicates a sharp turn. The directions R (right) and L (left) for the forward journey are above the Road Line, those of the reverse, below.

181

Measurements.

Aberdeen,* Market Street.
2 Woodside.*
6½ 4½ Dyce.
10⅜ 8⅜ 4⅜ New Machar Inn.*
18 16 11½ 7⅝ Old Meldrum,* Square.
26¾ 24¾ 20¼ 15⅜ 8¾ Fyvie,* Station.
34⅝ 32⅝ 28⅛ 23¾ 16⅝ 7⅞ Turriff,* High Street.
46 44 39½ 35⅝ 28 19¼ 11⅜ Banff,* Town Hall.

Principal Objects of Interest.—Fyvie; Castle. Turriff; Cross, Old Church ruins. BANFF; Duff House, Museum, Castle, Bridge of Alvah.

Hotels or Inns at places marked *, and at Blackbog.

247 ABERDEEN TO METHLICK.

Description.—Class II. Lumpy to Bridge of Don; thereafter the road is very fair, but undulating, the last section being through the grounds of Haddo House.

Gradients.—At 20½m. 1 in 23.

Milestones.—Measured from a point more than ½m. from Market Street,—correct.

Measurements.

Aberdeen,* Market Street.
2⅜ Bridge of Don.
8¼ 6⅛ Whitecairns.
14⅜ 12⅝ 6¼ Pitmedden.
21¾ 19⅝ 13½ 7¼ Methlick,* Church.

Principal Objects of Interest.—2⅜m. Brig o' Balgownie to W. 19¾m. Haddo House.

Hotels or Inns at places marked *, and at (Udny), and (Tarves).

248 NEWBURGH TO CULSALMOND, &c.

Description.—Class II. A fair cross country road, rather rough between Pitmedden and Old Meldrum; thereafter good surface to beyond Culsalmond, where join Route 245.

Gradients.—At 13m. 1 in 19.

Milestones.—After Old Meldrum, measured from Aberdeen; as Route 246.

Measurements.

Newburgh,* Cross.
7 Pitmedden.
12¾ 5¾ Old Meldrum,* Square.
23¾ 16¾ 11 Culsalmond School.
34¼ 27¼ 21½ 10½ Huntly,* Square.

Hotels or Inns at places marked *.

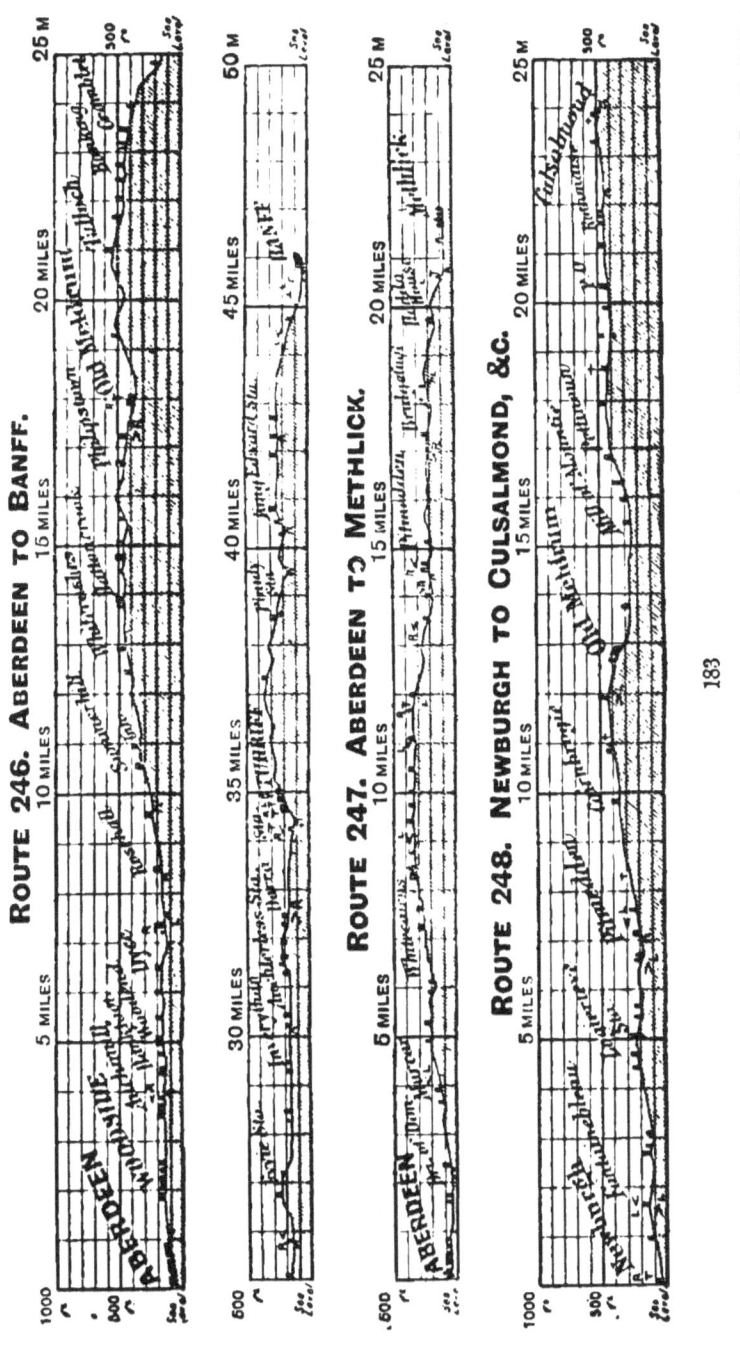

249 Aberdeen to Peterhead, &c.

Description.—Class I. A very undulating road. The surface is lumpy for a short distance, but after Bridge of Don it is very fine till within a few miles of Peterhead, when it becomes very rough owing to the Granite Quarries traffic. From Peterhead to Fraserburgh the road is very good.

Gradients.—At 17½m. 1 in 25; 25m. 1 in 23.

Milestones.—Measured from Aberdeen suburbs,—correct to Ellon, where another set is joined continuing to Peterhead; thereafter from Peterhead, correct to Lonmay.

Measurements.

Aberdeen,* Market Street.							
9⅜	Menzie Inn.*						
16⅜	7	Ellon,* Square.					
20¾	11⅜	4⅜	Birness, P.O.				
30½	21⅛	14⅛	9¾	Sterling.			
33¾	24⅜	17⅜	13	3¼	Peterhead,* Town Hall.		
43	33⅝	26⅝	22¼	12½	9¼	Crimond.	
51½	42⅛	35⅛	30¾	21	17¾	8½	Fraserburgh,* Cross.

Principal Objects of Interest.—2¼m. Brig o' Balgownie. Fine cliff scenery near Peterhead. 29½m. Bullers of Buchan.

Hotels or Inns at places marked *, (Port Errol), & Rathen.

250 Aberdeen to Fraserburgh.

Description.—Class I. As above to Birness; thereafter a magnificent road with splendid surface, but somewhat rough between Mintlaw and New Leeds.

Gradients.—Nothing above 1 in 25.

Milestones.—Measured from Aberdeen suburbs,—correct.

Measurements.

Aberdeen,* Market Street.			
16⅜	Ellon,* Square.		
30	13⅝	Mintlaw.*	
42½	26⅛	12½	Fraserburgh,* Cross.

Principal Objects of Interest.—As above to Birness. Mormond Hill is very prominent after Mintlaw.

Hotels or Inns where marked *, Mintlaw Sta., & Rathen.

251 Inverurie to Forgue.

Description.—Class II. The surface is fair, but the road is somewhat hilly nearing Forgue.

Gradients.—At 10½m. 1 in 26.

Milestones.—Measured from Inverurie Square.

Measurements.

Inverurie,* Square.			
10	Rothie* Inn.		
20½	10½	Forgue.	
26⅜	16⅜	5⅞	Aberchirder.*

Hotels or Inns where marked*, Badenscoth, & (Bogniebrae).

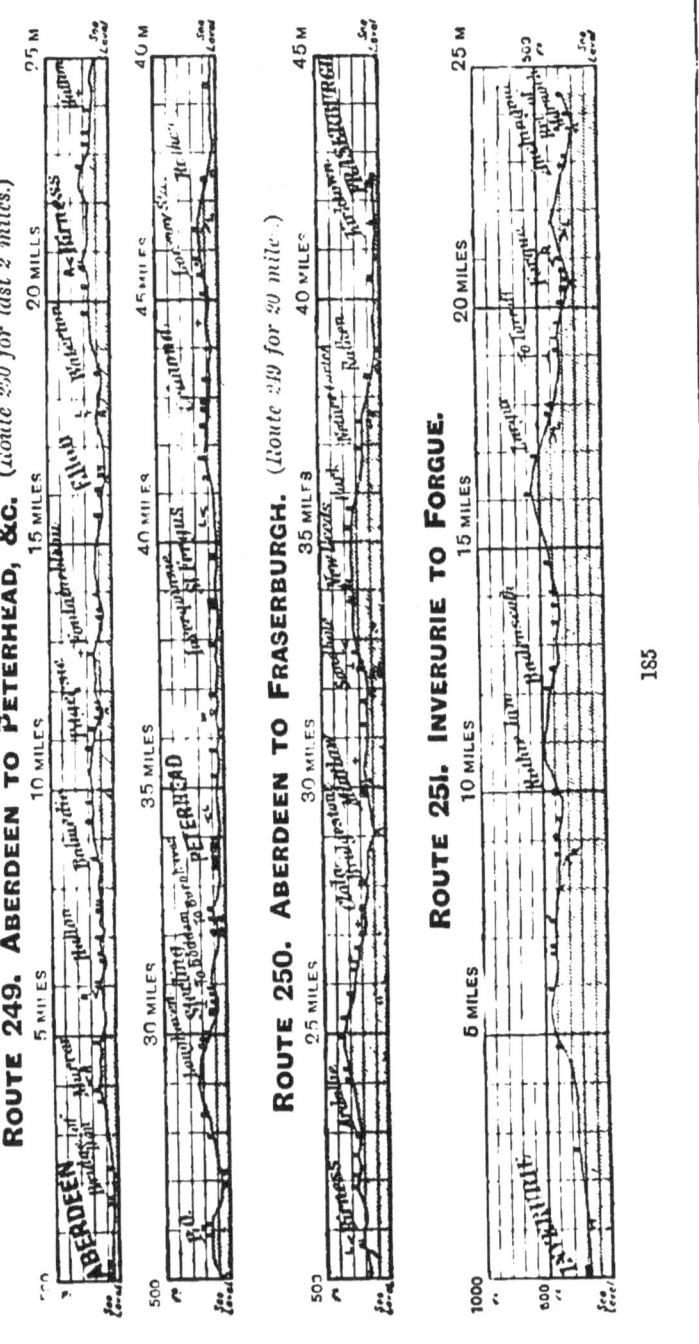

252 STONEHAVEN TO MILL INN.

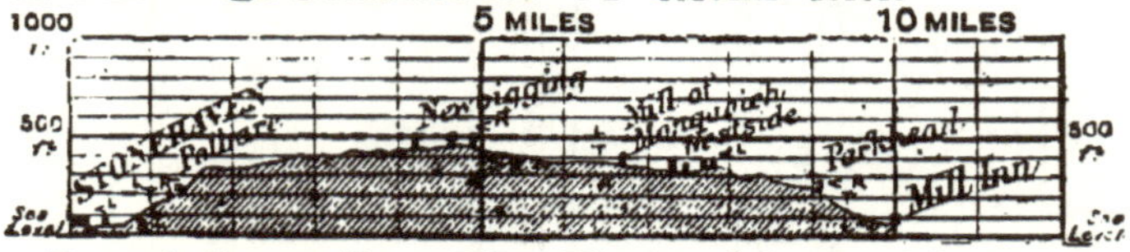

Description.—Class III. The road has a fair surface but is very steep at both ends.

Gradients.—At 1m. 1 in 21-12-14; 9¾m. 1 in 24-14.

Measurements.—Stonehaven,* Market Square.
10 Mill Inn.*

---

253 BALLATER TO BALMORAL.

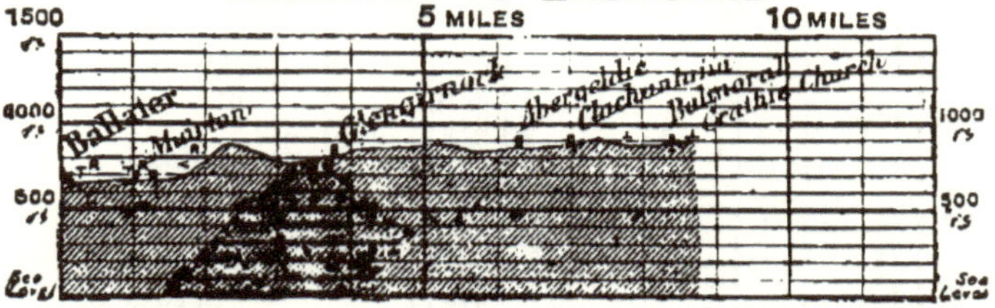

Description.—Class III. A fair road at first but it soon becomes very steep and soft, improving again after Abergeldie. Route 241 is the direct road.

Gradients.—At 2m. 1 in 16.

Measurements.—Ballater,* Church.
3⅞ Glengirnock.
8⅝ 4¾ Crathie Church.
17⅝ 13¾ 9¼ Braemar.*

Principal Objects of Interest.—1¾m. Knock Castle ruin. 6¼m. Abergeldie Castle. 8¾m. Balmoral Castle.

---

254 BRAEMAR TO INVEREY, &c.

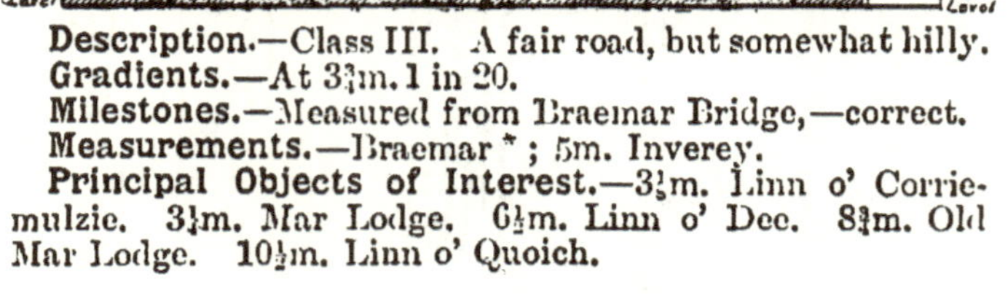

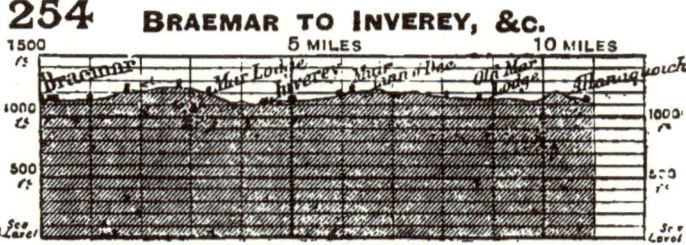

Description.—Class III. A fair road, but somewhat hilly.

Gradients.—At 3¾m. 1 in 20.

Milestones.—Measured from Braemar Bridge,—correct.

Measurements.—Braemar*; 5m. Inverey.

Principal Objects of Interest.—3⅛m. Linn o' Corriemulzie. 3¼m. Mar Lodge. 6½m. Linn o' Dee. 8¾m. Old Mar Lodge. 10½m. Linn o' Quoich.

INVERURIE TO ALFORD. 255

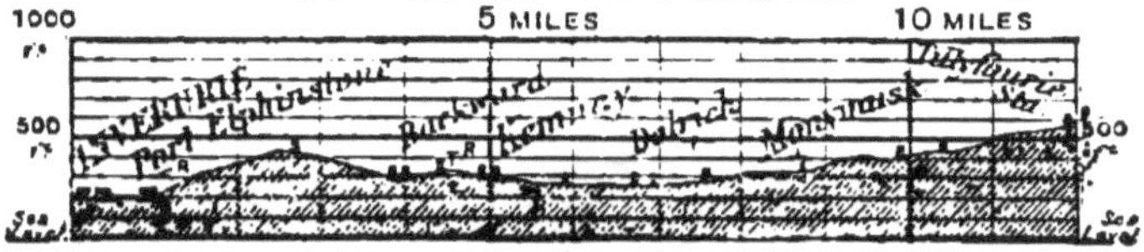

Description.—Class II. A very good road with remarkably easy gradients.

Gradients.—At 1¼m. 1 in 19.

Milestones.—Measured from Aberdeen *via* Blackburn, partly correct.

Measurements.—*Aberdeen.**

...	Inverurie,* Square.				
15⅜	5	Kemnay.*			
19⅛	8¾	3¾	Monymusk Roadend.		
22½	12⅛	7⅛	3⅜	Tillyfourie.	
27¾	17⅜	12⅜	8⅝	5¼	Alford * Hotel.

Principal Objects of Interest.—Fine views of the valley of the River Don.

ELLON TO METHLICK. 256

Description.—Class II. A good undulating road.

Measurements.—Ellon.*

4⅝	Ythanbank.	
8½	3⅞	Methlick,* Church.

Principal Objects of Interest.—The banks of the Ythan are very pretty, especially near Methlick.

TURRIFF TO BOGNIEBRAE. 257

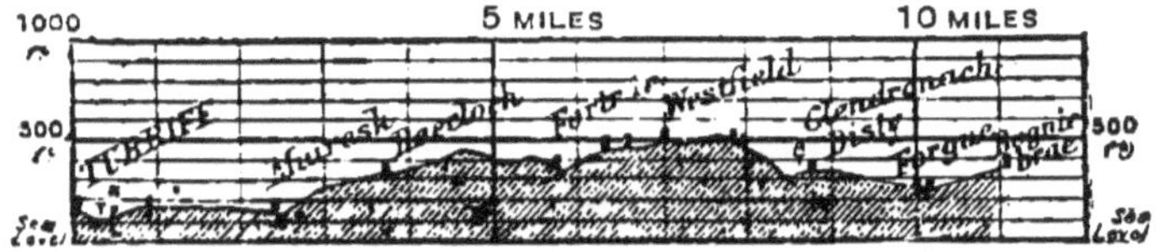

Description.—Class II. The road has a fine surface but is very hilly. Care must be taken at the turn at Turriff Station.

Gradients.—At ¼m. 1 in 20; 2¼m. 1 in 20-24; 4m. 1 in 25; 5½m. 1 in 17; 6m. 1 in 18; 8m. 1 in 17-11.

Milestones.—Measured from Turriff Station.

Measurements.—Turriff,* High Street.

5¾	Fortrie.		
10	4¼	Forgue.	
11⅛	5⅜	1⅛	Bogniebrae.*

258 PETERHEAD TO ELGIN.

Description.—Class I. This is a magnificent road with very fine surface nearly the whole way. It is a little lumpy after Brucklay Station, near Banff, Portsoy, and Cullen, but in the other parts the surface is mostly very good; between Cullen and Fochabers it is not quite so good.

Gradients.—At 27¾m. 1 in 25; 31m. 1 in 23-20; 35m. 1 in 16; 47¾m. 1 in 24; 48¼m. 1 in 21-19; 60¼m. 1 in 20.

Milestones.—Measured from Peterhead Church, to New Pitsligo; thereafter from Banff Town Hall, then from Banff, High Street, to Fochabers,—correct; thereafter from Elgin Cross,—correct.

Measurements.

Peterhead.*								
8⅞	Mintlaw.*							
18½	9⅝	New Pitsligo,* Market.						
33⅜	25	15⅝	Macduff,* Town Hall.					
34⅜	26	16⅜	1	Banff,* Town Hall.				
42¼	33⅞	24¼	8⅞	7⅞	Portsoy * Church.			
48⅜	29½	19⅞	14½	13½	5⅝	Cullen,* Town Hall.		
60¼	51⅞	42¼	26⅞	25⅞	18	12⅜	Fochabers,* Square.	
69½	60⅝	51	35⅝	34⅝	26¾	21⅛	8¾	Elgin,* Cross.

Principal Objects of Interest.—10⅝m. Abbey. 23¾m. Byth House. BANFF; Duff House, Bridge of Alvah. 37½m. Asylum. CULLEN; Cullen House. FOCHABERS; Gordon Castle. ELGIN; Cathedral. Macduff, Banff, Portsoy, and Cullen, are important centres of the fishing industry.

Hotels or Inns at places marked *, and at Inchgower.

259 ELLON TO NEWBYTH, &C.

Description.—Class II. This is a fair but hilly road, and though comparatively level to New Deer is somewhat rough. Thereafter it is a poor and very hilly road.

Gradients.—At 1m. 1 in 24; 4¾m. 1 in 19; 15⅜m. 1 in 21; 15¾m. 1 in 23; 18½m. 1 in 18-16-19; 19m. 1 in 19.

Measurements.

Ellon,* Square.				
8	Auchnagatt,* Station.			
12½	4½	New Deer,* P.O.		
19⅜	11⅜	6⅞	Newbyth,* Square.	
31⅞	23⅞	19⅜	12½	Banff,* Town Hall.

Principal Objects of Interest.—Fine views of the county after New Deer.

Hotels or Inns at places marked *.

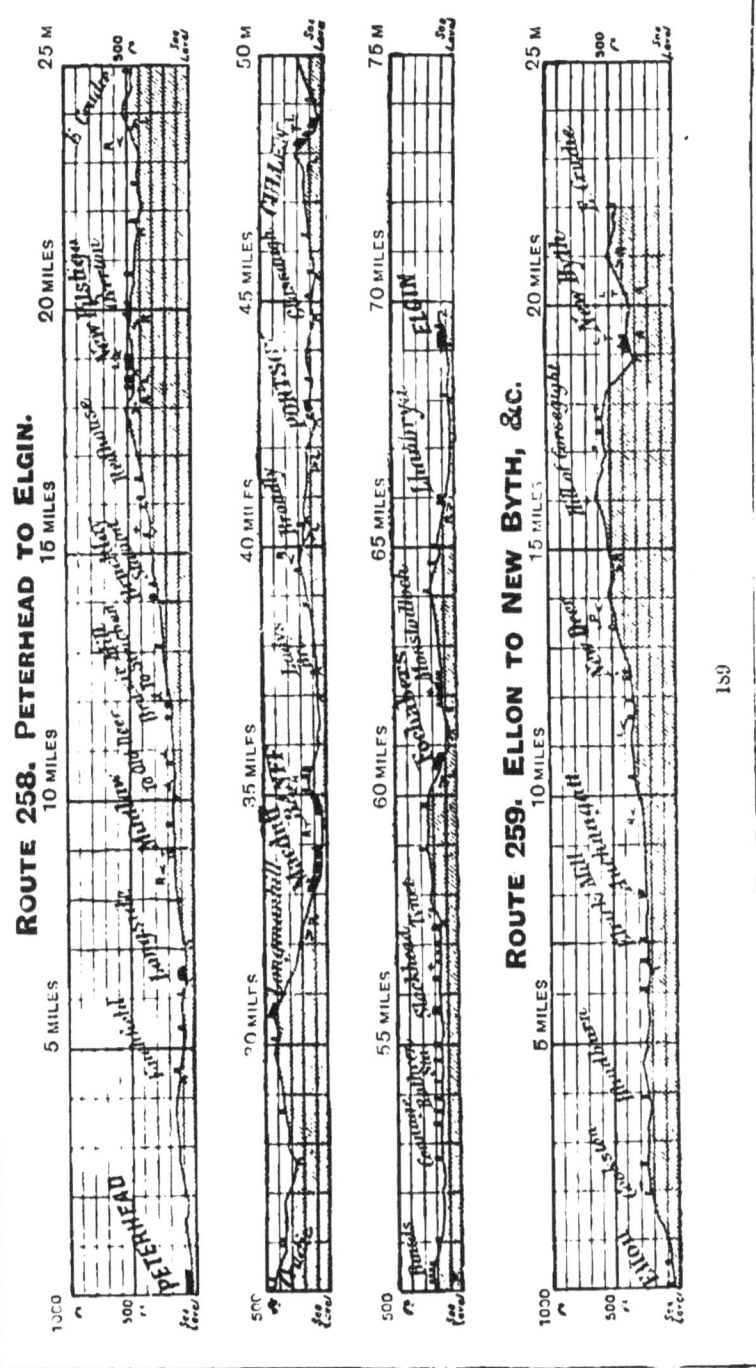

260 FRASERBURGH TO METHLICK.

Description.—Class II. & III. As far as Strichen the road is exceptionally fine, but thereafter though of fair surface it is more hilly, the last section being rather poor.

Gradients.—At 12m. 1 in 18; 20½m. 1 in 21; 22½m. 1 in 24; 22¾m. 1 in 22-19.

Milestones.—Measured from Fraserburgh Cross as far as Strichen; only odd ones thereafter.

Measurements.
Fraserburgh,* Cross.
   8¾   Strichen,* Town Hall.
  16¾ 7¾ New Deer,* Inn.
  23½ 14½ 6¾ Methlick,* Church.

Principal Objects of Interest.—Pleasant road through agricultural land. Methlick; Haddo House.

Hotels or Inns at places marked *.

261 FRASERBURGH TO TURRIFF.

Description.—Class II. & III. This is a fine but undulating road all the way. The best part of the road is between Fraserburgh and Newbyth; thereafter the surface and gradients are not so favourable. This is the usual road to Banff (25⅜m.), joining Route 258 close to Pitsligo.

Gradients.—Hardly any of note; except 6m. 1 in 20, and 7¼m. 1 in 15. The ascent up to Turriff is 1 in 20.

Milestones.—Measured from Fraserburgh Cross.

Measurements.
Fraserburgh,* Cross.
  15¾ Newbyth, Square.
  25¾ 9¾ Turriff,* High Street.

Hotels or Inns at places marked *, and at (Cuminestown).

262 FRASERBURGH TO BANFF, *Old Road.*

Description.—A fair road to Aberdour; thereafter it is a fearful and almost precipitous road till within a few miles of Macduff when it improves and is of good surface. As a through road between the two places it is almost never used—see previous route.

Gradients.—At 7¾m. 1 in 6; 8½m. 1 in 9; 10m. 1 in 10; 11m. 1 in 11; 11¾m. 1 in 7; 10½m. 1 in 16; 15½m. 1 in 11; thence mostly 1 in 20.

Milestones.—Measured from Fraserburgh Cross,—correct, and from Banff Cross—partly correct.

Measurements.
Fraserburgh,* Cross.
  7¾ Aberdour.
  13½ 5¾ Protstonhill.
  22¾ 14¾ 9¼ Banff,* Town Hall.

Principal Objects of Interest.—Fine cliff scenery.

Hotels or Inns at places marked *, and at (Gardenstown).

ROUTE 260. FRASERBURGH TO METHLICK.

ROUTE 261. FRASERBURGH TO TURRIFF.

ROUTE 262. FRASERBURGH TO BANFF (via Coast).

263 TURRIFF TO MINTLAW.

Description.—Class III. Care must be taken at the turn at Turriff Station. Thereafter the road is splendid to the fork at 2m., when the road becomes only fair, with some stiff hills to beyond Old Deer; where join Route 258.

Gradients.—At 6½m. 1 in 22; 7¼m. 1 in 18; 7⅞m. 1 in 25; 9¾m. 1 in 22; 11m. 1 in 23; 11½m. 1 in 19-16-17; 14¾m. 1 in 22.

Measurements.

Turriff,* High Street.					
7	Cuminestown,* P.O.				
13⅛	6⅛	New Deer,* Inn.			
15⅞	8⅞	2¾	Maud.*		
19⅜	12⅜	6¼	3½	Old Deer,* Church.	
21⅛	14⅛	8	5¼	1¾	Mintlaw.*

Principal Objects of Interest.—Old Deer; Abbey.

Hotels or Inns at places marked *, and at Mintlaw Sta.

264 TURRIFF TO KEITH.

Description.—Class III. As far as Marnoch the surface is good, but the road is very hilly; thereafter it is poorer till joining the Keith-Banff road,—Route 271.

Gradients.—At ½m. 1 in 21-19; 2m. 1 in 24-19; 6¾m. 1 in 17; 7m. 1 in 21; 8¾m. 1 in 21; 14¾m. 1 in 15; 17½m. 1 in 22; 18m. 1 in 20; 18¼m. 1 in 24.

Milestones.—Continuation of those from Aberdeen.

Measurements.

Turriff,* High Street.			
7¾	Aberchirder,* (Foggylone).		
16	8¼	Rothiemay Crossroads.	
23⅝	15⅞	7⅝	Keith.*

Principal Objects of Interest.—The road between Marnoch and Rothiemay is remarkably pretty.

Hotels or Inns at places marked *, and at (Rothiemay).

265 HUNTLY TO BANFF.

Description.—Class II. A remarkably good road, with comparatively easy gradients, in splendid condition.

Gradients.—At 5¼m. 1 in 24-22; 10¾m. 1 in 21; 13m. 1 in 24; 16¼m. 1 in 23; 18m. 1 in 18-17-23; 20m. 1 in 20.

Milestones.—Measured from Banff, High Street,—correct.

Measurements.

Huntly,* Square.			
6¼	Bogniebrae.*		
11¾	5½	Aberchirder,* P.O.	
20⅝	14⅜	9⅛	Banff,* Town Hall.

Principal Objects of Interest.—3½m. Lessendrum. 9m. Kinnairdy Castle. 18¾m. Bridge of Alvah. BANFF; Duff House, Museum, Castle.

Hotels or Inns at places marked *.

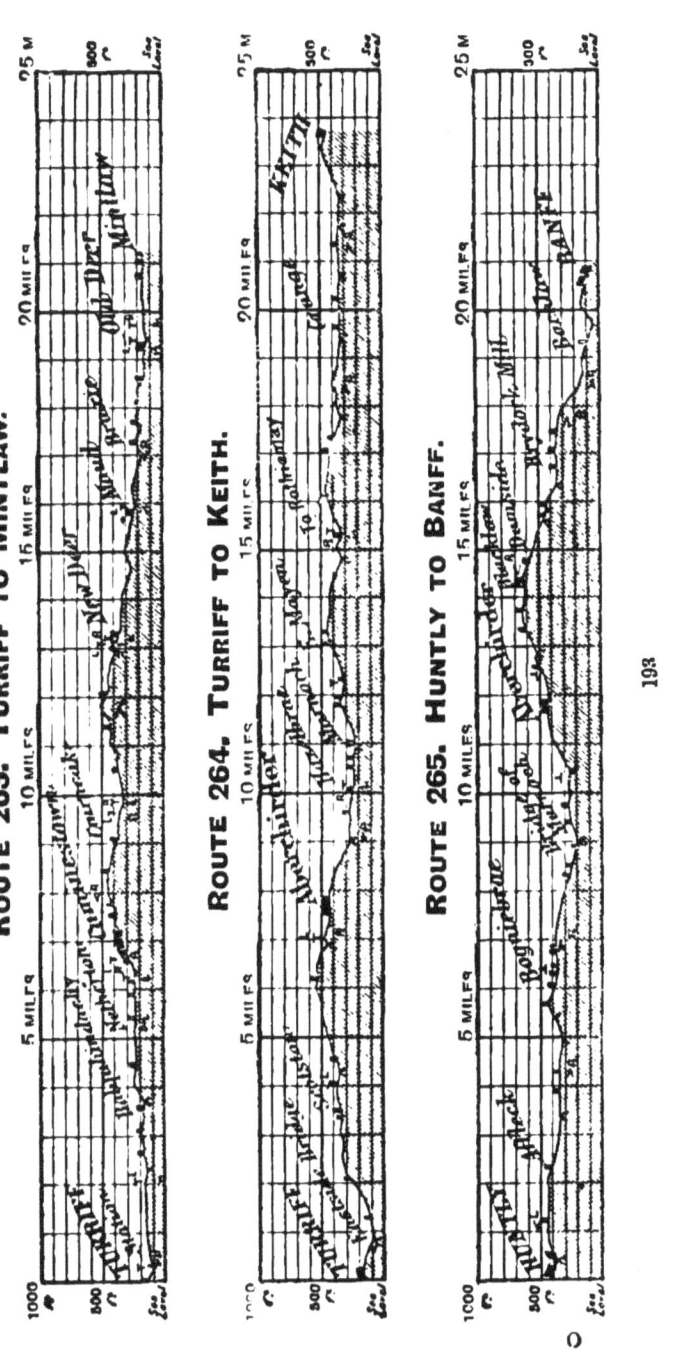

266 HUNTLY TO PORTSOY.

Description.—Class II. The surface is good till nearing Glenbarry, when it becomes rather poor for some miles; thence fair to Portsoy.

Gradients.—At 6m. 1 in 25.

Milestones.—At first measured from Banff; after Glenbarry, from Portsoy Square.

Measurements.

Huntly,* Square.			
6⅞	Rothiemay Crossroads.		
10¼	3⅜	Glenbarry * Inn.	
17⅞	11	7⅝	Portsoy,* Square.

Principal Objects of Interest.—Knock Hill is very prominent near Glenbarry.

Hotels or Inns at places marked *, and at (Rothiemay).

267 HUNTLY TO CRAIGELLACHIE.

Description.—Class III. The surface is very fine for 2½m.; thereafter is poor and very hilly—very bad at the summit—until near Dufftown, thence good to Craigellachie. There is a more direct road—1⅝m. shorter—to Milltown by Cairnford Bridge. It has one slight hill.

Gradients.—At 8¼m. 1/24; 9m. 1/17-23; 10½ to 11¼m. 1/17-23-12-19; 12½m. 1/13-15; 15m. 1/16; 17m. 1/19; 18m. 1/22.

Measurements.

Huntly,* Square.			
8¼	Market Inn.*		
15¼	7	Dufftown,* Tower.	
19¾	11⅜	4¾	Craigellachie.*

Principal Objects of Interest.—Rather pretty up the banks of the Deveron. 16m. Balvenie Castle, ruin.

268 HUNTLY TO INVERURIE.

Description.—Class II. The road has a good surface, but is undulating as far as Kennethmont; thereafter the gradients are almost imperceptible, and the surface is extremely good. Route 245 is more direct, but this has the advantage of a much easier climb.

Milestones.—At first measured from Aberdeen *via* Alford,—correct; after Insch—continuation of those from Aberdeen.

Measurements.

Huntly,* Square.					
5¼	Gartly,* Station.				
8	2¾	Kennethmont.			
14⅝	9⅜	6⅜	Insch,* Station.		
20¾	15½	12¾	6⅜	Pitcaple.*	
25½	20¼	17½	11⅛	4¾	Inverurie,* Square.

Principal Objects of Interest.—Rather monotonous scenery between Gartly and Insch.

Hotels or Inns at places marked *.

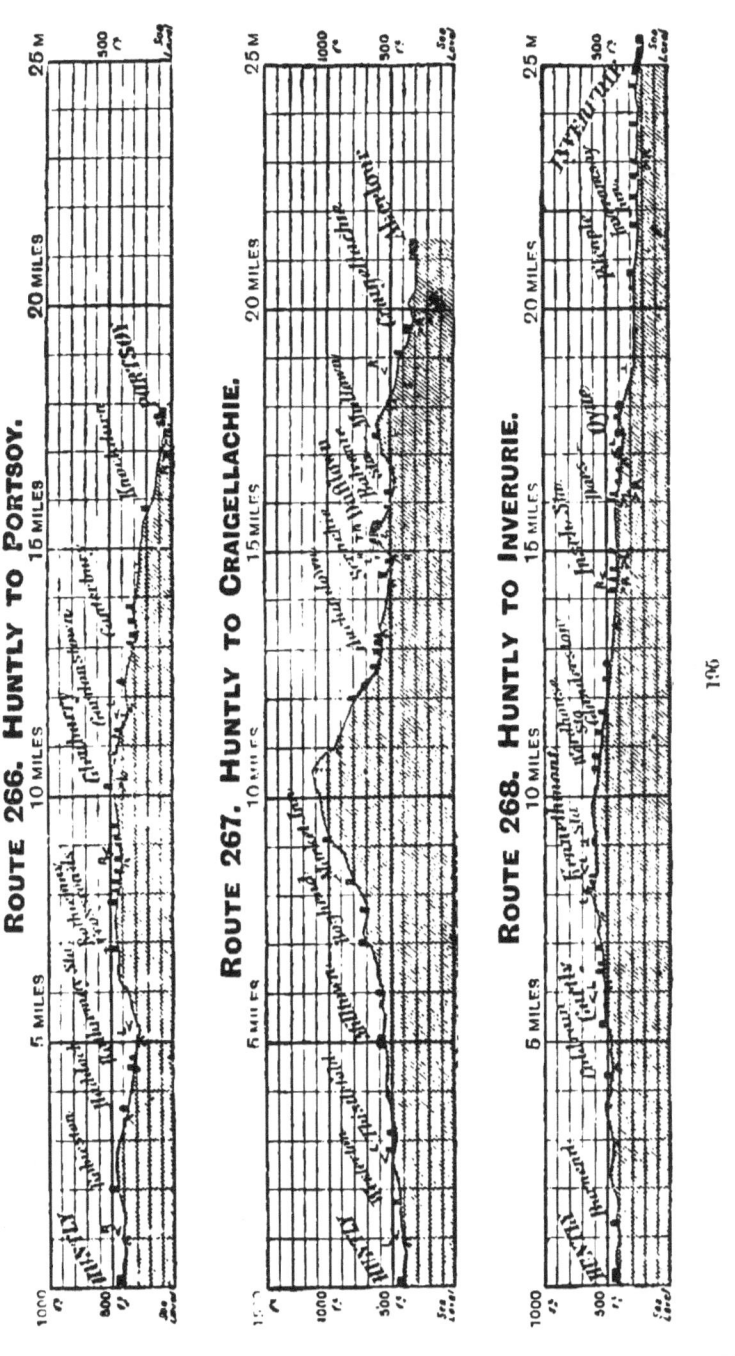

269 HUNTLY TO ABOYNE.

Description.—Class II. The road is undulating, with a very good surface to Gartly, after which it becomes hilly —with several stiff pulls—and has rather poor surface. Between Mossat Toll and Alford Bridge it is almost level, with fine surface ; thereafter the surface degenerates considerably, and is very rough on the hills on both sides of Crossroads. After Roadside the surface is very good.

Gradients.—6m. 1 in 23-21 ; 9½m. 1 in 19 ; 11m. 1 in 19 ; 21¾m. 1 in 25; 30½m. 1 in 12.

Milestones.—Continuation of those to Alford, from Aberdeen.

Measurements.

Huntly,* Square.						
5¼	Gartly,* Station.					
9	3¾	Rhynie.				
12⅞	7⅝	3⅞	Lumsden.			
20⅜	15⅛	11⅜	7½	Alford Bridge.*		
28½	23¼	19½	15⅝	8⅛	Crossroads.*	
37	31¾	28	24⅛	16⅝	8½	Aboyne,* Hotel.

Principal Objects of Interest.—11m. Craig Castle. Alford ; Scene of Skirmish. 27m. Craigievar Castle. 31⅝m. Peel bog. Pretty scenery near Alford.

Hotels or Inns at places marked *, and at (Alford).

270 KEITH TO CULLEN.

Description.—Class II. The surface is very good as far as Grange Crossroads ; thereafter for some miles it is rather poor, till nearing Cullen, when it becomes better.

Gradients.—At 3m. 1 in 21; 13m. 1 in 20-19.

Milestones.—Measured from Cullen Square,—correct.

Measurements.

Keith.*			
4¼	Crossroads.*		
9	4¾	Deskford P.O.	
13	8¾	4	Cullen,* Square.

Principal Objects of Interest.—Rather tame scenery at first. CULLEN ; Cullen House.

Hotels or Inns at places marked *.

271 KEITH TO BANFF.

Description.—Class II. The road has a very good surface to beyond Grange, but becomes slightly rough and hilly till near Cornhill, when the surface improves, and is very good nearing Banff.

Gradients.—At 20m. 1 in 16.

Milestones.—Measured from Banff.

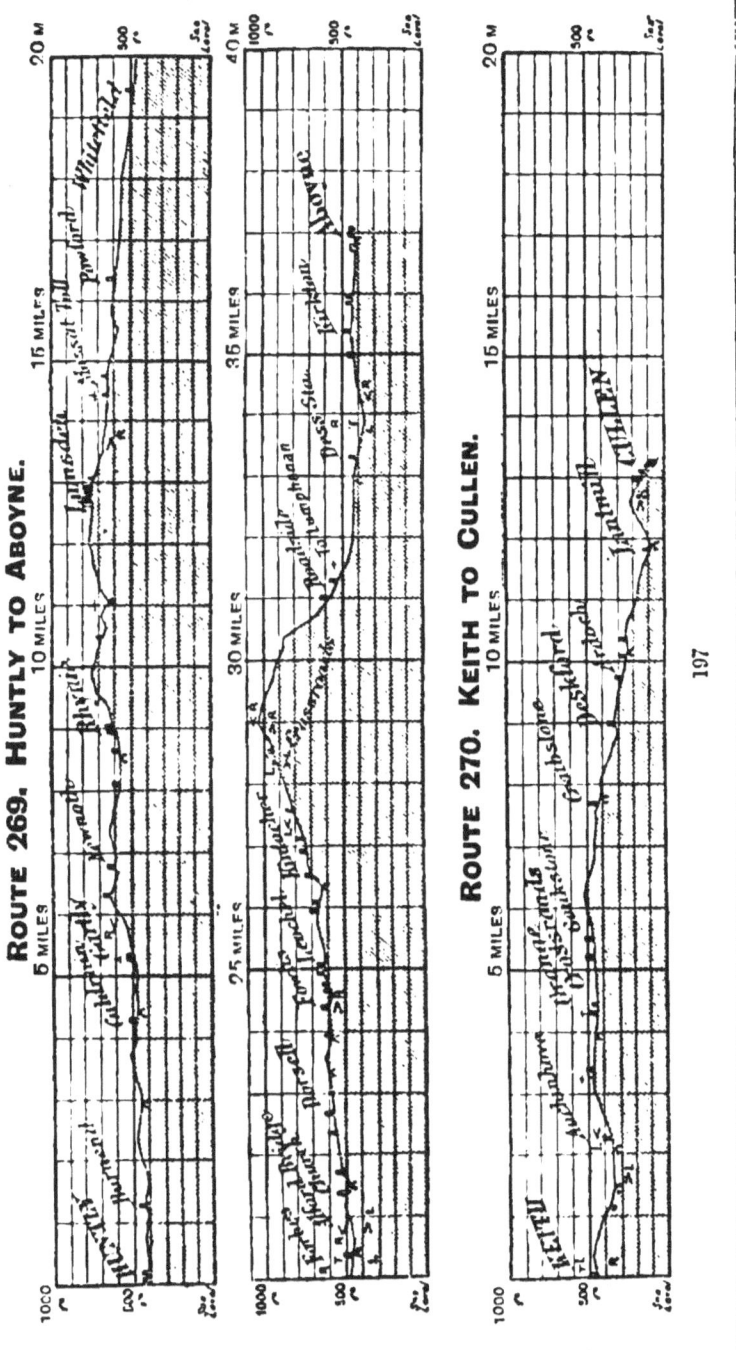

Measurements.

Keith.*
9 Glenbarry Inn.*
11⅞ 2⅞ Cornhill,* Inn.
20¼ 11¼ 8⅜ Banff,* Town Hall.

Principal Objects of Interest.—Knock Hill is very prominent near Glenbarry. 17¾m. Asylum. BANFF; Castle, Museum, Duff House, Bridge of Alvah.

Hotels or Inns at places marked *.

---

272 KEITH TO GLENLIVAT.

Description.—Class III. The road is fair, but very hilly to Dufftown; thereafter it gradually degenerates, and near the summit is very poor and soft.

Gradients.—At 6½m. 1 in 20-19; 9¼m. 1 in 20-18; 10½m. 1 in 16-22-17; 12¼m. 1 in 24; 13m. 1 in 17; 14¼m. 1 in 23; 16m. 1 in 24; 16½m. 1 in 20; 18¼m. 1 in 15.

Milestones.—Measured from Fife-Keith Square; after Dufftown, from the Tower at that place.

Measurements.

Keith.*
10⅞ Dufftown,* Tower.
19⅜ 8½ Craighead Inn.*
21⅝ 10¾ 2¼ Achbreck (Glenlivat).

Principal Objects of Interest.—Rather pretty scenery near Drummuir, and in Glen Rinnies. DUFFTOWN; Balvenie Castle, Auchindoun Castle.

Hotels or Inns at places marked *, and at Drummuir.

---

273 GRANTOWN TO ABERLOUR.

Description.—Class III. The road is comparatively level and has a fair surface to Dalvey; thereafter hilly and poor to Dalnashaugh. From this point the road is firmer but hilly, with a long steep descent to Aberlour.

Gradients.—At 13m. 1 in 21-19; 13¾m. 1 in 16-15; 16½m. 1 in 24-21; 17¼m. 1 in 22; 20½m. 1 in 19; 21¼m. 1 in 17.

Milestones.—Measured from Bridge of Avon, southwards,—correct.

Measurements.

Grantown.*
4⅝ Cromdale,* Inn.
10¼ 5⅝ Advie, P.O.
14 9⅜ 3¾ Dalnashaugh Inn.*
21¾ 17⅛ 11½ 7¾ Aberlour,* Square.

Principal Objects of Interest.—Very fine scenery in the Spey valley and at Dalnashaugh. The scenery at Craigellachie Bridge is also very fine.

Hotels or Inns at places marked *.

ROUTE 271. KEITH TO BANFF.

ROUTE 272. KEITH TO ACHBRECK (GLENLIVAT.)

ROUTE 273. GRANTOWN TO ABERLOUR.

274 GRANTOWN TO AVIEMORE.

Description.—Class II. A fine road with good surface and easy gradients the whole way. It is, however, somewhat rough for a few miles after Dulnan Bridge.

Gradients.—Nothing above 1 in 25.

Milestones.—Measured from Grantown Square,—correct to Kinveachy; thereafter from Inverness.

Measurements.

Grantown,* Square.			
3⅛	Dulnan Bridge.		
11	7⅞	Kinveachy.	
15	11⅞	4	Aviemore * Station.

Principal Objects of Interest.—Dulnan Bridge; Muckrach Castle. The Spey valley is finely wooded. Fine views of the Cairngorm range of mountains.

Hotels or Inns at places marked *, and at (Boat of Garten).

---

275 GRANTOWN TO AVIEMORE *via Nethybridge.*

Description.—Class III. A fair road at first but somewhat hilly; after Nethybridge rather soft in parts.

Gradients.—At 1¾m. 1 in 22; 13½m. 1 in 16.

Measurements.

Grantown,* Square.				
1¾	Grantown (Spey Bridge) Station.			
5⅞	4½	Nethybridge * Hotel.		
15¾	14⅜	9⅞	Coylumbridge.	
17⅝	16¼	11¾	1⅞	Aviemore * Station.

Principal Objects of Interest.—Fine woods near Nethy Bridge. Aviemore; Rothiemurchus Forest, and Loch-an-eilan.

Hotels or Inns at places marked *.

---

276 KINGUSSIE TO AVIEMORE *via Feshiebridge.*

Description.—Class III. The surface of the road is rather poor, and there are several rather dangerous hills, notably at Tromie and Feshie bridges.

Gradients.—No information obtainable. The steepest is 1 in 12, the others are about 1 in 15.

Measurements.

Kingussie,* Court House.			
2¾	Tromie Bridge.		
8⅝	5⅞	Feshiebridge.	
15⅛	12⅜	6½	Aviemore * Station.

Principal Objects of Interest.—1¼m. Ruthven Barracks, ruin. 13m. Loch-an-eilan to E., and Rothiemurchus Forest. The road passes through very pretty scenery.

Hotels or Inns at places marked *.

ROUTE 274. GRANTOWN TO AVIEMORE (direct).

ROUTE 275. GRANTOWN TO AVIEMORE via Nethybridge.

ROUTE 276. KINGUSSIE TO AVIEMORE via Feshiebridge.

277 FOCHABERS TO KNOCKANDO.

Description.—Class III. The surface is very fine to Mosstodloch where the road becomes undulating, but with good surface to Rothes. After Dandaleith the road becomes very hilly, with rather poor surface.

Gradients.—At 8m. 1 in 18; 12m. 1 in 15-14; 12¾m. 1 in 21; 14½m. 1 in 25; 16¾m. 1 in 24; 19m. 1 in 25; 19½m. 1 in 15.

Measurements.

Fochabers,* Hotel.					
6	Orton Station.				
9¾	3¾	Rothes * Square.			
12	6	2¼	Dandaleith Station.		
16⅛	10⅛	6⅜	4⅛	Archiestown.	
19⅝	13⅝	9⅞	7⅝	3½	Knockando,* P.O.

Principal Objects of Interest.—This is a pretty road up the left bank of the Spey; after Dandaleith it is high above the river.

Hotels or Inns at places marked *, and at (Craigellachie).

278 BALLINDALLOCH TO TOMINTOUL.

Description.—Class II. The road is fair at first, but there are some rather stiff hills in the first few miles. Thereafter the road is rather soft past Achbreck on to Tomnavoulin, where the long ascent begins; thence to Tomintoul is fair, sometimes rather rough.

Gradients.—At 1½m. 1 in 16-15; 4¾m. 1 in 19; 8¾m. 1 in 21; 9¼m. 1 in 22; 10m. 1 in 20; 11¼m. 1 in 19; 14½m. 1 in 24.

Milestones.—Measured from Ballindalloch Station,—correct.

Measurements.

Ballindalloch Station.					
1⅝	Dalnashaugh Inn.*				
5	3⅜	Downan.			
7⅜	5¾	2⅜	Achbreck.		
10¾	9⅛	5¾	3⅜	Knockandhu,* P.O.	
15½	13⅞	10½	8⅛	4¾	Tomintoul,* Hotel.

Principal Objects of Interest.—1¾m. Ballindalloch Castle. 5¼m. Drumin Castle. Glenlivet Distillery. Pleasant road up the valley, but dreary on the higher parts.

Hotels or Inns at places marked *.

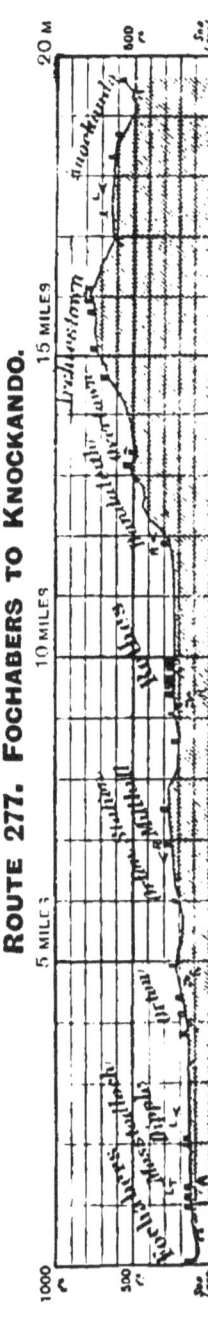

ROUTE 277. FOCHABERS TO KNOCKANDO.

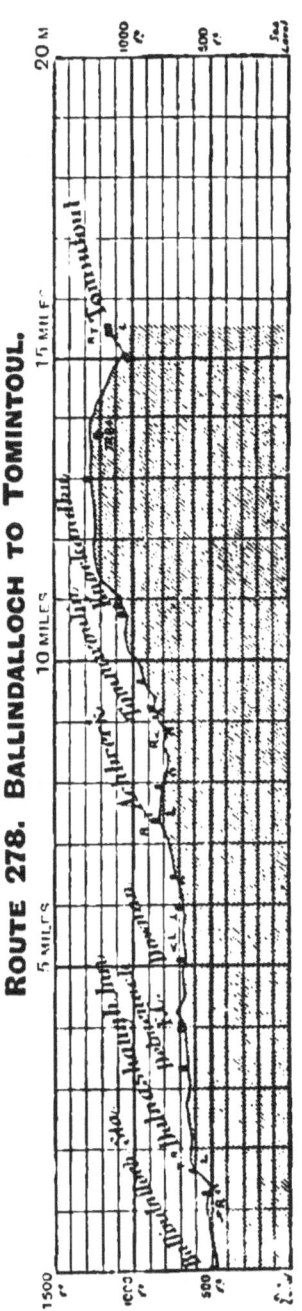

ROUTE 278. BALLINDALLOCH TO TOMINTOUL.

Signs: < Road Fork, forward journey, > ditto reverse, + Cross Roads, ⊥ Road Junction, ∩ Bridge, ⊤ indicates a sharp turn. The directions R (right) and L (left) for the forward journey are above the Road Line, those of the reverse, below.

203

279 KEITH TO CRAIGELLACHIE.

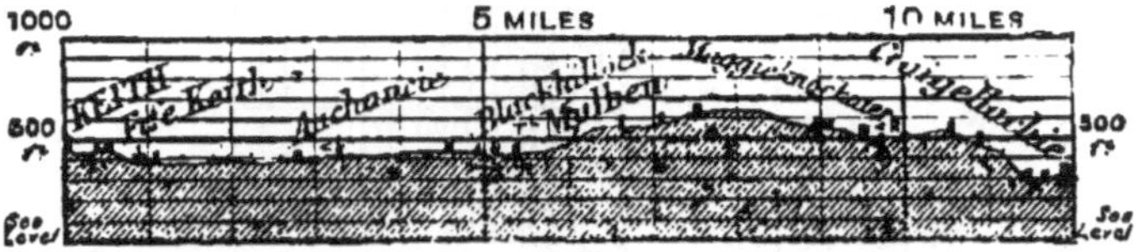

Description.—Class II. After Fife-Keith a fine smooth road as far as Mulben; thereafter hilly, with a steep descent to Craigellachie.

Gradients.—At 8½m. 1 in 25; 9½m. 1 in 16; 9¾m. 1 in 17; 11¼m. 1 in 14.

Measurements.—Keith.*
5¼ Mulben.
11⅞ 6⅝ Craigellachie.*

Principal Objects of Interest.—Fine scenery approaching Craigellachie.

280 GRANTOWN TO CARRBRIDGE.

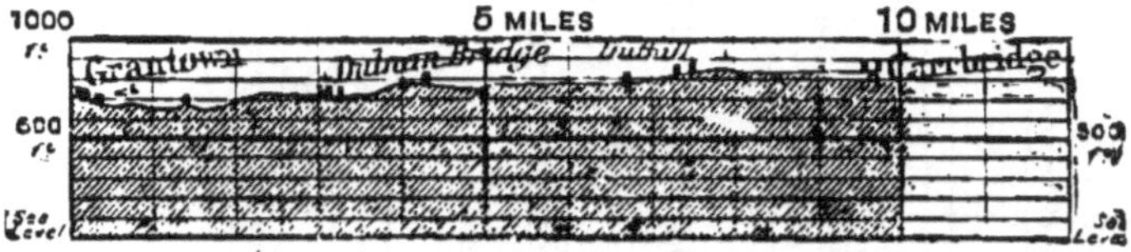

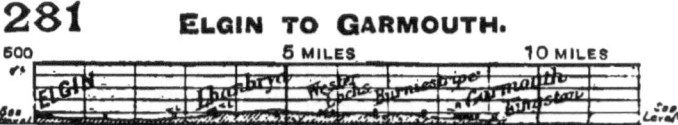

Description.—Class II. A fine undulating road all the way.

Milestones.—Measured from Grantown, after Dulnan Bridge from Carrbridge.

Measurements.—Grantown,* Square.
3½ Dulnan Bridge.
7¾ 4¼ Duthil.
9⅝ 6½ 2¼ Carrbridge,* Hotel.

Principal Objects of Interest.—The road is very pretty between Dulnan Bridge and Carrbridge.

281 ELGIN TO GARMOUTH.

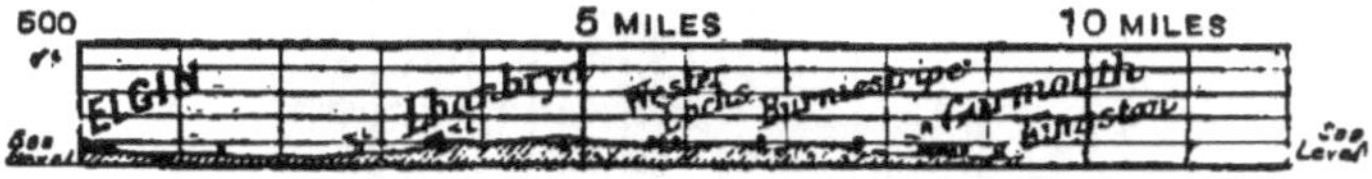

Description.—Class II. A very good undulating road.

Measurements.—Elgin * Cross.
3½ Lhanbryd.
8½ 5 Garmouth.*

Hotels or Inns at places marked *.

ELGIN TO DALLAS. 282

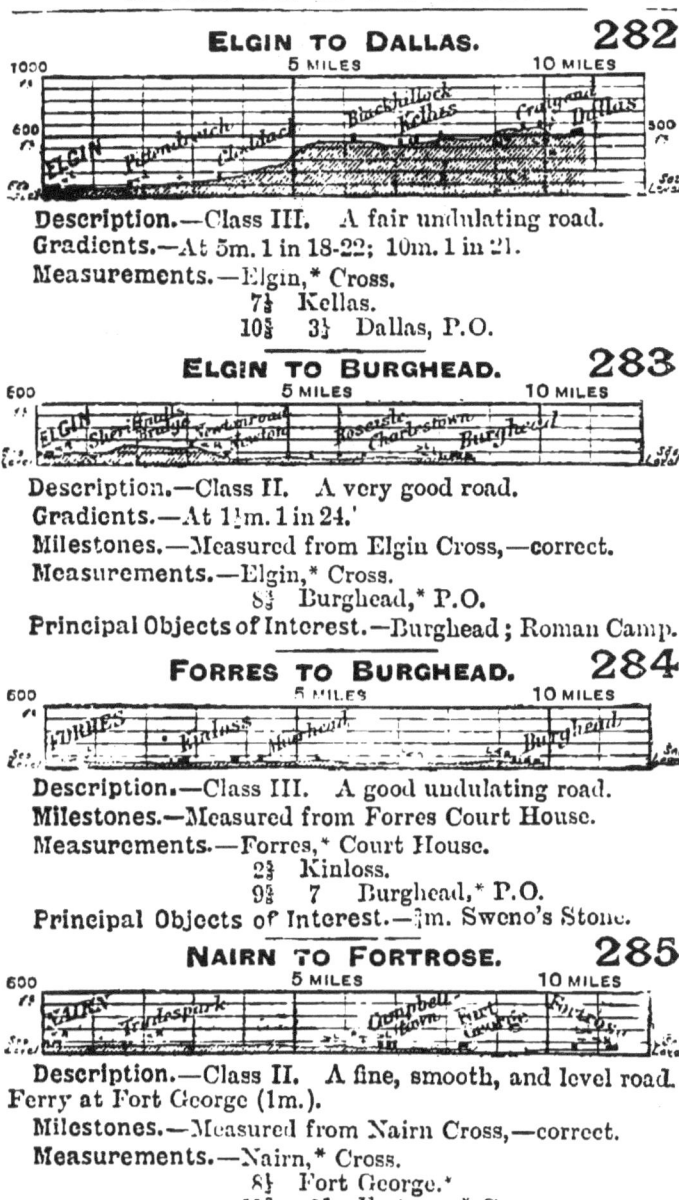

Description.—Class III. A fair undulating road.
Gradients.—At 5m. 1 in 18-22; 10m. 1 in 21.
Measurements.—Elgin,* Cross.
    7¾ Kellas.
   10⅝ 3⅓ Dallas, P.O.

ELGIN TO BURGHEAD. 283

Description.—Class II. A very good road.
Gradients.—At 1½m. 1 in 24.'
Milestones.—Measured from Elgin Cross,—correct.
Measurements.—Elgin,* Cross.
    8¼ Burghead,* P.O.
Principal Objects of Interest.—Burghead; Roman Camp.

FORRES TO BURGHEAD. 284

Description.—Class III. A good undulating road.
Milestones.—Measured from Forres Court House.
Measurements.—Forres,* Court House.
    2¾ Kinloss.
    9⅝ 7 Burghead,* P.O.
Principal Objects of Interest.—¾m. Sweno's Stone.

NAIRN TO FORTROSE. 285

Description.—Class II. A fine, smooth, and level road.
Ferry at Fort George (1m.).
Milestones.—Measured from Nairn Cross,—correct.
Measurements.—Nairn,* Cross.
    8¼ Fort George.*
   11¾ 2¾ Fortrose,* Cross.
Principal Objects of Interest.—Fort George; Old Fort. Fortrose; Cathedral.

286 ELGIN TO KEITH *via Mulben.*

Description.—Class II. Very good surface for several miles, then a fair undulating road to Orton. After the very steep hill past Boat of Brig, the road is good with slight undulations.

Gradients.—At 5m. 1 in 22; 10¾m. 1 in 13-16-14-16.

Milestones.—Measured from Elgin Cross, and from Aberdeen.

Measurements.

Elgin,* Cross.
9¼ Orton Station.
12⅝ 3⅜ Mulben, P.O.
18¼ 9 5⅝ Keith.*

Principal Objects of Interest.—Very pretty scenery in the Spey Valley.

Hotels or Inns at places marked *.

287 ELGIN TO ABERLOUR.

Description.—Class II. A fine undulating road to Rothes; thereafter level to Craigellachie, after which there is a short hill; thence level and very good to Aberlour.

Gradients.—At 1m. 1 in 25; 4¼m. 1 in 21-23; 8⅞m. 1 in 21; 9⅜m. 1 in 20-24; 13½m. 1 in 18.

Milestones.—Measured from Elgin Cross,—correct.

Measurements.

Elgin,* Cross.
10 Rothes,* Square.
12⅞ 2⅞ Craigellachie,* P.O.
14⅞ 4⅞ 2 Aberlour,* Square.

Principal Objects of Interest.—Very pretty scenery at Craigellachie.

Hotels or Inns at places marked *.

288 ELGIN TO FORRES *via Pluscarden.*

Description.—Class III. A fair undulating road to Pluscarden, then very steep; after Cantsford it is comparatively easy.

Gradients.—At 7¼m. 1 in 20-17-22; 8¼m. 1 in 13; 9¼m. 1 in 21; 10m. 1 in 16; 12¼m. in 20.

Measurements.

Elgin,* Cross.
6¾ Pluscarden.
15⅝ 8⅞ Forres,* Court House.

Principal Objects of Interest.—6¾m. Pluscarden Abbey, ruins. 12⅝m. Blervie Castle. FORRES; Nelson Monument, Sweno's Stone.

Hotels or Inns at places marked *.

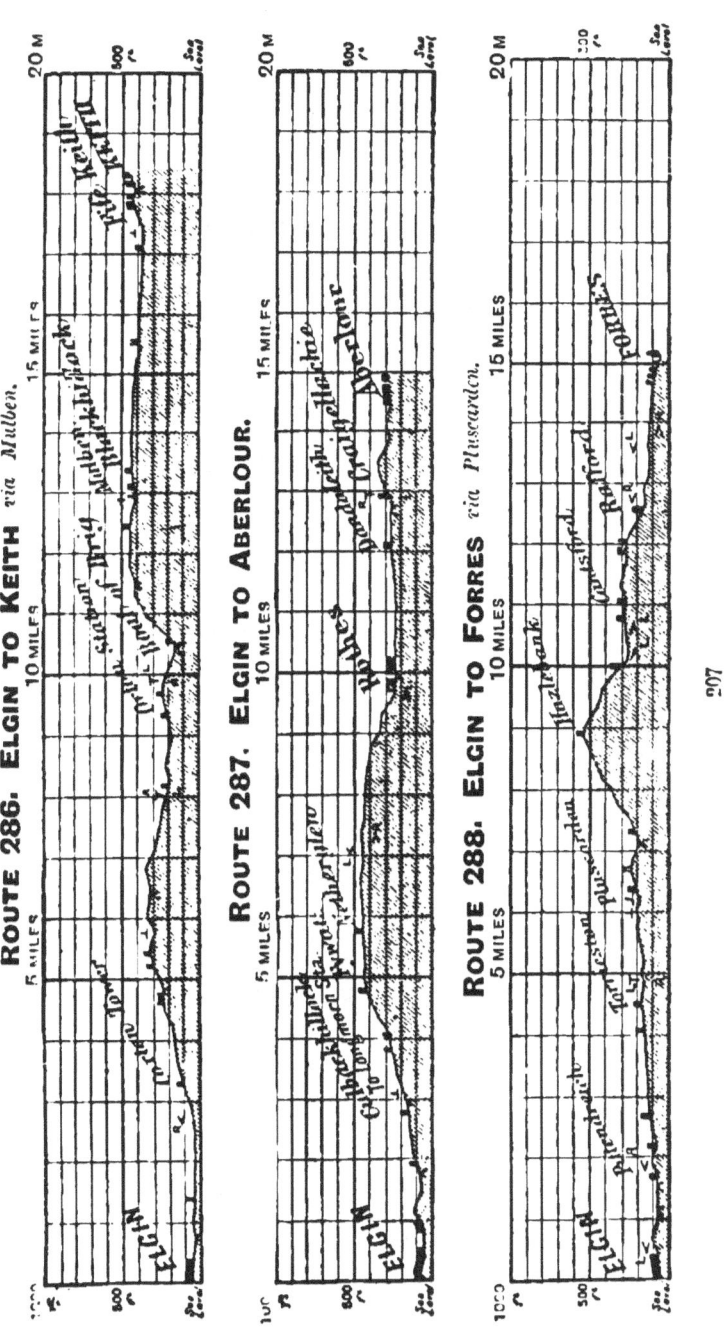

289 FORRES TO DALNASHAUGH.

Description.—Class III. The road has a fair surface to Dallas, but there are some stiff hills; thereafter rather poor surface and steep hills. After Knockando the surface is better, but the road is undulating. Ferry across the River Spey at Blacksboat.

Gradients.—At 3m. 1 in 20; 6¼m. 1 in 17; 8¾m. 1 in 19; 10½m. 1 in 15; 12¼m. 1 in 21; 13½m. 1 in 15; 15⅝m. 1 in 17; 18¾m. 1 in 17; 19½m. 1 in 11.

Measurements.

Forres,* Court House.				
8	Dallas, P.O.			
15½	7½	Knockando, P.O.		
19	11	3½	Blacksboat.	
21⅞	13⅞	6⅜	2⅞	Dalnashaugh Inn.*

Principal Objects of Interest.—2½m. Blervie Castle. 7½m. Tor Castle. Moorland on the higher parts.

Hotels or Inns at places marked*, and at Rafford.

290 FORRES TO GRANTOWN.

Description.—Class II. This is a fine road with very steady and comparatively easy gradients. The surface is very fine to Dunphail, then becomes rather poorer, with loose stones past Dava till nearing Grantown, when it becomes very fine.

Gradients.—At 6¾m. 1 in 23; 8½m. 1 in 24; 8⅝m. 1 in 19; 10m. 1 in 25; 14¾m. 1 in 14; 20¼m. 1 in 13.

Milestones.—Measured from Grantown Square,—incorrect between Dunphail and Dava.

Measurements.

Forres,* Court House.			
7⅝	Dunphail Station.		
14½	6⅞	Dava Inn.*	
21⅞	14¼	7⅜	Grantown,* Square.

Principal Objects of Interest.—Nelson Monument above Forres. Remarkably fine road through Altyre Woods. 6m. Randolph's leap to W. Dava; Loch-an-dorb to W. Very dreary moorland after Dava. Grantown; Castle Grant.

Hotels or Inns at places marked *.

291 FORRES TO DUTHIL.

Description.—Class III. The first 6 miles of the Grantown road are very good; thereafter to Ferness is fair but hilly, after which the road becomes very bad with loose stones, and is in a dreadful state till quite near Duthil. This last part is almost disused.

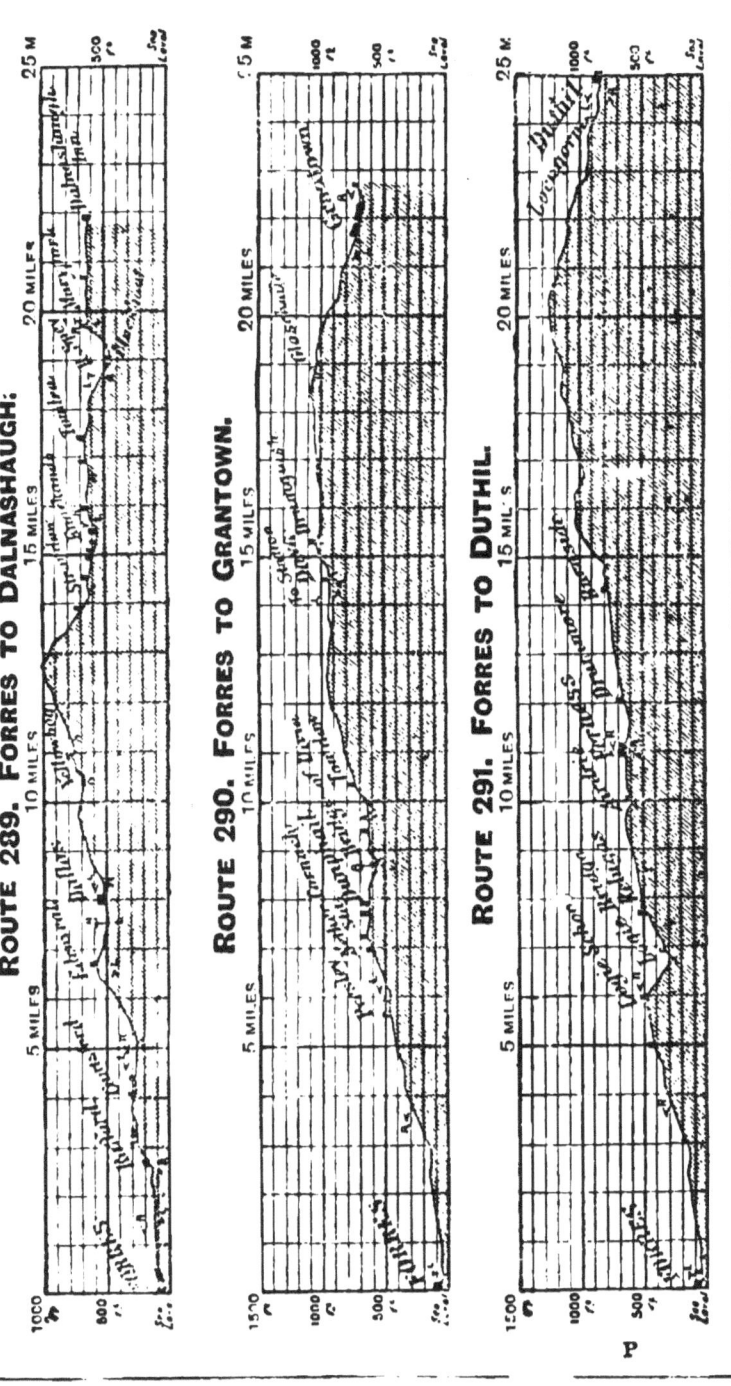

Gradients.—At 6¼m. 1 in 16-20-15; 7m. 1 in 23; 7¾m. 1 in 20; 15m. 1 in 14-23-20; 18¼m. 1 in 19; 20½m. 1 in 21; 22¾m. 1 in 15; 24m. 1 in 24.

Milestones.—To Ferness, measured from Grantown; thereafter from Nairn (Route 292).

Measurements.

Forres,* Court House.
7¾ Relugas.
11 3¼ Ferness, Crossroads.
25 17¼ 14 Duthil.

Principal Objects of Interest.—Very pretty near Relugas, dreary moorland after Burnside.

292 NAIRN TO DAVA.

Description.—Class III. The surface is good for the first eight miles; when the road descends steeply to Ferness Bridge with a corresponding ascent; easier thereafter, but with poor surface.

Gradients.—At 9¼m. 1 in 23-16; 10m. 1 in 14-25; 13⅛m. 1 in 20.

Milestones.—Measured from Nairn County Buildings; after Ferness, from Grantown Square.

Measurements.

Nairn,* Cross.
5 Littlemill.
10¼ 5¼ Ferness, Crossroads.
15⅝ 10⅝ 5⅜ Dava.
23¼ 18¼ 13 7⅝ Grantown,* Square.

Principal Objects of Interest.—Very fine scenery at Ferness Bridge; very dreary thereafter.

Hotels or Inns at places marked *.

293 NAIRN TO DAVIOT.

Description.—Class III. As far as Cawdor the road is of good surface, with easy undulations; thereafter it is rather poor, with a stiff hill past Galcantry.

Gradients.—At 9m. 1 in 25-13; 12m. 1 in 22. There are short hills of 1 in 24.

Milestones.—Measured from Nairn, Straths Monument,—correct to Cawdor.

Measurements.

Nairn,* Cross.
5⅝ Cawdor,* Bridge.
16⅝ 11 Craggie Inn.*
17½ 12⅛ 1⅛ Daviot Church.

Principal Objects of Interest.—4m. Brackla Distillery. Cawdor; Castle. 7½m. Kilravock Castle.

Hotels or Inns at places marked *.

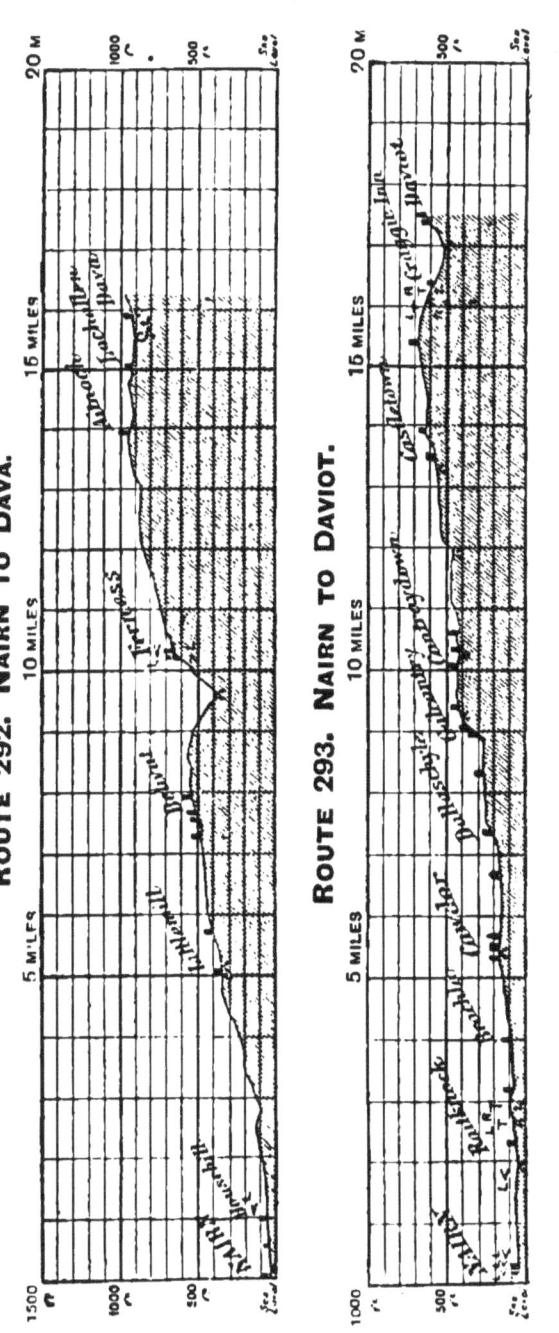

Signs: < Road Fork, forward journey, > ditto reverse, + Cross Roads, ⊥ Road Junction, ∩ Bridge, ⊤ indicates a sharp turn. The directions R (right) and L (left) for the forward journey are above the Road Line, those of the reverse, below.

294 Inverness to Elgin.

Description.—Class I. The road is rather lumpy at first, but after Culloden Station the surface improves, and is exceptionally fine to Nairn. Thence to Forres is very good, after which the road becomes more undulating, with a slight hill before Elgin.

Gradients.—At 36¼m. 1 in 24.

Milestones.—Measured from Inverness suburbs and Nairn Cross,—correct to Forres. Thereafter from Elgin Cross,—correct.

Measurements.

Inverness,* Town Hall.						
9¾	Lower Crossroads (*to Fort George Station*).					
15¾	6	Nairn,* Cross.				
18⅜	8⅝	2⅝	Auldearn P.O.			
26⅛	16⅜	10⅜	8	Forres,* Court House.		
32⅝	22⅞	16⅞	14½	6½	Alves.	
38	28¼	22¼	19⅞	11⅞	5⅜	Elgin,* Cross.

Principal Objects of Interest.—Culloden Station is some miles from the Battlefield. Auldearn; Battle, 1645. 22¼m. Brodie Castle, Darnaway Castle. FORRES; Sweno's Stone. The Nelson Monument is very prominent on the hilltop. ELGIN; Cathedral.

Hotels or Inns at places marked *.

295 Inverness to Nairn *via Culloden.*

Description.—Class III. The first few miles of the Perth road are very good; thereafter it is steep and with poor surface to Culloden Cairn, when it improves and continues of fair surface to Nairn.

Gradients.—At 2¾m. 1 in 18; 3¾m. 1 in 16.

Measurements.

Inverness,* Town Hall.			
5¾	Culloden Cairn.		
12	6¼	Clephanton.	
18	12¼	6	Nairn,* Cross.

Principal Objects of Interest.—Culloden; Battlefield, 1746. 6¼m. Cumberland Stone. 11¼m. Kilravock Castle.

296 Inverness to Kingussie.

Description.—Class II. The road is slightly rough at first but improves near Culcabock, and though the hills are long and very stiff, the surface is particularly good. The road is undulating with good surface past Moy, but after Freeburn Inn, becomes rather poor till nearing Carr-bridge when it improves. Thence to Aviemore the road is

Route 294. Inverness to Elgin.

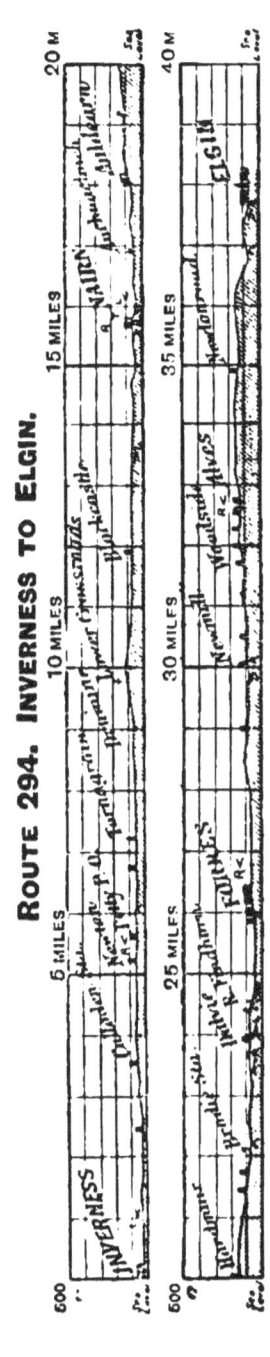

Route 295. Inverness to Nairn via *Culloden*.

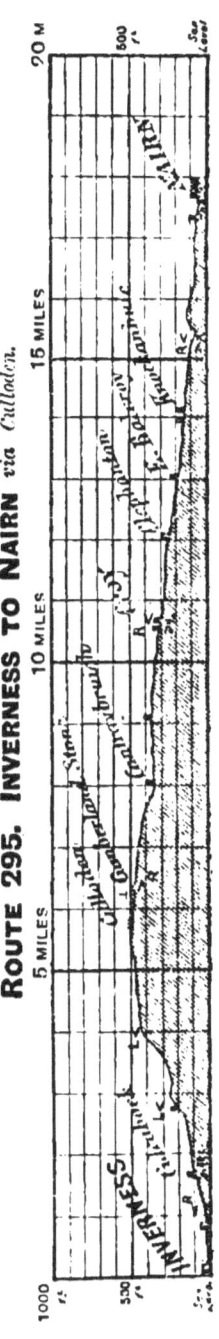

Signs: < Road Fork, forward journey, > ditto reverse, + Cross Roads, ⊥ Road Junction, ∩ Bridge ⊤ indicates a sharp turn. The directions R (right) and L (left) for the forward journey are above the line, those of the reverse, below.

very good, after which it is undulating with fair surface to Kingussie. This road is peculiarly liable to change according to the season. The direct but steep road Inverness to Culcabock is ½m. shorter.

Gradients.—At 3m. mostly 1 in 16; 6¼m. 1 in 23-20. 7⅞m. 1 in 25-13; 9m. 1 in 21-18; 19¾m. 1 in 24; 24m. 1 in 23-16; 27¼m. 1 in 18; 32½m. 1 in 18; 38¾m. 1 in 22.

Milestones.—Measured from Inverness suburbs,—correct.

Measurements.

Inverness,* Town Hall.							
7⅜	Craggie Inn.*						
11⅝	4¼	Moy,* Inn.					
15⅜	8	3¾	Freeburn Inn.*				
24¾	17⅜	13⅛	9⅜	Carrbridge,* Hotel.			
32	24⅝	20⅜	16⅝	7¼	Aviemore Station.		
34⅜	27	22¾	19	9⅝	2⅜	Lynwilg Inn.*	
44	36⅝	32⅜	28⅝	19¼	12	9⅝	Kingussie,* Court House.

Principal Objects of Interest.—2¾m. Culloden to E. Fine scenery in the valleys of the Rivers Nairn and Findhorn into which the road dips. Carrbridge; Old Bridge. Very picturesque scenery. Aviemore; Rothiemurchus Forest and Loch-an-eilan. 35m. Kinrara. 41¾m. Belleville House. Kingussie; Ruthven Barracks.

Hotels or Inns at places marked *.

297 CRAGGIE INN TO INVERFARIGAIG.

Description.—Class II. This is a well made road with easy gradients, but the surface is only fair to Flichity Inn; thereafter it is very rough and stony.

Gradients.—At 12¾m. 1 in 20; 13½m. 1 in 23; 14m. 1 in 21; 18m. 1 in 20-16-20-25-11.

Milestones.—Continuation of those from Inverness,—correct.

Measurements.

Inverness, Town Hall.*					
...	Craggie Inn.*				
15⅜	8¾	Flichity Inn.*			
22⅞	16¼	7½	Errogie Inn.*		
27⅝	21	12¼	4¾	Foyers Hotel.*	
28½	21⅞	13⅛	5⅝	⅞	Foyers Pier.

Principal Objects of Interest.—The scenery up Strath Nairn is very fine.

Hotels or Inns at places marked *.

298 INVERNESS TO FORT AUGUSTUS.

Description.—Class II. & III. At first the road has a good surface, but there are several slight hills to Dores. Thence along the shores of Loch Ness is undulating with fair surface to Inverfarigaig, when the road—leaving the

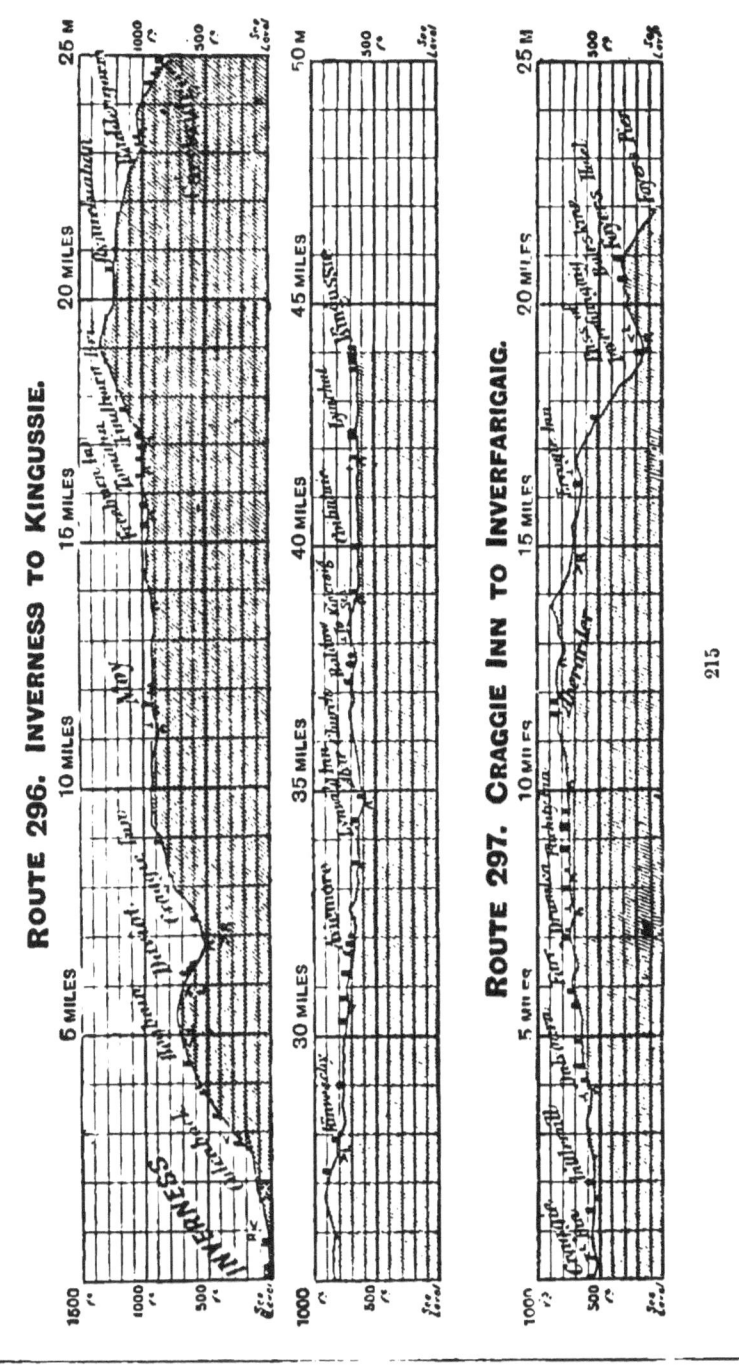

Loch—rises rather steeply to Foyers Hotel. Thereafter the road gets worse and worse, and after Whitebridge is a loose mass of stones, with very steep hills, the descent to Fort Augustus being almost precipitous at several points. At times the surface from Whitebridge to Fort Augustus is little better than a watercourse.

Gradients.—At 3¾m. 1 in 23; 6¾m. 1 in 15-25; 16¼m. 1 in 11; 16½m. 1 in 17; 17m. 1 in 11-24. At 19m. is 1 in 8; 20m. 1 in 10. After Whitebridge the grades average about 1 in 20; but are 1 in 13 at 25½m., and 1 in 10 at 27m. The descent begins with 1 in 15-13, and is 1 in 7 at 29¾m. and 31¼m., the rest being on an average about 1 in 11. These hills are of course highly dangerous.

Milestones.—Measured from Inverness suburbs,—correct to Foyers; thereafter from Fort Augustus,—correct.

Measurements.

Inverness,* Town Hall.				
8	Dores,* Inn.			
18⅝	10⅝	Foyers Hotel.*		
23¼	15¼	4⅝	Whitebridge Inn.*	
32⅜	24⅜	14	9⅛	Fort Augustus.*

Principal Objects of Interest.—2½m. Ness Castle. 19m. Fall of Foyers. The scenery about Foyers is very fine, and magnificent views are obtained of "Glen More."

Hotels or Inns at places marked *.

299 DORES TO WHITEBRIDGE.

Description.—Class III. This is a fearful road with very bad surface the whole way—stony at first, soft afterwards—the fine scenery is the only attraction.

Gradients.—At 1m. 1 in 13-9-26-15; 2¾m. 1 in 25.

Milestones.—After Torness, measured from Inverness *via* Essich; afterwards from Errogie Inn.

Measurements.

Inverness,* Town Hall.				
8	Dores,* Inn.			
14	6	Torness.		
17¾	9¾	3¾	Errogie Inn.*	
24⅝	16⅝	10⅝	6⅞	Whitebridge Inn.*

Principal Objects of Interest.—The road passes through very grand scenery.

Hotels or Inns at places marked *.

300 INVERNESS TO FORT WILLIAM.

Description.—Class II. A very undulating road with a number of rather abrupt turns. The road is undulating, but with comparatively easy hills at first, and has a fine surface as far as Drumnadrochit, when the hills become steeper and the road has a poorer surface. After Fort

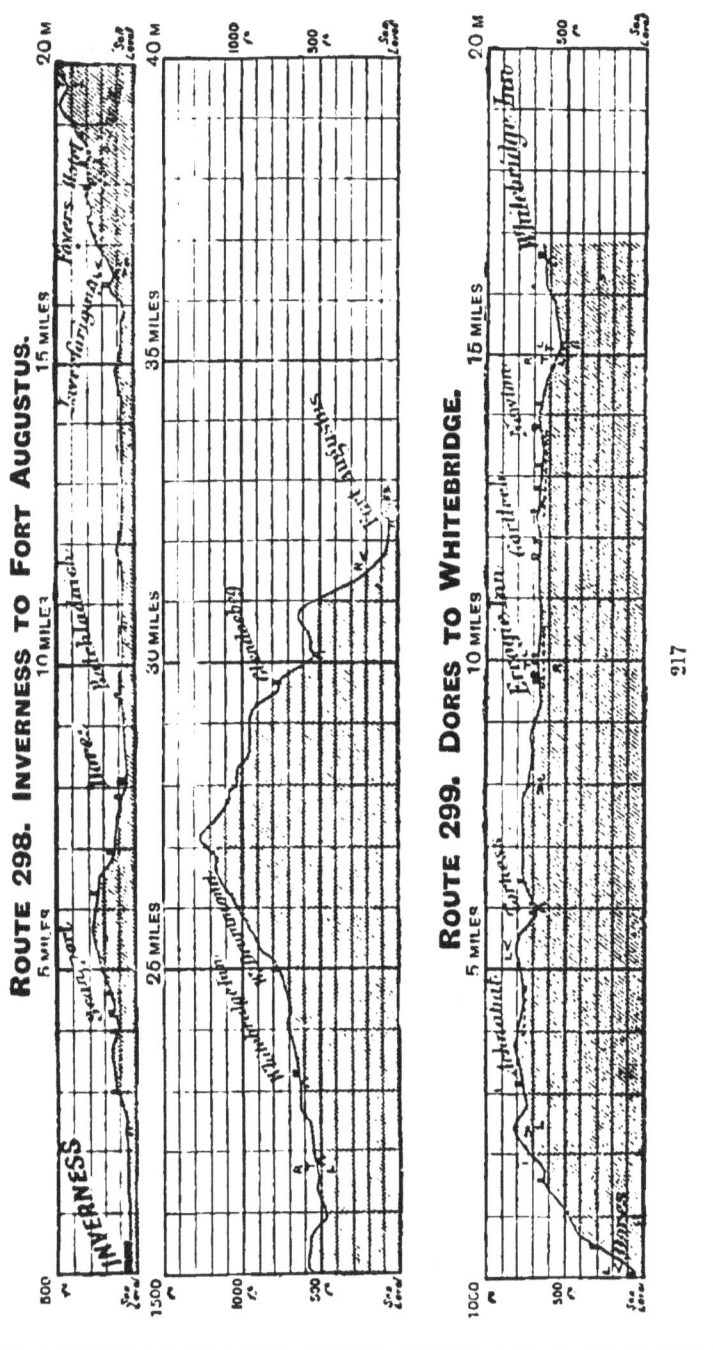

Augustus the road is rather better, but again degenerates beyond Letterfinlay. After Spean Bridge the surface is very good, and the grades are easy. There is a more direct road (Class III.), ⅜m. shorter between Fort Augustus and Letterfinlay, along the east side of Loch Oich; it is soft and hilly.

Gradients.—At 2¼m. 1/23; 3¾m. 1/24; 10¾m. 1/24; 12¼m. 1/22; 16¼m. 1/20; 17¼m. 1/20; 18½m. 1/22; 19m. 1/13; 19¼m. 1/15; 19½m. 1/21-10; 25¼m. 1/19; 26¼m. 1/23; 31¾m. 1/16; 32m. 1/22; 33½m. 1/20; 38¼m. 1/17; 39¼m. 1/25; 49½m. 1/14-23; 50m. 1/19-25; 31¾m. 1/25; 55¾m. 1/20-24.

Milestones.—Measured from Invermorriston Inn, northwards, and southwards to Invergarry; thereafter north and south from Spean Bridge,—correct.

Measurements.

Inverness,* Town Hall.							
6¾	Lochend Inn.*						
14½	7¾	Drumnadrochit Hotel.*					
27¼	20½	12¾	Invermorriston Inn.*				
33⅞	27⅛	19⅜	6⅝	Fort Augustus.*			
40⅞	34⅛	26⅜	13⅝	7	Invergarry Hotel.*		
56½	49¾	42	29¼	22⅝	15⅝	Spean Bridge.*	
66	59¼	51½	38¾	32⅛	25⅛	9½	Fort William,* Pier.

Principal Objects of Interest.—1m. Tomnahurich Cemetery. 5¾m. Dochfour. 6¾m. Lochend Castle. 16¾m. Castle Urquhart. 22m. Ruskich Inn; Ferry to Foyers. Fort Augustus; Monastery. 64m. Inverlochy Castle. Fort William; Fort (ruins), Ben Nevis, and Glen Nevis. The Caledonian Canal is crossed at 1¼m., 33¾m., 38½m., & 43⅝m.

Hotels or Inns at places marked *, and at Ruskich, and Letterfinlay.

---

301 INVERMORRISTON TO CLUNIE INN.

Description.—Class III. The road is well engineered and has very easy gradients, but it is in rather poor condition.

Gradients.—Nothing above 1 in 25 worth noticing.

Milestones.—Measured from Invermorriston Inn in Inverness-shire; in Ross-shire probably from Glenelg.

Measurements.

Invermorriston Inn.*		
8¼	Torgoyle Inn.*	
24¼	16	Clunie Inn.*

Principal Objects of Interest.—Glen Morriston is finely wooded at first—rather bleak afterwards.

Hotels or Inns at places marked *.

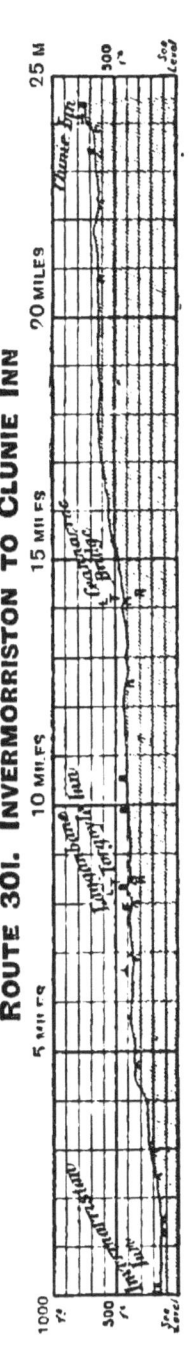

ROUTE 300. INVERNESS TO FORT WILLIAM.

ROUTE 301. INVERMORRISTON TO CLUNIE INN

Signs: < Road Fork, forward journey, > ditto reverse, + Cross Roads, ⊥ Road Junction, ∩ Bridge, T indicates a sharp turn. The directions R (right) and L (left) for the forward journey are above the Road Line, those of the reverse, below.

302 INVERNESS TO DORNOCH.

Description.—Class I. & II. The road has a very fine surface almost the whole way to Bonar Bridge, and is generally in very fine condition. There are slight rises after Bogroy, near Evanton, before Tain, and after Edderton, but these are very slight. After Bonar Bridge the road is rather hilly, but the surface is fair. By crossing at the Meikle Ferry at 48⅜m., the distance between Tain and Dornoch is reduced to 9½m.

Gradients.—At 13¾m. 1 in 25; 65m. 1 in 20; 65½m. 1 in 19; 66½m. 1 in 18; 66¾m. 1 in 20; 67¼m. 1 in 24; 68½m. 1 in 23; 69¼m. 1 in 18.

Milestones.—Measured from Inverness suburbs to Beauly—correct; then from Beauly Hotel. In Rosshire, at first, from Dingwall, Old Court House; they then become variable, but latterly are from Tain, County Buildings.

Measurements.

Inverness,* Town Hall.							
12½	Beauly,* Hotel.						
15½	3	Muir of Ord * P.O.					
18⅝	6⅛	Conon,* P.O.					
21⅛	8⅝	2½	Dingwall,* Old Court House.				
31¼	18¾	12⅝	10⅛	Alness * P.O.			
34¾	22¼	16⅛	13⅝	Invergordon * P.O.			
46⅜	33⅞	27¾	25¼	11⅝	Tain,* County Buildings.		
61⅜	48⅞	42¾	40¼	26⅝	15	Bonar Bridge.*	
71	58½	52⅜	49⅞	36¼	24⅝	9⅝	Clashmore Inn.*
74⅜	61⅞	55¾	53¼	39⅝	28	13	3⅜ Dornoch,* Co. Builds.

Principal Objects of Interest.—1m. Caledonian Canal. BEAULY; Priory, Kilmorack Falls. 25m. Fowlis Castle. Evanton; Glen Glass. Invergordon; Castle. 39¼m. Tarbat Ho. 40⅜m. Balnagown Cas. DORNOCH; Cathedral, Castle.

Hotels or Inns at places marked *, and at Bogroy, Maryburgh, Evanton, Kildary, and Ardgay.

303 BEAULY TO INVERCANNICH, &c.

Description.—Class II. The road is somewhat hilly at first, but has a fair surface; it then becomes more level but is apt to be soft. The last section is rather poor.

Gradients.—1½m. 1 in 23; 4m. 1 in 22-13; 5m. 1 in 25; 5½m. 1 in 19-20.

Milestones.—Measured from Inverness suburbs,—correct.

Measurements.

Beauly,* Hotel.			
10¼	Struy,* Hotel.		
17⅝	7⅜	Invercannich Hotel.*	
20	9¾	2⅜	Tomich.

Principal Objects of Interest.—2½m. Kilmorack Falls. 5¾m. Druim Falls. Very fine scenery in Strath Glass.

Hotels or Inns at places marked *, and at Wellhouse.

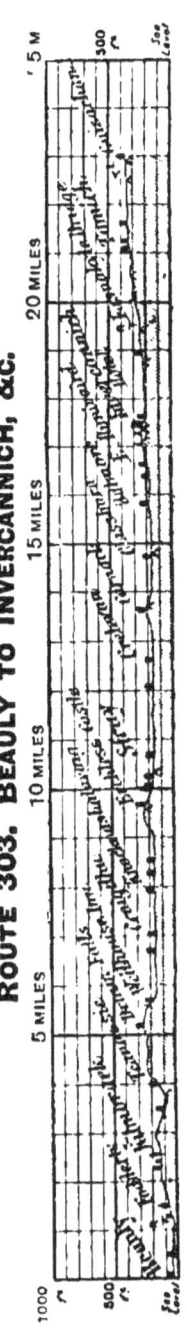

ROUTE 302. INVERNESS TO DORNOCH.

ROUTE 303. BEAULY TO INVERCANNICH, &C.

Signs: < Road Fork, forward journey, > ditto reverse, + Cross Roads, ⊥ Road Junction, ∩ Bridge, T indicates a sharp turn. The directions R (right) and L (left) for the forward journey are above the Road Line, those of the reverse, below.

304 INVERNESS TO INVERGORDON.

Description.—Class II. Good surface to Kessock Ferry (⅝m.), thence the road is very good to Munlochy, after which it becomes poor and hilly. Ferry to Invergordon (¾m.). The road more usually followed is by Fortrose; see Route 305.

Gradients.—At 3½m. 1 in 25; 9m. 1 in 19-15; 10½m. 1 in 22-12-17; 14½m. 1 in 17; 15m. 1 in 22.

Milestones.—Measured from Dingwall.

Measurements.

Inverness,* Town Hall.
6¾ Munlochy.
18¾ 12 Invergordon,* Tower.

Hotels or Inns at places marked *, and at Kessock.

305 INVERNESS TO CROMARTY.

Description.—Class II. Good surface to Kessock Ferry (⅝m.), thence the road is very fine, but slightly hilly to Avoch, where it becomes almost level. After Rosemarkie the surface is scarcely so good, and there are several stiff hills. A branch to Invergordon strikes off at 14¾m., and is more generally used than Route 304.

Gradients.—At 3½m. 1 in 25. To Invergordon at 15¼m. 1 in 17; 17½m. 1 in 14.

Milestones.—Measured from Dingwall.

Measurements.

Inverness,* Town Hall.
2 North Kessock.*
6¾ 4¾ Munlochy P.O.
12¼ 10¼ 5½ Fortrose,* Cross.
22 20 15¼ 9¾ Cromarty,* Pier; or,
22 20 15¼ 9¾ Invergordon,* Tower.

Principal Objects of Interest.—Fortrose: Cathedral. Cromarty: "The Soutars," Cromarty House, Hugh Miller's Monument.

Hotels or Inns at places marked *.

306 CONON TO CROMARTY.

Description.—Class III. The road has a good surface at first, but is hilly till past Balblair, when it becomes almost level with good surface.

Gradients.—At 6¼m. 1 in 22-17.

Measurements.

Conon * P.O.
8¾ Drumcudden Inn.*
12⅜ 4⅛ Balblair Inn.*
15 6¼ 2⅛ Jemimaville.
19¾ 11 6⅞ 4¾ Cromarty,* Pier.

Principal Objects of Interest.—Cromarty; as Route 305.

Hotels or Inns at places marked *.

Route 304. Inverness to Invergordon.

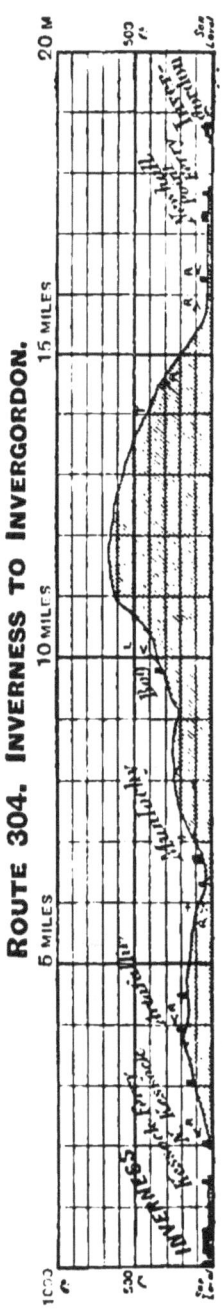

Route 305. Inverness to Cromarty. (Route 304 for 5 miles.)

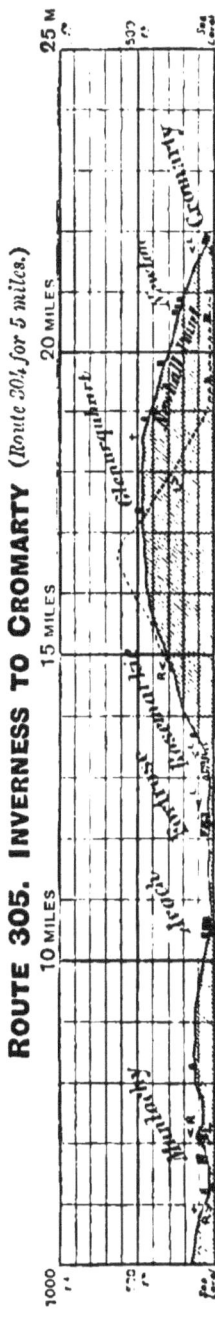

The dotted line is the branch road to Newhall, for Invergordon.

Route 306. Conon to Cromarty.

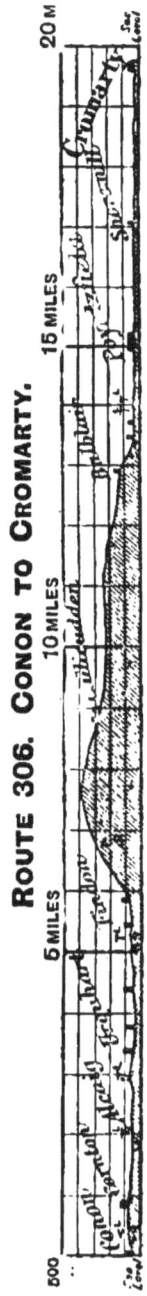

307 INVERNESS TO FORT GEORGE.

Description.—Class II. The road is rather lumpy at first, but improves after Culloden Station.

Milestones.—Measured from Inverness suburbs,—correct.

Measurements.—Inverness,* Town Hall.
    3½ Culloden Station.
    10¾   7½ Campbelltown.
    12¼   8¾   1½ Fort George.*

Principal Objects of Interest.—Culloden Battlefield lies nearly 3 miles to the south of the station. Glm. Castle Stuart. Fort George; Old Fort.

308 DRUMNADROCHIT TO INVERCANNICH.

Description.—Class III. As far as Glenurquhart the surface is good; but thereafter it is hilly and soft, with a dangerous descent to Strath Glass.

Gradients.—At 9¾m. 1 in 13; 10¼m. to 11¾m. 1 in 21-13-9-23-19 (dangerous).

Milestones.—Continuation of those from Inverness.

Measurements.—Drumnadrochit Hotel.*
    6½ Glenurquhart P.O.
    12½   6 Invercannich Hotel.*

309 INVERCANNICH TO AFFRICK LODGE.

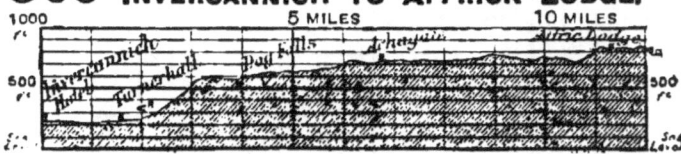

Description.—Class III. A fair undulating road for two miles, then a soft bad road most of the way.

Gradients.—At 3m. 1 in 12.

Measurements.—Invereannich Hotel.*
    12½ Affrick Lodge.

Principal Objects of Interest.—2½m. Chisholm's Pass. 4½m. Dog Falls. Exquisite scenery in Glen Affrick.

Dingwall to Inverness. 310

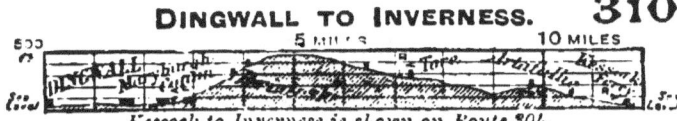

Kessock to Inverness is shown on Route 304.

Description.—Class II. This road has a splendid surface. Ferry at Kessock (¾m.).
Gradients.—At 3½m. 1 in 21-25-19-16-20; 4¼m. 1 in 16.
Milestones.—Measured from Dingwall.
Measurements.—Dingwall,* Old Court House.
        11¾   N. Kessock.*
        13⅜   2   Inverness,* Town Hall.

Tain to Cromarty. 311

Description.—Class II. This road has a very fine surface, and is level after Nigg Sta. Ferry to Cromarty (1m.).
Milestones.—Continuation of those on Invergordon Road.
Measurements.—Tain,* County Buildings.
        4¾   Nigg Station.
        11¾   7   Cromarty,* Pier.

Principal Objects of Interest.—CROMARTY; as Route 305.

Tain to Tarbat Ness. 312

Description.—Class II. A fine smooth road.
Milestones.—At first from Tain, County Buildings.
Measurements.—Tain,* County Buildings.
        9¼   Portmahomack,* Inn.
        12¼   3¼   Tarbat Ness Lighthouse.

Tain to Dornoch, &c. 313

The first 5 miles are shown on Route 317.

Description.—Class II. To Meikle Ferry, as Route 317; thereafter a fine road to Dornoch. The continuation past Little Ferry is in poor condition. Little Ferry (¼m.).
Measurements.—Tain,* County Buildings.
        9½   Dornoch,* County Buildings.
        17½   7⅞   Golspie,* Hotel.

Principal Objects of Interest.—Dornoch; as Route 302. Golspie; as Route 333.

314 STRUY TO MONAR LODGE.

Description.—Class III. This is not a good road. The surface is fair at first, but soon becomes soft and bad, and at several points is very loose.

Gradients.—At 13¾m. 1 in 17; is the only hill of note.

Milestones.—Continuation of those from Inverness.

Measurements.
Struy Hotel.*
14¾ Monar Lodge.

Principal Objects of Interest.—The scenery up this valley amply repays the tourist, but can hardly be considered equal to Strath Affric.

---

315 MUIR OF ORD TO STRATH CONON.

Description.—Class III. The road has a good surface as far as Clachuile Inn; but thereafter is slightly hilly, and with several rough parts. The driving road continues as far as Scardroy, 23¾m. from Muir of Ord.

Gradients.—At 4m. 1 in 25; 10½m. 1 in 16-19.

Milestones.—Measured from Muir of Ord Post Office,—correct.

Measurements.
Muir of Ord,* P.O.
5¼ Clachuile Inn.*
15¼ 10¼ Strathconon Inn.*

Principal Objects of Interest.—The scenery in Strath Conon is pretty, but at first there is little noteworthy.

Hotels or Inns at places marked *, and at Milton.

---

316 ALNESS TO BONAR BRIDGE.

Description.—Class II. The road rises with a stiff gradient at first, with fair surface, and then is a long and steady ascent. After Sittenham the surface degenerates, and is very poor past Aultnamain, with a rough and steep descent to Fearn Lodge. Thereafter the road is very good to Bonar Bridge.

Gradients.—At 1m. 1 in 17-19. From 12m. to 13½m. the ruling gradient is 1 in 17; at 12¼m. 1 in 13.

Milestones.—Measured from Bonar Bridge,—correct.

Measurements.
Alness P.O.
9¼ Aultnamain Inn.*
18¼ 9¼ Bonar Bridge.*

Principal Objects of Interest.—After Sittenham a very monotonous road. 3m. Ardross Castle to W.

Hotels or Inns at places marked *, and at Ardgay.

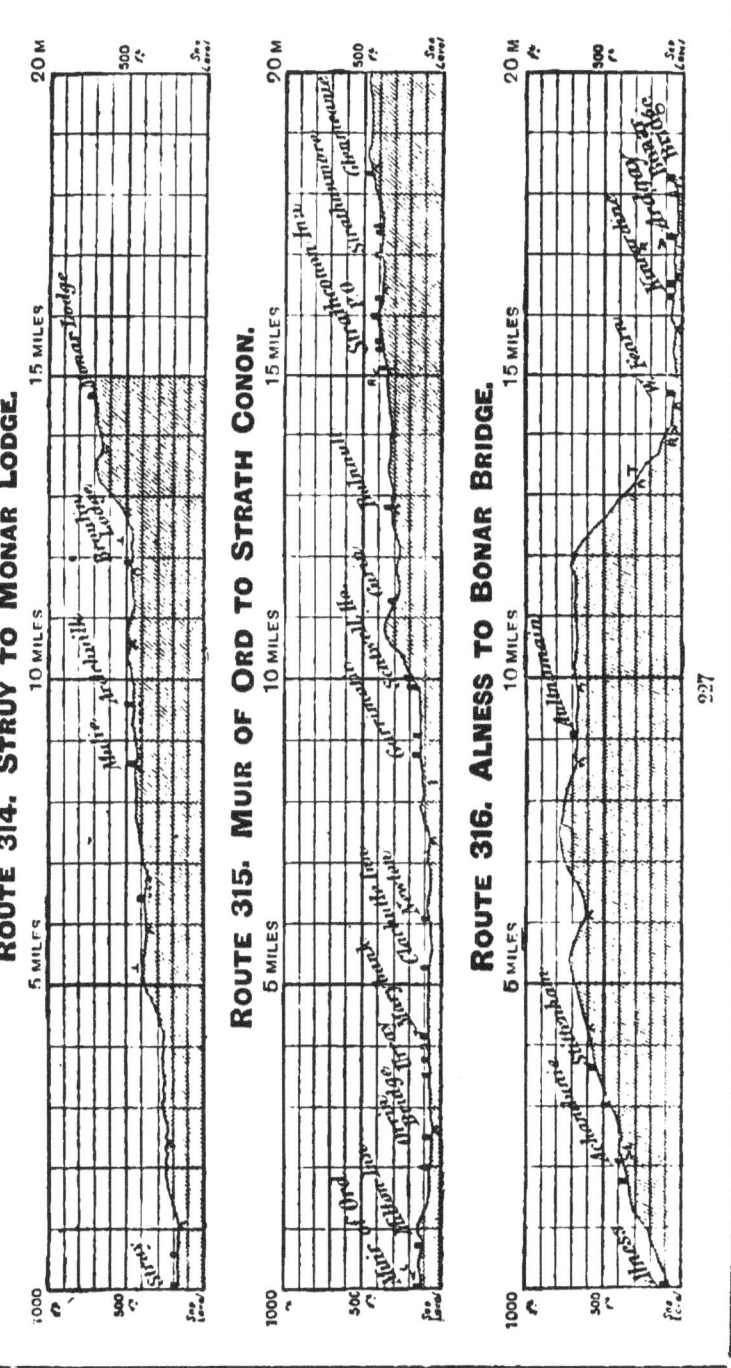

317 TAIN TO WICK.

Description.—Class II. Leaving the Bonar Bridge road at 2½m., it is a rough track down to the Meikle Ferry pier, where ferry across (⅝m.). Thence the road has a very fine surface, but is somewhat hilly between Evelix and the Mound, and between Brora and Helmsdale. From Helmsdale to Latheron over "the Ord" is most trying, and with some particularly dangerous hills, on which the surface is rough, but the more level parts are decidedly good. After Latheron the surface is very good.

Gradients.—At 10¾m. 1 in 20; 13m. 1 in 25; 20m. 1 in 23; 28¾m. 1 in 18-23; 30¾m. 1 in 20; 34¾m. 1 in 21. The ascent of the Ord has varying grades, and is 1 in 14 at 37½m.; and 1 in 15 at 38m.; and 1 in 16 at 39¾m. Berriedale Hill S. side 1 in 10-9-12; N. side 1 in 12. Dunbeath S. 1 in 14-17; N. 1 in 17-19. Latheronwheel S. 1 in 18; N. 1 in 17. These hills are highly dangerous,—those at Berriedale and Dunbeath having most dangerous turns.

Milestones.—At first from Tain, County Buildings. In Sutherland, measured from Bonar Bridge *via* Dornoch,—tolerably correct. In Caithness, from Wick, County Buildings,—correct.

Measurements.

Tain,* County Buildings.								
7½	Clashmore Inn.*							
15¼	7¾	Mound Station.						
19⅜	11⅝	3⅞	Golspie,* Hotel.					
25	17½	9¾	5⅞	Brora,* Bridge.				
36½	29	21¼	17⅜	11½	Helmsdale,* Hotel.			
56¾	49¼	41½	37⅝	31¾	20¼	Latheron,* P.O.		
60¼	52¾	45	41⅜	35¼	23¾	3½	Lybster,* Portland Arms.	
73⅜	65⅞	58⅛	54¼	48⅜	36⅞	16⅝	13⅛	Wick,* Co. Buildings.

Principal Objects of Interest.—12m. Skelbo Castle. 15m. "The Mound." Sutherland Monument on hilltop. 20½m. Dunrobin Castle. Helmsdale; Castle ruin. Berriedale; Castle ruin. Dunbeath; Castle ruin. After Berriedale the country is almost treeless, and has a most monotonous appearance. At the coast, however, there is some fine cliff scenery. WICK; "Trams," Harbour.

Hotels or Inns at places marked *, and at Meikle Ferry, Poles, Dunbeath, and Forse.

318 DORNOCH TO LAIRG.

Description.—Class III. A fine but hilly road at first, then fair surface past Rogart, but rather poor near Lairg.

Gradients.—1¼m. 1/24; 6¾m. 1/24; 7m. 1/19; 21m. 1/20.

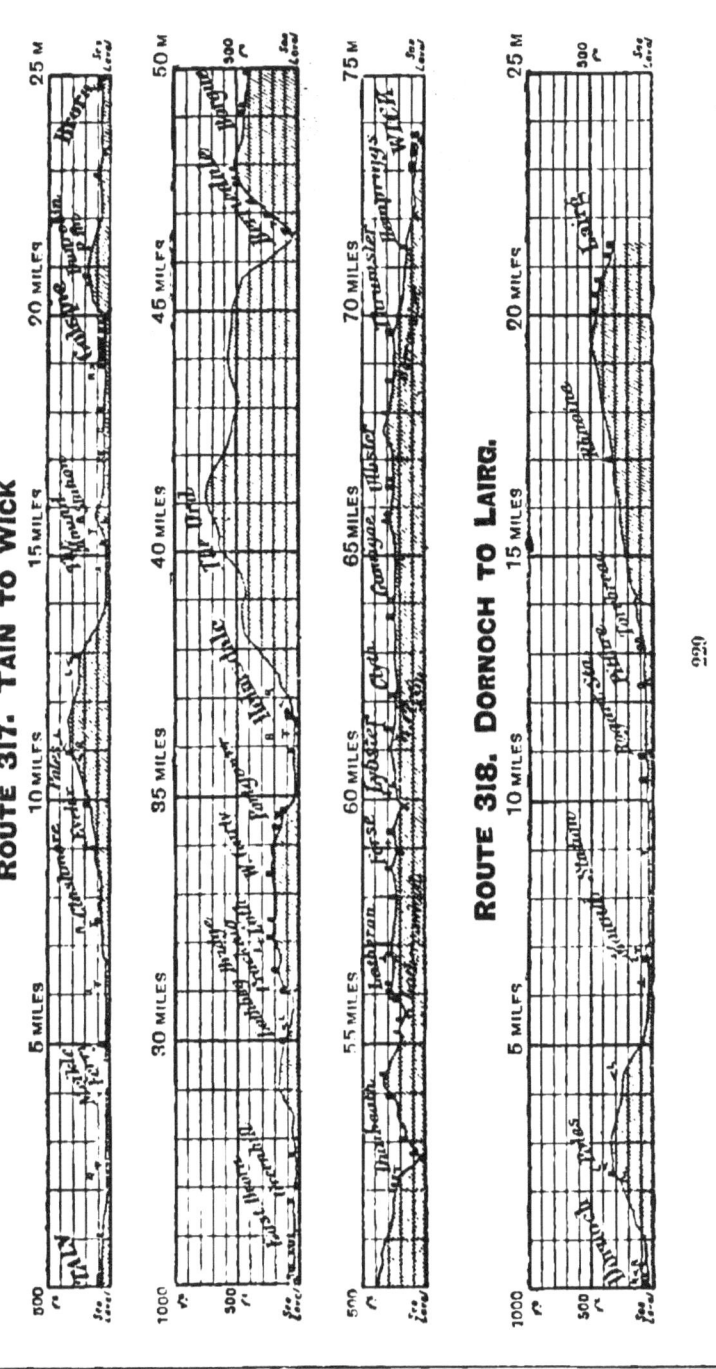

Measurements.

Dornoch,* County Buildings.			
6¾	Mound Station.		
10⅞	4⅛	Rogart,* Station.	
21½	14¾	10⅝	Lairg,* Hotel.

Principal Objects of Interest.—4½m. Skelbo Castle. 6½m. "The Mound." Very dreary road after Rogart.

319 HELMSDALE TO MELVICH.

Description.—Class III. This is a well made, but narrow road, up Strath Ullie and down Strath Halladale. The surface throughout is pretty uniform—fair, inclining to be soft. This route is sometimes preferred to the more direct road to Thurso *via* Latheron, as it avoids the nasty hills.

Gradients.—At 9¾m. 1 in 23; 23½m. 1 in 22; 27m. 1 in 15.

Measurements.

Helmsdale,* Hotel.			
9	Kildonan Church.		
24⅜	15⅜	Forsinard Hotel.*	
40¼	31¼	15⅞	Melvich,* Inn ; or,
43¼	34¼	18⅞	Reay,* Inn.

Principal Objects of Interest.—After Kildonan a most monotonous and desolate road for about 20 miles.

Hotels or Inns at places marked *.

320 WICK TO JOHN O' GROATS.

Description.—Class II. A fine road with smooth surface and easy hills to Freswick; thereafter rather steeper, but with good surface past Canisbay. A more direct road to John o' Groats has been constructed lately, but it is steeper, and the surface is hardly formed yet.

Gradients.—At 10½m. 1 in 16; 11½m. 1 in 23; 12¾m. 1 in 24.

Milestones.—Measured from Wick Cross,—correct.

Measurements.

Wick,* County Buildings.		
7¾	Keiss * Inn.	
17⅜	9⅝	Huna * Inn.
19¼	11½	John o' Groats * *via* Canisbay.
16⅞	9⅛	John o' Groats * direct.

Principal Objects of Interest.—1½m. Ackergill Tower. Girnigoe; Castle. Keiss; Castle ruin. Freswick; Castle. 16⅞m. "John o' Groats House."

Hotels or Inns at places marked *.

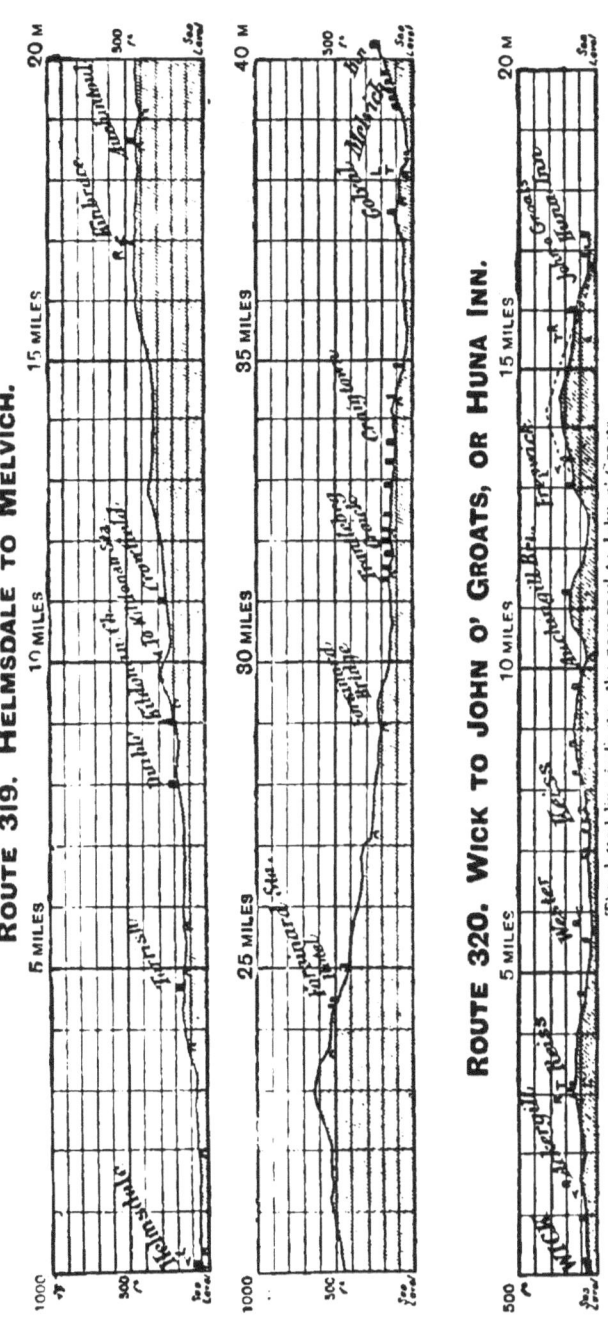

321 WICK TO THURSO.

Description.—Of the two roads that *via* Watten (Class II.) is the preferable, as it is rather better than that *via* Castletown (Class III). On both roads the surface is good.

Milestones (*via* Watten).—Measured from Wick Town Hall. (*Via* Bower)—measured from Wick Cross.

Measurements.

Wick,* County Buildings.				
7⅝	Watten Inn.*			
11⅛	3½	Dunn Inn.*		
15	7⅜	3⅞	Georgemas Inn.*	
20⅝	13	9½	5⅝	Thurso,* Post Office.

Wick,* County Buildings.			
10⅝	Thura Inn.*		
15¾	5⅛	Castletown,* P.O.	
20⅞	10¼	5⅛	Thurso,* Post Office.

Principal Objects of Interest.—Both roads are somewhat dreary, the country being very flat.

---

322 THURSO TO JOHN O' GROATS.

Description.—Class III. A fine road to Castletown; thereafter rather soft, but improving before Canisbay, thence good to John o' Groats.

Measurements.

Thurso,* Post Office.				
5⅛	Castletown,* P.O.			
8½	3⅜	Dunnet,* P.O.		
12¾	7⅝	4¼	Berriedale Arms Inn.*	
18⅜	13¼	9⅞	5⅝	Huna Inu'; or,
20⅛	15	11⅝	7⅜	John o' Groats Hotel.*

Principal Objects of Interest.—8½m. to Dunnet Head. 20⅛m. John o' Groats House.

---

323 THURSO TO LATHERON.

Description.—Class III. A good but narrow road with easy undulations. It is sometimes rather soft.

Gradients.—At 9m. 1 in 22; 23m. 1 in 21.

Milestones.—At first measured from Wick, County Buildings; after Georgemas, from Thurso.

Measurements.

Thurso,* Post Office.				
5⅝	Georgemas Inn.*			
10¾	5⅛	Mybster Inn.*		
17¼	11⅝	6½	Achavanich.*	
23⅜	17¾	12⅝	6⅛	Latheron,* P.O.

Principal Objects of Interest.—A very dreary road.

Hotels or Inns at places marked*.

Route 321. Wick to Thurso *via Bower.*

Via Watten.

Route 322. Thurso to John o' Groats.

Route 323. Thurso to Latheron.

324 Thurso to Durness.

Description.—Class II. & III. This is a fine road as far as Reay, but thereafter it becomes somewhat soft. At one or two points beyond Melvich the surface is fair, but the road is a constant succession of hills more and less steep with rough surface. Ferry at Tongue (¾m.). Thence to Hope Ferry is the long and arduous ascent of the Moine—rough and steep—after which, although the hills are not so long, the surface is not good till near Durness. The long round of Loch Ereboll may be shortened by 9 miles, by crossing at Heilem Ferry (⅝m.).

Gradients.—At 13m. 1 in 23; 16m. 1 in 22; 16¼m. 1 in 13; 17¼m. 1 in 24; 18m. 1 in 23; 20m. 1 in 21-16; 21m. 1 in 13-23-17; 24m. 1 in 14 (dangerous); 25m. 1 in 13-15; 27½m. 1 in 19; 28½m. 1 in 15; 30¼m. 1 in 16; 31m. 1 in 14-17; 34½m. 1 in 11; 36½m. 1 in 11; 38m. 1 in 14; 39½m. 1 in 16; 40½m. 1 in 18; 41¾m. 1 in 16; 43m. 1 in 10-14; 46m. 1 in 17; 48½m. 1 in 17; 52m. 1 in 8-10; 52½m. 1 in 15; 53¼m. 1 in 16; 53¾m. 1 in 11; 54¼m. 1 in 11; 55¾m. 1 in 13; 57½m. 1 in 14; 66¼m. 1 in 22; 69½m. 1 in 14; 69¾m. 1 in 17; 72m. 1 in 15; 72¼m. 1 in 15.

Milestones.—Measured from Thurso Post Office, as far as Melvich.

Measurements.

Thurso,* Post Office.							
10⅞	Reay Inn.*						
17⅞	7	Melvich Inn.*					
21⅛	11¼	4¼	Strathy Inn.*				
31¼	20⅜	14⅝	10⅛	Bettyhill Inn.*			
44⅝	33½	27½	23¼	13⅜	(Tongue Hotel).*		
57¼	50¼	46	41¾	26	15	Ereboll.	
72⅝	65⅝	61⅝	57⅛	41⅜	30⅜	15⅜	Durness Inn.*

Principal Objects of Interest.—The country through which this road passes is mostly moorland, with very frequent dips down into the different valleys. There being, of course, fine views of the coast from the more elevated parts. The Kyle of Tongue is rather pretty in contrast to the country just passed through, and is less barren than the neighbouring Loch Ereboll. The Smoo Cave at 71¼m. should not be missed.

Hotels or Inns at places marked *.

ROUTE 324. THURSO TO DURNESS.

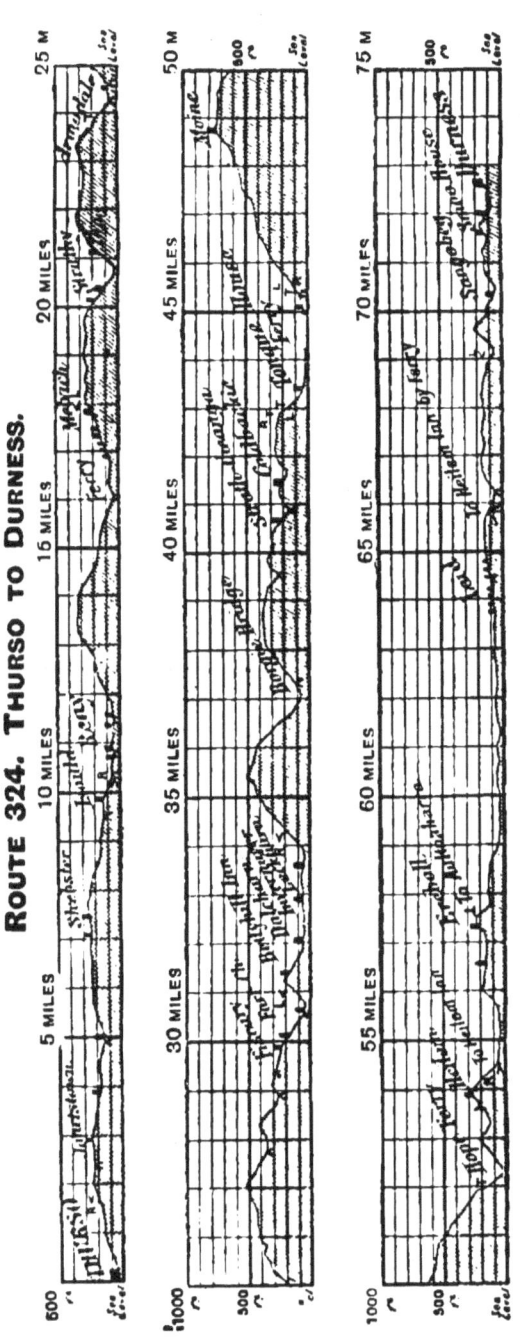

Signs: < Road Fork, forward journey, > ditto reverse, + Cross Roads, ⊥ Road Junction, ∩ Bridge, ⊤ indicates a sharp turn. The directions R (right) and L (left) for the forward journey are above the Road Line, those of the reverse, below.

325 THURSO TO WESTERDALE.

Description.—Class III. An undulating road with good surface.

Measurements.—Thurso,* Post Office.
    6¼   Halkirk,* Inn.
    11¼ 5   Westerdale.

326 THURSO TO REAY.

Description.—Class III. A more hilly road than Route 324, but the surface is good.

Gradients.—At 2m. 1 in 24; 5¾m. 1 in 22.

Milestones.—Measured from Thurso Post Office.

Measurements.—Thurso,* Post Office.
    5¾   Bridge of Forss.
    10¾ 5¾ Reay,* Inn.

327 BONAR BRIDGE TO CRAIGS.

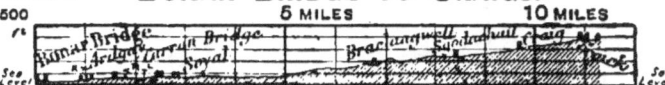

Description.—Class III. We have no information as to the state of this road, but believe it to be somewhat rough.

Milestones.—Measured from Ardgay Inn.

Measurements.—Bonar Bridge.*
    1   Ardgay,* Inn.
    9¼ 8¼   Craig House.
    11   10   1¼ Croick Church.

328 BONAR BRIDGE TO ROSEHALL.

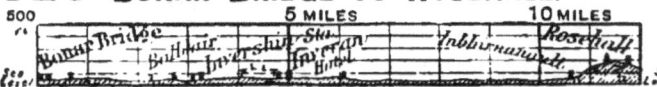

Description.—Class II. A fine road with slight undulations until just before Rosehall, when there is a stiff hill.

Gradients.—At 10¾m. 1 in 19-17.

Milestones.—At first measured from Bonar Bridge, afterwards from Invershin.

Measurements.—Bonar Bridge.*
    3¼   Invershin Station.*
    4¾ 1½   Inveran,* Hotel.
    11¾ 8¼ 7 Rosehall.*

Principal Objects of Interest.—Very pretty scenery between Bonar Bridge and Inveran, and at Rosehall.

BONAR BRIDGE TO LAIRG. 329

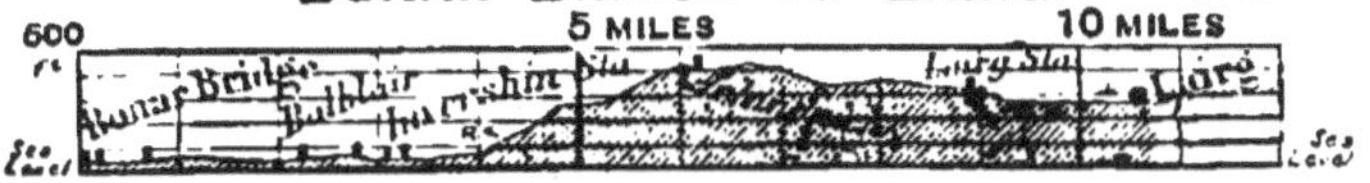

Description.—Class III. Although this is the direct road to Lairg, Route 334 is more generally followed. The surface is fair but the road is hilly.

Gradients.—At 4¾m. 1 in 17; 5¼m. 1 in 22.

Milestones.—Measured from Bonar Bridge,—correct.

Measurements.—Bonar Bridge.*

3¼ Invershin Station.*

8⅝ 5⅜ Lairg Station.

10⅝ 7⅜ 1¾ Lairg,* Hotel.

Principal Objects of Interest.—Very pretty scenery between Bonar Bridge and Invershin, dreary near Lairg Station.

TORNAPRESS TO APPLECROSS. 330

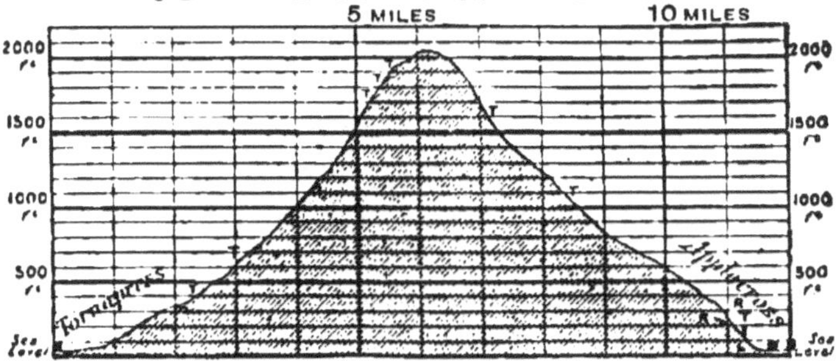

Description.—Class III. Although the road has been engineered by a series of zig-zags to ease the gradients as much as possible, nevertheless it is terribly steep, and the surface is wretched. There are a large number of dangerous turns at different points along the road. The road strikes off Route 346 at 10¼m.

Gradients.—The gradients vary considerably, but in the first 3½m. are not above 1 in 15; up to 4¼m. 1 in 11; at 5m. 1 in 7, then 1 in 10. The descent is at 7¼m. 1 in 8; at 8½m. 1 in 11; at 10½m. 1 in 16; at 11m. 1 in 9.

Measurements.—Tornapress.

12 Applecross,* Inn.

Principal Objects of Interest.—Magnificent view from the summit.

Hotels or Inns at places marked *.

331 DURNESS TO CAPE WRATH.

Description.—Class III. A good road to Keoldale, where Ferry (½m.). Thence the road has a tolerable surface, but there are some very steep hills.

Gradients.—At 1½m.1 in 17; 3m.1 in 10; 5m.1 in 10; 7¾m. 1 in 20; 9m.1 in 18; 10m.1 in 15; 12m.1 in 13; 12½m.1 in 17.

Milestones.—Measured from Cape Wrath Lighthouse,—correct.

Measurements.

Durness,* Inn.
   14   Cape Wrath Lighthouse.

Principal Objects of Interest.—Very fine cliff scenery at Cape Wrath.

---

332 DURNESS TO LAXFORD BRIDGE.

Description.—Class III. The road is fairly well engineered, and in good condition, except in the higher parts, and on the descent to Rhiconich; thereafter undulating but good surface to Laxford Bridge.

Gradients.—At 8½m.1 in 19-20; 12m.1 in 18; 13¾m.1 in 17; 15½m.1 in 21; 16¾m.1 in 16; 17m.1 in 23; 18m.1 in 12.

Measurements.

Durness,* Inn.
  14¼   Rhiconich Inn.*
  19¼   5   Laxford Bridge.
  26   11¾ 6¾ Scourie,* Hotel; or,
  56   41¾ 36¾ Lairg,* Hotel.

Principal Objects of Interest.—Characteristic Sutherlandshire loch scenery between Rhiconich and Laxford.

Hotels or Inns at places marked *.

---

333 BONAR BRIDGE TO GOLSPIE.

Description.—Class III. The ascent is very steep at first, but after passing the summit there is a long and comparatively easy descent to Mound, with rather soft surface; thence very good to Golspie.

Gradients.—At ¼m. 1 in 10-16; 2m. 1 in 13; 3½m. 1 in 20; 4¼m.1 in 15-23; 11¾m.1 in 17.

Measurements.

Bonar Bridge.*
  14   Mound Station.
  17¾ 3¾ Golspie,* Hotel.

Principal Objects of Interest.—A very dreary road. 14m. The "Mound." Golspie; Dunrobin Castle, Sutherland Monument on hilltop.

Hotels or Inns at places marked *.

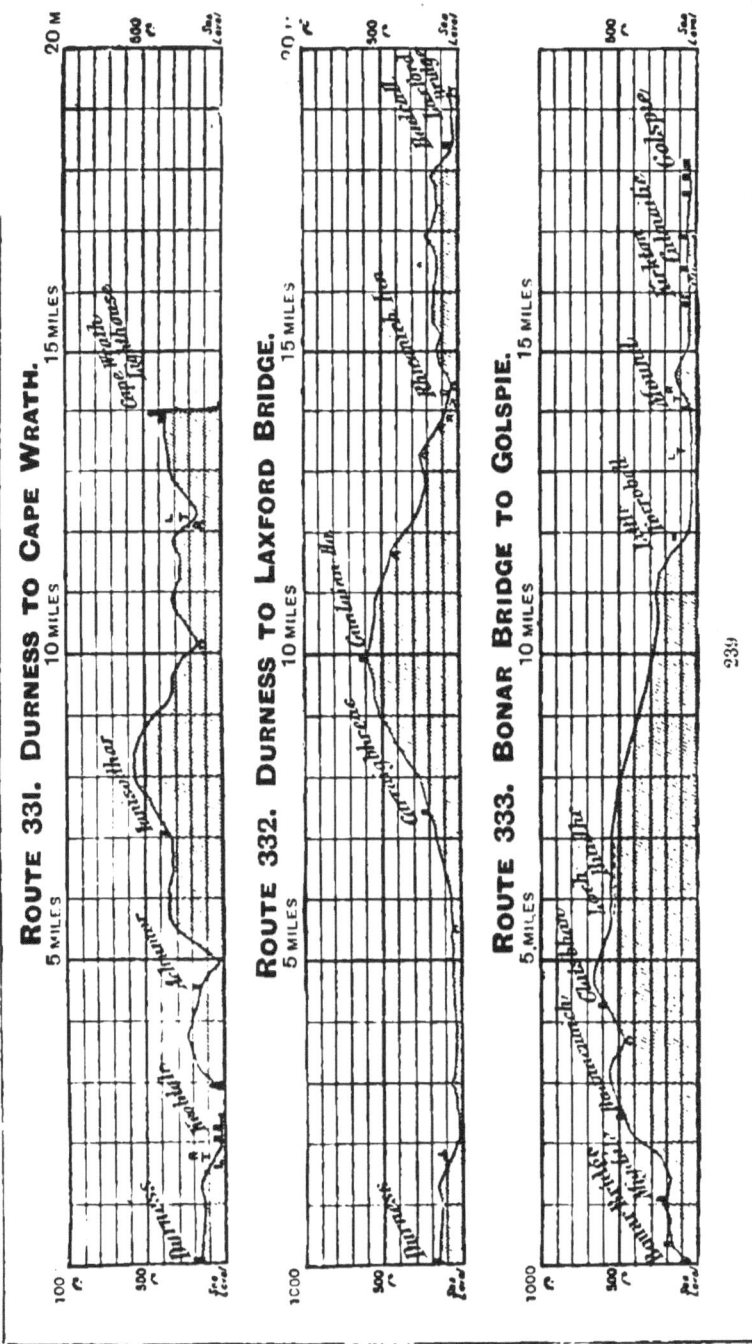

334 BONAR BRIDGE TO TONGUE.

Description.—Class II. The surface is very good and the gradients are very easy for some distance past Lairg, but the road becomes rather rough and steep near the Crask, and on the descent to Aultnaharra. Thereafter the road is soft at first, very good along Loch Loyal, then poor with steep descent to Tongue.

Gradients.—At 23m. 1 in 23; 25¼m. 1 in 20; 30m. 1 in 21; 32¼m. 1 in 19; 33¾m. 1 in 18; 37m. 1 in 22-18-22; 47m. 1 in 22; 48m. 1 in 24; descent to Tongue Ferry or Hotel 1 in 10.

Milestones.—Measured from Bonar Bridge *via* Lairg Station,—correct.

Measurements.

Bonar Bridge.*					
3¼	Invershin Station.*				
10¾	7½	Lairg,* Hotel.			
23¾	20½	13	Crask.*		
31½	28¼	20¾	7¾	Aultnaharra Hotel.*	
47⅞	44⅝	37⅛	24⅛	16⅜	Tongue,* Hotel.

Principal Objects of Interest.—Pretty scenery at first, but very barren moorland after Lairg until nearing Tongue, when a fine view is obtained.

---

335 AULTNAHARRA TO BETTYHILL.

Description.—Class III. This is a wretched road, badly kept, mostly on account of the absence of traffic. The last 5 miles nearing Bettyhill are in good order.

Gradients.—There are short hills but none of length.

Measurements.

Aultnaharra Hotel.*	
24⅜	Bettyhill Inn.*

Principal Objects of Interest.—A bleak, barren, and lonely glen, once well populated, now a Deer Forest.

---

336 AULTNAHARRA TO EREBOLL.

Description.—Class III. A poor road with soft surface, and a very dangerous descent to Ereboll. A considerable river has to be ferried across or forded.

Gradients.—At 11m. 1 in 23-24-13-19; 16¼m. 1 in 11; 17m. 1 in 13; 17½m. 1 in 15; 18m. 1 in 13; 19½m. 1 in 6, with some nasty double turns—exceedingly dangerous.

Measurements.

Aultnaharra Hotel.*		
20⅜	Ereboll.	
23½	3⅛	Heilem Inn.*
35¼	...	... Durness* *via* Laid.

Principal Objects of Interest.—A moorland road.

Hotels or Inns at places marked *.

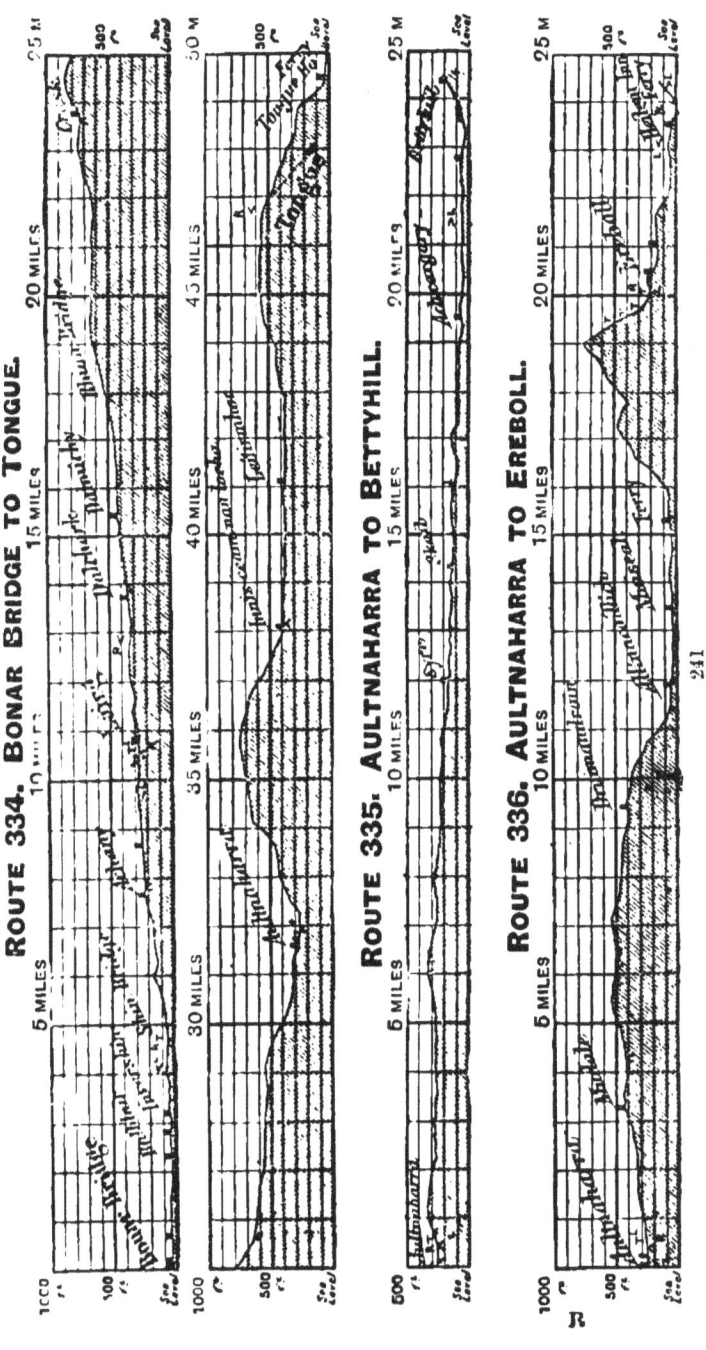

337 LAIRG TO SCOURIE.

Description.—Class II. The road has a very fair surface throughout but is narrow, and at several points is rather soft. There is a steep hill before Kinloch and also before Scourie. Laxford Bridge is only a central point—there are no houses—and it lies a little to the north of the road.

Gradients.—At 25m. 1 in 22-16; 31¾m. 1 in 20; 35½m. 1 in 19; 35¾m. 1 in 17; 42¾m. and 42¼m. 1 in 9-10.

Milestones.—Measured from Lochmore Lodge,—correct.

Measurements.

Lairg,* Hotel.			
15¾	Overscaig Inn.*		
36¾	21	Laxford Bridge.	
43½	27¾	6¾	Scourie,* Hotel.

Principal Objects of Interest.—The road lies near Loch Shin at first and is bleak, but after passing Kinloch the character of the scenery changes and becomes more attractive. Ben Stack is very prominent.

338 LAIRG TO LOCHINVER.

Description.—Class II. A narrow road like the most of the other Sutherland roads. Fair surface but long hill over to Rosehall; thereafter an undulating road, with surface inclining to be loose and gravelly according to season, almost the whole way to Lochinver. On the whole it is a very good road for this County. Care must be taken on the hill descending to Lochinver.

Gradients.—At 1m. 1 in 23; 2½m. 1 in 17; 3½m. 1 in 22; 6¼m. 1 in 17; 8¾m. 1 in 12; thereafter numerous hills—mostly short—up to 1 in 15; the only one specially noticeable being that at Lochinver 1 in 13.

Measurements.

Lairg,* Hotel.						
8¼	Roschall.*					
15	6¾	Oykell Bridge Inn.*				
25¼	17	10¼	Aultnacallagach Inn.*			
32⅞	24⅝	17⅞	7⅝	Inchnadamff,* Inn.		
35	26¾	20	9¾	2⅛	Skiag Bridge.	
46	37¾	31	20¾	13⅛	11	Lochinver,* Hotel.

Principal Objects of Interest.—9m. Cassley Bridge; Falls. Near Aultnacallagach fine views of Suilven and the neighbouring hills. 34¾m. Ardvreck Castle ruins. Charming scenery along Loch Assynt, and approaching Lochinver; also the extraordinary ridges of Suilven and Quinag.

Hotels or Inns at places marked *.

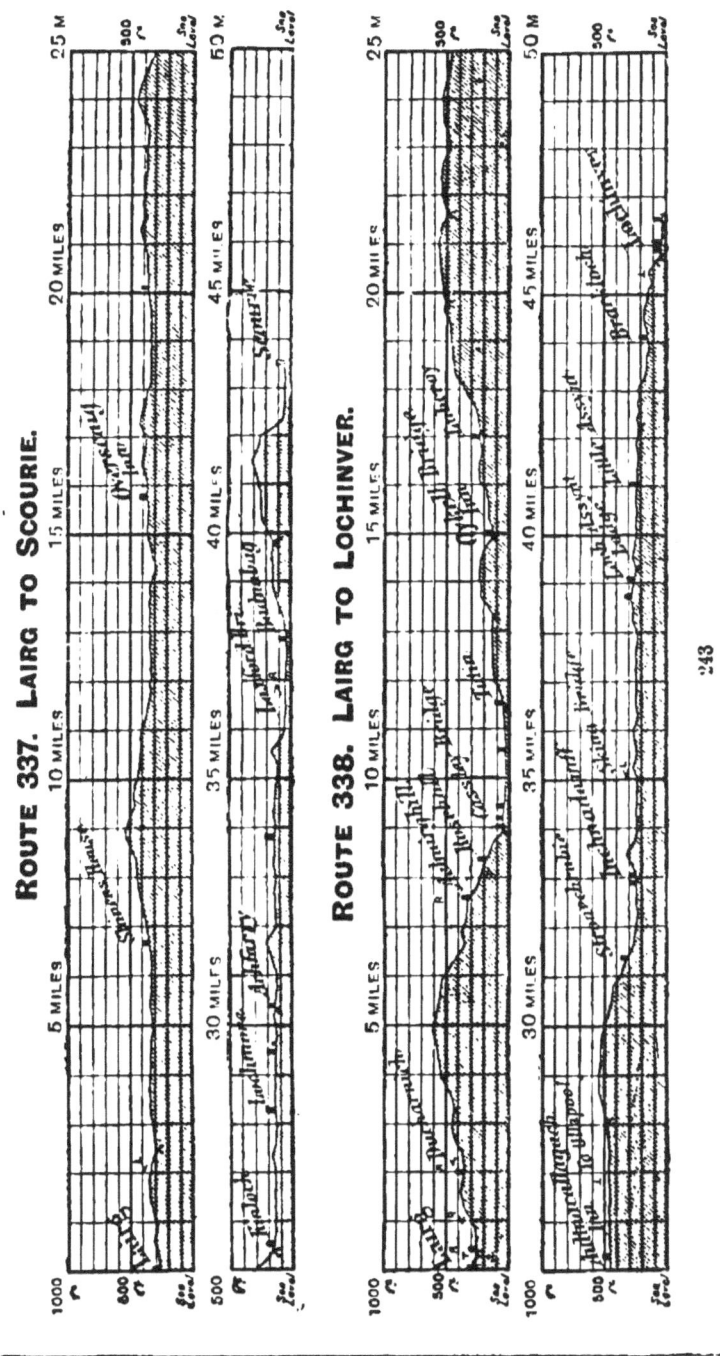

ROUTE 337. LAIRG TO SCOURIE.

ROUTE 338. LAIRG TO LOCHINVER.

339   Dingwall to Kyle Akin.

Description.—Class II. This is a fine smooth road as far as Strathpeffer, then becoming rather poor over the hill to Contin, when the road continues of fair surface to Garve. Thereafter until near Lochcarron is pretty well divided between good and bad, there being several rather loose and stony parts which are compensated by others in fair order. Between Lochcarron and Strome the surface is good. Ferry at Strome ($\frac{3}{8}$m.). Thence to Kyle, with the exception of the short and level part at Balmacara, is an exceedingly hilly road with very poor surface, especially after Balmacara. Ferry to Kyle Akin ($\frac{1}{2}$m.). After Strome Ferry the hills are nearly all dangerously steep.

Gradients.—At $4\frac{3}{4}$m. 1 in 17; 6m. 1 in 16; $17\frac{3}{4}$m. 1 in 23; $19\frac{3}{4}$m. 1 in 22; $39\frac{1}{4}$m. 1 in 25; $55\frac{1}{2}$m. 1 in 10; $56\frac{1}{4}$m. 1 in 16; 58m. 1 in 10; 61m. 1 in 16-10; 65m. 1 in 10; 66m. 1 in 14; $66\frac{1}{2}$m. 1 in 11.

Milestones.—Measured from Dingwall Old Court House, —correct to Auchnasheen, where there is a discrepancy, thence correct to Strome. Thereafter from Strome Ferry Post Office.

Measurements.

Dingwall,* Old Court House.
$4\frac{3}{4}$ Strathpeffer,* P.O.
$13\frac{1}{2}$ $8\frac{3}{4}$ Garve,* Hotel.
$29\frac{1}{2}$ $24\frac{3}{4}$ 16   Auchnasheen.*
$50\frac{1}{2}$ $45\frac{3}{4}$ 37   21   Lochcarron Inn* (Jeantown).
$55\frac{1}{4}$ $50\frac{3}{4}$ $41\frac{3}{4}$ $25\frac{3}{4}$ $4\frac{3}{4}$ Strome Ferry.*
$63\frac{3}{4}$ $58\frac{3}{4}$ $49\frac{3}{4}$ $33\frac{3}{4}$ $12\frac{3}{4}$ $8\frac{1}{2}$ Balmacara,* Hotel.
$70\frac{3}{4}$ $65\frac{3}{4}$ $56\frac{3}{4}$ $40\frac{3}{4}$ $19\frac{3}{4}$ $15\frac{1}{4}$ 7   Kyle Akin,* Hotel.

Principal Objects of Interest.—Strathpeffer; Spa, View Rock. $9\frac{1}{4}$m., to Rogie Falls. Between Garve and Craig Inn the road passes through rather desolate country, only broken by the change in scenery of some half dozen lochs which lie close to the road. Fine scenery thereafter, and there are fine views from the Strome Ferry and Kyle road. Kyle Akin; Castle Moil.

Hotels or Inns at places marked*, and at Achilty, Achanault, Craig, (Strathcarron), Strome, and Kyle.

ROUTE 339. DINGWALL TO KYLE AKIN.

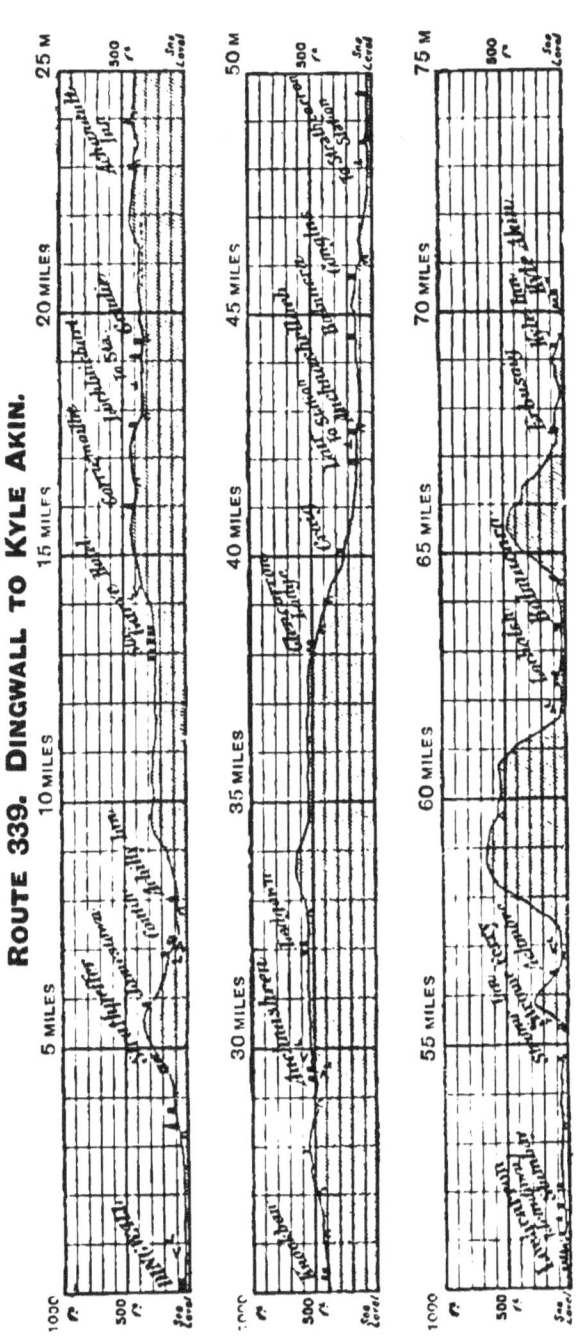

Signs: < Road Fork, forward journey, > ditto reverse, + Cross Roads, ⊥ Road Junction, ∩ Bridge, ⊤ indicates a sharp turn. The directions R (right) and L (left) for the forward journey are above the Road Line, those of the reverse, below.

340   GARVE TO ULLAPOOL.

Description.—Class II. The road branches off the Strome Ferry road ¾m. beyond the Hotel, and has a fair surface as far as Aultguish Inn, when it becomes looser, and on the summit is rather rough. Thereafter the surface improves a little, and is pretty fair on the steep descent from Braemore Lodge, when the road becomes undulating, with some sharp hills to Ullapool.

Gradients.—At 1m. 1 in 17; then a long and steady ascent; 20 to 21½m. 1 in 21-20-25-10-20-12-19; thereafter several short hills of 1 in 16; 31½m. 1 in 19.

Milestones.—Continuation of those from Dingwall, and measured from Dingwall Old Court House.

Measurements.

Dingwall,* Old Court House.
Garve Hotel.*
  9¾   Aultguish Inn.*
20   10¼   Braemore Lodge.
25¼ 15½   5¼   Lochbroom P.O.
32¼ 22½ 12¼   7   Ullapool,* Hotel.

Principal Objects of Interest.—After the first dozen miles this is a very desolate moorland road through a large deer forest. Close to Braemore Lodge are the most extraordinary "Measach Falls," which should not be missed, and here the change from the "Forest," just passed through, is most noticeable. The road runs at a considerable elevation above Loch Broom, and affords some fairly extensive views.

Hotels or Inns at places marked *.

341   ULLAPOOL TO SCOURIE.

Description.—Class III. The road has a rough surface at first on the steep hills near Ullapool, then improves considerably, but with some sharp pitches past Auchendrean, when the surface degenerates, and is a little rough passing Elphin. The Lairg-Lochinver road, joined after Elphin, has a fair surface, but on turning off it at Skiag bridge the road becomes very steep, with bad surface almost the whole way to Kyle Sku Inn, where Ferry (¼m.). The road still continues rough, but steadily improves in quality, and though hilly, is fair near Scourie.

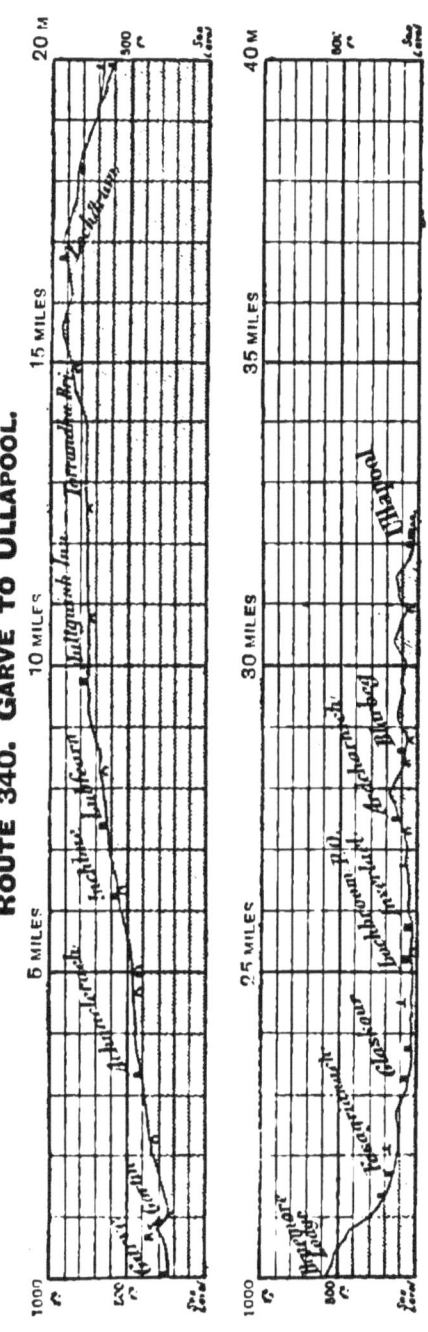

Signs: < Road Fork, forward journey. > ditto reverse. +-Cross Roads, ⊥ Road Junction, ∩ Bridge ⊤ indicates a sharp turn. The directions R (right) and L (left) for the forward journey are above the line, those of the reverse, below

247

Gradients.—At 1¾m. 1 in 16-12; 2¼m. 1 in 16-11; 3½m. 1 in 20; 4½m. 1 in 12; 5m. 1 in 23; 7m. 1 in 12; 7¾m. 1 in 22-13; 8¾m. 1 in 18; 11m. 1 in 21-15-18; 14¼m. 1 in 13; 22½m. 1 in 17; 25¼m. 1 in 15; 26½m. to 28m. 1 in 13-16-12-17-12; 30¼m. 1 in 12 (dangerous turn); 30¾m. 1 in 16; 31½m. 1 in 14; 32½m. 1 in 15; 33m. 1 in 10; 33½m. 1 in 10-19; 35m. 1 in 16-22-19-20; 37¼m. 1 in 17; 37½m. 1 in 13; 39¼m. 1 in 18-14; 43m. 1 in 15.

Measurements.

Ullapool,* Pier.						
7¾	Auchendrean.					
16¼	8½	Elphin School.				
(20	12¼	3¾	Aultnacallagach *).			
24⅜	16⅝	8⅛	...	Inchnadamff,* Inn.		
26½	18¾	10¼	...	2⅛	Skiag Bridge.	
34	26¼	17¾	...	9⅝	7½	Kyle Sku Inn.*
45½	37¾	29¼	...	21⅛	19	11½ Scourie,* Hotel.

Principal Objects of Interest.—The altitude of the road at first permits some extensive views, but after the Auchendrean until nearing Inchnadamff the country is bleak and uninteresting. Along Loch Assynt, however, there is some charming scenery, but after leaving the Loch there is little else than the wild rocky scenery of Quinag and Glasven. From the road fine views are obtained of Kyle Sku—hemmed in with steep rocky mountains—and the numerous small islands in Eddrachillis Bay.

342 ULLAPOOL TO LOCHINVER.

Description.—Class III. As Route 341 for the first ten miles, where this road turns off. This is a fearful road, with soft loose stony surface and very steep hills, but improving in quality near Inverkirkaig. Its only recommendation is the magnificent and varied scenery it traverses. A much better road is by Inchnadamff—37½ miles.

Gradients.—As Route 341 for 10 miles, thence varying grades of 1 in 10 and 1 in 12. There are very numerous short but sharp hills. Dangerous descent to Lochinver.

Measurements.

Ullapool,* Pier.		
27⅞	Inverkirkaig.	
31¼	3⅜	Lochinver,* Hotel.

Principal Objects of Interest.—As Route 341 for 10 miles; the remainder is most lonely, the only habitations visible for the next 17 miles being a couple of shepherd's cottages and a shooting lodge. The scenery is most varied, wild and beautiful alternately. A magnificent view of the fantastic peaks of Suilven, &c., is obtained.

Hotels or Inns at places marked *.

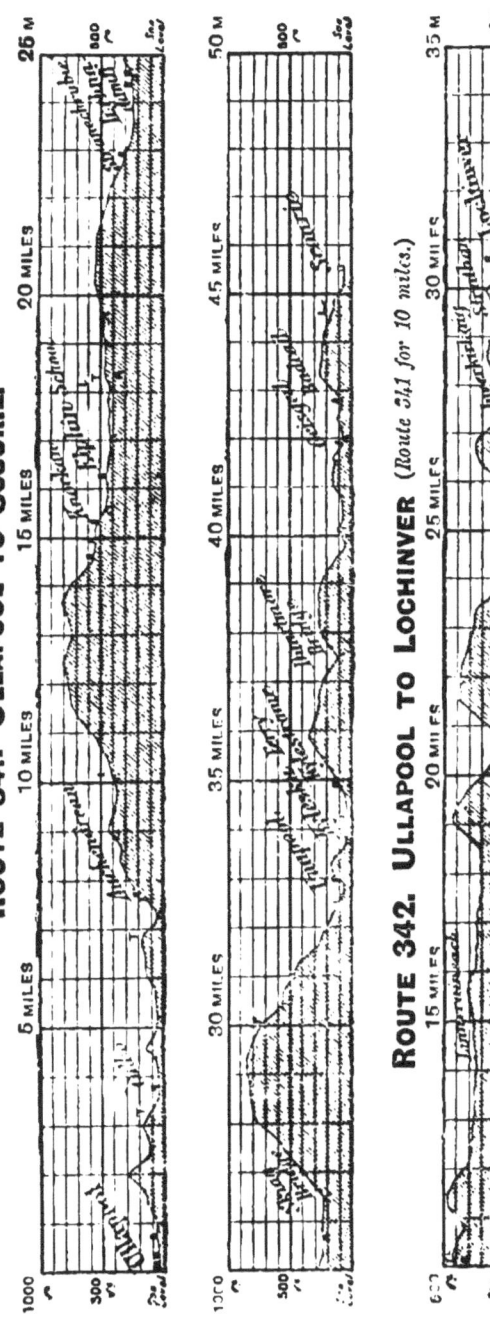

Signs: < Road Fork, forward journey, > ditto reverse, + Cross Roads, ⊥ Road Junction, ∩ Bridge, T indicates a sharp turn.

The directions R (right) and L (left) for the forward journey are above the Road Line, those or the reverse, below.

343 BRAEMORE TO DUNDONNELL.

Description.—Class III. The surface is good for several miles from Braemore Lodge, but then becomes very bad, even although the ascent is not very steep. This continues until within a few miles of Dundonnell Inn when it is very good.

Gradients.—At $2\frac{3}{4}$m. 1 in 24, and $4\frac{1}{2}$m. 1 in 17; these short pieces are the steepest part of the ascent on the east side. The long descent has several parts steeper than the rest, notably $8\frac{1}{2}$m. 1 in 16; $9\frac{3}{4}$m. 1 in 19; $10\frac{3}{4}$m. 1 in 15.

Measurements.
Braemore Lodge.
$13\frac{3}{4}$ Dundonnell Inn.*

Principal Objects of Interest.—Braemore Lodge; the extraordinary "Measach Falls" are crossed just after the lodge. Thereafter the road is chiefly remarkable for the fine views of the mountains, and of Little Loch Broom, which are obtained from the higher parts and approaching Dundonnell.

Hotels or Inns at places marked *.

344 AUCHNASHEEN TO GAIRLOCH, &C.

Description.—Class II. The road at first is slightly undulating, then becomes steep to the summit, with a correspondingly steep descent to Kinlochewe; thereafter the road is undulating with pretty good surface along Loch Maree, but becoming hilly over to the Gairloch. The road has a tendency to be soft. The Torridon branch has a good surface throughout.

Gradients.—At $4\frac{1}{2}$m. 1 in 22; $5\frac{1}{4}$m. 1 in 17; 6 to 7m. 1 in 15-23-12-17-12-20; $18\frac{1}{4}$m. 1 in 24; 22m. 1 in 15-24; $25\frac{1}{2}$m. 1 in 19; 28m. 1 in 22.

Milestones.—Continuation of those from Dingwall Court House,—correct till near Gairloch.

Measurements.
Auchnasheen.*
$9\frac{1}{4}$ Kinlochewe Hotel.*
$11\frac{7}{8}$ $2\frac{3}{4}$ Rhu Noa Pier.
$19\frac{1}{4}$ 10 $7\frac{3}{8}$ Loch Maree Hotel.*
$28\frac{3}{4}$ $18\frac{7}{8}$ $16\frac{1}{4}$ $8\frac{3}{4}$ Gairloch,* P.O,
$29\frac{1}{4}$ $19\frac{3}{4}$ $17\frac{3}{8}$ $9\frac{3}{4}$ $\frac{3}{4}$ Gairloch Hotel.*

Torridon Branch.
Kinlochewe Hotel.*
$10\frac{3}{4}$ Torridon,* Inn.

Principal Objects of Interest.—The scenery at Loch Maree is very fine. 25m. Falls. Gairloch; Flowerdale.

Hotels or Inns at places marked *.

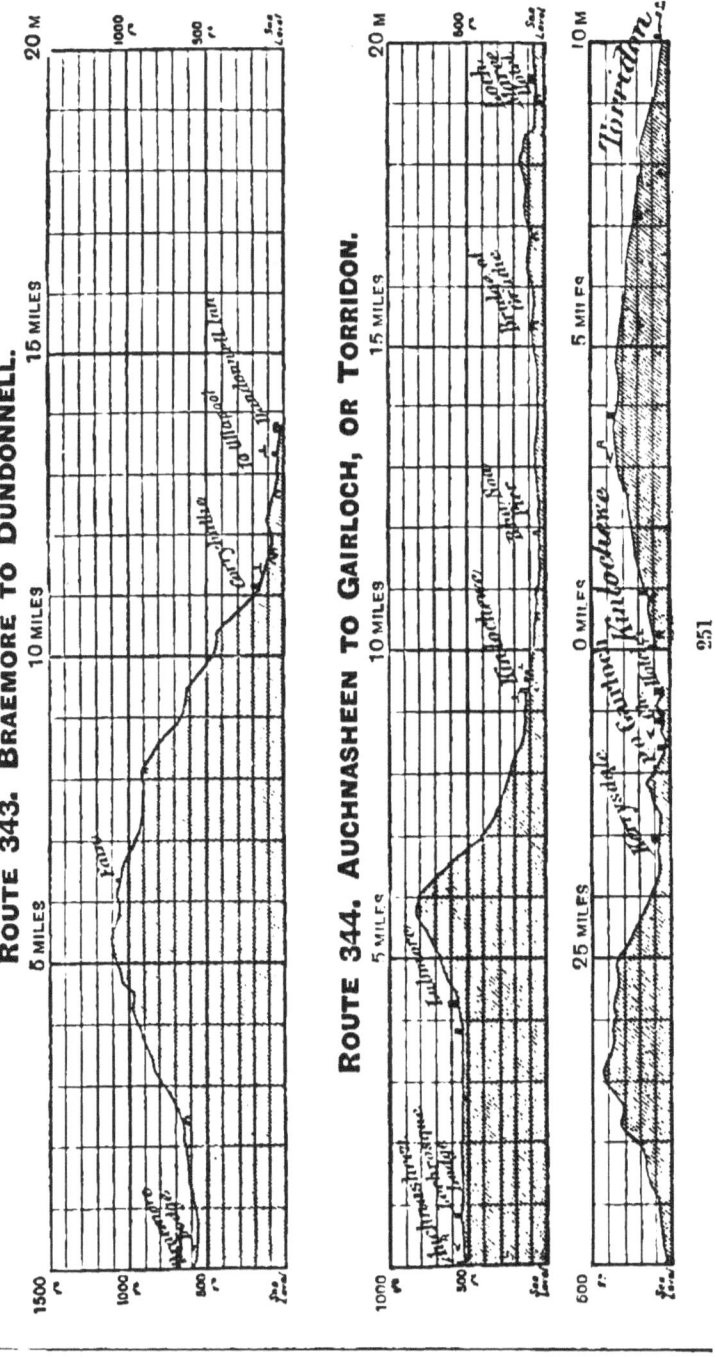

345 GAIRLOCH TO ULLAPOOL.

Description.—Class III. This is a very hilly road, crossing the shoulders of ranges of hills no less than six times. The surface is pretty fair as far as Laid, but then becomes somewhat rough with severe gradients, then improves, and is very fair for some miles before Dundonnell Inn. Thereafter the road is abominable, with a precipitous descent to Loch Broom—certainly vieing with the Foyers road as being the worst in Scotland. Ferry to Ullapool (1⅞m.). The usual road to Ullapool is by Braemore, but this short cut—saving 19m.—is in common use.

Gradients.—At ½m. 1 in 14; ¾m. 1 in 15; 1½m. 1 in 12-13-20, 3¼m. 1 in 15; 5m. 1 in 19; 5¾m. 1 in 10-12; 7¾m. 1 in 14; 9½m. 1 in 15; 12¾m. 1 in 21-16; 13¾m. 1 in 15-20; 15¾m. 1 in 24-19; 16⅝m. 1 in 17; 17¾m. 1 in 12; 18¾m. 1 in 8 (dangerous turn); 19m. 1 in 7-12 (dangerous turn); 20m. 1 in 13; 23½m. 1 in 12; 26¼m. 1 in 19-16; 33 to 34m. 1 in 20-10-15-10-16; 30½m. 1 in 16; 36½ to 37½m. 1 in 16-6-9-5, this last being at the foot. There are several turns which make this a terribly dangerous hill to descend.

Milestones.—Measured from below Gairloch Free Church,—correctly placed.

Measurements.

Gairloch * P.O.					
⅞	Gairloch Hotel.*				
6¾	5⅞	Poolewe,* Inn.			
(13½	12⅝	6¾	Aultbea,* Inn).		
31⅜	30½	24⅝	18¼	Dundonnell Inn.*	
38⅜	37½	31⅝	25¼	7	Ullapool,* Pier.

Principal Objects of Interest.—The view up Loch Maree just before Poolewe is remarkably fine; thereafter nothing beyond the fine coast scenery of Sutherlandshire.

Hotels or Inns at places marked *.

---

346 STRATHCARRON TO SHIELDAIG.

Description.—Class II. A good road as far as Lochcarron, then a precipitous hill followed by a long and easy descent; thereafter a fair undulating road to Shieldaig.

Gradients.—At 4¼m. 1 in 9-16-14-19-16 (dangerous); 6m. 1 in 18; 11¾m. 1 in 21; 14¼m. 1 in 20; 15m. 1 in 20-17.

Measurements.

Strathcarron,* Station.			
3¼	Lochcarron,* Inn.		
8⅝	5⅜	Kishorn P.O.	
18⅞	15⅝	10¼	Shieldaig,* Inn.

Hotels or Inns at places marked *.

ROUTE 345. GAIRLOCH TO ULLAPOOL.

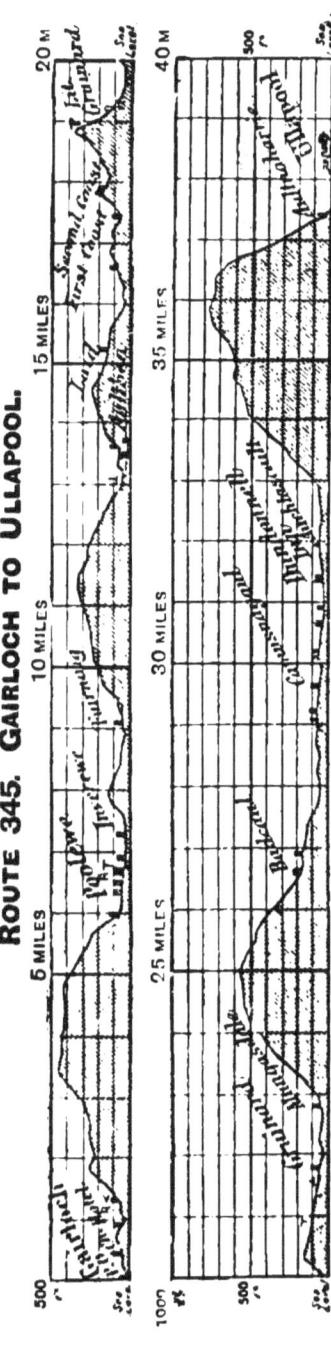

ROUTE 346. STRATHCARRON TO SHIELDAG.

Signs: < Road Fork, forward journey, > ditto reverse, + Cross Roads, ⊥ Road Junction, ⌒ Bridge ⊤ indicates a sharp turn. The directions R (right) and L (left) for the forward journey are above the line, those of the reverse, below.

347 INVERGARRY TO BALMACARA.

Description.—Class II. An undulating road with good surface as far as Tomdoun, then a wretched road—covered with loose stones—to Clunie Inn. Thereafter down Glen Shiel and on to Inverinate the surface is fair—good near Shiel Inn—but approaching Dornie there is a tremendous climb with a steep descent to that village. Thereafter it is a fine level road to Balmacara. Ferry at Dornie (⅓m.).

Gradients.—At 1⅓m. 1 in 12-23. The ascent from Tomdoun at 17¾m. is 1/17; 18m.-21m. mostly 1/21, in parts 1/16 & 13; 24m. 1/20; 26⅞m. 1/17; 27¾m. 1/13; 38¼m. 1/14; 39¾m. 1/12; 40½m. 1/11-16; 41½m. 1/10; 42½m. 1/13, both dangerous.

Milestones.—Continuation of those in "Glenmore" from Invermorriston as far as Cluny Inn; thereafter measured seemingly from Glenelg.

Measurements.

Invergarry.						
½	Invergarry Hotel.*					
10⅞	10¾	Tomdoun Inn.*				
21⅝	20⅞	10½	Clunie Inn.*			
33	32½	22⅛	11⅜	Shiel Inn.*		
42⅝	42⅛	31¾	21¼	9⅝	Dornie Inn.*	
47⅛	46⅝	36¼	25¾	14⅛	4½	Balmacara,* Hotel.

Principal Objects of Interest.—Pretty scenery in Glen Garry, but most desolate between Clunie and Tomdoun. 27¾m. Battlefield 1719. The scenery at Loch Duich is very pretty. Dornie; Eilan Donan Castle ruin.

---

348 SHIEL INN TO BROADFORD.

Description.—Class III. "Mam Ratachan" with its double turns is a most dangerous hill. The surface is abominable till within a few miles of Glenelg when it becomes good. Ferry at Kyle Rhea (⅝m.). Thereafter another fearful ascent with a long steady descent—a very rough road also—as far as Lusa Bridge, whence it is a good road to Broadford.

Gradients.—"Mam Ratachan" 1 in 15-10-7-10-8-17, descent mostly 1 in 12. From Kyle Rhea between 1 in 12 and 1 in 19, but 1 in 8 near summit, descent 1 in 15 at 17¼m.

Milestones.—From Glenelg?; in Skye from Broadford.

Measurements.

Shiel Inn.*				
10¾	Kyle Rhea Inn.*			
11⅝	⅝	Kyle Rhea Inn* (Skye).		
18⅛	7⅜	6¾	Lusa Bridge.	
22⅛	11⅜	10¾	4	Broadford,* Hotel.

Glenelg,* Hotel is ⅝m. distant at 8½m.

Principal Objects of Interest.—Fine views of Loch Duich and the Sound of Sleat. Bernera; Old Barracks.

Hotels or Inns at places marked *.

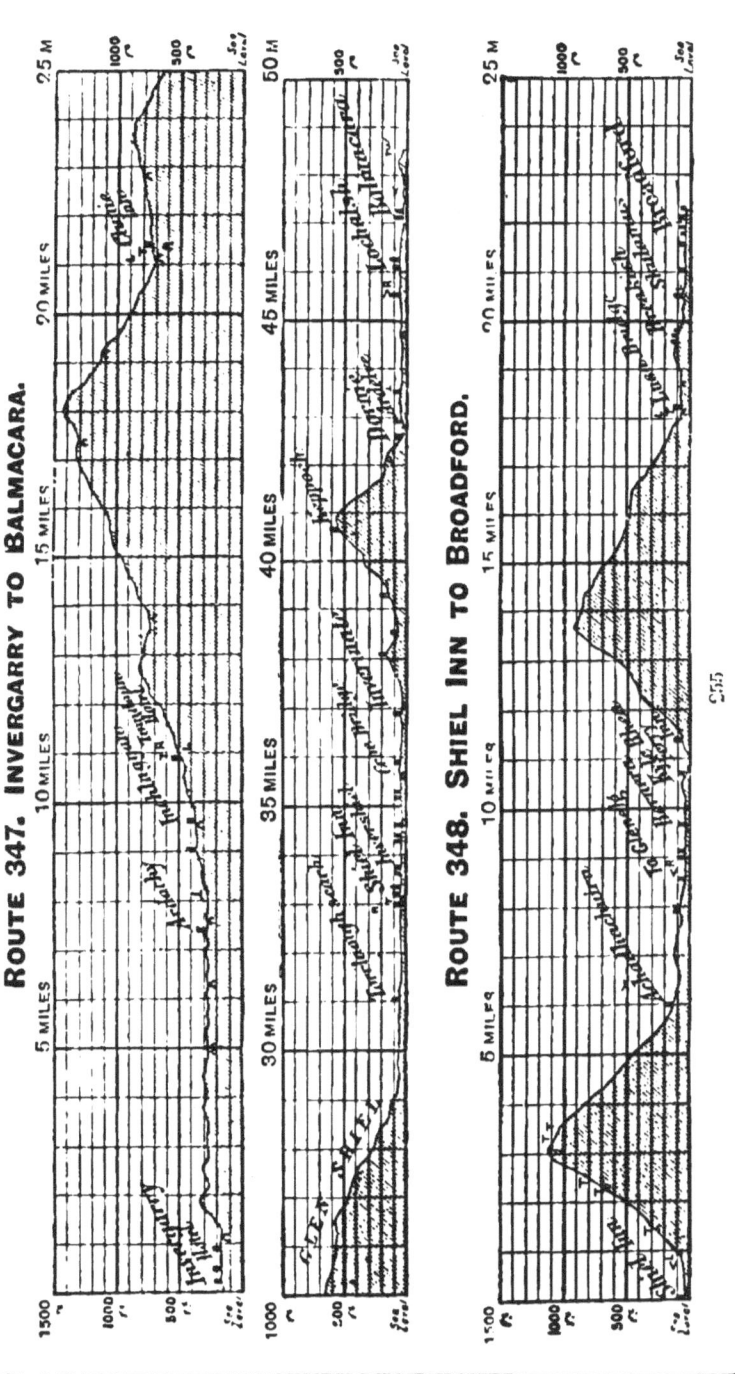

349 TOMDOUN TO KINLOCHHOURN.

Description.—Class III. A fair but narrow undulating road, with a very dangerous descent to Kinlochhourn. Carriages usually remain at the top.

Gradients.—13¾m. 1 in 12; 15m. 1 in 10-9.

Milestones.—Continuation of those from Invergarry.

Measurements.
Tomdoun Inn.*
9¾ Quoich Bridge.
15¾ 6 Kinlochhourn.

Principal Objects of Interest.—Magnificent scenery at Loch Hourn with its precipitous sides. The upper parts of Glen Garry are of no particular interest.

Hotels or Inn at places marked *.

---

350 PORTREE TO KYLE AKIN.

Description.—Class II. & III. A good road to Sligachan; thereafter there are some fearful hills—on which the surface is wretched—alternated with strips of good road. After Broadford, undulating but good surface.

Gradients.—At 9m. 1 in 22-19; 15m. 1 in 22-11-14; 16m. 1 in 8; 19m. 1 in 21-12; 20¾m. 1 in 17; 32½m. 1 in 23.

Milestones.—At first measured from Sligachan Inn, afterwards from Broadford Bridge. Near Kyle Akin measured from the Pier.

Measurements.
Portree.*
9¼ Sligachan Inn.*
25 15¾ Broadford,* Hotel.
29 19¼ 4 Lusa Bridge.
32¾ 23⅜ 7¾ 3¾ Kyle Akin,* Hotel.

Principal Objects of Interest.—The country is moorland, but the magnificent outline of the Cuillin Hills, and the "Inner Sound" with its numerous Islands backed by the Applecross Mountains, make attractive what would be a somewhat dreary road.

Hotels or Inns at placed marked *.

---

351 BROADFORD TO ARMADALE.

Description.—Class II. A fair road but inclining to be soft.

Gradients.—At 2½m. 1 in 22; 4½m. 1 in 24; 5¼m. 1 in 18-22; 11m. 1 in 12; 14m. 1 in 23; 15½m. 1 in 17; 16¼m. 1 in 12.

Milestones.—Measured from Broadford P.O.,—tolerably correct.

Measurements.
Broadford,* Hotel.
(9¾ Isle Ornsay,* Pier).
17½ 8¾ Ardavasar Inn.*

Hotels or Inns at places marked *.

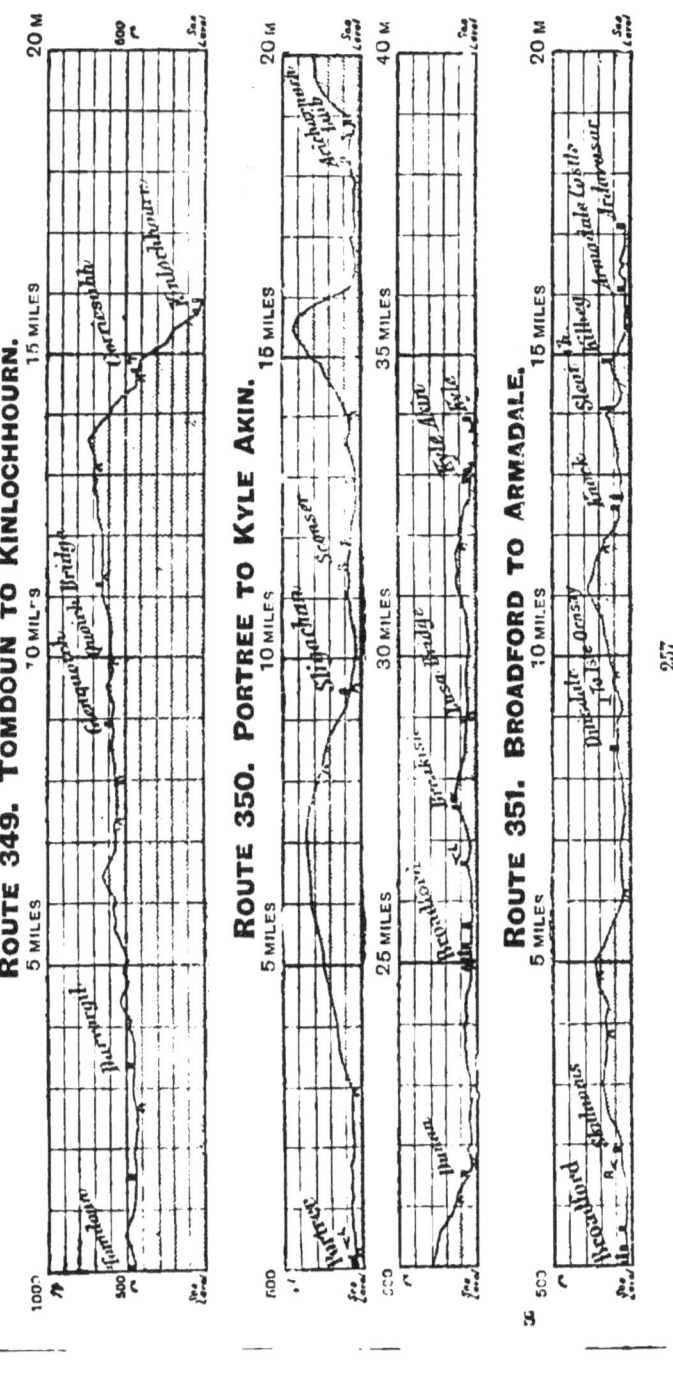

352 SLIGACHAN TO DUNVEGAN.

Description.—Class II. A hilly road, poor at first, but with fair surface between Bracadale and Dunvegan.

Gradients.—At ¼m. 1 in 16; 6m. 1 in 13-21; 6¾m. 1 in 14-15; 7¾m. 1 in 23; 11m. 1 in 17; 12m. 1 in 11 (dangerous); 14¼m. 1 in 15; 17m. 1 in 23; 17¾m. 1 in 18; 20m. 1 in 15.

Milestones.—Measured from Dunvegan Hotel.

Measurements.
Sligachan Hotel.*
14½   Struan Inn.*
24¾   10¼   Dunvegan,* Hotel.
25   10¾   ⅜   Dunvegan Pier.

353 PORTREE TO DUNVEGAN.

Description.—Class II. As far as Skeabost the road has easy gradients and good surface, but thereafter it is very hilly, with some rather stony parts after Edinbain.

Gradients.—At 2½m. 1 in 20; 8m. 1 in 21; 9m. 1 in 20; 10m. 1 in 19-15; 10½m. 1 in 15; 11¾m. 1 in 20; 16m. 1 in 16-24; 17m. 1 in 14; 18¼m. 1 in 14; 18¾m. 1 in 20; 20¼m. 1 in 19; 22½m. 1 in 15.

Milestones.—Measured from Portree as far as Tayinlone; thereafter from Edinbain Bridge.

Measurements.
Portree.*
4¼   Schoolhouse.
10¼ 6¼   Tayinlone Inn.*
14¼ 10   3¾   Edinbain Inn.*
22¼ 18½ 12   8¼   Dunvegan,* Hotel.

Principal Objects of Interest.—Dunvegan; Castle.

354 PORTREE TO THE QUIRANG.

Description.—Class II. & III. A good road with easy gradients till near Uig, then very hilly with dangerous descent to Staffin. The latter part is rather rough.

Gradients.—At 2½m. 1 in 20; 15m. 1 in 21-19-17; 16½m. 1 in 20-18 (dangerous turn); 21¼m. 1 in 11 (dangerous turns); 23m. 1 in 14-18-12.

Milestones.—Measured from Portree.

Measurements.
Portree.*
4¼   Schoolhouse.
6¾   2⅝   Kensaleyre Inn.*
15   10¾ 8¼   Uig,* Inn.
24¼ 20¾ 17¾ 9¼   Staffin Inn.*

Principal Objects of Interest.—Moorland road. 9½m. Kingsburgh Ho. Uig; Falls. 21¼m. Path to the Quirang.

Hotels or Inns at places marked *.

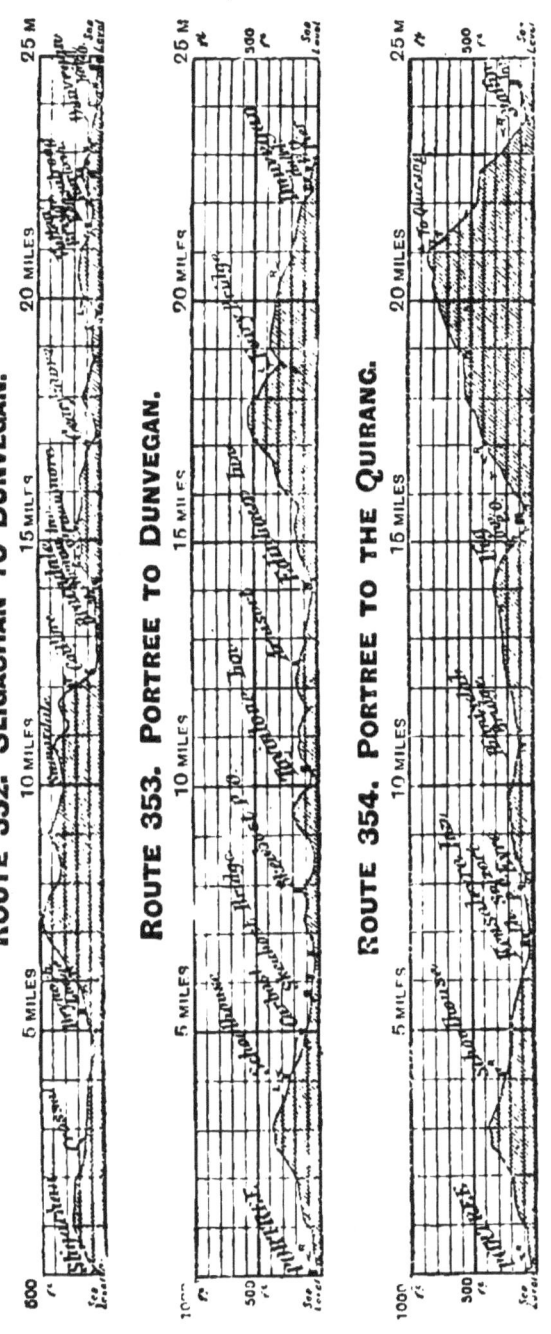

Signs: < Road Fork, forward journey, > ditto reverse, + Cross Roads, ⊥ Road Junction, ∩ Bridge, ⊤ indicates a sharp turn
The directions R (right) and L (left) for the forward journey are above the Road Line, those of the reverse, below

355 UIG TO DUNTULM, &c.

Description.—Class III. Rather a rough road, with a nasty turn 1⅝m. from Uig, and very hilly after Kilmaluag.

Gradients.—At 1¼m. 1 in 23-20-18-23 (dangerous); 2¾m. 1 in 20; 7¼m. and 7¾m. 1 in 13; 8¾m. 1 in 17; 9¾m. 1 in 16; 10½m. 1 in 14; 12¼m. 1 in 15-19; 13¾m. 1 in 13; 13m. 1 in 19; 13½m. 1 in 17.

Measurements.

Uig,* Inn.				
5½	Kilvaxter Inn.*			
10½	5	Kilmaluag,* Inn.		
(16⅞	11⅜	6⅜	Staffin Inn*).	
24¼	18¾	13¾	...	Uig,* Inn.

Principal Objects of Interest.—7½m. Flora Macdonald's Grave. 9m., to Duntulm Castle.

---

356 FORT WILLIAM TO ARISAIG.

Description.—Class II. This is a very fine smooth road as far as the head of Loch Eil, but then becomes rather soft, and beyond Loch Shiel is pretty hilly nearly the whole way to Arisaig.

Gradients.—At 17¾m. and 18½m. 1 in 16; 19¾m. 1 in 21; 21½m. 1 in 15-22-14-18; 28⅜m. 1 in 9; 29m. 1 in 13 (dangerous); 30¼m. and 30½m. 1 in 15; 31¼m. 1 in 19-12-17; 33m. 1 in 14; 34½m. 1 in 17; 35¼m. 1 in 20; 36¾m. 1 in 23.

Milestones.—Continuation of those from Fort William,—correct after Lochy Bridge.

Measurements.

Fort William,* Pier.					
3¼	Banavie Hotel.*				
4⅜	1⅛	Corpach Hotel.*			
18¾	15⅛	14	Glenfinnan Inn.*		
27⅞	24⅝	23½	9½	Kinloch Aylort Inn.*	
38¼	35	33⅞	19⅜	10⅜	Arisaig,* Inn.

Arisaig Landing-place is 3⅜ miles from the Inn.

Principal Objects of Interest.—1¾m. Inverlochy Castle. 3¼m. Caledonian Canal. 17⅝m. Prince Charlie's Monument. Magnificent scenery nearly the whole way.

---

357 FORT WILLIAM TO LOCH ARKAIG.

Description.—Class II. This is a fairly good road as far as Bunarkaig, beyond that it is rather poor.

Gradients.—Nothing very steep.

Milestones.—Continuation of those as Route 356.

Measurements from Fort William,* Pier.

3¼m. Banavie.* 12¼m. Bunarkaig. 15⅜m. Loch Arkaig foot. 9⅝m. Gairlochy Inn.* Spean Bridge* (by this road) 13⅜m. 12½m. Achnacarry P.O.

Hotels or Inns at places marked *.

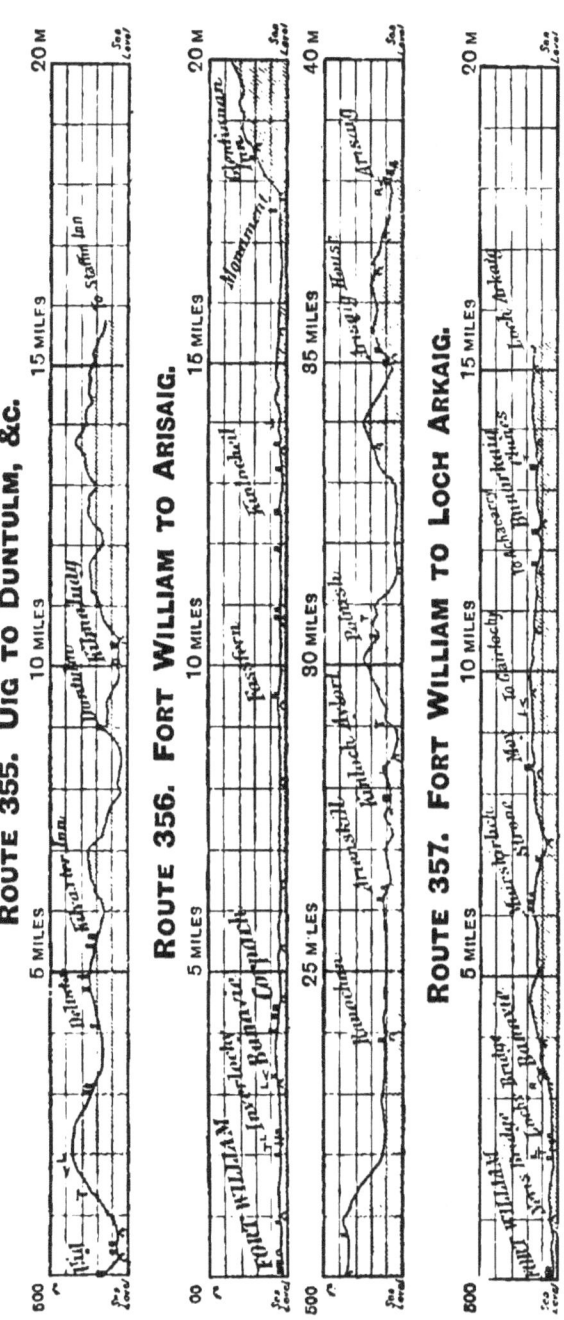

358 Fort William to Kingussie.

Description.—Class II. A fine smooth undulating road as far as Roy Bridge, when it becomes scarcely so good, and with a number of short hills, till past Laggan Inn. Thereafter the surface is very good, but with several short hills near Cluny Castle, after which it is smooth to Kingussie.

Gradients.—16½m. 1 in 25; 42¾m. 1 in 18.

Milestones.—Measured from Spean Bridge in both directions.

Measurements.

Fort William,* Pier.							
9½	Spean Bridge.*						
12¾	3¼	Roy Bridge,* Hotel.					
23	13½	10¼	Moy.				
31⅝	22⅛	18⅞	8⅝	Loch Laggan Inn.*			
38⅝	29⅛	25⅞	15⅝	7	Laggan Bridge.		
46¾	37¼	34	23¾	15⅛	8⅛	Newtonmore,* P.O.	
49½	40	36¾	26½	17⅞	10⅞	2¾	Kingussie,* Court House.

Principal Objects of Interest.—2m. Inverlochy Castle ruin. 3⅜m. Inverlochy Castle. Roy Bridge; Parallel Roads of Glen Roy to North. The rocky course of the River Spean and views of Ben Nevis should be noticed. 41m. Cluny Castle. The western end of Loch Laggan is rather tame, but there is pretty scenery near the Inn and near Laggan Bridge. Kingussie; Ruthven Barracks ruin.

Hotels or Inns at places marked *.

359 Ardgour to Morvern.

Description.—Class II. We believe this road is in good order as far as Lochaline, but pretty stony near Loch Uisge; thereafter poor surface and hilly.

Gradients.—At 7¼m. 1 in 11; 17¼m. 1 in 11-20; 21½m. 1 in 15-22-18; 25¼m. 1 in 13; 29¾m. 1 in 13; 32¼m. 1 in 21; 33½m. 1 in 17; 39¾m. 1 in 10-12.

Milestones.—Measured from Ardgour P.O.; after Clounlaid from Lochaline Pier.

Measurements.

Ardgour Hotel.*			
16½	(Kingairloch).		
31⅞	...	(Lochaline Pier).	
42¼	...	...	Drimnin P.O.

Hotels or Inns at places marked *.

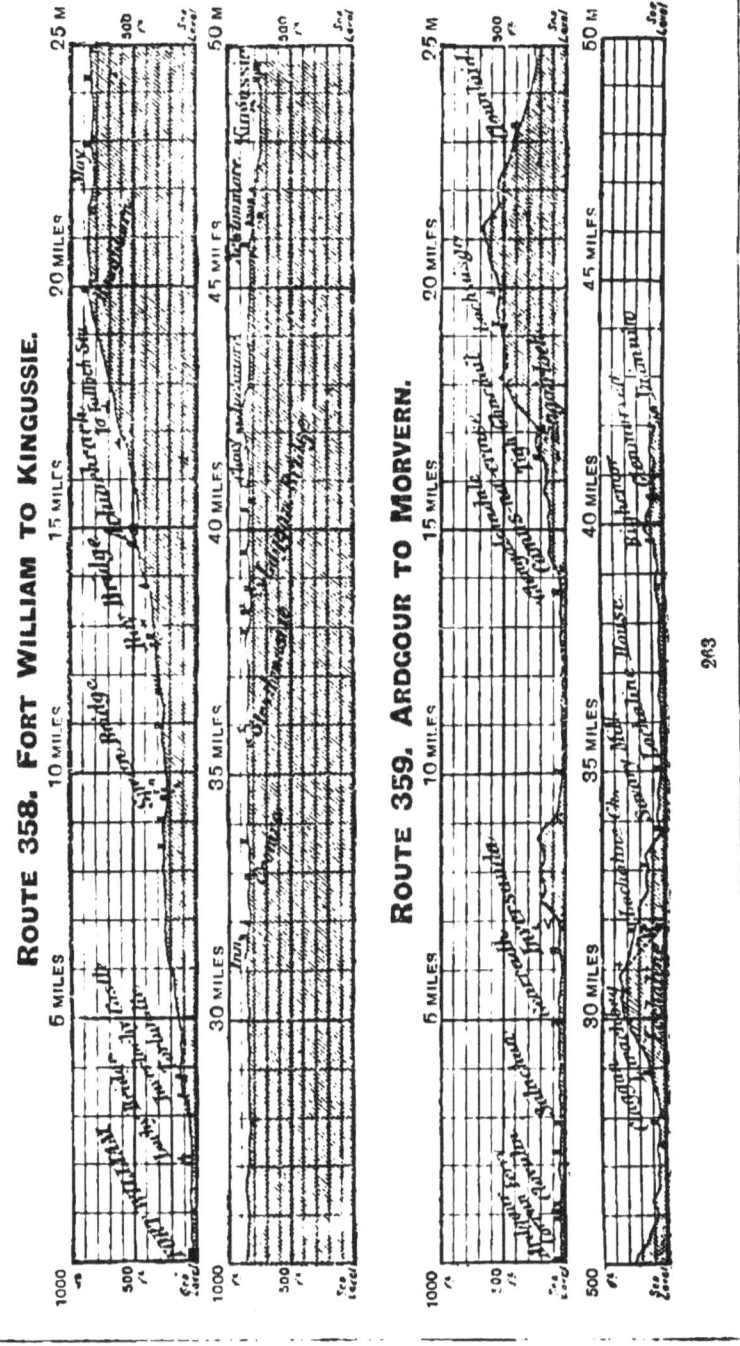

360 ARDGOUR TO MOIDART.

Description.—Class II. This is a fair road as far as Salen, then hilly and rough to Kinloch Moidart.

Gradients.—At 7½m. 1 in 17; 9m. 1 in 18-24; 12m. 1 in 23; 15m. 1 in 16; 16m. 1 in 18; then other short hills pretty steep till 25m. 1 in 23-18; 26¼m. 1 in 13-23; 30¾m. 1 in 15; 32¼m. 1 in 13; 32¾m. 1 in 14-17.

Milestones.—Measured from Ardgour Post Office,—correct.

Measurements.

Ardgour,* Hotel (Corran Pier).					
6⅜	Inversanda.				
14⅝	8¼	Strontian,* Inn.			
24½	18⅛	9⅞	Salen,* Inn.		
27⅞	21½	13¼	3⅜	Shielbridge Inn.*	
33¼	26⅞	18⅝	8¾	5⅜	Moidart P.O.

Principal Objects of Interest.—The scenery at Loch Sunart is charming. Ben Resipol is very noticeable.

Hotels or Inns at places marked *.

---

361 TOBERMORY TO SALEN BY ULVA.

Description.—Class II. & III. The road is very hilly, and there are a large number of abrupt and sharp turns for some miles on the north side of Dervaig, at which the greatest care should be taken. The road is somewhat easier between Dervaig and Calgary, and between Killiechronan and Salen; but the surface is only tolerable. Salen is known to the Post Office as Aros.

Gradients.—At ¾m. 1 in 8; then 1 in 13. Thereafter numerous and very variable grades, the most noteworthy of which are 4¾m. 1 in 10-17; 5½m. 1 in 15-19-16; 7½m. 1 in 20-14-12-14-11-12; 12¾m. 1 in 15; 15m. 1 in 18; 16m. 1 in 20-10-19; 17¼m. 1 in 14; 18½m. and 18¾m. 1 in 10; 26m. 1 in 14.

Measurements.

Tobermory,* Pier.				
8	Dervaig,* Inn.			
19	11	Kilninian Church.		
24⅜	16⅜	5⅜	Ulva Schoolhouse.	
34¼	26¼	15¼	9⅞	Salen,* Inn.
33	25	14	8⅝	Knock.

Principal Objects of Interest.—Tobermory; Falls, Glengorm Castle, Bloody Bay. 12¾m. Calgary Castle. There are magnificent views from this road, and the scenery of Ulva and Loch-na-Keal, with the numerous islands is very fine.

Hotels or Inns at places marked *, and on (Ulva Island).

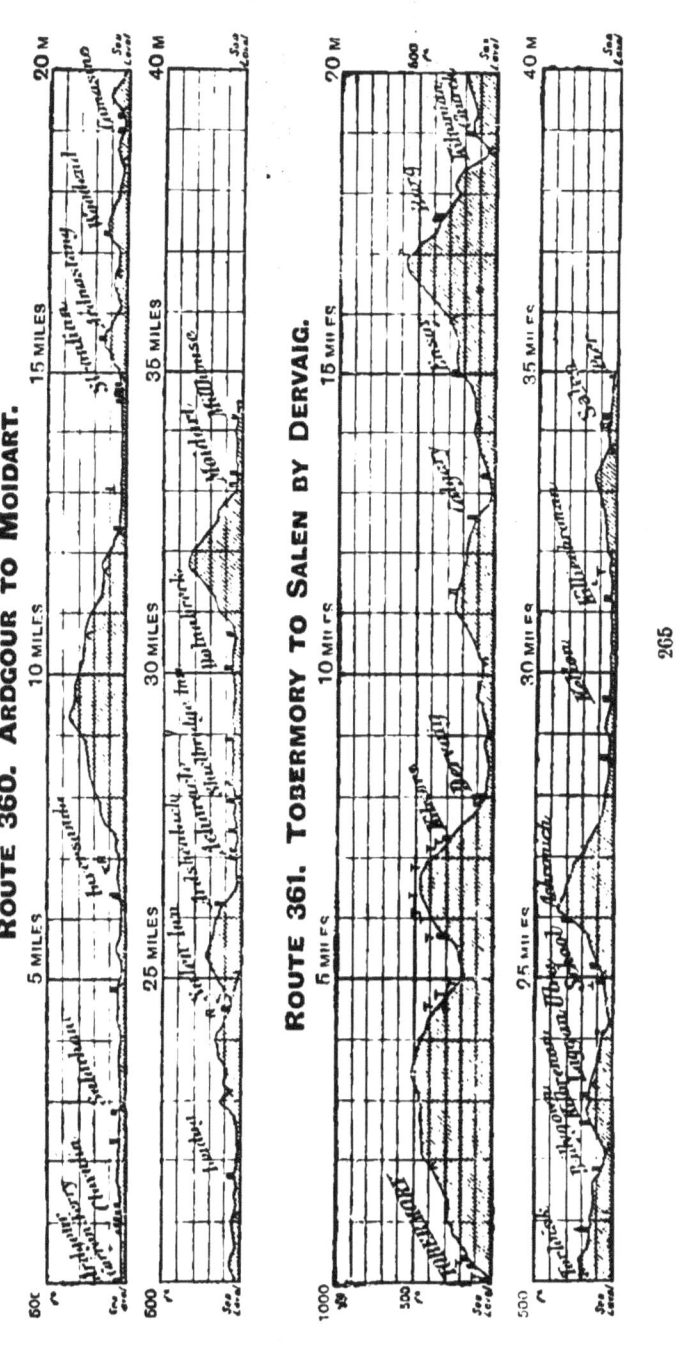

362 SALEN TO IONA.

Description.—Class III. This is a fair undulating road, but although it does not rise very high in many parts, there are a large number of short steep hills that are trying. After Pennyghael these are more so, although none are of any great length. Ferry to Iona ¾m. The steamer calls at Iona Pier—not at Fionphort.

Gradients.—It is impossible to detail the numerous gradients accurately, but the ascent at 12½m. is about 1 in 14; 33¼m. 1 in 13-17. The others are steep but none are of any great length.

Measurements.

Salen,* Inn.							
3⅞	Knock.						
16½	12⅝	Kilfinichen Church.					
21¾	17⅞	5¼	Kinloch Inn.*				
23¼	19⅜	6¾	1½	Pennyghael Bridge.			
33¼	29⅜	16¾	11½	10	Bunessan,* Pier.		
39	35⅛	22½	17¼	15¾	5¾	Fionphort Pier.	
40	36⅛	23½	18¼	16¾	6¾	1	Iona,* Hotel.

Principal Objects of Interest.—3¾m. Glenforsa House. Magnificent views of Loch-na-Keal, Ulva, Staffa, and further on of Loch Scridan. Iona; Cathedral. Ben More, the highest mountain in Mull, is very prominent near Bunessan.

Hotels or Inns at places marked *.

---

363 TOBERMORY TO SALEN, &C.

Description.—Class II & III. This is probably the best road in the island, and though it is pretty hilly, taken as a whole the surface is not bad; the best part is between Tobermory and Lochdonhead.

Gradients.—At ¼m. 1 in 9; 4¼m. 1 in 15; 5m. 1 in 16-21; 8m. 1 in 21-14-12; 17¾m. 1 in 14; 22m. 1 in 18; 23¼m. 1 in 16-14; 34¾m. 1 in 20.

Measurements.

Tobermory,* Pier.				
10½	Salen,* Inn.			
21⅝	11⅛	Craignure.		
24½	14	2½	Lochdonhead.	
40½	30⅜	18⅞	16⅜	Kinloch,* Inn.

Principal Objects of Interest.—¼m. Falls. 1¾m. Aros House. 8½m. Aros Castle ruin.

Hotels or Inns at places marked *.

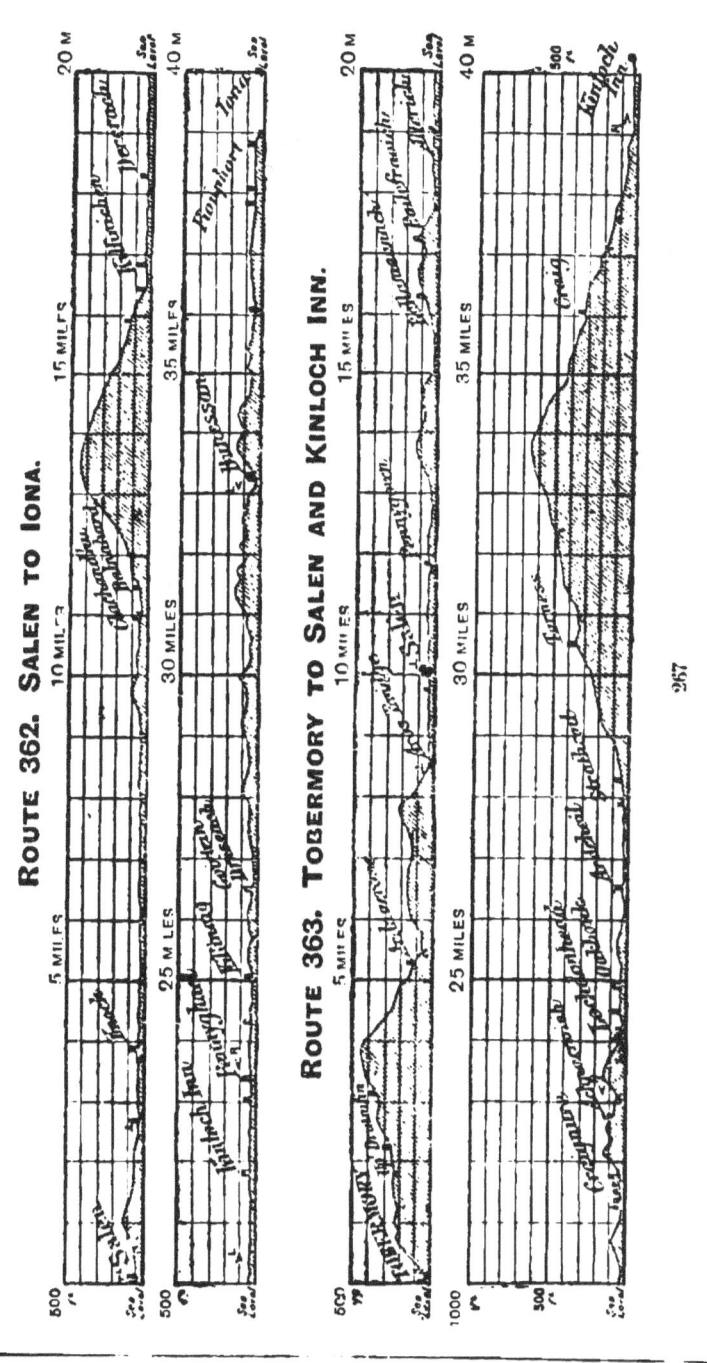

364 ROUND ARRAN.

Description.—Class III. At first there is a splendid stretch of level road to Sannox, when the surface begins to degenerate and is pretty rough on both sides of the hill over to Loch Ranza. Thence to Blackwaterfoot the road is undulating with fair surface, but there are some nasty and rough hills—short but very steep—cropping up at different points. Between Blackwaterfoot and Whiting Bay the road is rough and exceedingly hilly, with some most dangerous descents with sharp turns; but thereafter the surface is better, although both hills on the road between Brodick and Lamlash are dangerous to descend.

Gradients.—At 8m. 1 in 17; 10m. 1 in 16-10-11-21; 12m. mostly 1 in 14, maximum 1 in 11; 23¼m. 1 in 10 (?); 37m. 1 in 15; 39m. 1 in 14; 39½m. 1 in 14; 46½m. 1 in 15; 51m. 1 in 13; 52¾m. 1 in 11; 55½m. 1 in 10. These represent only the steep parts of the longer hills.

Milestones.—Measured from Brodick Old Pier round the island by Lamlash and Pirnmill, the last at Brodick Old Pier is therefore short.

Measurements.

Brodick,* Pier.								
6¼	Corrie,* Hotel.							
14¾	8½	Lochranza,* Pier.						
20¾	14½	6	Pirnmill.					
32	25¾	17¼	11¼	Blackwaterfoot Inn.*				
39⅛	32⅞	24⅜	18⅜	7⅛	Lagg Inn.*			
48⅛	41⅞	33⅜	27⅜	16⅛	9	Whiting Bay.		
52½	46¼	37¾	31¾	20½	13⅜	4⅜	Lamlash,* Pier.	
55⅝	49⅜	40⅞	34⅞	23⅝	16½	7½	3⅛	Brodick,* Pier.

The above is a recent Measurement by P. Jenkins, Esq., the Road Surveyor.

Principal Objects of Interest.—The road skirts the foot of the hills almost the whole way, so that no really fine views of the Arran Mountains are obtained, except perhaps at Glen Sannox, and descending to Brodick from Lamlash. 2¼m. Brodick Castle. Corrie; Glen Sannox. Lochranza; Fairy Dell. There is some rather pretty scenery about Lagg Inn. 44m. Kildonan Castle. Lamlash; Fort, fine view Holy Island. Brodick; Glen Rosa, Goat Fell, Glen Cloy, Brodick Castle.

Hotels or Inns at places marked*.

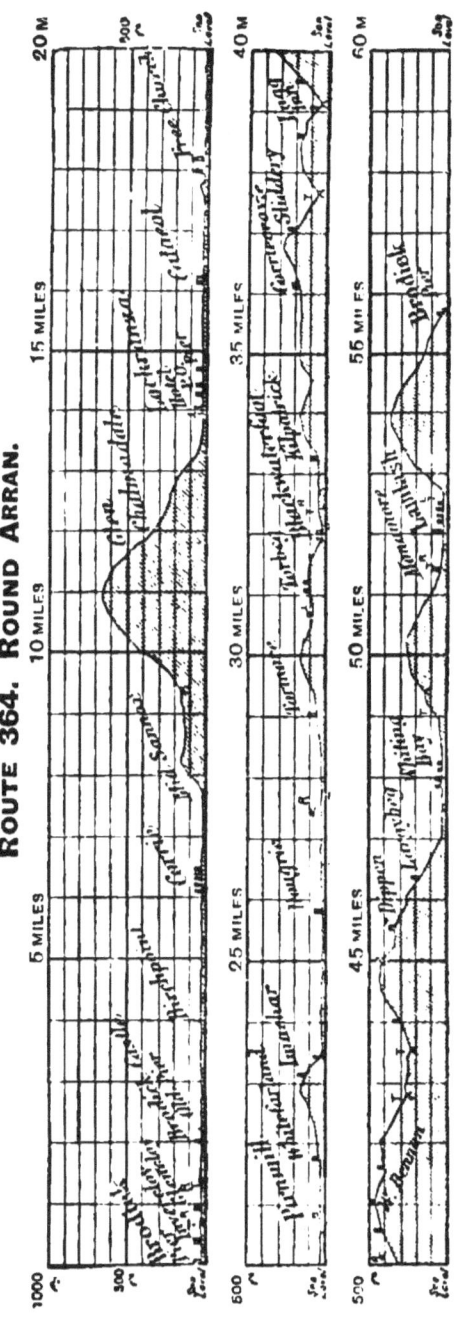

Signs: < Road Fork, forward journey, > ditto reverse, + Cross Roads, ⊥ Road Junction, ∩ Bridge, ⊤ indicates a sharp turn. The directions R (right) and L (left) for the forward journey are above the Road Line, those of the reverse, below.

269

365   Brodick to Blackwaterfoot.

Description.—Class II. This road although fairly well engineered, is very rough and stony on the hill, but improves near Blackwaterfoot.

Gradients.—Ascent at first 1 in 10-19-13, then 1 in 9. Descent 1 in 14-18-10-16-14.

Milestones.—Measured from Brodick Old Pier—near Brodick Castle.

Measurements.

Brodick,* Pier.
9¾   Shedog Inn.*
11   1½   Blackwaterfoot,* Inn.

Principal Objects of Interest.—The road affords fine views of Goat Fell and the neighbouring mountains.

Hotels or Inns at places marked *.

---

366   Bute.

The roads in this island are all in very good order, but they are pretty narrow and undulating.

The milestones are measured from Rothesay County Buildings.

The following are the distances from Rothesay,* Pier:—

Mount Stuart Lodge, 3¾m.   Kilchattan,* Pier, 8½m.
Kilchattan,* Pier, by Loch Fad, 8m.
Port Bannatyne Pier, 2½m (see Route 143).

Hotels or Inns at places marked *.

---

367   Great Cumbrae.

The road round this island is pretty soft at several points. The distance round the island is 10 miles exactly.

Appendix Routes.

368. Edinburgh to Innerleithen, 28⅜m.

Turning off Route 7 at 13½m. the road shortly becomes grass grown, but improves on the Peebles side about 6m. from Innerleithen.

369. Gifford to Duns.

Longformacus,* 13¾m.   Duns,* 20½m. This is a fearful road, with one hill 1 in 6, and another 1 in 9, but it is tolerable after Longformacus.

370. Grants House to Duns, 9½m.

A moorland road with poor surface, and very hilly.

371. Lockerbie to Eskdalemuir.

Boreland Inn, 6¾m.; Eskdalemuir, 14m. The surface at first is fair, but after Boreland the road is rough and hilly.

372. Moffat to Lockerbie (*Old Road*).

Wamphray Church, 7½m.; Lockerbie Town Hall, 16½m. This is the old Carlisle road, and it is undulating, but has good surface.

373. Dumfries to Castle Douglas (*Old Road*).

Lochfoot, 5½m.; Haugh of Urr, 12¾m.; Castle Douglas, 16¾m. The old military road; surface fair, but very hilly.

374. Maybole to Newton Stewart.

Crosshill, 2¾m.: Bargrennan, 25m. A good road until some miles beyond Crosshill, when the surface is wretched all the way to Rowantree. The hills are long and steep (1 in 11).

375. Strathavon to Muirkirk, 13¼m.

A good road, but with steep descent to Muirkirk, thereafter to Sanquhar (29½m.), is all grass-grown and disused.

376. Paisley to Greenock.

Port Glasgow, 13⅝m.; Greenock 16½m. This is the best road between these towns, and is quite level to the junction with the Glasgow Road.

377. Drymen to Rowardennan, 10¾m.

A fair road, but with numerous short hills.

378. Helensburgh to Luss, 9½m.

A good road, but with a somewhat steep hill (1 in 15), at Helensburgh.

379. Ardrishaig to Port Sonachan.

Ford, 14m.; Portinsherrich, 23½m.; Port Sonachan, 31¾m. A good road as far as Ford, thereafter rough and hilly.

380. Loch Katrine.

Loch Katrine Pier; Brenachoil, 2¾m.; Portnellan, 8¼m.; Stronachlacher, 12m. The cart road on the north side of the loch extends as far as Portnellan, but it is dreadfully rough and hilly; thereafter it is only a footpath, almost impassable in wet seasons. There is no road whatever on the south side of the loch.

381. Balquhidder.

Kingshouse Inn to Balquhidder Church, 1¾m.; Craigruie, 4¾m.; Rob Roy's House 8½m. Good to Balquhidder, then only fair to Craigruie, after which it is rough.

382. Callander to Comrie, 15½m.

This is only a cart road for about 3m. at the Callander end, and 7m. at the Comrie end; between the two is only a rough sheep track. The summit (1145 ft.) is reached at 5⅞m.

383. Comrie to Ardeonaig, 12½m.

A cart track for about 6m., the remainder is only an ill marked footpath. The summit (1700 ft.) is reached at 9¼m.

384. Glen Tilt.

Blair Athole to Forest Lodge, 7⅜m.; Summit (1647 ft.), 15¼m.; Bynack Lodge, 11⅝m.; Braemar, 28⅝m. The carriage road is private as far as Forest Lodge; thereafter it is only a footpath to Bynack Lodge, when a rough driving road is joined.

385. Ballater to Clova.

Falls of Muick, 5⅜m.; Spital of Muick, 9m.; Summit (2275 ft.), 13¼m.; Clova Inn, 18⅝m. A slightly rough road to the Spital, then a mere track to Glen Clova; a rough road is joined at 14½m.

386. Ellon to Old Deer, 11⅝m.

The old Fraserburgh road. Poor at first, but improving near Old Deer; the hills are long and stiff.

387. Braemar to Grantown.

Reinloan, 12⅝m.; Corgarff, 20¾m.; Summit (2091 ft.) 22⅜m. Tomintoul, 30m.; Grantown, 42⅝m. Ballater to Reinloan, 6½m. From both Braemar and Ballater to Reinloan (after striking off the Aberdeen road), is rough, then a fearful road almost all the way to Grantown, although the latter section is not quite so bad as the rest. The ascent northwards from Corgarff, known as "the ladder," is 1 in 8.

388. Glentromie and Glenfeshie.

Fair roads run up these glens leading to the shooting lodges.

389. Dalwhinnie to Fort Augustus (*Corrieyarrick Pass*).

Laggan Br., 8⅛m.; Summit (2543 ft.), 23¼m.; Fort Agustus, 32⅞m. To Laggan Bridge is steep and with rough surface, thereafter to Fort Agustus is only the remains of a road. There were once 12 zig-zags, on which the grade was 1 in 8, to take the road up the face of almost a precipice, but these are almost all washed away now as the road has been abandoned since 1830.

390. Balmacara to Invercannich.

Carnach Lodge, 15⅞m.; Summit (1095 ft.), 18¾m.; Lub-na-damph, 25m.; Invercannich, 38⅞m. A good road for 4m., then pretty rough to Carnach, from which there is a footpath to Lub-na-damph, where a rough road is joined once more.

391. Auchnashellach to Kinlochewe.

Torridon Road, 8¼m.; Kinlochewe, 11¼m. Long, stiff ascent at first, then easy descent, but the road is somewhat rough (it is really private).

392. The Larig Pass.

Aviemore to Coylumbridge, 1⅝m.; Summit (2771 ft.), 9½m.; Derry Lodge, 17¾m.; Braemar, 27⅜m. Good road to Coylumbridge, then only a path among the woods and heather until the summit, when it simply lies across the rocks at the bottom of the pass. A rough driving road, leading to Braemar, is joined at Derry Lodge.

INDEX.

The Route Numbers are given at each Name.

ABBOTSFORD, 55
Aberarder, 297
Aberchirder, 251, 264, 265
Aberdeen, 225, 240-250
Aberdour, 190
Aberfeldy, 197, 209, 210-12, 214, 216
Aberfoyle, 129, 168
Aberlady, 1, 27
Aberlemno, 224
Aberlour, 267, 273, 287
Abernethy, 196
Abington, 10, 50, 51, 52, 68, 121
Aboyne, 241, 269
Ach, see also Auch
Achanalt, 339
Acharacle, 360
Acharn, 213
Achbreck, 272, 278
Achnacarry, 357
Achoish, 151
Addiewell,
Advie, 273
Affrick Lodge, 309
Airdrie, 50, 124
Airth, 169
Aldbar, 226
Alexandria, 131
Alford, 244, 255, 269
Alloa, 24, 175, 176, 181, 189
Alloway, 96
Alness, 302, 316
Alt, see also Ault
Altnacealgach, 338
Alva, 174
Alves, 294
Alyth, 222, 228
Amisfield, 65
Amulree, 197, 205, 207
Ancrum, 6
Annan, 43, 62, 63, 64, 57, 58
Anstruther, 10, 187
Appin, 158, 161
Applecross, 330
Arbroath, 225, 234, 235
Archiestown, 277
Ardavasar, Skye, 351
Ardentinny, 147
Ardeonaig, 213
Ardgay, 302, 327
Ardgour, 359, 360
Ardlui, 132
Ardpatrick, 150
Ardrishaig, 144, 151, 152, 155

Ardoch, 172, 206
Ardrossan, 111
Ardtalnaig, 213
Ardwell, 88
Arisaig, 356
Armadale (Linlithgowshire), 124
Arnprior, 167
Aros, 363
Arran, 364-365
Arrochar, 131, 140-141
Ashkirk, 7
Assynt, 338, 341
Auch, see also Ach
Auchenblae, 238
Auchencairn, 74, 79
Auchinleck, 104
Auchmill, 245, 246
Auchnagatt, 259
Auchnasheen, 339, 344
Auchnashellach, 339
Auchterarder, 173, 198
Auchtermuchty, 174
Auchterneed,
Auchtertool, 183
Auldearn, 294
Auldgirth, 67
Ault, see also Alt
Aultbea, 345
Aultnaharra, 334-336
Aviemore, 274, 275, 276, 296
Avoch, 305
Ayr, 94-102, 119
Ayton, 3, 35

BADENSCOTH, 251
Baillieston, 124
Baldovie, 226
Balerno, 11
Balfron, 128
Balfron Station, 129
Ballachulish, 158, 186
Ballantrae, 89, 90
Ballater, 241, 243, 253
Ballindalloch, 278
Ballinluig, 200, 209
Balmacara, 339, 347
Balmoral, 241, 253
Balquhidder, 181
Banavie, 356, 357
Banchory, 237, 239, 240, 241
Banff, 246, 258, 262, 265, 271
Bankfoot, 200
Bannockburn, 15

T 2

Bargrennan, 92, 97
Barrhead, 114-118
Barhill (Ayrshire), 91, 92
Bathgate, 22, 124
Bearsden, 130
Beattock, 9, 51, 65
Beauly, 302, 303
Beeswing, 72
Beith, 116
Bellanoch (Lochgilphead), 152
Bellochantuy, 148
Bellshill, 123, 135
Benderloch, 159
Bentpath, 60
Berriedale, 317
Bervie, 225
Berwick, 33, 34, 36, 37
Bettyhill, 324, 335
Biggar, 10, 49
Birgham, 36
Birnam, 200
Birness, 249, 250
Bishopton, 115
Blackburn (Aberdeenshire), 245
Blackburn (Bathgate), 14
Blackford, 173
Blackridge, 124
Black's-boat, 289
Blackshiels, 4
Blackwaterfoot, 364-365
Bladnoch, 84, 95
Blair-Athole, 200
Blairgowrie, 201, 208, 221, 227, 228
Blairingone, 189
Blairmore, 147
Blantyre, 106
Bonar Bridge, 302, 316, 327-329, 333, 334
Bonchester, 39
Bo'ness, 22, 25
Bonhill, 167
Bonnybridge, 126
Bonnyrigg, 20
Bothwell, 121
Bower, 321
Bowling, 131
Bracadale, 352
Braco, 172, 206
Braemar, 201, 241, 254
Brechin, 202, 219, 224, 226, 234, 236
Bridgend (Islay),
Bridge of Allan, 172, 177
   ,,   Cally, 201, 227
   ,,   Earn, 17, 196, 198
   ,,   Marnoch, 251, 265
   ,,   Orchy, 164, 166
   ,,   Turk, 171
   ,,   Weir, 105
Broadford, 348, 350, 351
Brodick (Arran), 364, 365
Broomhouse, 121, 123, 135
Brora, 317

Broughton, 9, 49
Broughty Ferry, 4m. from Dundee
Broxburn, 124
Buchanty, 205
Buchlyvie, 128, 167
Buckie, 1¾m. distant at 53⅜m. on Route 258
Bunessan, 362
Burghead, 283, 284
Burntisland, 17, 18, 190
Burrelton, 202
Busby, 113
Butterstone, 208

CAIRNBAAN, 152
Cairndow, 141-142
Cairnryan, 89
Caldercruix, 124
Callander, 170, 171, 178-180
Cambuslang, 134
Campbeltown, 148, 149, 160
Campsie, 128
Camptown, 6
Canobie, 41, 43
Cape Wrath, 331
Caputh, 204, 229
Cardross, 140
Carfraemill, 4, 5, 6
Cargill, 201
Carlops, 10
Carlisle, 41, 51, 62
Carluke, 50, 123
Carnock, 175
Carnoustie, 233
Carnwath, 11, 123
Carr Bridge, 280, 296
Carradale, 149
Carron, 24
Carronbridge, 52, 67
Carron Bridge (Stirling), 23
Carrutherstown, 63
Carsphairn, 98
Carstairs, 99, 11
Castlecary, 125
Castle-Douglas, 70, 75, 76, 79, 80
Castletown, 321, 322
Cathcart, 133
Catrine, 2¾m. from Mauchline, 5⅜m. from Cumnock.
Causewayhead, 172-177
Cawdor, 293
Ceres, 186, 192
Chapelton, 120
Chirnside, 34, 35
Clachaig, 145
Clachan, 148
Clackmannan, 175, 176
Cladich, 153, 162
Clarencefield, 62
Clarkston, 113, 133
Clashmore, 302, 317
Clova, 231

INDEX.

Clovenfords, 47
Clunie Inn, 301, 347
Clydebank, 131
Clynder, 137
Coatbridge, 124
Cockburnspath, 3
Cockenzie, 1
Coldstream, 4, 36, 28
Colinsburgh, 19
Colintraive, 143
Collessie, 174, 185
Collin, 62, 63
Colmonell, 90
Colpy, 245
Comrie, 199, 206
Condorrat, 125
Connel, 157-158
Conon Bridge, 302, 306, 310
Contin, 339
Corgarff, 244
Cornhill, 36, 32
Cornhill (Aberdeen), 271
Corran Ferry, 166, 359, 360
Corrie, 364
Corsock, 71, 78
Corstorphine, 15, 124
Coulport, 137
Coupar-Angus, 202, 221, 229
Cove (Dumbarton), 137
Cowdenheath, 17
Coylton, 99
Coylum Bridge, 275
Craggie Inn, 293, 296, 297
Craigellachie, 267, 273, 279, 287
Craignure, 363
Crail, 19
Crailing, 38
Cramond Bridge, 16, 17
Crarae, 144
Crawford, 51, 52
Creetown, 70
Crianlarich, 132, 157
Crieff, 16, 172, 197, 199
Crinan, 152
Crocketford, 70, 71
Cromarty, 305, 306, 311
Cromdale, 273
Crook Inn, 9
Crook of Devon, 174
Crossford, 122
Crossgates, 17, 191
Crossmichael, 75
Croy, 295
Cullen (Banff), 258, 270
Culloden, 295
Culross, 190
Cults, 241
Cumbernauld, 50, 125
Cuminestown, 263
Cummertrees, 62
Cumnock, 99, 103, 104
Cumnock, New, 67, 104

Cupar, 18, 174, 186, 196
Currie, 11

DAILLY, 93, 96
Dairsie, 18
Dalbeattie, 72, 73, 74, 78
Dalguise, 210
Dalkeith, 4
Dallas, 282, 289
Dalmally, 153, 157, 164
Dalmellington, 93, 98
Dalnacardoch, 197, 200
Dalnashaugh, 273, 278, 279
Dalry (Ayrshire), 102, 112, 116
Dalry (Kirkcudbright), 75, 78
Dalrymple, 6m. from Ayr
Dalton, 64
Dalwhinnie, 200, 389
Darvel, 101
Dava, 290, 292
Daviot (Inverness), 293, 296
Deanston, 180
Denholm, 38
Denny, 23, 125
Dennyloanhead, 125, 126, 136
Dervaig, 361
Deskford, 270
Dingwall, 302, 310, 339
Dinnet, 241
Dirleton, 1, 2
Dollar, 174, 181, 182
Dolphinton, 10
Dores, 298, 299
Dornie, 347
Dornoch, 302, 313, 318
Dornock, 58
Douglas, 99
Douglas Mill, 99, 121
Doune, 170, 177, 180
Dreghorn, 108
Drem, 2
Drumclog, 101
Drummore, 88
Drumnadrochit, 300, 308
Drymen, 130, 167, 377
Dufftown, 267, 272
Dulnan Bridge, 274, 280
Dumbarton, 131, 167
Dumfries, 59, 62, 63, 65 to 67, 69-73
Dunbar, 1, 3
Dunbeath, 317
Dunblane, 172, 180
Dundee, 18, 203, 221-226
Dundonald, 109
Dundonnell, 343, 345
Dundrennan, 81
Dunecht, 244
Dunfermline, 16, 175, 176, 178
Dunkeld, 200, 208, 210, 229
Dunlop, 110
Dunnet, 322
Dunning, 198

INDEX

Dunoon, 138, 145-147
Dunphail, 290
Dunragit, 86
Dunscore, 69
Duns, 34, 35, 28, 369, 370
Duntulm, 355
Dunvegan, 352, 353
Durisdeer, 52
Durness, 324, 331, 332
Duror, 158
Durris, 240
Dyce, 246
Dysart, 19

EAGLESHAM, 106, 133
Earlston, 6, 31
Easdale, 154
East Calder, 12, 13, 14
East Kilbride, 106, 113, 120
East Linton, 3
Ecclefechan, 51
Echt, 243
Edderton, 302
Eddlestone, 8
Edinbane, 353
Edinburgh, 1-20, 124
Edrom, 34, 35
Edzell, 236, 237
Elderslie, 105, 116-177
Elgin, 245, 258, 281-3, 286-8, 294
Elie, 19
Ellon, 249, 256, 259
Elphin, 341
Elvanfoot, 51, 52
Ereboll, 324, 336
Errogie Inn, 297, 299
Errol, 10m. from Perth, 13m. from Dundee
Eskbank, 7
Eskdalemuir, 60, 371
Ettrick Bridge, 44
Evanton, 302
Eyemouth, 35

FAIRLIE, 107
Falkirk, 15, 23-25, 126
Falkland, 184
Fearnan, 212
Fenwick, 106, 119
Ferness, 291, 292
Feshie Bridge, 276
Fettercairn, 218, 220, 237
Fintry, 127
Fochabers, 245, 258, 277
Fordoun, 238
Ford, 379
Forfar, 202, 224, 232, 233, 235
Forgue, 251, 257
Forres, 284, 288-291, 294
Forsinard, 319
Forth, 12
Fortingal, 214

Fort Augustus, 298, 300
Fort George, 285, 307
Fortrose, 285, 305
Fort William, 166, 300, 356-358
Foulden, 34
Foyers, 297, 298
Fraserburgh, 249, 250, 260-262
Freswick, 320
Friockheim, 234, 235
Furnace, 144
Fyvie, 246

GAIRLOCH, 344, 345
Gairlochy, 357
Galashiels, 7, 46, 47
Galston, 101, 103, 108
Gardenstown, 9½m. from Banff
Garelochhead, 137, 140
Gargunnock, 167
Garlieston, 8½m. from Wigtown, 4¾m. from Whithorn
Garmouth, 231
Gartly, 268, 269
Gartmore Station, 129
Garve, 339, 340
Gatehouse, 70, 76, 82
Georgemas, 321, 323
Giffnock, 119
Gifford, 26, 27, 369
Girvan, 89-96
Glamis, 202, 217, 223
Glasgow, 115-131, and 133-135
Glenalmond, 265
Glenapp, 89
Glenbarr, 148
Glenbarry, 266, 271
Glencoe, 166
Glendaruel, 143
Glendevon, 16
Glenelg, 348
Glenfarg, 17
Glenfinnan, 356
Glen-Isla, 230
Glenlivet, 278
Glenluce, 86, 87
Glenlyon, 214
Glenmorriston, 300, 301
Glenorchy, 164
Glen Roy, 358
Glenshee, 201, 230
Glen Urquhart, 308
Golspie, 313, 317, 333
Gordon, 5
Gorebridge, 20
Gourock, 107
Grahamston, 24
Grandtully, 209, 210
Grangemouth, 25
Granton, 17, 18
Grantown, 273-275, 280, 290, 317
Grant's House, 3
Greenlaw, 4, 35

INDEX

Greenloaning, 172, 173, 206
Greenock, 105, 107, 115
Gretna, 51, 58
Guard Bridge, 19, 174
Guildtown, 201
Gullane, 1

HADDINGTON, 3, 27
Halkirk, 325
Hamilton, 14, 101, 106, 121-2, 134
Haugh of Urr, 78, 373
Hawick, 7, 38 to 42
Heilem Inn, 324, 336
Heiton, 38
Helensburgh, 140, 378
Helmsdale, 317, 319
Heriot, 7
Holytown, 135
Holywood, 66, 67, 69
Hounam, 30
Howood, 116
Huna, 320, 322
Hunter's Quay, 146, 147
Huntingtower, 199
Huntly, 245, 248, 266-269
Hurlet, 113, 118
Hurlford, 104, 108

INCHMILL INN, 231
Inchnadamff, 338, 341
Inchture, 203
Innellan, 138
Innerleithen, 47, 368
Insch, 268
Inveran, 328
Inveraray, 141-144, 139, 153
Invercannich, 303, 308, 309
Inverey, 254
Inverfarigaig, 297, 298
Invergarry, 300, 347
Invergordon, 302, 304
Inverkeilor, 225
Inverkeithing, 17, 190
Inverkip, 107
Invermorriston, 300, 301
Inverness, 294-305, 307, 310
Inveroran, 164, 166
Invershin, 328, 329, 334
Inversnaid, 168, 171
Inverurie, 245, 251, 255, 263
Iona, 362
Irvine, 102, 107, 108, 118
Islay,
Isle Ornsay, 351
Isle Toll, 66, 67, 69
Isle of Whithorn, 84, 87

JEANTOWN, 339, 346
Jedburgh, 6, 43
John o' Groats, 320, 322
Johnshaven, 225
Johnstone, 105

Johnstone Bridge, 51
Juniper Green, 11
Jura,

KAMES, 142
Keills, 152
Keiss, 320
Keith, 245, 264, 270-272, 273, 286
Kelso, 5, 29-32, 36-38, 46
Kemnay, 255
Kenmore, 212
Kennethmont, 268
Kennoway, 192
Kesssock, 304, 310
Kettle, 18
Kilberry, 150, 151
Kilbirnie, 117
Kilbride, East, 106
    „   West, 112
Kilchattan, 366
Kilchrennan, 162
Kilcreggan, 137
Kildonan, 319
Kilfinnan, 142
Kilkenzie, 148
Killearn, 128
Killiecrankie, 200
Killin, 132, 170, 212, 213
Kilmalcolm, 105
Kilmany, 193
Kilmarnock, 104, 108-110, 119
Kilmartin, 155
Kilmaurs, 110
Kilmelfort, 155
Kilmichael Glassary, 155
Kilmorack, 303
Kilmun, 147
Kilninver, 154, 155
Kilpatrick, Old, 131
Kilrenny, 18
Kilsyth, 126, 128
Kilwinning, 102, 107, 111
Kincardine, 136, 176
Kincardine O'Neil, 241
Kingairloch, 359
Kinghorn, 18
Kingsbarns, 19
Kingshouse, 163, 166
Kingussie, 200, 296, 258
Kinloch-Aylort, 356
Kinlochewe, 344
Kinloch Inn (Mull), 362, 363
Kinloch-Moidart, 360
Kinloch-Rannoch, 211, 215, 216
Kinnesswood, 194
Kinross, 17, 189
Kintore, 245
Kippen, 127, 167, 179
Kirkbank, 38
Kirkcaldy, 18, 19, 183, 191, 192
Kirkconnel, 67
Kirkcowan, 83

Kirkcudbright, 72, 74, 77, 80-82
Kirkfieldbank, 122
Kirkinner, 84
Kirkintilloch, 126
Kirkliston, 15
Kirkmichael (Perth), 227
Kirkmichael (Ayr), 97
Kirknewton, 14 ; 1½m. S.W. fr.9m.
Kirkoswald, 94
Kirkwall,
Kirn, 146-147
Kirriemuir, 223, 228, 230, 231, 235
Knockando, 277, 289
Knowe, 91
Kyle Akin, 339, 350
Kyle Rhea, 348
Kyle Sku, 341

LAGG INN, 364
Laggan Bridge, 358
Lairg, 319, 329, 334, 337, 338
Lamington, 10
Lamlash, 364
Lanark, 11, 12, 49, 50, 122
Langholm, 41, 60, 61
Larbert, 15, 136
Largo, 19, 186, 188, 194
Largs, 107, 117
Larkhall, 121
Lasswade, 20
Latheron, 317, 323
Lauder, 5, 6, 33
Laurencekirk, 202, 238
Laurieston (Falkirk), 15
Lawrieston, 76, 77
Lawers, 212
Laxford Bridge, 332, 337
Leadburn, 8, 9
Leadhills, 68
Ledaig, 158, 159
Leith, page 1
Lennoxtown, 127, 128
Leslie (Fife), 194
Leshmahagow, 121
Letham, 226
Leuchars, 19
Leven, 19, 194
Lhanbryd, 245, 258, 281
Linlithgow 15, 21, 22
Linlithgow Bridge, 15
Linton, East, 3
   ,,   West, 10
Livingston, 14
Loans, 102, 109
Lochaline, 359
Lochalsh, 339, 347
Lochawe Station, 157
Lochbroom, 340
Lochcarron, 339, 346
Lochdonhead, 363
Lochearnhead, 170, 199
Lochenbreck, 76

Lochee, 221, 222
Lochgair, 144
Lochgilphead, 144
Lochgoilhead, 139
Lochhournhead, 349
Lochinver, 338, 342
Loch Katrine, 171
Lochlaggan Inn, 358
Lochlee, 236
Lochmaben, 59, 64
Lochmaree, 344
Lochranza, 364
Lochwinnoch, 117
Lockerbie, 51, 57, 59, 61, 371, 372
Logierait, 209
Longforgan, 203
Longformacus, 369
Longniddry, 2
Longside, 258
Longtown, 41, 58
Lonmay, 249
Lossiemouth, 5¾m. from Elgin ; a fine level road
Loth, 317
Luib, 132
Lumphanan, 242
Lumsden, 269
Lundin Links, 19
Luss, 131, 378
Lybster, 317
Lyne, 123
Lynwilg, 296

MACDUFF, 258, 262
Machrihanish, 5¾m. from Campbeltown ; a good road
Macmerry, 3
Maidens, 95
Markinch, 194
Marykirk, 238
Mauchline, 100, 104
Maud, 263
Maybole, 94-96
Meigle, 202, 222
Meikleour, 229
Melrose, 46, 55
Melvich, 319, 324
Methlick, 247, 256, 260
Methven, 199, 205
Mid-Calder, 12, 13, 14
Mill Inn, 240, 252
Millerston, 125
Millport, 367
Milnathort, 17, 174, 194
Milngavie, 129
Milton, 128
Minard, 144
Minnyshant, 94, 97
Mintlaw, 250, 258, 263
Moffat, 9, 45, 65, 372
Moidart, 360
Moniaive, 53, 69

INDEX.

Monifieth, 6¾m. from Dundee; a good road
Monkton, 102, 119
Montrose, 219, 220, 225, 232, 238
Monymusk, 255
Morebattle, 30
Morvern, 359
Mossat, 244
Motherwell, 14, 123
Mound, 317, 318, 333
Moy, 296
Muchalls, 225
Muckart, 174
Muasdale, 148
Muirdrum, 225, 233
Muirhead, 221, 222
Muirkirk, 99, 100, 375
Muir-of-Ord, 302, 315
Mulben, 279, 286
Munlochy, 304, 305
Murthly, 204
Musselburgh, 1, 2, 3
Muthill, 16, 172
Mybster, 323

NAIRN, 285, 292-295
Neilston, 118
Nenthorn, 5
Nethy Bridge, 275
New Abbey, 73
New Aberdour, 262
Newarthill, 14
Newbigging (Lanark), 123
Newburgh, 185, 196
Newburgh (Aberdeen), 248, 13¼m. from Aberdeen
New Byth, 259, 261
Newcastleton, 40, 43
New Cumnock, 67, 104
New Deer, 259, 260, 263
New Galloway, 53, 71, 77, 98
New Galloway Station, 77
Newhouse, 14, 135
New Leeds, 250
Newmains, 13, 50
Newmill, 41
Newmilns, 101
New Pitsligo, 258
Newport, 18, 193
Newton Mearns, 119
Newtonmore, 200, 358
Newton-Stewart, 53, 70, 84-6, 92, 97
Newtyle, 217, 222
Nigg Station, 311
North Berwick, 1

OBAN, 154, 155, 157
Ochiltree, 99
Old Deer, 263, 386
Old Kilpatrick, 131
Old Meldrum, 246, 248
Onich, 166
Ordhead, 244

Orkney,
Ormsary, 151
Orton, 277, 286
Otter Ferry, 142, 145
Overscaig Inn, 337
Oykell Bridge Inn, 338

PAISLEY, 105, 113, 114, 116, 117. 376
Palnackie, 74
Palnure, 70
Parkgate, 65
Pass of Brander, 157
  „ Drumochter, 200
  „ Killiecrankie, 200
  „ Melfort, 155
Parton, 75
Pathhead (Edinburgh), 4
  „ (Fife), 18, 19, 192
Patna, 98
Paxton, 33
Peebles, 8, 47, 48, 49, 123
Penicuick, 8, 9, 10
Pennyghael, 362
Penpont, 53, 66
Perth, 17, 173, 196, 199-204
Peterculter, 241
Peterhead, 249, 258
Pinwherry, 90-92
Pirnmill, 364
Pitcaple, 245, 268
Pitlochry, 200, 211, 227
Pitmedden, 247, 248
Pittenweem, 19
Plean, 15
Pluscarden, 288
Pollokshaws, 118
Polmont, 15, 169
Poolewe, 345
Port Appin, 161
Portaskaig,
Port Bannatyne, 143
Port Charlotte.
Port Ellen,
Port Glasgow, 105, 115
Port Gordon, 5¾m. from **Fochabers** 10¼m. from Keith
Portmahomack, 312
Port Monteith, 168, 178
Portnahaven, 396
Port Sonachan, 162
Portobello, 1, 2, 3
Portpatrick, 89
Portree, 350, 353, 354
Portsoy, 258, 266
Port William, 85, 87
Poyntzfield, 306
Preston, 2
Prestonpans, 1
Prestwick, 102, 119

QUEENSFERRY (North), 16, 17
  „ (South), 16, 17, 21
Quirang, 354

RAFFORD, 288, 289
Rannoch, 211
Ravenstruther, 11, 99
Reay, 324, 326
Relugas, 291
Renfrew, 114, 115
Renton, 131
Reston, 3
Rhiconich, 332
Rhynie, 269
Rigg, 62
Ringford, 70, 77
Rogart, 318
Romanno Bridge, 9
Rosehall, 328, 338
Rosebearty, 4½m. fr. Fraserburgh; a good road
Rosemarkie, 305
Roseneath, 137
Roslin, 8; 1m. distant at 6¼m.; several steep hills
Rothes, 277, 287
Rothesay, 143, 366
Rothiemay, 264, 266
Row, 140
Rowardennan, 377
Roy Bridge, 358
Rumbling Bridge, 16
Rutherglen, 120
Ruthven, 228
Ruthwell, 62

SADDELL, 149
St. Andrews, 19, 174, 187, 188, 192
St. Boswells, 6, 46, 54
St. Catherine's, 139, 142, 143, 146
St. Cyrus, 225
St. Fillans, 199
St. Michael's Inn, 18, 19
St. Ninians, 15, 125
Salen (Loch Sunart), 360
Salen (Mull), 361, 362, 363
Saline, 182
Saltcoats, 107, 111
Sandbank, 145-147
Sanquhar, 67, 68
Scone, 201, 202
Sconser, 350
Scotlandwell, 194
Scourie, 337, 341
Scrabster, 2m. from Thurso
Selkirk, 7, 44, 45, 54-56
Shandon, 140
Shettleston, 124
Shieldaig, 346
Shiel Inn, 347, 348
Shotts, 14
Skeabost, 353
Skelmorlie, 107
Skene, 244
Skipness, 2m. fr. Claonaig (No. 149)
Slateford, 11

Sligachan, 350, 352
Smailholm, 31
Small Isles,
Snizort, 354
Sorbie, 84
Sorn, 100, 103
Southend, 160
Spean Bridge, 300, 358
Spinningdale, 302
Spital of Glenshee, 201, 230
Springholm, 70
Sprouston, 32
Staffin, 354, 355
Stanley, 204
Stenhousemuir, ⅞m. E. of Larbert
Stevenston, 107, 111
Stewarton, 110
Stirling, 15, 125, 167-177
Stobo, 49
Stobs, 40
Stonehaven, 202, 218, 225, 239, 252
Stonehouse, 13
Stoneykirk, 88
Stornoway,
Stow, 7, 33
Strachan, 237
Strachur, 142, 143, 146
Straiton, 8, 10
Straiton (Ayrshire), 93, 97
Stranraer, 86, 88, 89
Strathavon, 13, 101, 120, 375
Strathblane, 128, 129
Strathcarron, 346
Strathconon, 315
Strathdon, 244
Strathmiglo, 174, 184
Strathpeffer, 339
Strath Tummel, 211
Strathy, 324
Strathyre, 170
Strichen, 260
Strome Ferry, 339
Stromness,
Stronachlacher, 171
Strone, 147
Strontian, 360
Struan, 200, 215
Struan (Skye), 352
Struy, 303, 314
Swinton, 37
Symington, 49

TAIN, 302, 311-313, 317
Tannadice, 202, 228
Tarbet (Loch Lomond), 131, 132, 141
Tarbert (Lochfyne), 144, 148-49, 150
Tarbert (Harris),
Tarbolton, 7⅜m. from Ayr
Tarfside, 236
Tarland, 243
Tayinloan, 148
Taynuilt, 157, 159, 162

INDEX

Tayport, 19, 193
Tayvallich, 152
Templand, 64
Temple (Inverness), 300
Teviothead, 41
The Craigs, 327
The Mound, 317, 318, 333
Thornhill, 52, 53, 67
Thornhill (Stirling), 168, 179
Thornliebank, 113
Thornton (Fife), 18
Thurso, 321-326
Tighnabruaich, 142
Tillicoultry, 174, 181
Tillyfourie, 244, 255
Tobermory, 361, 363
Tomatin, 296
Tomdoun, 347, 349
Tomich, 303
Tomintoul, 278, 387
Tongue, 324, 334
Tongueland, 80
Tornaveen, 243
Torphichen, 22
Torphins, 242
Torrance, 127
Torridon, 344
Torryburn, 176, 190
Torthorwald, 59
Toward, 138
Tranent, 3, 26
Traquair, 48
Troon, 109
Trossachs, 129, 171
Tullibody, 175
Tummel Bridge, 197, 211
Turriff, 246, 257, 261, 263, 264
Tushielaw Inn, 42, 44, 48
Tweedmouth, 36
Twynholm, 70

Tyndrum, 157, 166
Tynninghame, 1

UDDINGSTON, 121
Uig, 354, 355
Ullapool, 340-342, 345
Ulva Ferry, 361
Uphall, 124

WALKERBURN, 47, 56
Wamphray, 372
Wanlockhead, 68
Watten, 321
Wemyss Bay, 107
West Calder, 12, 13
Westerdale, 325
West Kilbride, 172
West Linton, 10
Westruther, 33
Whistlefield (Argyle), 146-147
      ,,   (Dumbarton), 140
Whitburn, 14
Whitebridge, 298, 299
Whitehouse (Argyle), 148
Whithorn, 84
Whiting Bay, 364
Wick, 317, 320, 321
Wigtown, 83, 84
Wilkieston, 13, 14
Wilsontown, 12
Winchburgh, 15
Windygates, 192, 194
Wishaw, 13, 123
Woodside, 245, 246

YARROW, 45
Yetholm, 29
Yoker, 131
Ythanbank, 256

Railway Rates

FOR CONVEYANCE OF :—

Distances.	Bicycles.			Tricycles.		
	As Passenger's Luggage.	As Parcels. Owner's Risk.	As Parcels. Coy's Risk.	As Passenger's Luggage.	As Parcels. Owner's Risk.	As Parcels. Coy's Risk.
Up to 12 miles	6d.	9d.	1/-	1/-	2/-	3/-
12 to 25 ,,	9d.	1/2	1/6	1/6	3/-	4/6
25 to 50 ,,	1/-	1/6	2/-	2/-	4/-	6/-
50 to 75 ,,	1/6	2/3	3/-	3/-	6/-	9/-
75 to 100 ,,	2/-	3/-	4/-	4/-	8/-	12/-
100 to 150 ,,	2/6	3/9	5/-	5/-	10/-	15/-
150 to 200 ,,	3/-	4/6	6/-	6/-	12/-	18/-
200 to 250 ,,	3/6	5/3	7/-	7/-	14/-	21/-
250 to 300 ,,	4/-	6/-	8/-	8/-	16/-	24/-
300 to 350 ,,	4/6	6/9	9/-	9/-	18/-	27/-
350 to 400 ,,	5/-	7/6	10/-	10/-	20/-	30/-
Each additional 50 miles and portion thereof	6d.	9d.	1/-	1/-	2/-	3/-

Tandems, &c., 50 per cent. additional per seat.

CONTOUR ROAD BOOK OF SCOTLAND

DISTANCES BY RAIL.

```
Edinburgh.
 44 Glasgow.
131 153 Aberdeen.
 77  39 193 Ayr.
 98 102 229  93 Carlisle.
 89  82 229  60  33 Dumfries.
 59  82  71 122 158 160 Dundee.
 53  92 184 123  46  64 112 Hawick.
191 207 108 247 286 281 165 245 Inverness.
 52  63  90 103 148 140  21 101 144 Perth.
 37  30 123  70 118 107  54  89 177  33 Stirling.
 76 101  54 139 174 177  17 129 173  37  71 Arbroath.
 72  29 176  19 106  73 111  ..  236  92  59 Ardrossan.
 33  30 129  70 118 107  52  86 178  34   7 Alloa.
 58 102 190 140  92 111 117  47 250 105  94 Berwick.
181 203  50 243 279 279 121 234  72 140 173 Banff.
 68  84  78 124 166 160  27 121 150  20  54 Blairgowrie.
 94 115  46 155 192 191  35 147 154  52  85 Brechin.
 53  46 129  86 134 123  60 106 183  39  16 Callander.
109  97 240  80  53  20 169  83 301 157 126 Castle Douglas.
 45  68  86 108 143 134  15  98 168  24  44 Cupar.
 62  56 104  96 144 133  39 115 162  18  26 Crieff.
211 226 237 266 305 300 184 264  19 163 196 Dingwall.
 58  14 157  54 116  96  88 106 211  67  34 Dumbarton.
 29  73 160 106 127 119  88  ..  221  77  66 Dunbar.
 17  44 115  84 115 107  44  70 175  31  20 Dunfermline.
 64  80  91 120 162 152  37 117 128  16  49 Dunkeld.
180 196  71 235 278 271 153 232  37 132 165 Elgin.
 45  73 114 113 143 134  34  98 185  41  49 Elie.
 25  22 133  62 111 101  64  78 188  44  11 Falkirk.
 80  96  57 136 178 177  21 133 162  33  66 Forfar.
145 122 222 162 224 204 153 198 276 132 110 Fort William.
 34  73 165 112  65  ..   93  19 226  81  70 Galashiels.
 92  61 213  21 111  78 147 140 268 124  91 Girvan.
 63  20 161  40 123 102  96  ..  219  75  42 Greenock.
 39  11 153  50  93  82  86  ..  209  65  32 Hamilton.
 63  20 165  59 123 102  96 112 219  75  42 Helensburgh.
 70  27 178  11  99  66 109  ..  234  90  57 Irvine.
 56  96 187 135  75  92 115  28 248 104  93 Jedburgh.
 52  92 183 134  69  87 111  24 244 100  89 Kelso.
 67  24 177  15  91  58 106  ..  231  87  54 Kilmarnock.
 31  47 106  86 129 121  35  84 161  17  24 Kinross.
 26  56 105 102 124 116  33  80 176  32  40 Kirkcaldy.
 32  29 147  46  78  67  98  ..  221  76  44 Lanark.
 78 109 208  93  22  ..  137  38 269 125 114 Langholm.
 18  30 131  69 114  ..   60  71 192  48  19 Linlithgow.
 37  77 163 116  61  79  96  16 229  85  74 Melrose.
 63  64 178  95  42  31 134  ..  257 109  80 Moffat.
 89 117  41 156 203 193  30 143 149  51  87 Montrose.
177 193  93 231 275 266 150 230   5 129 162 Nairn.
139  97 261  71  83  50 190 113 315 171 138 Newton Stewart.
 23  67 154 105 111  ..   82  ..  214  70  59 North Berwick.
123 101 200 156 203 183 131 176 254  96  87 Oban.
 50   7 158  34 103  85  89  ..  214  70  37 Paisley.
 27  54 153  75  83  75  87  37 219  75  63 Peebles.
175 197  44 235 273 265 115 228 140 134 167 Peterhead.
 55  79  85 118 154  ..   13 108 179  35  55 St. Andrews.
 40  79 171 119  70  ..   99  26 231  87  76 Selkirk.
114 137  16 176 213 214  55 167 125  74 107 Stonehaven.
141  98 251  58 106  74 180 137 305 161 128 Stranraer.
353 368 260 407 447 442 326 406 161 305 338 Wick.
```

Ferries and Ferry Charges.

This list has been made up in response to numerous requests, but as the Author's Memoranda relating to some of the Ferries have been mislaid, it is not quite complete.

Owing to some oversight in the Local Government Act of 1889, the Ferries are no longer under responsible control, and travellers may be mulcted of a somewhat higher sum than that given below. The prices also at the same Ferry may vary considerably, but this refers mostly to those in the out-of-the-way parts. It is right, however, to state that many of these are patronised so seldom, and so irregularly, that there is no inducement for young and strong men to take it up as a permanent occupation, and the work is therefore left to the old men, boys, and loungers who are willing to earn occasional small sums. This is in explanation of much of the seeming extortion that is indulged in. The busier ferries have no excuse whatever for higher rates, and in fact are the least troublesome. The ferrymen also, on the longer crossings, do not care about single passengers, and often delay in the hope of having a full boat-load.

Passengers before 6 a.m. and after 9 p.m. are usually charged double.

The summer service of steamers usually extends from 15th May to 15th September. Some are earlier, some later.

The term "Irregular Ferry" denotes a ferry that is only occasionally used.

On comparing notes with tourists we find a considerable variation in the rates charged; those noted below must therefore be considered approximate; but usually the fare in boat ferries is 2d. to 6d. per passenger, and 6d. for bicycle. Chain pontoons are usually ½d. and 1d per passenger, and 1d. or 2d. for bicycle. As a cycle is not an article on the tariff boards, the charge is variable.

The Author would therefore feel obliged for further information and details. Parties so doing will receive a copy of the revised List.

Disused Ferries.—The following ferries marked on many maps are now disused:—Achnacloich (Loch Etive) and Ardchattan; Keills and Lagg (Jura); Strachur, across Loch Fyne; Dalpatrick, over River Earn, near Crieff; Knockdown, across Cree, near Creetown.

Alloa and South Alloa.—Steam launch nearly every half-hour, 2d.; Bic. 3d.

Ballachulish Ferry.—Boats of various sizes on both sides, 6d.

Blacksboat (River Spey), Route 289.—Chain boat for vehicles.

Boat of Garten (River Spey).—Chain boat for vehicles.

Bonawe (Loch Etive).—Boats of various sizes at the Bonawe side.

Broughty Ferry—Tayport.—Steamer. See Railway Time Tables. Fare, 6d. and 4d.; Bic. 6d.

Burntisland.—*See* Granton.

Colintraive.—Boats of various sizes.

Coulport Ferry.—Boats. Probably closed this year.

Connel Ferry.—Boats at both sides, 2d.; minimum, 3d.; Bic. 6d.

Corran Ferry.—Boats at both sides.

Cregan Ferry (Loch Etive).—Boats at northern side.

Cromarty Ferry.—Boats.

Cromarty-Invergordon.—Steam launch 3 times daily, 1s.; Bic.

Dornie Ferry.—Boats, 6d.
Dornie—Totaig Ferry.—Boat usually at Totaig, but often at Dornie, 1s.
Dundee—Newport.—Steamer every hour, Fare, 4d. & 3d.; Bic. 2d.
Durness Ferry.—Boats, 1s.
Erskine Ferry (River Clyde).—Steam Ferry boat.
Fort George—Chanonry (for Fortrose).—Boat at Chanonry Point, 1s.
Foyers—Ruskich.—Boat.
Granton—Burntisland.—Steamer 6 times daily. *See* Railway Time Tables. Fare, 10d. and 5d.; Bic. 6d.
Greenock—Helensburgh.—Steamer eight times daily. *See* Railway Time Tables.
Hellem Ferry.—Boat, 1s.
Helensburgh—Greenock—Steamer eight times daily. *See* Railway Time Tables.
Hope Ferry.—Chain boat, 4d.
Inveraray—St. Catherine's Ferry.—Mail steamer twice daily. Ferry boats at all times.
Invergordon—Newhall Ferry.—Boat, 6d.; Bic. 6d.
Invergordon—Cromarty.—Steam launch 3 times daily, 1s.; Bic.
Inversnaid (across Loch Lomond).—Boats at Inversnaid only. Irregular Ferry.
Kessock Ferry.—Boat every hour, Bic. 6d.
Kincardine—Higginsneuk Ferry.—Boat 8 times daily. *See* Railway Time Tables. 6d.; at any time on hoisting signal on south side, 1s.
Kyle and Kyle Akin Ferry.—6d. In connection with Railway.
Kyle Rhea Ferry.—Boats on both sides, 1s. Irregular Ferry.
Kyle Sku.—Boats at south side, 6d.
Lismore—Appin Ferry.—Boats on both sides.
Little Ferry.—Boats, 6d.
Logierait.—Chain pontoon from north side, 2d.
Meikleour Ferry (River Tay)—Chain pontoon for vehicles, 2d.
Meikle Ferry.—Boats on north side, Bic. 6d.
Newburgh and Errol.—No information.
Newport and Dundee.—Steamer every hour. Fare, 4d. and 3d.; Bic. 2d.
Otter Ferry.—Boats at both sides. Irregular Ferry.
Parton Ferry (across Loch Ken).—Chain pontoon for vehicles.
Portincaple Ferry (across Loch Long).—Boats at Portincaple. (No road to Lochgoilhead.)
Port Askaig (Islay).—Boat.
Port Sonachan—Taychreggan.—Boats, and steamer during summer. Fare,
Queensferry and North Queensferry.—Steamer six times daily. Fare, 4d.; Bic. 6d.
Renfrew—Yoker (River Clyde).—Steam Ferry, ½d.
Row—Roseneath Pier.—Boat, 2d.; Bic. 6d.
Rowardennan to Inverbeg (Loch Lomond).—Boat.
Strome Ferry.—Boats at north side, summoned by horn, 6d.
Shian Ferry.—Boats at north side, summoned by semaphore, 3d.; Minimum, 6d.; Bic. 6d.
Tayport.—*See* Broughty Ferry.

Tobermory Drimnin.—Mail steamer daily.
Tongue Ferry.—Boats, 6d.
Totaig—Dornie (Ardelve).—Ferry boat at Totaig, summoned by horn, if at Dornie, 1s.
Torridon and Shieldaig.—No Ferry; hire fishing boat.
Ullapool Ferry.—Irregular Ferry; hire fishing boat, 1s. to 2s. 6d.
Tummel Ferry (east end of Loch Tummel).—Chain pontoon for vehicles, 2d.; and boat.

STEAMERS ON LOCHS, &c. (See Railway Time Tables.)

Loch Awe.—Summer service four times daily between Loch Awe station and Port Sonachan; twice daily to Ford.
Loch Eck.—Summer service only in connection with coach.
Loch Etive.—Summer service twice daily.
Loch Katrine.—Summer service 6 times daily. Fare, 2/6; Bic. 1/-.
Loch Lomond.—In summer three times daily; thrice a week in the winter months. Fares, 6d. to 3s.; Bic. 6d. and 1s. Note there is no road to Balloch Pier, from which the steamer starts; train must be taken to or from Balloch station, half a mile off.
Loch Maree.—Summer service.
Loch Ness and Caledonian Canal.—Summer service of fast steamers three times daily; winter service of fast steamer (on Loch Ness only) once daily, and of slow steamers twice a week.
Loch Tay.—Four times daily in summer; twice daily in winter. Fares, 3s.; B'c. 1s. 6d.
Crinan Canal.—Summer service. Cycles are not taken on the steamer.

THE CLYDE.—There is a splendid service of steamers all the year round between the various points. See Railway Time Tables.
THE FORTH.—In addition to the Granton and Queensferry ferries, there are summer steamers from Leith to Stirling, Queensferry, Aberdour, Kirkcaldy, Elie, and North Berwick.
THE TAY.—A summer steamer runs between Dundee, Newburgh, and Perth.
BEAULY FIRTH.—A summer steamer runs between Inverness and Fortrose; and to Cromarty and Invergordon.
WESTERN HIGHLANDS.—Service of steamers all the year round between all Islands.
ORKNEY AND THURSO.—Mail steamer daily.

PIER DUES.

At nearly all the Piers there is a Pier charge of a 1d., and usually 2d. for a Bicycle. At several piers the toll is as high as 4d.

The Rates for Cycles by Macbrayne's Steamers are:—

	Bicycles.	Tricycles.		Bicycles.	Tricycles.
Up to 10 miles,	1/-	1/6	Up to 100 miles,	4/-	6/-
,, 20 ,,	1/6	2/6	,, 200 ,,	6/6	9/-
,, 50 ,,	2/6	4/-	,, 300 ,,	7/6	10/-

Cyclists should note that on most steamers scarcely any care or protection is given to their machines notwithstanding the high rates charged. In time this may be remedied, but the matter is notorious.

Lamp=Lighting Tables.
(See Index of Towns on next page.)

The time of sunset for each date varies from year to year, these Tables therefore are not absolutely exact, but give an average which is never more than a few minutes out, on any date.

To use the Tables.—Find the district required on the next page, and add the time allowance to the column named, and opposite the required date. For example, the average time for lighting lamps at Edinburgh on June 21 is obtained as follows:—Edinburgh, add 13 minutes to column B on June 21, which is 9.41. The average hour for lighting lamps is therefore 9.54 p.m.

For dates not in Table take the proportion between the two nearest.

Date.	55° A P.M.	56° B P.M.	56½° C P.M.	57° D P.M.	58° E P.M.	Date.	55° A P.M.	56° B P.M.	56½° C P.M.	57° D P.M.	58° E P.M.
Jany. 1	4.35	4.28	4.25	4.21	4.13	July 2	9.32	9.39	9.42	9.46	9.54
,, 9	4.47	4.40	4.37	4.33	4.26	,, 11	9.26	9.32	9.35	9.39	9.46
,, 15	4.57	4.50	4.47	4.44	4.37	,, 18	9.19	9.25	9.28	9.31	9.38
,, 20	5.6	5.0	4.58	4.55	4.49	,, 23	9.11	9.17	9.19	9.22	9.28
,, 24	5.14	5.9	5.6	5.3	4.57	,, 28	9.4	9.9	9.11	9.14	9.20
,, 28	5.22	5.18	5.16	5.13	5.8	Aug. 1	8.57	9.1	9.3	9.6	9.11
Feby. 1	5.30	5.25	5.23	5.21	5.16	,, 5	8.50	8.54	8.56	8.58	9.3
,, 4	5.37	5.33	5.31	5.29	5.25	,, 8	8.42	8.46	8.48	8.50	8.54
,, 8	5.44	5.40	5.39	5.37	5.32	,, 12	8.35	8.39	8.40	8.42	8.47
,, 11	5.51	5.47	5.46	5.44	5.40	,, 15	8.27	8.31	8.32	8.34	8.38
,, 14	5.57	5.54	5.53	5.51	5.47	,, 18	8.20	8.24	8.25	8.27	8.31
,, 17	6.3	6.1	6.0	5.58	5.54	,, 21	8.14	8.16	8.17	8.19	8.23
,, 19	6.9	6.7	6.6	6.4	6.2	,, 24	8.6	8.9	8.10	8.12	8.14
,, 22	6.15	6.13	6.12	6.11	6.8	,, 27	7.59	8.2	8.3	8.4	8.7
,, 25	6.21	6.19	6.18	6.17	6.14	,, 30	7.52	7.54	7.55	7.56	7.59
,, 28	6.27	6.25	6.24	6.23	6.21	Sept. 2	7.46	7.48	7.49	7.50	7.52
Mar. 2	6.32	6.30	6.29	6.28	6.27	,, 4	7.39	7.41	7.42	7.43	7.44
,, 5	6.37	6.35	6.35	6.34	6.32	,, 7	7.33	7.34	7.34	7.35	7.37
,, 7	6.42	6.41	6.41	6.40	6.39	,, 10	7.26	7.27	7.27	7.28	7.29
,, 10	6.47	6.46	6.46	6.45	6.44	,, 12	7.19	7.20	7.20	7.21	7.22
,, 13	6.52	6.51	6.51	6.50	6.50	,, 15	7.12	7.13	7.13	7.14	7.14
,, 15	6.58	6.57	6.57	6.57	6.56	,, 17	7.5	7.6	7.6	7.6	7.7
,, 18	7.2	7.2	7.2	7.2	7.2	,, 20	6.59	6.59	6.59	6.59	6.59
,, 20	7.7	7.7	7.7	7.7	7.7	,, 22	6.53	6.53	6.53	6.53	6.53
,, 23	7.13	7.12	7.12	7.12	7.12	,, 25	6.46	6.46	6.46	6.46	6.46
,, 25	7.17	7.18	7.18	7.18	7.19	,, 28	6.40	6.30	6.39	6.39	6.38
,, 28	7.22	7.23	7.23	7.24	7.24	,, 30	6.33	6.32	6.32	6.31	6.31
,, 30	7.27	7.29	7.29	7.30	7.31	Oct. 3	6.26	6.25	6.25	6.24	6.23
April 2	7.33	7.34	7.34	7.35	7.36	,, 5	6.19	6.18	6.18	6.17	6.16
,, 5	7.38	7.39	7.39	7.40	7.42	,, 8	6.12	6.11	6.11	6.10	6.8
,, 7	7.42	7.44	7.45	7.46	7.47	,, 11	6.7	6.5	6.4	6.3	6.2
,, 10	7.47	7.49	7.50	7.51	7.53	,, 13	6.0	5.58	5.57	5.56	5.54
,, 13	7.53	7.54	7.55	7.56	7.59	,, 16	5.54	5.51	5.50	5.49	5.46
,, 15	7.58	8.1	8.2	8.3	8.6	,, 19	5.47	5.44	5.43	5.42	5.39
,, 18	8.4	8.6	8.7	8.9	8.11	,, 22	5.41	5.38	5.37	5.35	5.33
,, 21	8.10	8.12	8.13	8.15	8.19	,, 25	5.33	5.31	5.30	5.28	5.24
,, 24	8.15	8.18	8.19	8.21	8.25	,, 27	5.27	5.24	5.23	5.21	5.17
,, 27	8.21	8.25	8.26	8.28	8.32	,, 30	5.21	5.17	5.15	5.14	5.10
May 1	8.27	8.31	8.32	8.34	8.39	Nov. 3	5.14	5.10	5.9	5.7	5.2
,, 4	8.34	8.38	8.40	8.42	8.46	,, 6	5.7	5.3	5.1	4.59	4.55
,, 8	8.41	8.45	8.47	8.49	8.54	,, 9	5.0	4.56	4.54	4.52	4.47
,, 11	8.47	8.52	8.54	8.57	9.2	,, 13	4.54	4.50	4.48	4.45	4.40
,, 16	8.54	8.59	9.1	9.4	9.10	,, 17	4.47	4.42	4.40	4.37	4.31
,, 20	9.1	9.7	9.9	9.12	9.18	,, 21	4.41	4.35	4.33	4.30	4.24
,, 25	9.9	9.15	9.18	9.21	9.28	,, 26	4.35	4.29	4.26	4.23	4.16
,, 31	9.18	9.24	9.27	9.31	9.38	Dec. 2	4.29	4.23	4.20	4.16	4.9
June 10	9.28	9.35	9.38	9.42	9.50	,, 11	4.24	4.17	4.14	4.10	4.2
,, 21	9.34	9.41	9.45	9.49	9.57	,, 21	4.26	4.18	4.14	4.10	4.2

CONTOUR ROAD BOOK OF SCOTLAND.

Index of Towns—Lamp-lighting Tables.

(See previous page.)

Town.	Minutes.	Col.	Town.	Minutes.	Col.
Aberdeen,	add 8 to	D	Huntly,	add 11 to	D
Aberfeldy,	,, 15 ,,	C	Inverary,	,, 20 ,,	B
Airdrie,	,, 16 ,,	B	Inverness,	,, 17 ,,	E
Alloa,	,, 15 ,,	B	Irvine,	,, 19 ,,	B
Annan,	,, 13 ,,	A	Islay,	,, 25 ,,	B
Arbroath,	,, 10 ,,	C	Jedburgh,	,, 10 ,,	A
Ardrossan,	,, 19 ,,	B	Johnstone,	,, 18 ,,	B
Arran,	,, 21 ,,	B	Kelso,	,, 10 ,,	A
Ayr,	,, 18 ,,	A	Kilmarnock,	,, 18 ,,	B
Ballater,	,, 12 ,,	D	Kingussie,	,, 16 ,,	D
Banff,	,, 10 ,,	E	Kinross,	,, 14 ,,	B
Bathgate,	,, 14 ,,	B	Kirkcaldy,	,, 13 ,,	B
Beauly,	,, 18 ,,	D	Kirkcudbright,	,, 16 ,,	A
Berwick,	,, 8 ,,	B	*Kirkwall (Orkney),	,, 12 ,,	E
Blairgowrie,	,, 13 ,,	C	Kirriemuir,	,, 12 ,,	C
Brechin,	,, 10 ,,	C	Lanark,	,, 15 ,,	A
Callander,	,, 17 ,,	B	Langholm,	,, 12 ,,	A
Campbeltown,	,, 22 ,,	A	Largs,	,, 19 ,,	B
Carlisle,	,, 15 ,,	A	Lauder,	,, 11 ,,	B
Castle Douglas,	,, 16 ,,	A	†Lerwick (Shetland),	,, 5 ,,	E
Coatbridge,	,, 16 ,,	B	Linlithgow,	,, 14 ,,	B
Coldstream,	,, 9 ,,	A	Lockerbie,	,, 13 ,,	B
Crieff,	,, 15 ,,	C	Lossiemouth,	,, 13 ,,	E
Cumnock,	,, 17 ,,	A	Mauchline,	,, 17 ,,	A
Cupar Angus,	,, 13 ,,	C	Maybole,	,, 18 ,,	A
Cupar,	,, 12 ,,	B	Melrose,	,, 11 ,,	A
Dingwall,	,, 18 ,,	E	Moffat,	,, 14 ,,	A
Dollar,	,, 15 ,,	B	Montrose,	,, 10 ,,	C
Dumbarton,	,, 18 ,,	B	Motherwell,	,, 16 ,,	B
Dumfries,	,, 14 ,,	A	Muirkirk,	,, 16 ,,	A
Dunbar,	,, 10 ,,	B	Nairn,	,, 15 ,,	D
Dunblane,	,, 15 ,,	B	New Galloway,	,, 17 ,,	A
Dundee,	,, 12 ,,	C	Newton Stewart,	,, 18 ,,	A
Dunfermline,	,, 14 ,,	B	North Berwick,	,, 11 ,,	B
Dunkeld,	,, 14 ,,	C	Oban,	,, 22 ,,	C
Dunoon,	,, 20 ,,	B	Peebles,	,, 13 ,,	A
Earlston,	,, 11 ,,	A	Perth,	,, 14 ,,	C
Edinburgh,	,, 13 ,,	B	Peterhead,	,, 7 ,,	D
Elgin,	,, 13 ,,	E	Pitlochry,	,, 15 ,,	C
Falkirk,	,, 15 ,,	B	Portree,	,, 25 ,,	D
Forfar,	,, 11 ,,	C	Rothesay,	,, 20 ,,	B
Forres,	,, 14 ,,	E	St. Andrews,	,, 11 ,,	B
Fort Augustus,	,, 19 ,,	D	‡Sanquhar,	,, 16 ,,	A
Fort William,	,, 20 ,,	D	Selkirk,	,, 11 ,,	A
Fraserburgh,	,, 8 ,,	E	Stirling,	,, 15 ,,	B
Galashiels,	,, 11 ,,	A	Stonehaven,	,, 9 ,,	D
Girvan,	,, 19 ,,	A	Stornoway (Lewes),	,, 25 ,,	E
Glasgow,	,, 17 ,,	B	Stranraer,	,, 20 ,,	A
Grangemouth,	,, 15 ,,	B	Tain,	,, 16 ,,	E
Grantown,	,, 14 ,,	D	‡Thurso,	,, 14 ,,	E
Greenock,	,, 19 ,,	B	Tobermory,	,, 24 ,,	C
Haddington,	,, 11 ,,	B	Troon,	,, 19 ,,	B
Hamilton,	,, 16 ,,	B	Turriff,	,, 10 ,,	D
Hawick,	,, 11 ,,	A	Ullapool,	,, 20 ,,	E
Helensburgh,	,, 19 ,,	B	§Wick,	,, 12 ,,	E
Helmsdale,	,, 14 ,,	E	Wigtown,	,, 18 ,,	A

* Add 3 min. in Jan., 21 min. in June. † Deduct 14 m. in Jan., add 19 m. in June.
‡ Add 9 m. in Jan., 19 m. in June. § Add 7 m. in Jan., 17 m. in June.

Suggested Tour.

The following suggested Tour will cover the leading points of interest, and the best scenery, in the course of about three weeks, and those following it will get a very fair idea of the prettier parts of the country. The average day's ride should not exceed 40 miles, especially for Photo-cyclists. This tour is divided into comfortable stages; tourists may often find it convenient to adopt other stopping-places from those mentioned.

DAY.
1. Edinburgh to Doune, 43¾m., Routes 15 and 170, visiting Linlithgow Palace, Stirling and Castle, &c., Doune Castle.
2. Doune to Callander and the Trossachs, back to Callander, 27m., Routes 170-171; splendid scenery.
3. *Callander to Crieff, 44m., Routes 170 and 199, visiting Pass of Leny, Strathyre, Rob Roy's Grave, along the beautiful shores of Loch Earn to St. Fillans and Crieff.
4. Crieff to Perth and Dunkeld, 32¼m., Routes 199-200; uninteresting to Perth; very pretty near Dunkeld.
5. Dunkeld to Pitlochry (Falls of Tummel), Queen's View of Loch Tummel, back through the Pass of Killiecrankie to Blair Athole, where train to Kingussie, 28½m., Routes 200 and 211
6. Kingussie to Inverness, 44m., Route 296.
8. Inverness to Fall of Foyers, 18½m., Route 298, thence steamer to Laggan Lock, whence ride to Fort William, 21m., Route 300; fine scenery, total, 39½m.
9. Fort William to Ballachulish, thence visit Glencoe, returning to Ballachulish, 24¼m., Route 166, whence ride to Appin, 16¼m., Routes 158 and 161, and take steamer to Oban.
10. Oban: numerous excursions in vicinity.
11. Oban, through the wild Pass of Brander, to Dalmally, 26m., Route 157, where train to Crianlarich, thence ride to Arrochar, 18¼m., Routes 131-132, visiting Falls of Falloch. Beautiful road along Loch Lomond.
12. Arrochar to Helensburgh, 17¼m., Route 140, either by Loch Long or Loch Lomond, 19m., Routes 131, 378. Sail on the Clyde by steamer.
13. Cross to Greenock, and ride by fine coast road to Ayr, 49m., Routes 107, 102.
15. Ayr: visit Burns' Haunts, Burns' Cottage, Alloway Kirk, &c., on to Barhill by Maybole and Girvan, 34½m., Routes 96, 94, and 91.
16. Barhill to Newton Stewart, 21½m., visiting Loch Trool; rather pretty scenery.
17. Newton Stewart to Dumfries, 51½m., Route 70, visiting Dirk Hatteraick's Cave and Threave Castle; fine scenery to Gatehouse.
18. Dumfries: visit Burns' Mausoleum, &c., thence to Moffat, 21m., Route 65.
19. Moffat to Selkirk, 34½m., Route 45, by St. Mary's Loch (visit if possible the Grey Mare's Tail); a charming road alongside the Loch, and through "Yarrow."
20. Visit Abbotsford, Melrose Abbey, and Dryburgh Abbey, and return to Edinburgh, 50m., Routes 55, 46, and 33.

* An alternative road, quite as pretty, is to go from Callander to Killin, thence by Loch Tay, Kenmore, and Aberfeldy, to Dunkeld

ADVERTISEMENTS.

ESTABLISHED 1824.

CAPITAL, SIX MILLIONS STERLING.

BONUS YEAR, 1899.

Total Funds,　　-　-　-　-　£4,672,700.

SCOTTISH UNION AND NATIONAL
INSURANCE COMPANY.

LONDON—　　　　　　　　GLASGOW—
3 King William Street, E.C.　　150 West George Street.

Head Office—35 ST. ANDREW SQUARE, EDINBURGH.

Directors—

Wm. White Millar, Esq., James D. Lawrie, Esq., T. Hector Smith, Esq., A. D. M. Black, Esq., John Mackenzie, Esq., William S. Davidson, Esq., Walter Thorburn, Esq., M.P., Hon. James W. Moncreiff, And. Jameson, Esq., Sir Arthur Halkett, Bart., John Jordan, Esq.

Secretary—J. K. Macdonald.　*Actuary*—Colin M'Cuaig, F.F.A.
General Manager—A. Duncan.

LIFE ASSURANCE.

EARLY BONUS SCHEME (E.B.)

The following among other special advantages apply to ordinary Policies issued under this Scheme. Besides being payable immediately on proof of death and title, they are, *at the end of Three years from their date,*

Entitled to rank for Bonus Additions;

Indisputable on the ground of Errors or Omissions;

World-Wide without Extra Charge; and

Liable only to Reduction in Amount on Non-payment of the Premiums.

At the Division of Profits for the Five years ending 31st December 1894, Ordinary Life Policies under this Scheme received a BONUS ADDITION of £1, 10s. per cent. for each year since they were entitled to rank.

SPECIAL BONUS SCHEME (D.B.)

Under this Scheme Profit Policies are issued at Rates which do not exceed, and in many cases fall short of, the Non-Profit Rates of other Offices.

They share in the Profits when the Premiums received, accumulated at 4 per cent. compound interest, amount to the Sum Assured.

Policies issued at these very economical Rates practically receive a large Bonus at the outset.

At age 30, £1200 with right to Profits can be insured for the same Premium as would be charged for £1000 under the usual Profit Schemes of most Offices.

Policies of this class which have for the first time become entitled to rank for Bonus, have received additions at the rate of £10 per cent. at least, besides a further progressive addition of £1 per cent. per annum, and Policies which participated at last division received a further addition of £2, 10s. per cent., and to those which then received a contingent addition a Bonus at the rate of 10s. per cent. in respect of each year which elapsed since the date of their commencing to rank was added.

FIRE INSURANCE.

Almost all descriptions of Property insured on the most favourable conditions.

Reference Guide Books.

PRICE 6d. (originally published at 1/-).

Pollock's
Guide to the Lothians
and Dictionary of the Forth.
WITH SIX MAPS.

This admirable guide book is arranged Alphabetically, so that by turning up any desired place, full information as to its history, associations, and the places of interest in the locality can be found in a moment.

The volume is designed to cover that section of Scotland in which lies the Basin of the River Forth, and thus covers the counties of Linlithgow, Edinburgh, Haddington, the extreme South of Perthshire, North Stirling, Clackmannan, and the coast line of Fife.

The actual limits are: all the towns from Callander to Crail, and from Aberfoyle to Dunbar.

"Of great value to any one planning a holiday."
—*Weekly Scotsman.*

PRICE 6d.

Pollock's
Guide to the Clyde.
WITH FIVE MAPS.

This volume, uniform with the above, and arranged Alphabetically also, deals with all the towns on the River Clyde, from its source. It includes Arran, the county of Bute; the Dumbarton, Renfrew, Ayrshire, and Argyle-shire coasts, and the larger part of Lanarkshire.

"Its success is well merited."—*Scotsman.*

"A storehouse of valuable fact and fancy connected with the Clyde."—*Glasgow Herald.*

POST FREE, 8½d. EACH.

GALL & INGLIS, 20 Bernard Ter., Edinburgh;
And London.

ADVERTISEMENTS.

ESTABLISHED 1809.

NORTH BRITISH & MERCANTILE
INSURANCE COMPANY.

Fire—Life—Annuities.

TOTAL ASSETS exceed	£12,950,000
REVENUE, 1896, Over	£2,980,000

LIFE BRANCH—Important Features.
All Bonuses vest on Declaration.

NINE-TENTHS of the WHOLE PROFITS of the LIFE ASSURANCE BRANCH are allocated to PARTICIPATING POLICIES.

Claims paid *on Proof of Death and Title.*

Attractive Threefold Option Scheme.

The policy secures a capital sum payable at death or on the attainment of an age (say 55, 60, or 65) specified at the time the policy is effected; but the assured may, on attaining that age, elect to receive either:—

1. Immediate payment of the capital sum; *or*
2. An Annuity (equal in amount to Interest on the Capital Sum at the rate of 4 per cent.) payable during the remainder of his life—payment of the Capital Sum being deferred until his death; *or*
3. An Annuity of larger amount (in lieu of Capital and Interest) payable during the remainder of his life.

NOTE.—In the case of a Policy, say for £1000, if, on attaining the age agreed upon, the Assured should elect to take an Annuity of £40 for the remainder of life and £1000 at death, he may at any time thereafter take payment, in whole or in part, of the capital sum, continuing to draw interest at 4 per cent. on the balance, if any, remaining in the Company's hands. Capital once withdrawn cannot be re-invested with the Company.

Prospectuses and every Information may be had at the Chief Offices, Branches, or Agencies.

CHIEF OFFICES—

EDINBURGH, ...	64 Princes Street.
LONDON	61 Threadneedle Street.

THE
Continuous Strip Maps

By H. R. G. INGLIS.

On a long Tour everyone has felt the nuisance of carrying a large number of Maps for the purpose of showing a single route. By a simple and novel arrangement the following Roads—on the very large and detailed scale of half an inch to a mile—have been issued in pocket form, and although they are from 4 to 16 feet in length their bulk is no greater than a single Map.

The Map turns over page after page
JUST LIKE A BOOK,
And never requires to be unfolded.

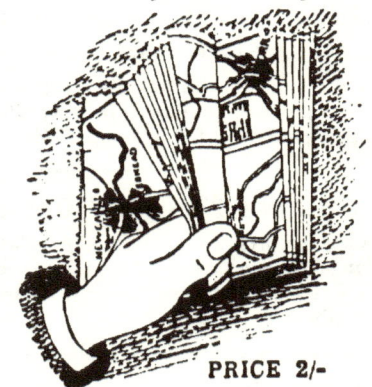

PRICE 2/-

A Key Map at the beginning shows what page to turn to. Each Map is a continuous strip of our ½-inch Map, joined together so as to produce a neat Map pocket size, showing the Road, and about 6 miles on each side.

GREAT NORTH ROAD MAP, London to York, Newcastle, and Edinburgh, 2/-

HOLYHEAD ROAD MAP, London to Birmingham, Shrewsbury, Holyhead, and Dublin, 2/-

BATH ROAD MAP, London to Newbury, Bath, and Bristol, 1/-

EXETER ROAD MAP, London to Salisbury and Exeter, 1/-

LAND'S END TO JOHN O' GROATS, in 8 Sections—
1. Land's End to Exeter, Bristol, Worcester, and Birmingham, 2/-
2. Worcester to Warrington, Preston, Carlisle, Edinburgh, or Glasgow, 2/-
3. Edinburgh to John o' Groats in preparation.

GALL ND INGLIS, LONDON AND EDINBURGH.

ADVERTISEMENTS.

SHETLAND SPENCER. *(Grey, Brown, or White.)*

4 to 6 Oz.   Price, 6/6, 7/-, 7/6.   Free by Post, 2d. extra.

Invaluable for Cyclists when resting during the ride; worn under the Norfolk Jacket, it is as warm as an Overcoat, and takes up no room in the haversack when riding.

It is well known to the Officers of H.M. Army for wearing under the uniform.

JOHN WHITE & CO.,
10 FREDERICK STREET, EDINBURGH.

ADVERTISEMENTS.

GALL & INGLIS'
TOURISTS' MAPS
Of Scotland.

SCALE: HALF AN INCH TO A MILE.

INDEX MAP.

Printed on Strong Paper, Roads Coloured, each Sheet, 1/-
In Cloth Cover, Mounted on Cloth, ,,   ,,   ,,   1/6

NEW LARGE SHEETS.
From the Latest Surveys, and Revised to date.

56. GALLOWAY DISTRICT.
69. OBAN DISTRICT.
70. SCOTTISH LAKE DISTRICT.
71. FIFE, FORFAR, AND EAST PERTH DISTRICT.

57. DUMFRIES DISTRICT.
60. AYR DISTRICT.
61. EDINBURGH DISTRICT.
62. BERWICK DISTRIC
64. GLASGOW DISTRICT.

Half Sheets, Price 6d. each, or on Cloth, 1/- Each.
66. ARRAN AND BUTE.   67. THE CLYDE WATERING PLACES.

Other Half-Sheets of TROSSACHS, STRATHTAY, EDINBURGH TO GLASGOW, STIRLING, and MELROSE DISTRICTS are published.

Large Map of London, with Handbook, containing Guide-Book, Index to Streets, and 3 Maps. Price 1/-.

Tourists' Maps of England. See Special List.

GALL & INGLIS, 20 Bernard Ter., Edinburgh.
AND LONDON.

ADVERTISEMENTS.

The "Half-Inch" Map of
ENGLAND.

SCALE: HALF AN INCH TO A MILE.

Printed on Strong Paper, Roads Coloured, each Sheet, 1/-
In Cloth Cover, Mounted on Cloth ,, , ,, 1.6

Each Sheet covers an area of 40 by 50 miles.

C. T. C. Gazette.—"Their value has long been admitted."

MAP LISTS AT ALL BOOKSELLERS.

For Edinburgh Cyclists.

OVER FIFTY MAPS AND PLANS.

PRICE 6d.; on Thin Paper, Cloth Covers, 1/-

Short Spins Round Edinburgh.

A Local Supplement to The 'Contour Road Book of Scotland,'

By HARRY R. G. INGLIS.

"Visitors to Edinburgh will find much to interest them in this publication."—*Edinburgh Citizen.*

"Will be found of the greatest service to pedestrians in their rambles round the country."—*Edinburgh Evening News.*

"Buy 'Short Spins'—you won't regret it."—*Scottish Cyclist.*

GALL & INGLIS, 20 Bernard Ter., Edinburgh

LEITH and LONDON.

The London & Edinburgh Shipping Co.'s
First-Class Steamships

FINGAL (New Steamer),

IONA, MALVINA, and MARMION,

(Lighted by Electricity), or other of the Co.'s Vessels, are intended to Sail (Weather, Casualties, and Strikes excepted) from

VICTORIA DOCK, LEITH,

Every WEDNESDAY, FRIDAY, and SATURDAY; and from

HERMITAGE STEAM WHARF, WAPPING, E.,

Every TUESDAY, WEDNESDAY, and SATURDAY.
For times of Sailing see Handbills.

FARES—First Cabin, including Steward's Fee, 22s. Second do. 16s.
RETURN TICKETS, available for 12 Months (including Steward's Fee both ways)—First Cabin, 34s.; Second Cabin, 24s. 6d.
Provisions, &c., may be had from the Steward on moderate terms.

Apply in London to LONDON AND EDINBURGH SHIPPING CO., Hermitage Steam Wharf, Wapping; M'DOUGALL & BONTHRON, 72 Mark Lane, E.C. Edinburgh—COWAN & CO., 5 Princes St. Glasgow—COWAN & CO., 23 St. Vincent Place. Greenock—D. MACDOUGALL, 1 Cross Shore Street.

THOMAS AITKEN, 8 & 9 Commercial St., Leith.

ADVERTISEMENTS.

BALLATER, NEAR BALMORAL.

THE
INVERCAULD ARMS HOTEL

The Hotel is pleasantly situated on the Banks of the Dee, in the midst of the finest scenery on Deeside, and most centrically and conveniently situated for parties visiting the Royal Residences, neighbouring Mountains, and other principal places of interest on Deeside. Golf Course ten minutes walk from Hotel.

The Hotel has recently undergone extensive alterations and improvements, and for comfort will compare favourably with any First-Class Hotel in Scotland.

POSTING IN ALL ITS BRANCHES.

By Special Appointment POSTING MASTER to HER MAJESTY THE QUEEN.

COACHES DURING THE SEASON TO BRAEMAR, BALMORAL, BLAIRGOWRIE, & DUNKELD.

EXCELLENT SALMON FISHING.

LETTERS & TELEGRAMS PROMPTLY ATTENDED TO.

ALEX. M'GREGOR, *Proprietor*.

ROYAL HOTEL, CRIEFF, N.B.

Under new management. Fishing, Golf, Headquarters C.T.C. Brake to St. Fillans, Mondays, Wednesdays, and Saturdays during the Season. Posting in all its branches.

DONALD LAMONT, Proprietor
(Late of Lamont's Hotel, Ellon).

PALMER'S TEMPERANCE HOTEL, DUMFRIES.

Established 16 Years. Every Convenience for Cyclists.

MODERATE TERMS.

E. PALMER, Proprietor.

Braid Hills & Barnton Hotels
EDINBURGH.

THESE Hotels are new and beautifully situated among lovely surroundings. They both lie in the immediate suburbs, one to the South and one to the West. Easy and continuous access to City. Splendid Cycling Roads.

MODERATE TARIFFS.

APPLY TO MANAGERS FOR BROCHURE.

ADVERTISEMENTS.

Philp's Dunblane Hydropathic,
PERTHSHIRE.

Unquestionably one of the Best in Britain.

Physician—DR. DEWAR.

Newly erected, a Special Stalled Depot for Cycles.
The Engineer on the Premises executes Temporary Repairs.
Perthshire possesses some of the finest Roads and Scenery in the Kingdom for Cycling.

PROSPECTUS FROM MANAGER.

Glenburn Hydropathic,
ROTHESAY.

Bicycle Stables under the Charge of Engineer, who can undertake Repairs.
Splendid Cycling Roads all over the Clyde District.

ELECTRIC LIGHT. ELEVATOR. SEA WATER.
TURKISH, RUSSIAN, & OTHER BATHS.

DR. PHILP, *Resident Physician.*

ADVERTISEMENTS.

EDINBURGH.

THE COCKBURN HOTEL.
(Adjoining Waverley Station.)

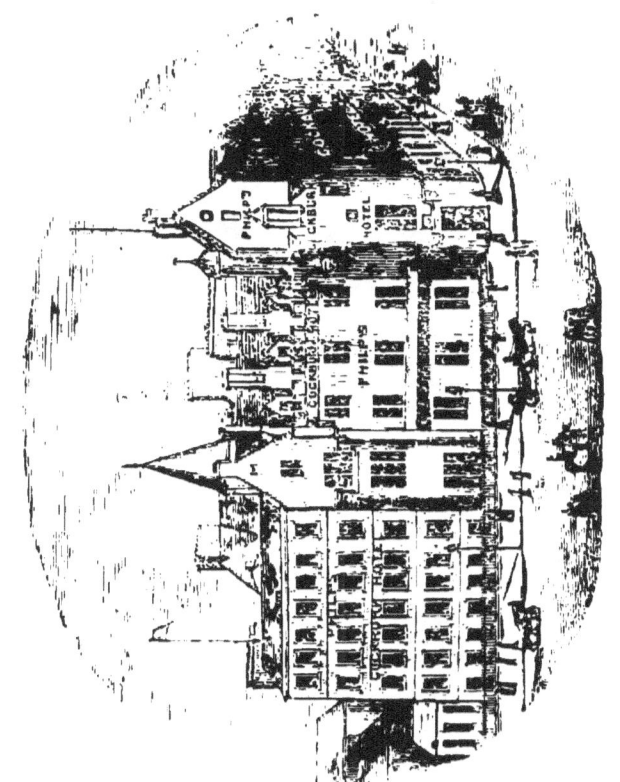

Passenger Lift.   Electric Light.

Tariff on Application.

No Intoxicating Drinks.

THORNTON & CO.,
Limited,
Patentees and Manufacturers of
REGISTERED WATERPROOFS.

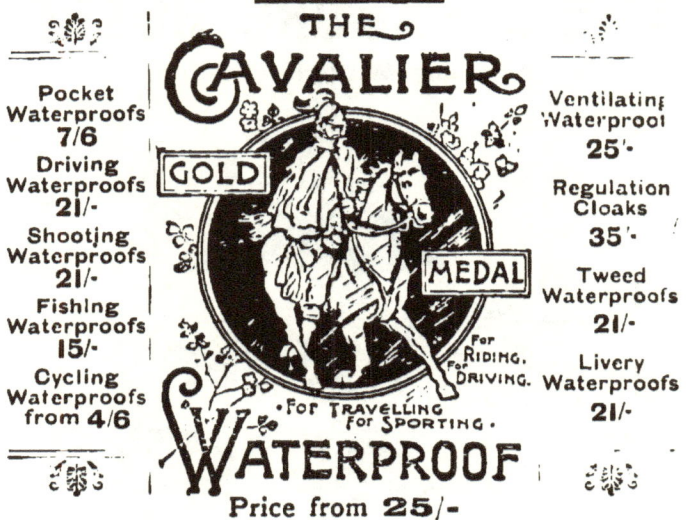

Pocket Waterproofs **7/6**
Driving Waterproofs **21/-**
Shooting Waterproofs **21/-**
Fishing Waterproofs **15/-**
Cycling Waterproofs from **4/6**

Ventilating Waterproof **25/-**
Regulation Cloaks **35/-**
Tweed Waterproofs **21/-**
Livery Waterproofs **21/-**

THE CAVALIER — GOLD MEDAL — WATERPROOF
For Riding, For Driving, For Travelling, For Sporting.
Price from **25/-**

CYCLISTS' WATERPROOFS.

FOR LADIES—
  Light Waterproof Capes, 4/6
  Fine Gossamer Capes, 6/6, 7/6
  Fancy Waterproof Tweed, 12/6, 18/6

FOR GENTLEMEN—
  Light Poncho Shape, 4/6
  Fine Waterproof Tweed, 8/6, 10/6

Specialities in Cycling Waterproofs of Superior Make and Finish.

THORNTON & CO.,
Limited,
Patentees and Manufacturers,
78 PRINCES STREET, EDINBURGH.
(Opposite the Mound.)

131	Glasgow to Tarbet	21
132	Tarbet to Crian	17
157	Crian to Oban	42
157½	Oban to Connel	5½
158	Connel to Balla.	22½
166	Balla to Ft W	13
300	Ft W to Inver	66

Inverness — to Blair athol

384	to Brorenr	38
441	to aberdn	58¼
	to Dunbar	27

Montrose
to   29½   good
Dundee

Taypole
to
Thurdon   16th

.9½   St Andrews
       to   20
     ?????

18   Kirkcaldy
        to   18¼
       Edin

7   Edin
       to   33
      Eula

       Eula
46   to   17½
      Kelso

       Kelso
36   to   23½
      Berwick

www.ingramcontent.com/pod-product-compliance
Lightning Source LLC
Chambersburg PA
CBHW030003240426
43672CB00007B/810